AMERICAN POETRY: THE NEXT GENERATION

EDITED BY
GERALD COSTANZO
AND
JIM DANIELS

CARNEGIE MELLON UNIVERSITY PRESS
PITTSBURGH 2000

ACKNOWLEDGMENTS

The publication of this book is supported by a grant from the Pennsylvania Council on the Arts.

Library of Congress Catalog Card Number 99-74773
ISBN 0-88748-337-2
ISBN 0-88748-343-7 Pbk.
Copyright © 2000 by Gerald Costanzo and Jim Daniels
Printed and bound in the United States of America.

10 9 8 7 6 5 4 3 2

Contents

Introduction

In a period in which the proliferation of poetry is widely acknowledged, in an era of "National Poetry Month" and of the "Favorite Poem Project," it's probably not an original notion to set out to edit an anthology of younger poets, those of the generation succeeding our own. But in fact it has been twenty-five years since poets in the "under forty" age group have been comprehensively anthologized. American society has undergone substantial changes in the past quarter century; it comes as no surprise that among these has been the direction of its poetry, and the diversity of its poets. One of our challenges was to select representative poems from perhaps the broadest range of styles ever extant at a single period in our history—a poetry which spans the spectrum from "performance" to "language" to the "new formal" and so on. Some of these poets acknowledge in their published books not only the literary journals in which the poems were first published, but the names of bars and clubs in which they were performed.

Initially, we located and exchanged the books from our own collections which we knew were written by poets born in 1960 or later. Because we surmised the number of these poets would make for an unwieldy anthology, we decided to limit our selections to those who had already published a full-length book with a trade, independent, or university press. Then we wrote to approximately 250 "established" poets—both those within the academy and outside—and to publishers across the country, soliciting suggestions for the names of poets who fit our criteria. Many of the poets we identified made additional suggestions. To each of those who responded to our requests we owe our gratitude; it was a lengthy period of correspondence, and the response yielded a number of books far in excess of our own predictions. We agreed also to consider manuscripts which were under contract for publication at about the time this anthology appears.

To begin with, we both read every book. As the number of books grew, it became clear that a division of labor was necessary, and we each began taking our own stacks of books home, then returning to discuss them in the University Press office, which remains awash in books, manuscripts, and correspondence. In the midst of that chaos, we read each other's selections aloud, shared our discoveries with energy and passion—the same energy and passion we felt as young poets ourselves. The office was a happy disaster, full of fascinating, provocative poets who might never share the same space again.

In the world of poetry, it is tempting to become cynical about our relatively small readership, and about the egotism and jealousy which can infect any creative field in any generation. We are extremely grateful to the poets for renewing our excitement about poetry. We hope our readers find themselves equally renewed.

As part of our selection process, we asked each poet for a list of poems which she or he considered representative. We made our own selections, then compared them with those of the poets. It quickly became apparent that we were editing a democratic compilation; that *inclusion* rather than *exclusion* would be the theme; that our limitation would be one of length of selection, rather than any limitation on the number of poets. Lastly, we took an ad in one of the trade journals in an effort to uncover any poets we might have missed. We offer our apologies to the poet born in or after 1960 who publishes a first book next week or next year; your absence from these pages is our loss. Clearly, as poets ourselves, we have preferences. While our biases may reveal themselves in the poems we have selected—we offer no apology for that—we hope the range of poets and styles is still readily apparent.

Despite the idiosyncratic nature of the publishing industry during the past two decades, and poetry's place in that industry, it has been widely held that the publishing of poetry has shifted from commercial publishers to the university presses. As the poets gathered here continue to establish themselves, no doubt these percentages will change, but our discoveries have amazed us: 49 percent of the books we read were published by independent and small presses; 43 percent by university presses; and 8 percent by trade publishers. This means that 92 percent of the books published to date by this age group have been produced outside of New York and Boston! The "burden" has shifted to places such as Minneapolis/St. Paul, Buffalo, Salt Lake City, Kansas City, Houston, Rochester, Chicago, Baton Rouge, Madison, Washington, DC, Louisville, Philadelphia, Columbus, Los Angeles, and Berkeley. Kalamazoo, Athens (Ohio and Georgia), Fayetteville, Oxford, Emporia, Cheney, Greensboro, Marshfield, East Lansing. And Pittsburgh. The emergence of Tia Chucha and Manic D, New Issues, Hanging Loose, and other such presses has expanded the literal and the figurative landscape of contemporary poetry. Not only is poetry alive and well in the provinces, the provinces have become the reason it is well and alive.

We offer our gratitude to our associate editor, Kathy Samudovsky, and to Press editors Cynthia Lamb and Irma Tani for their diligent efforts; and our thanks to Keya Brown of the Carnegie Mellon Department of English, and to University Press intern Karen Rigby for their efforts on behalf of this project. To Jared Cohon, President, and Paul Christiano, Provost of Carnegie Mellon University, our appreciation for their continuing support of poetry and the University Press.

Gerald Costanzo
Jim Daniels

Pittsburgh
November 10, 1999

AMERICAN POETRY:
THE NEXT GENERATION

RICK AGRAN (b. 1960)

WEARING DAD'S WHITE SHIRT BACKWARDS

That substitute teacher in art, you could tell she was strange.
Black hair pulled back so tight her eyes slanted,
her ponytail bobbed as she walked the halls.

Her teeth brilliant and pointy, she chewed gum
that cracked in the corners of her red mouth.
She made everyone else spit theirs out.

Sitting crisp in a chair, she crossed her legs
at the knee wearing red rubber flip flops,
a red color we'd never seen before.

Today, class, we'll paint the foot, she said.
Extending her long, pale leg,
her ruby big toenail pointed straight toward us.

Billy dipped his brush in lumpy blue tempera
and ran it along the clean arch of her right foot.
Her head dropped to one side,

and she sighed at the paint's coolness.

CAKES CONTINUE TO RISE

A pancake with its burnt side down
is still burnt.
No amount of syrup can hide it.

And the heel of stale white bread
is not camouflaged
inside the peanut butter and jelly sandwich.

I've jumped in front of the oven.
Cakes never fall
as you have always threatened.

And baloney is not enhanced by frying it.

Spoonfeed me a rich tapioca

of truth.
I swear, I can take it.

Help me cut my uncertainties
into littler pieces.
You've always been afraid I'd choke.

Give me the lollipop of life
and I promise
I will run with it in my mouth.

SWIMMING WITH SEIGER

As a girl she body surfed on the tidal sandbars,
the crest of wave and foam bearing down on her,
the fluid twist, lunge, and launch, the rush
of being borne away, salt water calling back and forth
through her skin.

After years in New England, she moved back
to Wrightsville, but the beach is a different place
to be now, her lost breast harder to hide.
A navy blue one-piece replaces her floral bikini
covering the zipper stitches of surgery.

She rented a beach cottage to hear the waves at night,
a gentle pull toward the water like a calling.
I coaxed her back into the ocean with strong marijuana
the day the reprieve of her remission was revoked.
She was tentative at the edge, back and forth,

until the longing overwhelmed her.
The waves spread and respread themselves
on the shore in inches of foamy smoothness,
came toward us in perfect curls
unrolling glassy green and blue.

Holding hands we went to meet them,
diving under the curls,
waiting for the perfect one to break and carry us.
And it came, gathered us, sucked us up,
turned us over and shot us out toward the shore,
arms out ahead in a hurtling horizontal dive

and then gone,
momentum slowing,
water quieting,
bodies smoothed.

Doors Thrown Open to Daisies

Warm slipperiness of us in the car's backseat
hot July afternoon coming home and we cannot wait
for bed's winding sheet and mirror's last glance before we fall.
Instead we have each other smelling of coconut lotion,
spangled with sand and salt crystals, wild wind-styled hair,
bathing suits damp, still cooling our bodies.

White cotton shirt ties arms entangled in hurry,
the light and dark of us tanned and not,
worn like smooth and seamless suits, marks that never leave
our skin, necks salty and offered, the back of this field
haven enough for this whirl of us in a moment of surrender
we practice like children with a white flag.

Elizabeth Alexander (b. 1962)

Stravinsky in L.A.

In white pleated trousers, peering through green
sunshades, looking for the way the sun is red
noise, how locusts hiss to replicate the sun.
What is the visual equivalent
of syncopation? Rows of seared palms wrinkle
in the heat waves through green glass. Sprinklers
tick, tick, tick. The Watts Towers aim to split
the sky into chroma, spires tiled with rubble
nothing less than aspiration. I've left
minarets for sun and syncopation,
sixty-seven shades of green which I have
counted, beginning: palm leaves, front and back,
luncheon pickle, bottle glass, etcetera.
One day I will comprehend the different
grades of red. On that day I will comprehend

these people, rhythms, jazz, Simon Rodia,
Watts, Los Angeles, aspiration.

MINNESOTA FATS DESCRIBES HIS YOUTH

I've been eating
like a sultan
since I was two days old.

I had a mother
and three sisters
who worshipped me.

When I was two years old
they used to plop me
in bed with a jillion

satin pillows
and spray me
with exotic perfumes

and lilac water,
and then
they would shoot me the grapes.

ASPIRIN

Bayer's children's aspirin is cheaper
than St. Joseph's, I know, because
Bayer's is what we buy, so I want
St. Joseph's, the tiny peach teeth,
the chalky crumble.

       Sometimes I long
for the fevers of my childhood.
I'd turn radiant and magenta
and see cheetahs in my bedroom,
the grey rug turned to elephant
hide, damp sheets, mosquito net—

I miss actual delirium,
the hot brain burning through its caul
to imagination.

SHERMAN ALEXIE (b. 1966)

DEFENDING WALT WHITMAN

Basketball is like this for young Indian boys, all arms and legs
and serious stomach muscles. Every body is brown!
These are the twentieth-century warriors who will never kill,
although a few sat quietly in the deserts of Kuwait,
waiting for orders to do something, do something.

God, there is nothing as beautiful as a jump shot
on a reservation summer basketball court
where the ball is moist with sweat
and makes a sound when it swishes through the net
that causes Walt Whitman to weep because it is so perfect.

There are veterans of foreign wars here,
whose bodies are still dominated
by collarbones and knees, whose bodies still respond
in the ways that bodies are supposed to respond when we are young.
Every body is brown! Look there, that boy can run
up and down this court forever. He can leap for a rebound
with his back arched like a salmon, all meat and bone
synchronized, magnetic, as if the court were a river,
as if the rim were a dam, as if the air were a ladder
leading the Indian boy toward home.

Some of the Indian boys still wear their military haircuts
while a few have let their hair grow back.
It will never be the same as it was before!
One Indian boy has never cut his hair, not once, and he braids it
into wild patterns that do not measure anything.
He is just a boy with too much time on his hands.
Look at him. He wants to play this game in bare feet.

God, the sun is so bright! There is no place like this.
Walt Whitman stretches his calf muscles
on the sidelines. He has the next game.
His huge beard is ridiculous on the reservation.
Some body throws a crazy pass and Walt Whitman catches it with
        quick hands.
He brings the ball close to his nose
and breathes in all of its smells: leather, brown skin, sweat, black hair,
burning oil, twisted ankle, long drink of warm water,

gunpowder, pine tree. Walt Whitman squeezes the ball tightly.
He wants to run. He hardly has the patience to wait for his turn.
"What's the score?" he asks. He asks, "What's the score?"

Basketball is like this for Walt Whitman. He watches these Indian boys
as if they were the last bodies on earth. Every body is brown!
Walt Whitman shakes because he believes in God.
Walt Whitman dreams of the Indian boy who will defend him,
trapping him in the corner, all flailing arms and legs
and legendary stomach muscles. Walt Whitman shakes
because he believes in God. Walt Whitman dreams
of the first jump shot he will take, the ball arcing clumsily
from his fingers, striking the rim so hard that it sparks.
Walt Whitman shakes because he believes in God.
Walt Whitman closes his eyes. He is a small man and his beard
is ludicrous on the reservation, absolutely insane.
His beard makes the Indian boys laugh righteously. His
        beard frightens
the smallest Indian boys. His beard tickles the skin
of the Indian boys who dribble past him. His beard, his beard!

God, there is beauty in every body. Walt Whitman stands
at center court while the Indian boys run from basket to basket.
Walt Whitman cannot tell the difference between
offense and defense. He does not care if he touches the ball.
Half of the Indian boys wear T-shirts damp with sweat
and the other half are bareback, skin slick and shiny.
There is no place like this. Walt Whitman smiles.
Walt Whitman shakes. This game belongs to him.

FATHER AND FARTHER

> *Such waltzing was not easy.*
> —Theodore Roethke

1.

In McNeil Island Prison for bad checks, my father worked to pay
back his debts. One morning, a few weeks before his scheduled
release date, he climbed the power tower for some routine line repair
and touched a live wire. Unconscious and burned, he fell five feet
before his safety line snapped taut.

2.

My father knows how to jitterbug.
How many Indians can say that?

3.

He attended Catholic school on purpose. There, the nuns taught him
how to play piano. He refuses to play now, and offers no explanations
for his refusal. There is a photograph of my father and his sister sitting
side by side at a piano. She is wearing a silk dress. He is wearing a coat
and tie. Did she know how to play the piano? I assume she could. She
attended the same Catholic school as my father. She died in 1980.
My father stood beside her coffin and did not sing.

4.

Late night, Yakima Indian Reservation, my father drunk, telling sto-
ries. We had traveled there to play in an all-Indian basketball tourna-
ment. My father was the coach. I was the shooting guard. We had a
bad team and were eliminated quickly. We camped in a cheap hotel.
Four players to a room, though my father and I were alone for some
reason. "Listen," my father said, "I was a paratrooper in the war."
"Which war?" I asked. "All of them," he said.

5.

My father drinks cough syrup
because he believes it heals everything.

My father drinks cough syrup
because he watched RFK's last news conference.

My father drinks cough syrup
because he has a tickle in the back of his throat.

My father drinks cough syrup
because he has survived twenty-three car wrecks.

My father drinks cough syrup
because he wants to stop the influenza virus at the door.

My father drinks cough syrup
because he once saw Lana Turner in a parade.

My father drinks cough syrup
because he is afraid of medicine.

6.

Of course, by now, you realize this is a poem about my father. It could
also be a series of exaggerations and outright lies. I might be talking

about another man who wears my father's mask. Behind that mask, he could be anybody.

7.

Summer evening, 1976. Our father is thirsty. He knows his children are thirsty. He rummages through our house in search of loose change. He finds a handful of coins. He walks to the Spokane Tribal Jail which, for some unknown reason, has the only soda pop machine on the reservation. My father has enough change for six Pepsis. It is quiet. We can hear mosquitoes slamming against the screen door. The jail is only a few hundred feet from our house. If we listen closely, we can hear our father dropping change into the machine. We can hear the sodas drop into the dispenser. My father gathers the cans. He carries them back to us.

8.

Basketball is
a series of prayers.

Shoot the ball
and tell me

you believe
otherwise.

My father
shoots the ball.

As it spins away
my father prays.

9.

My father often climbed into a van with our crazy cousins and left us for days to drink. When he came back, still drunk, he always popped "Deer Hunter" into the VCR. He never made it past the wedding scene. I kept watching it after he'd passed out. Halfway through the movie, John Savage and Robert De Niro play a sick game of Russian Roulette while their Vietcong captors make wagers on the probable survivor. De Niro asks for more bullets. Two bullets, three. He knows the odds. He holds the gun to his head. He has a plan.

10.

As he dribbles
past you, into the
paint, then stops, pivots

and gives the big man
a head fake, you must
remember that my
father can shoot with either
the right or left hand.

11.

During the World's Fair in 1974, my father and I rode over Spokane Falls
in a blue gondola. No. It was more like a chair. Our legs and feet
floated free. I looked down into the water. My father held his left arm
around me. He must have been afraid of gravity. Then my left shoe
came loose because the laces were not tight enough. My shoe would
have slipped from my foot if I hadn't pressed my other shoe against it.
My father told me to hang on. He was smiling as I struggled to keep my
shoe. I had written my name across the top of it. I looked down into
the water. My father was laughing. The chair was blue. It was 1974.
The entire world was walking the streets below us. My mother was
dancing for tourists in the Native American exhibit. My siblings were
sleeping in the station wagon. Gravity. The water. My shoe. I looked at
my father. He held me tightly. He told me to hold on.

RICK ALLEY (b. 1963)

THE CANARY MAN & YOU

He hunched a broomstick
behind his neck,
balanced his cages
and left town.
A riot of mosquitoes
paraded him away.
You sucked ice slivers
on the Methodist's porch,
watching evening slide
into a black lake.
Your hand, cold from the ice,
slipped into your pants
like someone else.
The whole town buckled.

A blue hound was nibbling
on a plate of grass

when it found the stiff yellow clumps
which it brought, one by one,
to your feet.
Summer withered by the mossy bog,
his hand an empty space in yours.

DISSECTING UNCLE SORROW

His night job is insomnia.
He seals pacts with a wink.
In all the lit buildings
of all the lit towns
he's got pillow-punching down
to a faith. His songbook includes
"I'll Be Happy, Soon"
and "The Amazing
Night-Blooming Tear."
At dawn, he's the woman
with the strong, small hand
holding her robe closed.
"What else do you want?"
I scream at her face
and the hand tightens its grip.
If that's not enough
he's the tepid coffee
I drink and return to the next day.
He's the guard in the park
walking alone
and he can walk a very long way.

CLEANING

The yard, littered
with dimpled pears, could drowse

for the rest of the day.
White in a field, a claw-footed tub

is reborn as a trough for the cows.
Spent a moment picking up

a perfect ash; it crumbled,
a storm between fingers.

Just now, my hands
in the blue dishwater, I heard

the house settle, complaining old wood.
For a second, the smell of a just-cut field

is a friend who died as a girl.
Easily lost, the mowers call

to each other, waving their shirts.
I'd forgotten voices could travel so far,

that they lose so little on the way.

THE GROWING DAYS

were becoming less sane.
We stayed clear
of the wasp's nest.
When it rained, we watched
from behind a screen
on a porch, getting wet.
My thin aunt was sick at night.
We could hear her smooth gown.
We knew we'd all change someday;
sometimes, we compared our hands.
The growing days grew without us
till some of us left, waving.
With paper hips, the wasp flew close
to our eyes, our moving hands.

ALICE ANDERSON (b. 1966)

LICKING WOUNDS

James went first because James always went first. The year I was
    six
and he eight, when we invited all the kids on the block—Linda
    and Lisa,
little Amy, Jenna and Adie and her brother Ludie the snake boy—
    over

to slide on our Slip-n-Slide in the backyard. James pulled the
   orange slip
out of the garage in a wrinkled heap and brought it out back by the
   long, still
fishpond. The pond where I fed my favorite fish too much and
   he drowned.

Those were the years we still had money, when Mom still carved
   my dresses
out of conspicuous bolts of brushed silk, linen, and furry, beige
   lambs-wool.
James held one end, and Ludie the other, backing away from each
   other, their

long arms outstretched but bent at the elbows as if pulling hot
   cupcake pans
from an oven. They layed the Slip-n-Slide out across the lawn,
   screwed in
the garden hose to the orange plastic nozzle, and watched as the
   chalky plastic

filled and shone with warm and then cold summer hose water.
   James went first because he always went first—not because he
   was the oldest or
the tallest or the least smart of all the kids. He went first because
   he liked

the protest, the jerking one-footed whines of girls with smaller
   faces, smaller
voices, and smaller, whiter thighs. I was obsessed with germs that
   year,
wouldn't have eaten at all if I had known that to make it, someone,
   somewhere

had to take it into hands. The butcher, with slabs of meat and bone,
   wrapping it up
in gleaming, invisible cellophane. The maid, washing lettuce,
   tearing it to shreds
before washing it again and placing it in a heap in the crisper. Even
   my mother,

washing the boneless pork under the faucet before dipping it into silt
   white flour,
turning it over, and over, and again, before laying it softly in the

sizzling copper pan.
At dinner, when no one was watching—no one ever did—James
would lean over

and let out his long, hot tongue. He'd lick his lips, my meat, the
edge of my milk
glass, or the tight, cold corner of my mouth. So he slid first down
the Slip-n-Slide.
He backed up to the fence and took off full speed, tight-fisted and
leaning into the leap,

belly-down, sliding in a jagged, wild line. And his sudden wailing
scream seemed
to come from somewhere in his shining, glassy eyes. It took hours
for the doctors
to extract the shards of glass from his chest and stomach, his skinny
thighs.

A broken jar? Camping lamp? No one knew. But when I went,
finally, to that
tall white bed where he lay for one long afternoon, I let out my
small, cool tongue
and ran it up his peach-fuzzed arm from wrist to elbow to shoulder
bone

and for just one day, I was first, and no one was looking.

THE SUICIDE YEAR

That fateful year I wished for you, flushed
the tiny orange pills away, listening to the rushing

whirl as I fixed my lipstick before coming to bed.
I wanted to give in, finally, and be the woman

I thought I should be. I kept you secret, held you in
for weeks, my angel, savior, twin. Finally, I had

a silent friend. As I broke the blade from
the plastic pink razor, I thought only of my

teen-age years, how I stayed home weeks at a time,
fake-sick and in love with my mother. We'd go

on long car rides and she'd talk, turning the radio
lower and lower, slowly, until it was off.

*We're leaving him soon. I'll sleep with you until then
so he won't. I don't blame you anymore, I don't.*

She spoke so quietly. Not crying. Just talk and pauses.
I wasn't to agree or not agree. She ached at imperfection,

but disappointment broke her. It was late and in
the bathroom when, six years after she did, I balanced

my white wrists atop my spare knees and began.
She never left him. She said he had a good

heart, though he drank himself into silence after five.
At least, she said, silence was safe. At least

she would always have me and that, she said, should be
enough. Her eloquent handwriting slid perfectly across

the notes she sent me back to school with. The notes without
her real voice, echoing, *Fathers just love their daughters*

in a special kind of way. I'm not jealous. And it wasn't
that I wanted to die. I wanted to wear heels with

a pencil skirt. I wanted to cook perfect casseroles
and be alright if friends dropped by. I wanted to be her,

not write these poems of death and erotic families.
But my cuts were so shallow I hid them in shame and

never even cried until several days later, when you slid out
of me and into water which I set swirling red, my little twin.

When I watched you wash away I thought I heard
a voice cry, *Better to die than to be loved.*

DANIEL ANDERSON (b. 1964)

EXECUTIVE GEOCHRONE
A map shop in December

The local peddler of geographies
Has hung a world which darkens by degrees
And lightens, also, as a sine wave glides
Over islands, continents, and still seas.

Occasionally browsers stop to ask
The idle clerk about the sine wave's task,
Though anyone could patiently observe
Its job is first to mask and then unmask

This planet with a corresponding light
To dusks that fall and mornings that ignite.
And calmly as that map grinds down its days
We view our lives as from a placid height.

Beyond the store's plate glass the first snows drift,
Blanketing streets like ash. The awnings shift
And signposts swagger in rank bursts of wind.
On Christmas Eve, in search of one last gift,

A globe, perhaps, a flag, or travel book
To gather dust in someone's inglenook,
Each customer compares the worlds he wants
As Argentina's turquoise buttonhook

Is cloaked in evening not yet reaching here.
A blue wine spills over this hemisphere,
Has washed across Bermuda's jagged coasts,
And hints of our own nightfall edging near.

One sees in this illuminated chart
Both time and place made graspable by art
And how each unveiled strip of morning light
Is balanced by a darkling counterpart.

Tomorrow when the presents are all passed
Around the living room, a low broadcast

Of caroling will chime the morning out;
The ornaments, which once seemed colorfast,

Will hang less brightly. Silences will stoke
The ghosts that January grays provoke,
And all soft essences that charged the air,
Of pine bough, holly wreath, and chimney smoke

Will be remembrancers of what has gone,
While through the sash that frames a snowy lawn
We'll watch a day that darkens by degrees
And witness something darker drawing on.

The Nightly News

Today, in the war-torn state, the nightly news
Reports the dead have numbered only one,
Which isn't bad, one has to think, for the land
Ravaged in shards and dust and overrun

By love of country. The television glows
With puddled streets, abandoned garden carts,
And the bullet-stippled window of a shop—
The landscape of a million hollow hearts.

The young married couple squander the night
Bickering over their standard of living
And how even making love has turned out sour.
Between the pair they've given up on giving.

They go bitterly through their dinner time,
Riddled by silence and the anchor's voice
Which tells them in a stark non sequitur
How they bear all their grievances by choice.

But all of this is nature's sleight:
While through this scene an abstract ache goes throbbing,
In the unremitting fever of some dark
The mother of that casualty lies sobbing.

Talvikki Ansel (b. 1962)

Flemish Beauty

Yesterday, all winter,
I had not thought of pears, considered:
pear. The tear-shaped, papery core,
precise seeds. This one channelled
through with worm tunnels.
Bruises, a rotten half—
sometimes there's nothing left
to drop into the pot.

             That phrase
I could have said: "you still
have us. . ."
         The knife
slides easily beneath the skins,
top to base, spiralling
them away.

The insubstantial us.
It could as well be the pear
talking to the river, turning to
the grass ("you still have us").
Besides, it's just *me*
a pear in my hand (the slop bucket full
of peels)—and sometimes, yes, that
seems enough: a pear—

              this larger one,
yellow-green, turning to red:
"Duchess" maybe, "Devoe,"
or what I want to call it: "Flemish
Beauty."
        When I can't sleep,
I'll hold my hand as if I held
a pear, my fingers mimicking
the curve. The same curve
as the newel post
I've used for years, swinging
myself up to the landing, always
throwing my weight back. And always
nails loosening, mid-bound.

Afterwards: Caliban

I learned to name them—brown-nut-warm, wide
Hipped, *horses*, on legs Thin as saplings.
They have smooth knocking, beach-stone Hooves,
Are made to pull carriages, carry wood
Across London's dull paths. Ears like the hare
They speak a Soft Language. Sweet Breathers:
They exist solely on the Insubstantial
Grass, dusty Grains. The head is small—the size
Of an owl, a keg. I think once they owned
This island. In the warm ear of the one
That stops at The Bridge, I whisper: "wave"
"Oat cake," "the world is whip-less," "blue grey,"
I can see suns, a seed, clouds in its Eye,
From its Flank, it shivers off a sweat Fly.

★ ★ ★

What does it matter if you can tell False
Visions, swell the air with your Words, make Tales
Intoxicate. What matters is what's here:
Spring veal and Peas, a warm bed, ale, the day
When you Wake, quarreling sparrows in the Eaves.
Or what's not here, my Island—is it still
There? A boat of five Years ago couldn't See
Its Bluffs. Perhaps eaten? Prospero ate
All the Mussels from the rocks where the Plover
Slept; perhaps Sunk under the Waves. When I
Think of it, it's in Days before they came,
When ginger root still bloomed at the cave.
It's the past, in my Head, Pictures: the bright
Metal brought from the Stone called Memory.

★ ★ ★

The boxwoods loom in the Dusk: dark
Beasts, elephants, a triangular monster,
Forgetful ostrich. Under my foot the shells
On the Path shift and crunch. So much one says
Like Seed, does not come True. Should I say *island*?
The Cook, squeezing a green Cabbage worm, would not
See *that* Bay, that particular promon-
tory. Talk, His barren talk, and Oaths. It seems
My island grows smaller, not Fixed

In Rhumb-lines on any Map. The Reare-mice
On leather wings, the Hedges, dissolve into
Night. My cane-taps sound far away.
What I tell you, what I tell you—
It is so much smaller than what I can not tell you.

AARON ANSTETT (b. 1968)

PHARMACY

If, at the pharmacy, I say to the woman
frowning behind the counter, "My heart's
a bad check, make good on it," will that mean
a kind of November has settled in my blood

and I'll be ready then to never lie again?
If, with my change, she offers me matches,
will she want to live with me forever
and together we'd love everything we touched?

"I'm no good for you," I'd say, holding the flame
just under my cigarette. Then, like some tough guy,
I'd breathe in hard, pulling the fire up.
If I lit it first try, would things work out between us?

Would she give me a pill that could keep me from yelling,
"We're all dying! Help!" in emergency rooms for fun?
Would she have another we could split?
Would we find our way back to the world

inside this one, and our pure happiness catch on
with the druggist, who'd start crazily ringing
his mortar and pestle? As we linked arms at the exit,
wouldn't he give us that music for our wedding?

MAN SAVES OWN LIFE

In the morning, before breakfast, I save my own life,
then walk around the house all day a hero.
Friends come by and ask how it feels.

I say it just happened. I couldn't help it.
They'd do the same in my shoes. I don't tell them how,
before I knew it, something raced down my fingers
and my feet. Something made me strong.
It crowded itself in my arms and my heart
and filled me up with as strange and kind a feeling
as I could remember, and suddenly I knew nothing
but I had to help that guy. It wasn't words. No voice
told me. It was more like light behind my eyes, weight
pressing in from every direction. High notes pierced me,
and it was clear what I had to do.

SHIFT

A little snow blew in where we stood.
Our boots squared off at the toe.
The doctors, said John Flowers,
didn't know fuck-all. Surgery
worsened something in his daughter.

John Flowers spat his cigarette
between the trailer and the bay door,
squinted his eyes and lit another.
He asked me if I'd ever killed a man.
All I wanted was a pallet

of certain-size parts unloaded
so I could run them to the floor.
He scratched his stomach, said he had,
one punch to that man's solar plexus,
back in Missouri, an accident. *I boxed,*

he said, and made me feel the arm.
He made me say I believed him.
Management could kiss his ass.
They weren't paying towards her bills.
He'd drive his forklift drunk or sober.

Hell if he wouldn't, he whispered,
holding me in a bear hug. *Some days,
son of a bitch,* he said, *it's like losing your wallet
and there's no proving who you are anymore.*
Close to my ear he called me *Kid.*

WORRY

Say you want to sing right now,
over and over, the name of an old lover.
Aren't you afraid the neighbors will hear
your voice shaking a little, the way you shook
in that lover's arms, the night you started
losing one another? If you were me, you felt
a lessening no talking could lessen, a sense
the motel television made sense just then,
with its wash of poorly adjusted color
lighting the room. Between leaving
for more ice and forcing a toast
to the future, plastic glasses patting
and sloshing, you thought, "This
is what we're entitled to."

If, unlike me, you had pulled the curtains open,
overhead lights might have glinted
off the balcony railing for you
and exposed the courtyard, the shutdown
fountain. The two of you might have danced
down there, slowly and close. The two of you
might have rescued something beautiful.
If you were me, you wouldn't sing
that name either. You'd worry
about the neighbors. You'd worry like I do.

CRAIG ARNOLD (b. 1967)

THE EXTRAVAGANCE OF ZOOS

Here in the dry consump-
tive desert, past a spray
of fountains that both day
and night are set to pump

whole reservoirs of water
straight up, in palm-tree feathers
the thirsty air withers
so quickly almost a quarter

is lost, our zoo teems
with legions of the blond
children we have spawned
to spectate, for whose games

this is an exercise
—accustomed watchfulness
will fit them to replace
their big brothers, sentries

at the frontier's most remote
outposts, who seldom wear
the regulation footgear,
or take time to vote,

but have instead married
the indigo-tattooed
natives, eaten their food,
engendered half-breed

children who play with pebble
chessmen and recite
their classics in the flat
unmodulated babble

of a second language. Lax
as we've become, we put
up with them for the tribute
they pay, by way of tax:

big wicker baskets full
of snakes, arm- and thigh-thick,
an ostrich, a rare black
leopard, a docile bull

elephant grown shabby
and ragged about the ears
from a close cage. Last year's
delivery, a baby

river-horse, recoiled
back in its box and had
to be pushed out with a prod,
trembling, into the cold

of its new mountain home.
It sat, and could be seen
most days, under the green-
corroded metal dome

(the local copper baron's
bequest) for the better half
of a year, its funny cough
much aped, its disappearance

not much noticed. But pity
is lost on the innocent,
the ingenuous, the infant
heir to some petty

title, whose first step
came only just in time
to allow him to climb,
all by himself, the steep

stairs to the guillotine,
shivering at the air
cool on his neck's clipped hair,
the raw shaved skin.

WHY I SKIP MY HIGH SCHOOL REUNIONS

Because the geeks and jocks were set in stone,
I, ground between. Because the girls I ate
lunch with are married now, most out of spite
—because the ones I spurned are still alone.
Because I took up smoking at nineteen, late,
and just now quit—because, since then, I've grown
into and out of something they've never known.
Because at the play, backstage, on opening night
she conjured out of the vast yards of her dress
an avocado and a razorblade,
slit the one open with the other, flayed
the pebbled skin, and offered me a slice

—because I thought that one day I'd say *yes*,
and I was wrong, and I am still afraid.

DAVID BARATIER (b. 1970)

AMERICAN STANDARD

It's the kind of place where
everyone's mother works there.
They fly a clean flag
each morning. So damn incestual,
I don't want to know what drugs she's taking
or some new growth located where. Top it off
with a daughter sitting to my left
who's a single mother with five kids under ten
jittered out on 14 hours straight-time, telling me
she's working extra for a gun to change her ex-
husband's mind about alimony. Makes
me nervous. The only way to get away from it all
is the men's bathroom, and they took me aside
about that yesterday.

THE FALL OF BECAUSE

A revelry was had. The chair came to pieces.
A miniature trapeze was confiscated
as well as a kilo of sassafras allegedly for soup.
What a chance to perfect our loutishness
with maximum suavity. We even truncated a few
humans. And what else could we do?
They were real scum, using popular science
to spank the glitch. We hate to cut the life of
the story but they were stealing the sense of gun
safety out from under us. Bloody boots aside,
look at the damage, the proliferation of
adverbs on terminal lines, a rise
in alcoholics drinking the blue sky.
For the proof, what else do we need?

ESTRELLA'S PROPHECIES #47

Someone will consider something you do prolific
until you stop doing it. Then someone who fell
in love with your potential will leave and go

shopping. Since life hasn't been easy, it's
no wonder shopping is not your bag. To cover
the loss take up a sport which fits the stereotype
people have of people like you. People with
mercantile difficulties need to teach their inner
child to buy through visualization, which also
costs less. Replaceable things fall through your
fingers over and again until you lose them. Throw away
your Isotoners this spring. In the next life larger
gloves are necessary. You have a fine mind but it
cannot be seen. Except on the third Saturday of this month.
Drop another coin in the slot and I will tell more.

SHE WANTS

him the way we leave a porchlight on
when we want a lover the way we leave
a porchlight on him. She walks her dog past
the door three times each day. Paper curls
in repetition. The admired fruit of neighbors
cleaned, cooked until the muscles simmer
down from the shelf of puritan cookbooks
into jars. Exploited is that fresh thing.
Which he understands, he is a crystal samurai
of juggernauts using fresh hair to reproduce
from flour small figures in bread for art.
Which means there is time. He is filling
her notebooks. For those dainty napkins;
food of all we've done.

DAVID BARBER (b. 1960)

THE SPIRIT LEVEL

You kept your tools sequestered,
out of sight. And to this day, the flinty logic
of the ratchet and the crescent
wrench evades me, I'm unable to brandish
a saw or drive a batch of penny nails
without a passing twinge of sheepishness.
But the spirit level, let me tell you,

is another story: so ingenious in the essence
        of its unvarnished purpose, it's practically
child's play. Yours was as long as your arm:
        a perfect makeshift shotgun for a boy
like me. But slipping downstairs first thing
        Sunday mornings, bent on infiltrating
the inspired clutter of your basement sanctum,
        I found it even more ingratiating
for what it was, for how its stripped-down upshot
        was both transparent and inscrutable.
Winking in their banded tubes of tinted glass,
        those emerald bubbles never burst
or vanished, no matter how savagely I shook
        or how doggedly I worked to tilt
and drown them. It seemed to me there had
        to be some clever dodge concealed
in its sundry uses, like umbrellas that sheath
        a well-honed blade, or the dining
table's folded wings. Still, such artfulness
        as I could grasp held all the thrill
of uncanny sorcery: the fingernail flecks
        of captive air always at the ready,
the stringent tension, streamlined to divine
        absolute vertical, true horizontal,
the furtive thrust of angles. Did I ever
        tell you that the basement floor
slumped faintly, here and there, the beams
        betrayed a hair's-breadth slant?
Did I already tell you that every doorframe
        would make those bubbles tremble,
as if the house were just then beginning
        to sink down on one knee?

NOCTURNE

The papers say the heat is here to stay.
Every window in the house thrown open
to a child's durable choruses.
He should be sung to. All of us should be.
The one good lullaby my mother knew
harbored a line in the distance darker
than the others, processions of ridges.
Some were scored with horses, or so I heard.

And I seem to recall braids of smoke, towns
in the strongholds of rivers, those slow blues.
But I could be mistaken. As children,
we wake in what we come to call the woods.
No faces, no dim outlines of bodies.
No lacework of stars: the trees are that thick.
Only a strand of song, that one refrain
that could still the eyelids at midsummer.

Nights I can't sleep, I know my mother sings.
I stray outdoors in hopes of hearing her.
There are the towns and there are the horses.
And there's a road I must have missed before.
Chimneys ghost on; ladles chime off kettles.
A local cradling kindling shuffles by
with a nod, whistling ferociously.
It isn't summer here. It never was.

LITTLE OVERTURE

A shimmering in the scrub-brush
Beside the tracks, a pleasing silken weft
Of stray raiment amid the rubbish.

Grace is like this: a scrim
Materializing in a strip of stubbly weeds.
It comes, it goes, a glint, a form

Of counterpoint and seduction.
Or call it a sampler, the handiwork
Of spring's first spiders practicing deception.

Now come closer. If it's silver lining
You want, it seems you have been hoodwinked.
Knots of kids have strewn

The slick innards of unspooled cassettes
Over the brambles as they wended
Home from school along the tracks.

Whose loss is it? Grace is like this.
Railway perennials shine in the wind.
Threads recur; pop songs persist

In telling us what we wish were true.
Trains storm by on time but you still wander,
Nodding to a beat you cannot hear.

SMALL HOURS

When the dark is wise to us, what is memory
But what the body agrees to abide by?
What comes upon us in a rush? Afterwards,
She talked and he listened. It was the year
Of her birth. The melons were prodigious
That summer, and the heat off the charts.
She likes the story best about her father
Fishtailing into a farmstand lot to purchase
A historic watermelon, thumping it gravely
With a knuckle before hugging it to his chest,
Though the contractions by that time
Were fierce. She likes the thought
Of newspapers spread on the tailgate
All delivery long. The Rambler parked
In the shade by the hospital. Her father
Slicing away. An overpowering sweetness.
She got out of bed to open the window.
Her body was darker than the rest of the room.
Then he talked and she listened. He likes
How inside the lumpishness of melons
Brightness waits like a seemly thought
Right before the tongue fleshes it out.
The way it lurks. The way it takes us back.
If loving is always groping in the dark,
If the heart keeps us on tenterhooks,
Then at times the body we find beside us
Will be the only steady source of light
At the back of the cave. He doesn't like
To call it a shining or a glowing.
It's more tacit than that. More ulterior.
Root and vine, bed and spade, curve and heft.
Something opens and we see.

PAUL BEATTY (b. 1960)

INDEPENDENT STUDY

everydays homecoming at sidewalk university / harlem campus

shreds of yellow newspaper
instead of tree leaves
tumble thru broken fields of glass
to quiet autumn touchdowns

if cat stevens
lived in harlem
he wouldn't have to ask *where do the children play*
they play in the streets
two-hand touch
purple and green nerf spirals
three completes first
take two steps turn around

i was open on that last play
the only thing open was your nose
you just stay back and block

> sidewalk chickenhawks
> begin to line the parade route

> hot dog   sauerkraut

the brownstone stoops are grandstand pigeon coops
a place to coo n schmooz the harlem blues
a wc handy place to wait for the chickens to come home to roost
remember when x said that about kennedy
at temple 7

> now theres a rhode island red sittin on his chest
> singin fight songs at the high jumpin sun

> i guess thats what happens
> when you strut n buck
> the pecking order

standing behind invisible police barricades
the crowds wave

as the drop tops
coast by

      prize winning floats
      metallic *im drivin you not* boasts

and you know niggas be scopin
heads out the windows
pick up lines and oldies
on harlem days that *float   float on*

               aquarius   and my name is ralph . . .
                            now i like a woman
                            who loves her freedom

the nigger please cheerleaders laugh
at this old straightjacket rap
these new age african harriet houdinis
with comeback lines like bobbipins
free themselves from the claptrap

cartwheels and handsprings
propel them awwwwww beepbeep down the street

sometimes bullshit walks
carryin a box   *naw baby for real   my carz in the shop*
then the love lyrics drop

libra   and my name is charles   now i like a woman whos quiet
        a woman who carries herself like mrs. universe

      my fathers name is charles
      and my mother is quiet

      but he didnt like her cause she carried
      herself like herself

thru the balloonless halftimes between riots
uprisings when neighborhood drill teams
marched thru cannon smoke

throwin flaming twirling molotov batons
way up in the air

then watched them hit the ground
crazy   i aint catchin shit

        a hunchedback drum major
        highsteps over the ashes
        blowin the whistle on the revolution

its the homecoming queens
day off from burger king
a rest from the constant *push up* codas

        I'LL TAKE AN ORANGE SODA   what size
        BOUT YOUR SIZE   that be about a medium

she rides on the hood
of a red on red gypsy cab
naugahyde interior
her long legs crimp styles

if you spliced speaker wires
to the lonely pop pop pops of hearts

cancer and my name is larry

the trip light sparks
in the mack daddies eyes
would walk right up to the side of her ride

grab the door handles
dapper dan secret service agent style
hoping to protect her from the whispering bullets of jive
thanks   but she got a bulletproof vest called pride
her bald headed driver smiles

his liver wrapped
in a brown paper bag
neil diamond on the radio
a mid-term in a community college intro to eastern religion on his mind
the bhagavad-gita on his lap
and aint harlem just like the parade of ants

Why That Abbott and Costello Vaudeville Mess Never Worked with Black People

who's on first?
i dont know, your mama

Stall Me Out

why you   no rhythm

afraid of women asexual pseudo intellectual
bald mt. fuji shaped head

            no booty havin   big nose
        size 13 feet   pigeon toed crook footed

taco bell burrito supreme eatin
            day dreamin

                        no jump shot   cant dunk
comic book readin
nutrition needin

knock kneed sap sucker
non drivin

                    anti fashion
        constantly depressed   clumsy no money mutherfucker

                        take your weak ass poems
                        and go back to los angeles

Joshua Beckman (b. 1971)

Lament for the Death of a Bullfighter

For David Avidan

1

At the news of your death
children could hold back their giggling no more
and fits of laughter spread like chicken pox

all over this country
and at first no one noticed
because kids are always doing stuff like that,
but soon there was no stopping them
no quieting them down at all
and then the sky turned dark
and authority slunk away
like the man who never wanted to be sheriff
and the kids stayed outside
floating down the streets in boats made from junk
and when the moon showed up
they finally went in
left their soaking clothes at the door
and headed straight for their computers.
And then we had lost them to you
their eyes glued to the screen
their fragile hearts pumping with electric blood
their thousand little thumbs
frantically bouncing up and down.

2

At the news of your death
pardon me, the mail is slow from there to here,
a giant wave finally reached our country
and sat his big gray body down
next to the few people left
who hadn't run away in fear
(again like the movies)
and the wave told such a captivating
intercontinental story that we didn't notice
him turning to mud like an ice cream cone
and when we looked, all that was left
were a dozen pie-shaped jellyfish,
but the ocean took those back quickly,
before any trouble got started.

3

At the news of your death
the computers at the phone company
all over New York City
and the surrounding area
went on strike
and had to be replaced
with people,
who made every connection

and answered every question,
much to the surprise of the callers
who had become accustomed to automation,
and no matter how many people called
(and once the lonely bachelors found out
there were a lot)
everything went smooth as could be
due to the courtesy and stealth of those young operators
and although things got back to normal the next day
—no reflection on you—
more than a few romances
budded from the sparks of that confusion.

4

At the news of your death
couples who had never heard of you
kept walking
and were only dragged back
by the nagging sensation
that after hundreds of miles
they had left homes and families unattended.
And one source stated
that a woman in her early thirties
after returning and finding that she
had not left her oven on,
headed directly back out
and has not been heard from since.

5

At the news of your death
in every hospital in America
and all at once
babies were born
and then slapped on the butt,
and preschoolers woke up early from their naps
and the more teachers yelled
and snapped their red rulers
the more riled up the little ones became.
At home, all they would have for dinner was chocolate milk
and they threw their pajamas out the window
and snuck dirty books to bed
and the next day everyone wore
their crusty fake mustaches to school
and answered their teacher's questions
in rhyme.

6

At the news of your death
not a good poem was written
not in your country or mine
not by any of the famous poets from anywhere,
no, we all just sat down and had a good cry,
even the ones who didn't think so much of you
got up from their chairs, misty,
thinking it was their wives or their age
or the millennium
and no matter what we did,
none of us could get back to it,
not for a good long while.

7

At the news of your death
everyone turned on the TV
and left the room
at the news of your death
everyone took pictures
that would come out blurry
at the news of your death
every dinner, no matter curried or cajun,
came out sweeter, unbelievably sweeter
than anyone could have imagined.

8

At the news of your death
on the day that you died
the paper came with a little note
saying that you were a crazy and good man,
which I knew
and that you were a talented poet
with thirty books to your credit,
which I knew
and saying that you were dead,
so I went out and threw it in the street.
Later the neighbors would mention it
and I would get sad, and wouldn't explain,
and I expect it will be a point of contention for a while.

9

David, at the news of your death
the trees became sad,

not all of them of course,
but a few in every country,
and they decided to skip summer
and drop their leaves right then
and despite confusion on the ground,
birds in naked nests, and wind with nothing to do
all over the world they have proposed to keep this up.
You see, being trees they can't believe you're not coming back.
They say they will do this year after year,
stubborn and ignorant trees that they are.
They have promised to keep this up, David,
despite official protest and calm pleading of every kind.
Yes, they are determined to keep this up
until you return.

ERIN BELIEU (b. 1965)

PART OF THE EFFECT OF THE PUBLIC SCENE
IS TO IMPORTUNE THE PASSING VIEWER

For Example:

walking past the Ritz a girl may be sitting on the last step crying
as if alone and you notice, even in this cocktail-hour light, the
little rips and shreds of her chapped lips and that she has no
Kleenex and no one stops to offer one and you feel damned if you
do or don't, not wanting to intrude, as a man is standing maybe
only three feet away, his profile approximating a little shame,
some discomfort, but mostly a sphinx-like composure, or
boredom, perhaps, indicating they *are* together, together in that
way you're not completely sure you'll ever want to know about
again and you're ashamed, too, with nothing to offer but to gaze
intently at the fascinating streetlamp as you walk by.

Probably You've Caused a Scene Yourself:

public or private, at a bar or in a strange apartment, when
suddenly you became conscious of the drama, of the real pleasure
in your tears, the catharsis of the wail and rage, the screams, the
"trashing of the joint," because that's what's next, snipping up
his Liberty of London ties, ripping off her nightgown, pushing

her out naked on the patio for the neighbors' judgment who are
there, to be sure, either by accident or rubbernecked design,
keeping score or scared for their own property. Or instead you've
been the impetus, unfaithful, deceitful, maybe only the hapless
object of some other person's desire thinking that, for all their
protestations of love, you might as well be a bathroom fixture or
bookend. In either case,

It's Hard to Make a Graceful Exit:

as all scenes peter out in awkward ways. Someone's left thinking
of the perfect remark, a remark that'll sink like an ax blade, the
kind that are never on hand when needed, so that you end up
shouting, spluttering *Oh yeah?! Oh Yeah?!* like a moron,
like a damn fool, crying on the last step, in front of strangers,
without a Kleenex.

THE MAN WHO TRIED TO RAPE YOU

When he appears a block away, you know.
Like when you watch a made-for-TV movie
and guess the ending in a minute,

or how, if you're listening, you'll almost hear
a pulse, a muted beat inside your head,
announcing the return of what's been coming.

Surprisingly, you think, it takes the form
of what's most obvious: the backlit shape
of trouble—first a faceless outline,

as if whoever drew this couldn't find
the way to fill it in, the buzzing mist
of streetlamps making ghosts of all his edges.

And then that ghost you've always feared is coming,
is walking toward you up the sidewalk, up
from childhood and books and all the movies

with which you've ever scared yourself, purposeless
as ghosts are, vaguely sad and understanding
in a way, as if he, too, knows a thing

about what's inevitable. The pause
before he grabs for you is awkward as

a school dance. It's like that, you think, a dance:

his arms heavy at your waist, the way he
smells not unpleasant, pulls you toward
his hips, which, in another case, might please

or thrill you. But now that thrill is fear, or
maybe it always was. The dance goes on
a moment more and you're not screaming, only

saying *No* and *No* and *No*; this becomes
a rhythm, like breathing, just as quiet,
as if you'll go on saying *No* forever,

and then he stops. Lets go. You wonder later
if it's your business to be generous.
And that you're sad and frightened, but not angry.

And where he went, pathetic silhouette,
the man who walked away, back to the dark;
how, after, even streetlamps seemed too bright

to fall on him. His face turning away.

How the Elderly Drive

You'd think this piece of road
just a dream for the old
woman coaxing her Bonneville
like a dangerous ghost down I-80.

Only her head appears above
the door panel, disembodied
by sundown, floating somewhere
above the thin string of her neck.

The way the elderly drive,
with their disheartened climbs
and slow-motioned maneuvers, it seems
they've only a mile to go down

soft, dirt roads, so that even Aunt
Pearl, her head sawed neatly from
her shoulders on the interstate last

winter, smiled down at the salad

she brought home from the luncheon
instead of tapping her brakes
gently when the semi tried to merge.
You'd think old people had no sense

of speed or the lateness of the day, or
where we all must get to, their magnified
eyes peering, inscrutable above
their steering wheels, tuberous hands

shaking, faintly shaking,
guiding their phantoms home.

MOLLY BENDALL (b. 1961)

CONVERSATION WITH ISADORA DUNCAN

How do you move?
  birds leaving water   mildly

What are your props?
  windmills   waves rising   columns   sky

What do you see there?
  the silhouette of a man sitting in an olive grove

Where are your children?
  when they call   gold leaves fall from their mouths

What was the dance you performed?
  the peasants plant their seed   I hold out my hands

What is death like?
  another dance   light falling on white flowers

What does the audience do now?
  laughter   uprising   I come at them headless

AFTER ESTRANGEMENT

You should know the kind
of morning it is—
one gods have argued over for years.

But I've decided I'm under
a Byzantine curse out of which endings
situate themselves
like deep forests.

The players are strewn
in the empty heart
of a house.
She's called up her lost cat
who kept her comfortable
when the weather wouldn't.
His promises are like an addict's;
they hang camouflaged
in the lying air.
They both bend close
to a package of undone letters.
(Remember, I've a knack for detecting
in those faint, desirous courtyards
where love once happened.)

You've argued for your eloquent society,
your chronic politics,
yet still you're fazed
by your worldly withdrawals
because the whole of us
can't seem to make you gloomy enough.
I take to the armchair
and look at the two of them from here.
They're out of step, gothic.
I've always cherished the dark rivers
of what's unfashionable.
Even the fireplace is complicit
as it gives up its last bouquets.
She wants one to hold
against him and the room's operas.

As sure as you held the moon
in your perverse opal,
their outcome is apparent.
Their planned departure is just

ahead of them: she'll harness
the gentle ribs of her cat
and leave in her most unseasonable dress.

What nonsense.
They only want to starve their history,
watch it dwindle
against the southeast light.
A shame—they'd seemed so sea-worthy.

Now, as voyaging linens precede
the stairs, the morning lingers
like trouble,
and they nod off.
The troubadours, too,
have neglected them.
Who can help them
to summon the illusion of desire?

MATINÉE IDYLLS

My window, barely attached by its butterfly hinge,
still reveals the shabby green awnings
across the street. If someone would only
mend the place. What's the latest in traffic?

I'm tucking away a few numbers on scraps and try
not to notice the black complacency of my phone.
Then I imagine his arrival:
He appears like a museum exhibit, hunted and ambushed

and always, graceful.
My face feels taut. I'm turning into brass.
I've kept his stash in my purse since
Wednesday—the litany—black beauties, white crosses.

But I can't live ashamed anymore.
In my letter to the city I say,
        "Dear ornamental pear, Dear old park at my disposal,
I need a new coat with thick cuffs,

I need walls with a real paint job. . ."
While I practice a stance,
my appliances only throw their color to each other
begging for words like   Bakelite   glamour.

★ ★ ★

Why don't we sit down at our usual place—
the hat-box-of-a-table, and retrieve

a momentary thing, like a Tuesday.
I am fond of your jacket, but I do think the darkness

should go down the front.
Midsummer has turned a suspicious cheek to me

rather than become the relief I'd counted on.
The turbaned one by your aqua pool?

A business associate?
I heard the snap of her compact

when I swung the gate. I could have been her,
and worn the gold sandals that light up against

the floral tiles. (That's another
reward I give myself when I need some mercy.)

You've carved an almost tropical
space around yourself.

It's all blurry to you. But look, past the verandah,
above the jasmine,

where the horizon is tissue paper thin,
that's where I'll help you one last time.

★ ★ ★

". . . yes, I left my martini back there on the vanity."
The mirror doubling her, her glass.
"Only a past to conceal. . ."

She crosses herself with her perfume.
He's getting ready, rushing in a belted coat
around a medley of packages and boxes.

"I'll send for the rest."
"On your way out, notice the trumpet vine,
it's so skillfully tangled."

Now their predicament, their cigarette smoke—they're so cavalier.
Once they'd rendez-voused to suit themselves
and left the misled behind.

Even their seaside table had risen
into the cloying sky. The diving pelicans
and yachts, aloof in their hemispheres.

The two of them had thrown their last worries
into the ocean of disapproval
leaving a cool, rational sound on the air.

DINA BEN-LEV (b. 1964)

BROKEN HELIX

The sexy talk show host nods and nods. Beside her
a bald man begs to meet the mother he's never known.
Slowly, in front of fourteen million, the curtain
rises with applause—surprise! Before a camera closes in,

I shut my eyes. Down in deepest Florida, in a hospital
winged with a sanatorium, you named me Cheryl.
Then signed me away. At 22, were you tired
of trailer parks, truck stops, drive-thru

windows of worry? Did an old, world-weary nurse
warn, Only one skill you'll be properly paid for. . . .
Impressive, said a man with his hand on my resume. . . .
But hell, you'll ruin marriages

with such heavenly hair. Walking out of that white room
and out of that black building, I thought of your leaving—
thirty years ago, those minutes it took
to exit, empty-handed but for one slim bag.

In the cool, antiseptic lobby, you might've stopped
at a fountain. Bending, maybe you moved your whole
face into the water. Were you glamorous in sunglasses,
pushing open the door to the heat? You'd never see

your daughter settled in Seattle, where sun's uncommon
and painful. Never know her new name. Did you
ride a bus alone through battering light, past the hundred
hotels of Miami? At 20, after phoning and phoning and failing

to find you, I fell off a chair in the Fontainebleau.
Pink drinks paid for by a lawyer who liked me best
on my knees. Did my father rub your feet
when you returned? Or did you dream

all night, alone, one light left on?
Blurry on gas, I spread for suction
and scalpel. A nurse held my head. . . .
At 24, with a Master's in Fantasy, I ached for escape

from the dirtiest, snowiest section of Syracuse.
A taxi took me home, where sleep came on a green
Goodwill couch—bought with the man of my dreams
who later burned poems in the bathtub,

shot fist-wide holes through my Nova.
And the next day, did you turn to the TV
for comfort? And now, half a lifetime later,
in the kitchen / livingroom / bedroom / only room,

watch the same talk show host? How she moved
a microphone to the mouth of the bald man's mother?
How she asked, OK tell me, would you do it again?

A SENSUALIST SPEAKS ON FAITH

The path the stream scribbles
is perfect. In summer when crows

lower themselves on the branches,
Italian plums rain. This is what I call

luck. Don't refrain from falling
in love with the Tunisian woman's black hair

in the window, her careful displays
of coconut loaves, pistachio crowns.

Smile at the way fingers anticipate
the shining cold curves of doorknobs.

If you should walk through a spiderweb,
pity how it will miss

the saffron perfume of a butterfly.
If you lie down with words that are ugly,

close your eyes—imagine
a time when no one was

guilty or clever.
Inhale deeply, again

and again, and in that breathing
hear the wordless faith

of our first ancestors—
the ones who forgave

their fins and swam to shore,
the ones who didn't question

a beginning made on sand.

JACQUELINE BERGER (b. 1960)

GETTING TO KNOW HER

Sometimes it's salt
from the V of bones at the collar,
sometimes it's the peppery smell of the scalp,
bitter chocolate of the inner ear,
the almost sugar of the lower back.
From one angle she looks like a boy,
from another like a workman,
and face to face she looks like the girl
who left home at sixteen
to live in a trailer on the outskirts of town
where factories sent petticoats of smoke into the dark sky
and where for a time she changed her name

from Martha to Anew.
We haven't touched yet, therefore I haven't sucked
the ends of her hair, little paint brushes,
or licked her palms, pressing them open
the way one coaxes the pages of a book
to lie flat so one can read. Something about her
reminds me of small streets I have stumbled upon
where the trees nearly grow together,
making a canopy of greens to walk beneath.
Already I have catalogued these smells on her: coffee,
cigarettes, beer, soap, leather. Leaving the sexual
air of the bar, we step into the differently
sexual air of the night, wet and cool, we hold onto
each other's sleeves as though in our absence
the sidewalk had turned to ice.
The moon is made of fish bones, it dangles
between buildings, its light comes down like snow.
We walk back to the car, sliding together
while the tectonic plates of crust beneath the earth
move like barges in their jelly.

THE GUN

The first time I held a gun,
the man asked me if I wanted to
and took the bullets out before
placing the heavy dark thing in my hand,
I cocked it and pulled the trigger, pointing it
away from and then toward myself.
Our life holds our death like a card
slipped into the center of the deck.
The man and I had been talking about art,
how each brush stroke is a record
of itself being made,
it surprised me when he said he had a gun,
we were up on the roof of his loft,
he had taken his clothes off
and was encouraging me to do that same.
Below us the yards were planted with corn,
the neighborhood bars were dark
and cool, you could slug back a beer
under a poster of a busty Mexican woman
draped in bullets.
Anything is harmless going at the right speed,

the bullets in my hand rattled like dried corn,
they were gold and heavy
rocking back and forth,
nestled like baby hamsters.
What followed was the usual
debate about guns and violence,
maybe it's foolish not to have a gun,
I can start thinking that way too,
a woman needs a gun,
I was ambivalent
about how much further
I wanted this to go,
he had nothing left to strip out of,
it would have been my turn.
I had no reason to trust him,
nor for that matter, not to.
Sometimes I think it would be great
to have a gun, but I know myself,
I'd spend all night looking at it,
turning it in my hand,
thinking, this is the small door
my death could walk through.
Sometimes I can't go even an hour
without putting something in my mouth,
sometimes the human
capacity for cruelty stuns me.
A woman gangraped in a stairwell
she was led to by a man she knew,
when he told her to wait there
for a minute, she waited,
he came back with his buddies
and they sealed off the exits,
and were on her like dogs
tearing into garbage,
she made herself lie still,
maybe they would leave
if they thought she was dead.
How many guns
were there, did she have a gun,
did she wish she had a gun,
did she know how to use a gun?
A man takes his clothes off
on the roof of his loft, below him,
the silk of corn, the blare of the street,
the day unraveling its light.
There is a gun in every drawer in America,

there is no way to forget this,
he took the bullets out
but the gun still sang
its dark power in my hand.

BETWEEN WORLDS

The doctor gave them what he thought was enough
to bring on the end, the flimsy door between worlds
easily pushed in, but the morphine rattled
in their mother's body for hours
until finally they turned her on her stomach,
as one latches the screen door
banging in the storm, to help her die.
An ordinary story, the way someone dies,
as women share stories of delivery
with bravado, at the baby shower.
Mine took twelve hours one woman says,
twelve is nothing, another claims
hers took twenty-four, and then it builds to two days,
several false starts, traffic to and from the hospital,
no epidural, it feels like fire
a woman with three boys tells a woman with no children,
like someone lit a match to your cunt,
she uses the hard Anglo-Saxon name,
this is the beginning of life.
They put their mother on her stomach to stop
the raking-leaves-on-concrete sound of her breath.
Death came like the tremble of rain on water,
then steam rising off the pond when it's through.

CAROLE BERNSTEIN (b. 1960)

THE CUP OF COFFEE

I sat on the couch. Sullen, young,
the young teenager. My mother had been dead
for three and a half hours. I was staring
at the couch arm, its orange threads,

and my own arm lying on it, bare.
It was summer. It was six in the morning.
My aunt and grandmother were there,
in my grandmother's apartment. They kept offering

food. Oatmeal, bananas. Gross. As if
I could eat. They tried to make me lie
down on Grandma's bed. "The puffy
pillows you loved to punch . . ." If I lay down I would die.

Some time passed. Neighbors left, came in,
cleared their throats, talked in murmur-voices.
I tried to remember "America" by Allen
Ginsberg, a boy had shown me. To block the noise.

I was starting to realize I could never go home.
That they were stuck with me, my aunt was.
The one who understood me was gone.
I narrowed my eyes to watch the room dissolve.

Then someone spoke to me. Would I have coffee.
It piqued my interest. I began to lift my face
slowly, carefully, neck stiff,
nearly paralyzed, I stood and took a place

at the kitchen table, where the cups
were passed to each and one came to me.
I had never tasted it. Of course a mess
of milk and sugar had been dumped
in mine, to lighten, sweeten. But beneath
was grateful, plain, essential bitterness.

When My Grandmother Said "Pussy"

It was when we were living
in the Rochdale Avenue projects,
right after we moved in. She was bringing us
a *mandel* bread wrapped in tinfoil.
She had walked up the three flights. That stairwell
wasn't the cleanest: a smell of burned food,
bubbled green walls seared with loopy graffiti.
She hobbled in shaking her head. *"Poosy!"* she spat.
"For vat do they hev to write this? What for, *Poosy?*
All over," she waved to *all over*

with the pointy bread, "it says, *Poosy!*
It's disgustinck!" she yelled. "It could
make you *zeeck!*" My mother laughed
a little, looked down,
took her coat.
My sister and I would snicker about it for days,
but then we smiled stupidly, painfully,
utterly paralyzed
to hear her speaking—*shouting*—such a word.

How unlike her it was, who never complained,
who shushed my grandfather's hoarse diatribes
against Capitalism, never read the paper,
pretended my cousin Roberta wasn't a lesbian.
At the funeral the rabbi called her a "Yiddishe Mama"—
yes, the well-scrubbed house, Passover feasts
where no one could get her to sit;
she was fed by watching us eat,
she'd hurry back to the kitchen, offer more.

It must have been indignation, that day,
about what we kids had to see. Still, it's a strange
keepsake of her. The past runs through our fingers
like flour, leaving a hard little packet
of surprising jewelry someone's buried. . . .
Roberta had me look at an old photo, once,
of my grandmother dressed up for Purim, as a boy.
Chubby in plaid knickers, cap, hair twisted up,
she's smiling, thrilled, at the photographer.
I could feel Roberta feeling she saw something
hidden to everyone else:

a quality she longed to find
in my grandmother, beneath the disguise.
And I look back, too, to pluck and pluck
embarrassment's twangy piano string,
to when she named it—my grandmother
for an instant becoming dangerous
as the writing on the wall:
to say she was pushing back
against all that was trying, and would try,
to claim my attention and consume me.

CAUGHT

The 1928 film star's breasts—
nipples poking through
the sheerest gossamer wrap—seem oddly modern,
as though people from the past's bodies aren't supposed
to look like ours. The photo dates,
explains the film book, from before
movies were made suitable for family viewing,
and even the actress's strands and strands of pearls
hide little, like the pearls I wore last night as I
hung over my lover and dragged them
down the dark field of his body,
slowly let them comb the delicate hairs
until they roped and held him, and as we smiled,
suddenly I remembered
the necklace had been my grandmother's.

I was quiet for a moment, like a child
listening at a locked door
who tenses for a cry—again—
then nothing, nothing out of them,
as if they've gone to sleep. And the cry recalled,
beyond belief, soon flies out the window.
When they pose for me it's always in the kitchen:
her paisley apron strains around her middle,
his back brace squeaks, he leans with a glass
to enlarge a column of *Yiddishe Zeitung*.
And the creased family photos glaze over
like a fisheye in the sun:
like something caught, that turns
to resemble abalone, mother-of-pearl.
So cloudy and so clear.

PROFANING THE DEAD

You died young, uncle, only fifty-two.
Heart stopped, you stared through the windshield at Avenue L.
Now dozens of cars wind faithfully after your funeral.
It's seven years since my last run-in with you;
Fourteen, parents just buried, I got screwed
Several afternoons a week before my aunt got home—
In her bed, I confess, fed a shotglass of Amaretto
While you tongued my reluctant feet. Oh, I was a "prude,"

You'd coo, and love would tingle from head to toe.
For years you sneered I'd come back. True, I couldn't miss
The end of the road for you. I'll bet it was rough:
Death licked its chops, preparing to swallow you whole,
Its massive paws on your chest, just scratching your tit—
It sniffs at you. It decides you're old enough.

MARK BIBBINS (b. 1968)

THE PATHOLOGY OF PROXIMITY

I stink to make you bitch
is as good a reason as any—

he can't see through pockets,
but then, that's the point.

He knows by now that keys
make a distinct music,

different from, say, two dimes
and a quarter. Ranting, he trudges

the middle of the avenue
in his pajama bottoms—

to have that much room to one's self—
the cars always go around.

Two kids argue on the corner
like actors picking parts

of scenery from between their teeth.
Once the idea of blue

hair belonged to old women
and everyone got along

just fine, but that was before
any of us met. Up there,

Midtown East hoists itself, dull
and lovely, into air thick as roux.

I push a shopping cart along
the bottom of the fusty river,

adding things as I go, removing
others to make room. Exhausting.

Here a box spring, a softball, a muffler.
They all want to go home with me.

As bubbles stampede toward whatever
light they can, a noise like *yet*

crackles with possibility, but is more
likely only some bird's beak

plunging after mercurial fish,
or a coin thrown in for luck.

GEOMETRY CLASS

Mark is a fag scratched in blue ink
        on the surface of a desk, and true

enough. Trust letters and numbers,
        if not hands that form them,

geometries of loss worked out
        on cool green skins of slate.

Clap these woolly erasers together,
        inhaling ashes of a dead theorem

as they slide down rulers of light
        slowly to the linoleum floor.

Trust what lines do to each other:
        they are creatures lacking malice.

DAVID BIESPIEL (b. 1964)

THERE WERE NO DEER IN THE THICKET

As if to draw the light to the body.
As if to draw the light.
As if through the hand that is music, that is stillness.
The bedrock we sat on thrummed like the light.
Air knew of long presences breaking near the heart.

Yesterday is already given up,
Like a body passing through another,
The voices dissolving the way light falls on the hand,
The way humility is given up.
You said the poplars made a music like daylight—

What the black spot in the eye catches—
Strumming the afternoon fissure to an answer.
You said the grass was not familiar,
That the ruminant undercurrent slapped at the green blades.
The wind was not an answer, not a music.

You said: *Look, deer!*
You said: *Give me your hand again.*
What of the light, full of voices, blowing streaks
Through the vigil-less holes in every moment?
Give me your hand again.

You slept, light softest on your closed eyelids.
Your breath.
Gray dimming in the bedrock.
There were no deer in the thicket, teething the grass,
Lying in the lion's sun.

Always someone is missing whom I'll never meet again, never touch.
Even the poplars are full of grief.
You said the light was like Canada, vast.
You said the heart will break for anyone,
Never more than a body from another.

WHITE ROSES

Men truck I-45 up and down Oklahoma,
Love the railroad, women, and wave ballcaps
To the sunburnt trains. Prairie
Spreads toward mute corn,
Sunflowers, pigsties.
In front lots, bus parts
Scatter like bred dogs.

Out of the caboose one man
Is like a menagerie. Trains chugging
Past towns with decent names,
Sunday to Friday. Whistleblast:
A reminder of old wins
Or terror a veteran
Won't even tell his new wife.
She knows something's happening
Already to their marriage.

His people adore her Chickasaw hair.
She loves the doctor's white roses
And the wood bird,
With the plastic spinning wings,
Poking out of the planters. The withered
Petals, she calls, *etudes.*

LILACS
Allston, Massachusetts, 1985

Leeward of the house is nothing but the tip-
Tapered leaves and the sweet blooms' purple
And white pyramidal clusters. In the shade
The petals are dark as plums or thumb-sized
Knots of blackberries, though in the sun
They're gray as sea water almost rippling.
When she comes to pick them after school's out,
They lean, as if to weep, into her palms, a few
Sprigs falling to the concrete, the flesh of each

Touching as companions touch. She must know
They'll die, though it's summer she feels
In the smooth oval green when she cracks the stems.
Above her hair that falls straight and black,

Above the wide petals of the early evening
Primrose, right and left of the lilac bushes,
There are only waves of clouds that crumble,
Bulge, and subside. I don't think she cares
About the clouds. They bloom and fall.

She's found a heaven to put in the window.
And I know she doesn't think of my father
At the salvage tug's anchor cable,
Near the Korea Strait's eastern channel.
It's 1951, the sky filled with a close knowledge
Of the gunfire's blue-red clusters of smoke.
He's at the winch, watching the hawser slacken
As it hooks in the damaged vessel.
Punctures the size of plums or blackberries.

Two men, to the right and the left
Of my father, will be shot. They will die.
Cut down, he'll say. Unlike the primrose
On each side of the lilacs. So dark,
The top ones beyond any reach or pull
But the wind's, and visible in the lamplight
Where the great clouds span like phantoms
Bearing blood, water, flower, sky.
Those things we never give up.
Be it late spring. Be it cloudy weather.

THE HEAT SOURS

And squeezes through the blinds of the open window,
The light foliated, inflamed. The heat turns
To dust over the sliced lemons
And saddens itself. Its breath like a child's
Sleeping breath, sleeping on the grass,
Oak-shadow and windbreak driving away
The gnats coming on with the sun.
With the waxwings: if one let me crawl within the sound

Of its breathing, its brown, warm belly
Rising and falling, would the song in its voice
Settle? And rest? Would it fly to a willow twig
And call out to the wounds of heaven,
Heaven on earth, earth we give our bodies to?
Or I put an ear to the grass, accepting
The urge not to cry again? At anything?

RICHARD BLANCO (b. 1968)

EL MALIBÚ

Papá smelled of fine *tabaco* and the dried blood
stains on his pants and underneath the fingernails
of his tender and pink meat-locker hands.
After four years as head butcher at *el mercado*,
he saved enough cash for a deal on a '72 Malibu,
two door, plush vinyl, with FM and lighter,
eight-track tape player under the driver's seat.

We rode in style that first summer vacation,
the copper-brown metallic finish of *el Malibú*
glimmering over turnpike tarmac and grove hills,
eight tracks of melancholy boleros playing
through cypress swamps and billboard holler
on a whirlwind of motel pools and theme parks:
goldfish worlds under glass-bottom boats,
enchanted castles, fireworks, and roller coasters,
water-ski pyramids of bathing caps and ruffles,
reenactments of Wild, Wild West shoot-outs.

Cruising our new country in our new car,
through attractions and distractions, convinced
we'd made it so many years since *la Revolución*—
Papá held to his leather-wrapped steering wheel
like a worn matador to red wine, denying loss,
denying the scented hills remind him of his hills—
his hands clean and manicured, free of blood.

THE SILVER SANDS

Before the revival of quartz pinks and icy blues
on this neon beach of Art Deco hotels and boutiques,
there were the twilight verandas lined with retirees,
the cataract eyes of Mrs. Stein who would take us
for mezzanine bingo and pancakes at Wolfies;
I remember her beautiful orthopedic wobble.

Before sequined starlets popping out of limousine doors
and booze on the breath of every glitter-paved street,
there were the five-year-old summers of flamingo towels,

transistor radios blaring something in Spanish we ignored,
only curious of driftwood, washed-up starfish and jellyfish,
the beauty of broken conchs and our moated sand castles.

Before the widened sidewalks and pretentious cafés
where I take my cappuccino sprinkled with cinnamon,
our mothers were peacocks in flowered bathing caps
posing for sandy Polaroids like pageant contestants;
there were fifteen-cent Cokes to their ruby lips
and there was nothing their beauty couldn't conquer.

Before the demolition of the Silver Sands Hotel,
our fathers spun dominos under the thatch-palm gazebos,
drank then insulted the scenery: *Nada like our Varadero,*
there the sand was powder; the water truly aquamarine.
I remember the poor magic of those voices—
how beautifully they remembered beauty.

SHAVING

I am not shaving, I'm writing about it.
And I conjure the most elaborate idea—
how my beard is a creation of silent labor
like ocean steam rising to form clouds,
or the bloom of spiderwebs each morning;
the discrete mystery of how whiskers grow,
like the drink roses take from the vase,
or the fall of fresh rain, becoming
a river, and then rain again, so silently.
I think of all these slow and silent forces
and how quietly my father's life passed us by.

I think of those mornings, when I *am* shaving,
and remember him in a masquerade of foam, then,
as if it was his beard I took the blade to,
the memory of him in tiny snips of black whiskers
swirling in the drain—dead pieces of the self
from the face that never taught me how to shave.
His legacy of whiskers that grow like black seeds
sown over my cheek and chin, my own flesh.

I am not shaving, but I will tell you about the mornings
with a full beard and the blade in my hand,
when my eyes don't recognize themselves

in a mirror echoed with a hundred faces
I have washed and shaved—it is in that split second,
when perhaps the roses drink and the clouds form,
when perhaps the spider spins and rain transforms,
that I most understand the invisibility of life
and the intensity of vanishing, like steam
at the slick edges of the mirror, without a trace.

JOE BOLTON (b. 1961; d. 1990)

FIN DE SIÈCLE

In the twilight of the nineteenth century,
    Chekhov's peasants
Are gazing across the river and dreaming
    The afterlife begins
In the belfry of the church with five domes.
    In Moscow one longs
For the provinces, and in the provinces
    One longs for Moscow.
This is the desire that makes life at once
    Irresistible and unbearable.
A man takes his lover's soft shoulder in his hands,
    Her hair gone suddenly gray.
In the chiaroscuro of the first snows of autumn,
    In the boom and heave
Of ice breaking up on the river in spring, you hear
    Your life passing like a song.
Near Petersburg, the women go mad trying to keep
    The geese out of the garden.

THE LIGHTS AT NEWPORT BEACH

If there were time for everything
(And there is); if that phosphorescent light
Stunning the Pacific meant anything
(And it does); if all this world of worlds might
Become more than the museum for something
We have lost (and it will)... but not tonight.
Tonight, love, Newport Beach is simply on fire,
The buildings blazing up under the sky,

The streets running headlong into the sea.
If we were more than the sum of our desire
(But we're not); if there were a language I
Could find to get beyond the opacity
Of zero. . . . But I'm tired of words and all we turn
Away from. I just want to watch it burn.

In Memory of the Boys of Dexter, Kentucky

West of Murray, just off 641,
It is forever summer in my mind.
I see land darken under a red sun
And hear lost music drift back on the wind.
Blind fingers read the initials D.P.
Carved in the oak from which he was found hung;
In the creek, J. holds his breath endlessly.
Did they think they were late, leaving so young?—
Chain-smoking only to bypass cancer,
Washing down pills with whiskey, wrapping cars
Round poles like a girl's love ring. . . . In answer,
The sky fades like a chord behind first stars.
Their dying, it seems now, started at birth—
Dying to find out what their lives were worth.

The Parthenon at Nashville

Late December noon, near freezing—
Maple and sweetgum bare, but the grass green yet
In sunlight, and warmth of light wearing away
At the frail scythe's-edge of ice
Around the pond. On her lunch hour,
Parked in his car, they tossed the last
Of their sandwiches to ducks that bobbed and fussed
In the smaller oval of water not frozen over.
They were beyond being
In love, but not quite ready
To look past the end of the affair.
Across the water, reflected in the water,
Risen stone:
Columns swelling with light,
The stylized figures restored
To the frieze—an order
Called into question

By the troubled surface of the pond.
They remember wondering
What happened to the ducks
Come autumn. Now they know: nothing.
And now a solitary jogger pushes his breath
Past them, as the traffic continues
Out on West End.
They sense that something
Needs to be done or said—
Anything but this feeling of themselves
As figures held in the motion
Of some lost moment.
And yet they can't seem to move, to speak,
Maybe thinking they won't have this clarity
Again for a long time, maybe amazed
At the distance from which they see themselves:
Luminous, hardly human,
And already half in love with the beautiful ruins.

AMERICAN TRAGEDY

The Chevrolet fires past two blond children
Eating mud in the ditch by a dirt road.
Kentucky, midsummer, sun going down—
Day like an empty shotgun shell, still warm,
Fragrant with dog shit and honeysuckle.

The skinny girl inside the white trailer
Is drinking gin and torturing herself
With a cigarette: nipples, navel, crotch.
The screen door hangs by one broken finger.
Past dark, a light comes on. Nothing happens.

GAYLORD BREWER (b. 1965)

MOUNTAINS

On a Sabbath late
    in a French embassy sedan
    on good roads from Tepoztlan

The woman beside me
      through thick English
      telling stories of a club singer
      who ruled Paris by voice

Mentions the loss
      of Raymond Carver laughs
      at how I say Rimbaud

We're soiled from climbing
      and the Mexican mountains
      we note together

Aging as they darken
      maintain a fair distance
      leave room for breathing
      for living

Unlike other mountains
      we could name

THE JOURNALS

Say you needed some ideas
about what your life had been.
In three notebooks are
details of all the adventures
to bring you back. They're a bit
roughed up. One with the unicorn
pacing inside a fence, another
of spring in the Han palace,
a third with red fishes jumping.

Say if you opened them,
all that you required would leap
to your fingers. It's your
life, you paid for it, so why not
look? Why be ashamed? Everyone
was young once. Strawberries
in Berlin, there was night music,
someone cried. Much you don't
remember—fences, palaces, water.

Say you knew what came next.

Teen Drowns in Rehabilitation Camp Days Before 17th Birthday, Questions Persist

I'm going under were the last words,
a friend swimming nearby
could do nothing—*I can't breathe*—
before the river swallowed the shadow

The mother speaks between pauses
I was going to take him a birthday cake
I don't know how to say it, it's not good
None of this is good

Her loss is palpable, real loss
But your pain is your own and enough
It sears away all excess, leaving
only a blue flame in water

Joel Brouwer (b. 1968)

Conservatory Pond, Central Park, New York, New York

The model yachts contend in seas sheltered
from any wave while their captains fidget
on the concrete shore, fingers sticky

with ice cream and Cracker Jack, less intrigued
by the tiny jibs and rudders of their ships
than their grandfathers would like.

Beyond the armada, on the far shore,
a flock of birders flutters into view.
They snap together telescopes and tripods,

screw four-foot lenses into cameras,
and vanish in a thicket of magnification
just as their quarry, a red-tailed hawk, dives

from his nest high above Fifth Ave., snatches
a squirrel off the grass not ten feet away,

and banks into an oak to eat. Equipment

superfluous, the birders stare up rapt.
The crowd grows fast: yuppies on mountain bikes,
Haitian nannies pushing strollers, some drunks,

the young skippers, their rankled guardians.
Fifty heads tilt and swivel like radar
as the hawk drags its prey from branch to branch.

A woman in a filthy Mets sweatshirt
stops tossing popcorn to the chipmunks, screams
Drop it, fucker! Go back to the goddamn forest!

She hurls rocks, misses. But the hawk, flustered,
bobbles, and the torn gray rag falls
at her bandaged feet. Guts shiny with blood. Eyes

augered out. The crowd looks around. We see
how close we're standing, begin to inch apart.
In the pond, the abandoned boats collide, go down.

Steve's Commando Paintball, San Adriano, California

no red ammo spells a tin sign screwed
to an oak. I ask the owner why. *It stains,* he says.
He pockets my twenties, thrusts

a heavy black gun into my hands, barks down
the list of rules: no close-range fire,
goggles on at all times, etc. *Sissy stuff,*

he adds, apologetic. I load up my gumball
bullets, unbloody yellows and greens.
A burst of full-auto—like popcorn—echoes

from the practice range. I'm here to chaperone
six kids from the school where I teach.
They haven't done this before, but assured me

It's cool. I suggested mini golf. Fat chance.
When the plastic trumpet squawks to signal
the war's begun, they melt into the brush, lose

me instantly. So here I am, alone on a dazzled
spring morning high in the Santa Cruz mountains,
sweating under goggles, helmet and face mask,

the redwoods full, I know, of salesmen and mechanics
who mean to point their guns at me and shoot. I buy it quick,
in the stomach, a bee sting under my sweater, and trudge

to the Dead Zone, fingering the wet white blot
and yelling as I've been taught: *Dead man! Dead man
coming through!* This keeps you from dying twice.

You can smoke once you're dead. And there are chairs.
The afterlife is bounded by orange traffic cones.
A teenage St. Peter with walkie-talkie checks your weapon

when you enter. *Safeties on in the Dead Zone!*
he scolds, if a corpse wanders in with his gun still hot.
I talk with a travel agent from San José.

Though allegiance means nothing to the dead,
I'm glad his armband matches mine. *Every human
has the instinct to hunt,* he says. *Better to get it out here*

than go psycho in McDonald's or the post office.
The trumpet blares for rapture, and we rise from our seats.
One of my kids turns up with his throat shot blue.

Having fun? I ask. He nods. Solemn. Says *Yes I am.*

SPACE MEMORABILIA AUCTION, SUPERIOR STAMP AND COIN, BEVERLY HILLS, CALIFORNIA

For Jim Richardson

When I bid my wad—forty bucks—on a helmet
with smoked-glass faceplate
and Soviet hammer and sickle stenciled

over the ears in—what else?—red,
I assumed I'd be outdone. But no one lifted
an eyebrow or wiggled a finger—not

the medal-spangled Air Force colonel, not the bored
old actress in the pink chiffon, not her poodle,

also pink. Imagine my triumph when the gavel fell,

but still, I wondered, what gives?
A single foil pouch of freeze-dried ice cream product
had gone for three grand just minutes ago.

I asked the guy next to me what was up,
and he explained through his cucumber sandwich
my helmet was training-camp stuff,

prototypical—in short, it had never left
the earth. I had stumbled on the odd economy
of space memorabilia: value rests not

in what, but how far. Thus no one bid a dime
for the set of Cape Canaveral silverware,
but a used washcloth from Mir nearly caused a riot.

Hilarious, I thought. Grown men and women
scribbling zero after zero on their chits
for golfballs, tubes of toothpaste, socks.

I wandered over to the display table
and tried on a glove from the Soyuz mission.
Used in three space walks, the catalog said.

Inside its eighteen heat-retaining layers
my hand felt suddenly absent, as if I'd thrust it
into another world. A quiet one. One above

all hungers, above the contorted atmosphere,
from which the earth would seem mercifully simple.
Yes, I thought, I'd buy this if I could.

STEPHANIE BROWN (b. 1961)

I WAS A PHONY BALONEY!

I was a real phony baloney.
I was not a, never was a, member of the Republican party
But I was a real phony baloney.
I pretended to be meek but I was not

I pretended to be silent but I was seething
I thought I was confessional but I was teething
On my gristly, phony baloney.
I cared about my shoes (I was chattering) not really
As much as you might have thought:
Oh, sure I was (fill in the blank) and I was (fill in this spot)
But I was a real phony baloney.
I was thinking of how to overthrow the power plot
While I pretended to tend to my petty thoughts
My eyes were narrowing into harmful harmless slots
I took it out on (Blank) and (Her name I forgot)
I was a real phony baloney.
I pretended to be meek but I was not
I pretended to be weak but I was a block
Of solid phony baloney.

Envoi:
I pretended to be sighing but I was enjoying my lot:
I was a sorry, sorry. (Baloney.)

FEMININE INTUITION

I. Little Red Riding Hood

Astrid comes from upstate New York.
She comes from distress.
She's enthusiastic about it.
She doesn't belong, but she tries hard.
Her husband hurts her, but they have a drug-free life.
They roller skate and take up fads enthusiastically,
Neon clothing and the like.
He's an air traffic controller, so they move constantly.
This time it's California. After the picnic
I said, "She reminds me of Little Red Riding Hood."
My husband said, "Yeah."
We were doing the dishes.
I can't say some other things, so I say this.

II. Plastic Surgery, Skipped Dessert

That simple woman thought I was simple, but I was not.
I was never simple.
Not trees, stars, plot.
She smoked her fingers down to the yellow.
She had the harsh hearty laughter

Of the women who believe the men will leave them.
All the mothers I knew went nuts.
Hair the color of a screwdriver.
It's a cliché, but it's an altar.
Cotton candy spun into a knot.
Especially rich women, with art.
Kimono, muumuu.
Ice cubes.
But I was never simple. I was never simple.
The way I was raised, the men never leave a woman.
She was a woman: I could not trust her.

III. A Woman Clothed with the Sun

Imagine, all over America, women are losing bone mass.

Brittle old ladies: we create them.
Coiffured movie sirens lounging around the pool transmogrify
into brittle old sea hags.
(They don't know anything; they just nag.)
Let's let them swim out to sea.
Let's give them a spiny seahorse to ride on.
"Good-bye brittle old ladies, beautiful ones—
Ride out against the horizon and the orange sun!"

MARGINALIA

You know, we looked at, touched carefully, and studied a copy of
Erasmus' *Praise of Folly* with marginal drawings by a young
Holbein. I gave the seminar an analysis of Holbein's early
woodcuts, made around the same time as the marginal drawings.
I knew Holbein as a young man, I thought. A different man than
the one who painted "The Ambassadors," a mature artist so
aware of the complexity of his craft, I said. The marginalia
included a friar wearing an ass' head while giving a sermon. In
pen and ink, yet! They were, I noted, "small, personal, intimate,
and funny." Folly is pictured as a woman with visible and nicely
proportioned breasts. (Remember the great marginalia in MAD
magazine?)

Then my brain felt clear like whiteness, glass, snow fields. I felt
adrenaline surges. I never had to leave the Library. I loved the

travel books with tiny foldout maps of the sixteenth-century sea.
I compared them to the first edition of *Gulliver's Travels*. I really
loved that closed quiet. Around rare books you can only write in
pencil. Finally, though, I had enough when I finished my
degree. You know, at a Christmas party a year after this time I
joked, "It was like I was in the Brain Olympics." I said, "I could
be a good amateur but never a professional." Then my brother
spoke in reply.

Still, I knew how to browbeat the others. I knew how to
outargue the point. I knew how to see the meaning of nudity in
the marginalia in the late editions of Books of Hours. Women in
tubs with fashionable distended stomachs surrounding the
prayers. My professor was often astonished at my leaps between
ideas; she was a very nice woman who wanted me to get a Ph.D.
I talked a lot about Erasmus because I was the only one who'd
read him. I was the kind of person people make fun of.

So, I was reading this *Ripley's Believe It or Not!* book in the
bathroom at my work. I work in a public library. I read a little
mortality tale about objects swept off to sea: they mean nothing,
therefore. Objects die too. You can't believe in them. When I
imagine myself in a future war, I always think of myself as being
one of those people who will be useless in the new society:
arcane knowledge about manuscripts, and typesetting, indeed! I'll
be one of the first to be killed if this happens.

Because, I am very far away from someone with hungry,
American immigrant needs. My family is now decadent. We're
serving the purpose of useless details. Did I have a certain
purpose? A dignity? All those things revolutionaries don't need.
Revolutionaries don't need toy stores. Revolutionaries don't need
me. Would I plead, *I never harmed anyone!* I did, of course. Most of
all, I would have harmed the soldier whose job it was to kill me.

It Took A Village

Every village has its village idiot.
Its Frankenstein, the monster, and the mob.

Fakelore, faxlore, bumper sticker wisdom.
I hope your own mom and dad tried to love you more.

LISA BUSCANI (b. 1964)

BAREFOOT IN THE CITY

You can't walk barefoot in the city.
Or your can,
if you're willing to chance. . .

The city covers its base
with things that stay with you,
with dog shit, with trash, with glass.

But still, you'll go where you'll go.

They say that the foot
is the soul of the body.
No pun is intended.
The center of everything is felt at the bottom.

The heat we've covered with concrete
is still with us.
We feel what's living and vital
underneath a face that would destroy us.

It's amazing what we'll do for warmth.

DOWNTIME

Catch me glassy vapid,
catch me mooning wordless,
catch me offtime-focus,
know me blessed and blessed.

There I am:
discordant, nouveau hooligan,
arched hands skeening bitchy on a steamy guitar.
My days whore short-lived syncopation;
I beat a nasty fractured push.

There I am:
Spring-coiled, muscled-up graceful,
the fruit of playground's labor caught in coursing,

Gravity's bastard with no legitimate ties,
I fly, I stuff, two. . . two. . .

There I am:
Babylon's worldly window,
stilettos staccatoing out
blood sharp swivels.
Mouth and mind and timing to match,
I'd love to kiss ya but I just washed my hair.

Catch me slack–move stupid,
catch me maw–deep living,
catch me slow–break gaping,
Know me blessed and blessed.

MISS MARY MACK

Nadine held my hand when we were kids.
When she stopped I thought she didn't love me anymore.

    Can I braid your hair?

We used to call my grandma "the Hoover,"
because her kisses were like a vacuum.

    I love you, a bushel and a peck, a bushel and a peck and
    a hug around the neck . . .

When I lost my virginity in a less–than–romantic manner, Fiona
put the tea pot on.

    He's an asshole. Need a hug?

Val took me to the campus clinic. They had a VHF Viewmaster
that showed the pap smear process up close and personal.

    Maybe we should tone it down a bit . . .

When her husband died, Mrs. Goldberg broke down over the
thought of going on their upcoming trip to Europe solo.

    I held her. She felt small.

I lay in my mother's bed, it was her bed then,
and I told her I was ugly and nobody liked me.

    My darling, you will always be beautiful to me.

ANTHONY BUTTS (b. 1969)

THE NATURE OF BRAILLE

She smelled like bananas just as sure
as if she'd sneaked into her mother's
refrigerator and scooped out a smooth
handful of pudding—rubbing it
between her breasts. She was retarded
and blind and couldn't have known
that she was the prettiest girl in fifth grade.
Her smile was the blueprint for guilt,
my guilt at wanting to have that scent
near me—dreaming of the glossy gray
veils obscuring her eyes, her tears
of irritation from medicines like the tears
of a young woman awaiting the end
of her boyfriend's year-long trip to Bulgaria.
Such was the dirt in my dreams, that silent
yet desperate need to make it all
right. I stand there with Becky against
the brick wall where we wait
for our taxi for the blind;
she has no idea I've closed my eyes
to that October day's sunshine.

A POE STORY

Three a.m. smoke rises from underground
gas lines, the hissing louder than the murmurs
of pigeons, louder than the white winter
clouds passing, heavy with the burden of snow,
nothing released here in Kalamazoo,
neither snow, nor rain, nor any item dropped
from the clenched purse of a woman walking
to her car, footsteps growing louder, quickening
as she spots me walking towards her, towards
the computer center, open twenty-four hours
for people like me, her car between us, gun metal
gray and slush beneath the fenders, the sky
forbidding as my brown face must seem,
her legs making ostrich strides, high heels
scraping the pavement, maybe thinking

my University book bag isn't a knapsack
but a rucksack concealing a gun or knife
bigger than any she's seen in any beefcake
action film where the hero can save a woman like her
from a guy like me, as beautiful as any Poe story,
the spires growing steeper, the icy
smoke of winter puffing faster through her lips, my strides
lengthening like any man who's tried to avoid looking
like a criminal, easing and slowing down as if the indictment
has already been filed, as if suspicion alone
could sentence a man before the crime,
before the thought has entered his mind, before the need
to steal ever took him from the arms of the starving children
he hasn't fathered, or from the woman waving good-bye
to her mother in the window of that first foster care home.

SKIN

In this world, shadows do not speak to us.
But when I write in shadows they call out
to me. I feel guilt for talking back,
        which should prove my humanity.

They move. The wings
of monarch butterflies flitter down into the fields
like leaves in autumn. Wings are shadows
        in my throat and they speak with me.
        They write their names on my skin
        as fervently as my brother did.

I have been a rapid angel since ending his game:
my awkward insides weren't really all mine. I would
disappear when he carved his name on my skin.
        He showed me I was just one word
        and I was made to never speak of it.

He told a lie to cover me up; I would never own
a unique body of cells. I'm dark and unseen
unlike the Christmas boxes
        in my dreams with their fervent stripes
        of pink and white skin. He was so happy
        about my insides that he would write
on me; and his name was silence.

The world of desire is too strong

for my body, but I can no longer sing of it
backwards, the falsetto scales
        of troubled notes; I was upside down for him,
        disappearing. I feel him ascending now
        out of my body unlike some finger
that he would slip in; his name passes up
and away through trails in my skin.
True memories are fires within.

        New hair curls his name backwards.
        And I will flitter now as I couldn't before;
lives are born and born again.

I have been a rapid angel since falling
        to earth; this paper, this skin, is mine.

THE BELLE ISLE MEN

Over by the horses,
        by the giant yellow slide,
the shoed but sockless
        men pace through the sundried dirt,
        through humid air lighting
on all those black legs
        sweating into the basins

of dress moccasins. Their mustaches
        are kept thin and close to the lip,
        close to the transplanted smiles
of Detroiters born in the Carolinas,
        of men who've learned to swallow everything.
The dusk blown into their eyes is the drought
        of women twisting in the shoreline silence,
        of cool evenings dying on the vines

of morning glories. The hum
        of lungs, of the larynx, murmuring low
aren't calls from pens of happy animals
        or from the reclusive river skulking
        in the crevices of rocks.
Those murmurs are the revenge of lust
        exchanged like rage, like the world when viewed

from horizontal, the big scoop
    of sky turning over the soil
    as if the coming of day
would cover them.

RAFAEL CAMPO (b. 1964)

THE LOST PLAZA IS EVERYWHERE

The protected Venezuela, the rare,
Scarlet birds everywhere—I see it now.
To have a memory is cloudless air
And greenest streets, to have it all right now,
Again, is true abundance! I walk where
Huge mangos sway in every tree, and leaves
Are bigger than my hands, and women swear
At dusty streets clamoring at their feet for laundry
Balanced on their heads, out of reach, in mountains
Crumpled as the Andes. If there are boundaries
To this place, or if really there are fountains
In grand plazas brimming with equator
And the sun the light in every face, I cannot say.
I lived there only as a child. I remember seeing waiters
Dressed in white, bringing demitasse on small black trays,
The wind a vast white hand across the plaza
Touching, for a moment, the café.

BELONGING

I went to Cuba on a raft I made
From scraps of wood, aluminum, some rope.
I knew what I was giving up, but who
Could choose his comfort over the truth? Besides,
It felt so sleek and dangerous, like sharks
Or porno magazines or even thirst—
I hadn't packed or anything, and when
I saw the sea gulls teetering the way
They do, I actually felt giddy. Boy,
It took forever on those swells of sea,
Like riding on a brontosaurus back
Through time. And when I finally arrived,

It wasn't even bloody! No beach of skulls
To pick over, nothing but the same damn sun,
Indifferent but oddly angry, the face
My father wore at dinnertime.   I stripped
And sat there naked in an effort to
Attract some cannibals, but no one came;
I watched my raft drift slowly back to sea,
And wished I'd thought to bring a book
That told the history of my lost people.

FROM *Ten Patients, and Another*

XI.   JANE DOE #2

They found her unresponsive in the street
Beneath a lamplight I imagined made
Her seem angelic, regal even, clean.
She must have been around sixteen. She died
Who knows how many hours earlier
That day, the heroin inside her like
A vengeful dream about to be fulfilled.
Her hands were crossed about her chest, as though
Raised up in self-defense; I tried to pry
Them open to confirm the absence of
A heartbeat, but in death she was so strong,
As resolute as she was beautiful.
I traced the track marks on her arms instead,
Then pressed my thumb against her bloodless lips,
So urgent was my need to know. I felt
The quiet left by a departing soul.

LOST IN THE HOSPITAL

It's not that I don't like the hospital.
Those small bouquets of flowers, pert and brave.
The smell of antiseptic cleansers.
The ill, so wistful in their rooms, so true.
My friend, the one who's dying, took me out
To where the patients go to smoke, IV's
And oxygen in tanks attached to them—
A tiny patio for skeletons. We shared
A cigarette, which was delicious but
Too brief. I held his hand; it felt

Like someone's keys. How beautiful it was,
The sunlight pointing down at us, as if
We were important, full of life, unbound.
I wandered for a moment where his ribs
Had made a space for me, and there, beside
The thundering waterfall of his heart,
I rubbed my eyes and thought, "I'm lost."

MY VOICE

To cure myself of wanting Cuban songs,
I wrote a Cuban song about the need
For people to suppress their fantasies,
Especially unhealthy ones. The song
Began by making reference to the sea,
Because the sea is like a need so great
And deep it never can be swallowed. Then
The song explores some common myths
About the Cuban people and their folklore:
The story of a little Carib boy
Mistakenly abandoned to the sea;
The legend of a bird who wanted song
So desperately he gave up flight; a queen
Whose strength was greater than a rival king's.
The song goes on about morality,
And then there is a line about the sea,
How deep it is, how many creatures need
Its nourishment, how beautiful it is
To need. The song is ending now, because
I cannot bear to hear it any longer.
I call this song of needful love my voice.

WHAT THE BODY TOLD

Not long ago, I studied medicine.
It was terrible, what the body told.
I'd look inside another person's mouth,
And see the desolation of the world.
I'd see his genitals and think of sin.

Because my body speaks the stranger's language,
I've never understood those nods and stares.
My parents held me in their arms, and still
I think I've disappointed them; they care
And stare, they nod, they make their pilgrimage

To somewhere distant in my heart, they cry.
I look inside their other-person's mouths
And see the sleek interior of souls.
It's warm and red in there—like love, with teeth.
I've studied medicine until I cried

All night. Through certain books, a truth unfolds.
Anatomy and physiology,
The tiny sensing organs of the tongue—
Each nameless cell contributing its needs.
It was fabulous, what the body told.

NICK CARBÓ (b. 1964)

IN TAGALOG IBON MEANS BIRD

Carmencita said I had a small ibon
hiding between my legs. I was eight years old,

smiling at our three maids eating
their dinner of dried salted fish and warm white rice.

My parents were out at the Adamsons'
for cocktails, red snapper, or mahi-mahi.

It was a Friday night when Carmencita asked if I could show
the ibon inside my pajamas. *Hold him tight*

so he won't fly away. I felt a small stirring—
anticipating a sudden flutter of wings

like the little brown birds that would fly
past my window in the morning. *Look,*

your ibon must be hungry, feed him
some of this rice, and watch, he will grow.

I watched my ibon peck at the white grains
offered by her outstretched palm. His belly grew fat

but he was not really eating. Maybe he wanted
some kind of seeds, peanuts, or a little water.

Your ibon is very pretty, his lips are red, one day he will sing
to a beautiful woman and she will fall in love

with your ibon and she will kiss him all night long.
Carmencita, Nora, and Rosita giggled to each other

as they told me to hide my agitated ibon
because he was about to escape. I went back

to my room hungrier than when I woke up.

CIVILIZING THE FILIPINO

> *"I find this work very monotonous,*
> *trying to teach these monkeys to talk.*
> *The more I see of this lazy, dirty, indolent people,*
> *the more I come to despise them. I am becoming*
> *more and more convinced that for years and years*
> *to come, the only business Americans ought to have*
> *over here is to rule them with severity."*
>
> —Harry Cole, teacher on the island of Leyte, 1903

I remember the time I was called
to the Principal's Office
in fourth grade. I was accused

by Kevin Stapleton of stealing
his gold Parker pen.
The American principal grabbed me

by the cuffs of my shirt,
called me a "dirty, lying Filipino"
when I told him I was not the one

who stole the pen.
that was the first time I learned
about brute force, about how the color

of my skin makes me a more likely
suspect for a crime, about how it feels
to be picked up by two white

fists and thrown to the ground.
I cried, said I had stolen
the gold pen and that I had lost it

in the playground. The principal said
my parents had to buy Kevin
a new pen or pay for its replacement.

The next day I went straight
to the office with two hundred pesos.
I was ashamed that I lied to my parents

about why I needed the money,
ashamed that I was too scared
to tell the truth

about my innocence,
ashamed that I had become
a dirty, lying Filipino.

LITTLE BROWN BROTHER

I've always wanted to play the part
of that puckish pubescent Filipino boy

in those John Wayne Pacific-War movies.
Pepe, Jose, or Juanito would be smiling,

bare-chested and eager to please
for most of the steamy jungle scenes.

I'd be the one who would cross
the Japanese lines and ask for tanks,

air support, or more men. I'd miraculously
make it back to the town where John Wayne

is holding his position against the enemy
with his Thompson machine-gun. As a reward,

he'd rub that big white hand on my head
and he'd promise to let me clean

his Tommy gun by the end of the night. But
then, a Betty Grable look-a-like love

interest would divert him by sobbing
into his shoulder, saying how awfully scared

she is about what the "Japs" would do
to her if she were captured. In one swift

motion, John Wayne would sweep her off
her feet to calm her fears inside his private quarters.

Because of my Hollywood ability
to be anywhere, I'd be under the bed

watching the woman roll down her stockings
as my American hero unbuckles his belt.

I'd feel the bottom of the bed bounce off my chest
as small-arms fire explodes outside the walls.

KENNETH CARROLL (b. 1960)

DC NOCTURNE

For my son

i have found myself
praying to your sleeping
countenance
have reached out
stroked your face
& asked for a miracle
to save you from the
world.

THEORY ON EXTINCTION
(Or what happened to the dinosaurs?)

For my son, thomas

they were crushed by a gigantic meteor
they froze to death
they starved to death
they didn't wash their hands
they didn't brush their teeth
they got really bad report cards
they believed in gods that did not look like them

they evolved
they assimilated
they died waiting for john brown/jesus christ/& forty acres & a mule
they died fighting someone else's war
they didn't eat their vegetables
they used porcelana & faded to death
they overdosed on activator
they wanted to be white or arab or greek
they wanted to be anything but dinosaurs
they never read dinosaur history
they never read dinosaur literature
they read ebony and thought they had it made
they read jet and thought they had made it
they joined the republican party
they kept shooting at their own reflections
they got nose jobs/lip jobs/hip jobs
they would do anything for a job
they were scared of revolution
they thought malcolm x was a fashion statement
they stopped shouting in church
they were mis-educated
they pissed off the great dinosaur gods
they wanted to be like the people who despised them
they were, when they were here, a strange species
they are long gone son,
but you can see them,
at the smithsonian
just ask for the
great
negrosaurus wrecks.

In
dreams
diving deeper
than my disbelief,
your hungry shadow,
Dabo, finds the one spot
where the darkness shears apart
like a swimmer's hand cutting water.
In pointilliste indigo, you won't let me go,
your words bloating like bubbles: *Ra-ppe-lez-moi!*
you murmur through night's oscultations,
weird as the moon's coming between
us and the desert sun the day
you shaved my licey skull;
the sky blackened
with bleatings
and cocoricos
greeting death.
The moon caught
the sun in its paws,
let it slip to quick light.
And a boy goatherd emerged
for my shavings, eyes pleading *trust:*
C'est pou gris-gris M'sieu, pou la savance.
When I swept my hair up for him like mere dust,
you raged at my offering the self's secrets
to be braided with who-knows-what.
I beg it all back with interest
compounded in Arabic or
lizards' feet: Matthew,
Mark, Luke, John
bless the bed
I sleep
on.

The delta.
Itch of cayenne,
salt-stench of dried fish,
air thick and bouillon-cubed,
we bought grouper, okra and
field peas. The heat stirred
its tea down zinc-roofed
stalls' dirt streets,
Than a quick beat—
drums and balaphone.
Here come Marie Laveau
wit' a crowd followin' her,
"We goin' to see Papa Limba!"
"You come on in here Eunice!
Don't you know Papa Limba is
the devil?" (The Devils in Hell
want have nothin to do but punch
you. Stay Out.) Way high on stilts,
mud-cloth and black silk, that fierce
mask, ostrich-plumed, all horny with
cowries, let folk know spirits are real.
He fixed on you the moment a woman
panicked at your side, no devil—machete-
flashing spirit in stilted dance of the dead,
calling every coin we had to hover and nest
in his outstretched palms. Travelers spared no
terms on the Voodoo's praises, perfections of form.
They said she was a hundred years old.
She had shrunken from her skin
like a turtle. Still a faint
shadow of
quick power
on the face,
spark of an
old fire in
the sunken,
glistening
eyes.

ALL-YOU-CAN-EAT

catfish houses
along the river
from St. Louis
to New Orleans
where plates fill with hushpuppies,
cole slaw, catfish & greens, get eaten
& filled up again. The trick is not to
eat so much you can't beat busboys
waitress and cooks to the parking
lot (bred n bawn in de back seat
sezee). *Vous voyez je suis plus*
smart que vous, donc je vous
remercie du bon diner que
j'ai fait chez vous. If the
bush crack—you gots to
go. *Foofu la leeb doxe*
tabbi geej, (Here the
tale falls in the sea)
and that's the end
of that story says he.

HAYAN CHARARA (b. 1972)

THINKING AMERICAN

For Dioniso D. Martinez

Take Detroit, where boys
are manufactured into men, where
you learn to think in American.
You speak to no one unless someone
speaks to you. Everyone is suspect:
baldheaded carriers from the post office;
old Polish ladies who swear
to Jesus, Joseph and Mary;
your brother, especially your brother,
waiting in a long line for work.
There's always a flip side.
No matter what happens,
tomorrow is a day away,
or a gin bottle if you can't sleep,

and if you stopped drinking,
a pack of cigarettes. After that,
you're on your own, you pack up
and leave. You still call
the city beside the strait home.
Make no mistake, it's miserable.
After all, you bought a one-way
Greyhound ticket, cursed each
and every pothole on the road out.
But that's where you stood
before a mirror in the dark,
where you were too tired
to complain. You never go back.
Things could be worse. Maybe.
Detroit is a shithole, it's where
you were pulled from the womb
into the streets. Listen,
when I say Detroit, I mean any place.
By thinking American, I mean made.

My Father Breaks the Neighbor's Nose

Behind the screen door,
my mother sobbing
in the kitchen, I watched
my father strike
an old acquaintance
across the face
with a snow shovel.
I don't remember
the reason, but he did it,
and the old Polish ladies
who sold Avon products
called the police.
My father waited
on the porch while his friend
pressed a bloody towel
against his broken nose.
When he moved out,
our next door neighbor
told my mother not
to worry, that he was
an asshole—he laughed
and went on feeding

his dogs. That was in
1976, I was four years old.
Now and then, at Joe & Ed's,
I'd see the man my father
hit, and nod, as if to say
let bygones be bygones.
After my mother died,
he showed up at our house,
kissed my father
on the cheek, drank coffee
without saying a word,
excused himself and left.
It was the first time
my father saw him
in almost twenty years.
He remembers him well,
and when he tells the story
of their reacquaintance,
even to strangers, he can't help
but smile. I broke his nose,
he says, and wipes his tears.

On the Murder of an Ice Cream Man

You turned down the wrong street,
misread the directions, drifted
out of work into a lazy place.
Chance gives you up. A hand grasps
the throat, across the truck door
your stomach dragged, and a bullet
to the back out through the belly,
flat against the Detroit asphalt.
When the news broadcasts on the TV,
if you are lucky, your mother will
be watering tomatoes in the garden,
your father in the old country.
Those tuned in might recall that
Sunday for several days, bring it up
in empty conversations. In mid-July
at two hours past noon, you became
an incident, something odd to most
people, too familiar to others, a past
that sinks and dissolves inward
in lost memories. You made a mistake,

had to stare at the windshield's
reflection—that corner of an eye,
hair on the cheek—counted each last
breath. You did all this, and despite
that, I never learned your name.

HOLY WATER

Uncle Hussein mails his underwear,
linen trousers and business shirts
with straight collars, packed
tightly in cardboard boxes marked
BEIRUT, LEBANON.
In a week he'll be out of Detroit.
He is leaving America forever.
Up until days ago he was an engineer
selling auto insurance. We are
in the patio eating ripe cantaloupe.
My uncle says, "Israel stole water
from us." He means Arabs, he means
the Lebanese. There are rivers, he says,
that turn deserts into orchards of figs
and olives and dates. "We left them alone,
we didn't use them." Still he means Arabs,
the Lebanese. "Israel ran pipes through
the mountains straight into the hotel
faucets of Tel Aviv." He laughs, then asks
about my trip to New York. See,
an Arab sometimes laughs and changes
the subject when speaking about
a paradise gone wrong. How else can
Uncle Hussein keep face or myself
for that matter, knowing Jiddi lies
on his back with his stomach cancer,
dreaming of clean tomatoes and a glass
of cold water, pure without rust or dirt,
while ten miles south of his village,
an Israeli soldier pours water over
his boots to clean off the dust?

LISA D. CHAVEZ (b. 1961)

CLEAN SHEETS

Next door a woman is hanging
wet sheets on a line. Billowing
and snapping, tongues of clouds
fallen to earth, I try to understand
their language, but the whiteness
rebukes me. Today,
your letter came. I will say
it doesn't matter, but these sheets—flags
of cloth too pure for any
lover—seem enormous, an empty
page I cannot fill.

THE WOMAN WHO RAISED DOGS

Most people don't know
about Akitas. Big dogs—fighting
dogs—inscrutable eyes and broad,
bear heads. I raised Dobies
before. They're too high-strung
and nervous, like a woman who's been
beat too much. Akitas are tough,
quiet. I like to see them
in the kennels, a row of spiral tails
curling over broad backs.

Kenji, the pinto male
didn't place last show.
The judge took me aside, said
build up a little bulk,
run him five miles every day.
So I take him out,
watch his muscles snap and pull
as he runs, tongue like a ribbon,
beside the car. I don't get out
much else since Bob left.

Even if I could wash away
the smell of dog, pluck the hairs
from my clothes, what man

would understand? Bob said
if I paid him half as much
attention as those dogs, he'd never
have gone. The week
he left, Kenji got loose, nearly
killed the neighbor's shepherd.
He just flipped that dog over,
went for its throat. I understood.
It's not meanness; they're just eager,
wanting to test their strength
against anything else. Good-natured
killers. Jade, the fawn bitch,
will come into season soon.
Today, she snarls when Kenji approaches,
but tomorrow she may turn her tail
towards him, waiting.
The change is that quick.

AFTER THE PROM

Michael didn't want to go.
A few months shy
of dropping out, he spends
most nights cruising, dealing
"crystal" from his primer grey
Chevelle. I'm a senior—
one last shot at high school
anonymity before the hazy
day-to-day of the life after.
Mom saved her tips from cocktailing;
I bought a second-hand dress
and teased my hair.
Michael rented a tux and wore
a fake diamond earring.
To please me. Then it turns out
to be the same old shit:
Disapproving teachers
tense as we pass, and the school's
stuck-up royalty strutting
towards college—a future
I earned but couldn't afford.
We cut out early.

Driving across town, the Chevelle
shaking at 95, "Freebird" on the radio,
the lights on South Mountain
rising like phantom skyscrapers,
I wish we'd just keep on—
flying through the night
towards death or something
equally dramatic. We don't.
Michael stops for a six-pack
at a place sure to sell it.
Outside, there's a man
leaning against a shopping cart
flooded with blankets. He's so drunk
he sinks to the sidewalk.
He's got a pillow on the bottom
rack, a big feather pillow
like the one on my bed.
That really gets me.
Michael hands him an Old Milwaukee.

Later, I sit in the backseat
of the cooling car, dress rumpled
around me. Michael's pants circle
his knees; he lights a joint,
smoke suspending the air.
And I think of that pillow
bursting in a spray of feathers.
A blinding bouquet.

JUSTIN CHIN (b. 1969)

NIGHT

The light from the street lamp shines
through the window and shades your face.
In this dull shadow, you look different,
disfigured like the gargoyles I saw
at the museum today; it was
a visiting exhibition, next week
there will be something from South America.

As you sleep, cradled in my body,

your breathing is rhythmic. Listening
to your soft breath, I breathe
in time with you, counting the number
of breaths each minute, 17.

You look so small when
you're asleep. I wonder
what you're dreaming, and if you'd remember
the dream when you wake.

I dreamed of Dorothy Parker.
She came to me and said *bitch*; then
spiders gathered around me. Dorothy
Parker was wearing a dress with spider prints
on it. I thought it was curtain material.
I woke and saw your monster features
tucked in me and I was frightened. I
wanted to scream but did not want to wake you.

The clock glares its red eyes at me
and says *sleep*.
I glare back and say *count the time, count.*
The clock says *I will.*

A woman looks in from the window,
she doesn't say a word; I think
she is crying. She stands and we look
at each other for a while before she melts
into the shape of a spider on the window,
lost, homeless, and probably hungry.

I offer it my blood to suck but it declines;
it only wants blood from flying organisms.
I cannot fly
even if in dreams I flew
off a tall blue building, listening
to Patsy Cline records. I glided
for a while, then plummeted to my sheets,
wet and shivering.

The cat enters the room, looks
at us. He jumps on the bed, licks his paws
and smiles at me like he knows something
I don't. He winks at me, blows me a kiss, moves
to the window, kills the spider with a swat

of his paw, yawns and disappears through the window.
I see him flying upward, soaring like
a plastic toy aeroplane.
He tells me of the neighborhood
in the darkness of the nearly morning,
the little contained in each shoebox, all
kitty litter, all waiting
for the morning, to
be taken all away.

BERGAMOT

In the beauty shop, the saleswoman dabs
a touch of bergamot to my right wrist;
I grind the spot staining
my thin skin and vulgar veins
stretched across my carpus to the left
of its image; the friction
spreads the scent into my pulse
and I bring my newly aromatic
joint to my face.

This was before I knew the name
of that heady scent spilling
from teacups filling cafés
in steam and clink of pastry plates.
Before how the smell of a big pot
of chicken soup cooking in my kitchen
changed. Before I knew how
perfumous desire was, before I knew
the whiff of missing a lover.

WHY HE HAD TO GO

First of all, I could never get a straight answer. I'd ask, what day is it
today? He'd say something like, "Everyday with you is the Summer of
Love." He said it with all seriousness and sincerity which I try to repli-
cate now but it just makes my face hurt.

Why he had to go is a mystery. Some say it was because of
UFOs, the gravitational pull of Mercury in retrograde or those incurable
boils on his dick.

It could be because his mother said so, his wife said so, his other
lover said so, 'the voices' told him to, because all good things come to an

end and we're at the Dumbo Yellow section of the parking lot waving a fond farewell to the Magic Kingdom, the Happiest Place On Earth.

Maybe it was because I wanted to fuck with those Mickey Mouse ears on. Maybe I shouldn't have told him I wanted to do those four things that I haven't done in five positions.

Maybe that Tony Robbins seminar he took triggered it. 'Ask Isadora' thinks it might be the pre-mid-life crisis or the parole violations, we need to communicate she said, and she's got a book and tape that just might help.

I'm told he had to go because he had to find himself, that he took too many pills, drank too much & refused to share any of it, because he bought a bandana for his dog at the street fair, and he shaved his balls obsessively, more so than any man should.

He had to go and now he's gone, and friends say, *You're better off without him. It's his loss. If you love somebody, let him go . . . There are other fish on the bus.* But all I want to do is lie in the dark with my Roberta Flack records, just me, Roberta, a grand piano and her giant afro, plotting how to destroy his property, rip his piercings out and give him herpes all because he had to go and I wanted to go first.

A. V. CHRISTIE (b. 1963)

IN MY DREAM

you live in the thousand rooms
behind the Medusa doorknocker. Verdigris spills
its shock of turquoise through her skull, twists
in the fist-held braids coiling into serpents.
When I knock, you turn more and more to stone.

You tell me the angels are following:
I hear their wings beat in your breath.
Turning your clothes on the line to flame,
you watch ash spiral up, catch in the branches
outside your window. *They were too heavy*, you say.

The moon flashes like a lure, gloves my hands
as I reach past its light to cover you.
The back of your head is gone: your skull a thick frieze
of angels chiseled deeply. You mutter in sleep:
what's rustling, dead pockets, black wings.

All afternoon you strip the oleander of leaves.
Such are the messages received from songs, an overlapping
of strings insisting. You send me the last leaf, enclose
a poem about how my hands, in the moon's white gloves,
settle in your dreams. They are a kind of invitation.

I am holding a mirror in my palm.
The streetlight shines from it into her face
blooming with ruin. She neither leaves
nor speaks. Her bronze lips reveal nothing.
Already it is hard to make your heart move.

Midnight: a hollow sound, your piss
in the toilet too loud through the walls of my room.
I look out over the courtyard. All stone, you stand
in the fountain—the arc of water shining.
I toss my lucky coin and the house falls down.

BELONGINGS

I put aside the swim team ribbons,
crimped and shimmering, the varsity letters
like thick carpet over your wild heart.

I could string them to your memory, lift you
high on the breeze for everyone to see. It would be easy.
A shaking of heads, words like *shame* or *fine young man*.

They wouldn't know how you clung to a bar
all afternoon, hung there until you couldn't feel your arms,
at Stanley Junior High, a new Iron Man.

No, these honors flash a long tail of hurt in the sun.
Better to use them like shining lures, like junk
that catches the fish's eye, to troll the silence.

In your bottom drawer I find the heavy box of bullets,
spill them, a school of minnows on the rug.
I want your tallest fishing rod.

I want the few glittering feathers left
from your fly tying. How the hooked insects appeared
in your hands, a little thread and there were wings.

And give me the blues harp. You had it a long time.
I smell your cigarettes when I breathe in,
and again in the flat wail of the tune.

We make our own stories
of where these things have been, how very close
or in just what inner pocket you kept them.

I keep the cardboard scrap. On it a quick list
before one of your disappearances: *matches, peanut butter,*
hard boiled eggs, cigarettes, twine, matches.

This can mean what I want—bonfire, plea,
you repeatedly cradling the wan flame in your hands
and standing against the wind.

I reach down to your underwear, limp on the floor;
I take them—a litter of blown flowers—
and throw them away.

JOSHUA CLOVER (b. 1962)

THE INSTITUTE FOR SOCIAL CHANGE

It's too much, B writing to A's wife
of her resemblance to Katharine Hepburn.
We think of the pressed paper crossing the Straits
of Lavender, dragging an entire boat
behind it, racing October into the city
before it comes to rest on a foyer table
at the heart of the world of things:
What's this, a love letter? Well—.
Such a thing could turn a ring
of Saturn into an iron hotel railing.
Ten weeks later A to B (arctically): *You there,*
Felizitas sends her finest, much blue
has departed our celestial
quarters, the conspiring waitresses
downstairs are named Beatriz and Laura, think
of it! Next year will be a joke.

Family Romance

I am a service
revolver in a swimming pool.

The father is a chalk outline on the street
sealed with yellow tape.

Whatever passes as the mother has dropped
below the line of sight.

She's left behind some yarn & a machine
which plays to the father songs.

I don't mean to brag
but I am a love letter.

The noise which is not an echo?
      (Because it happens at the same time
      as the song but off to the side
      or behind like a shadow)
That's the father sleeping.

When father comes to we'll get
drunk & act out scenes from The Classics.

Sometimes we arrive at
the island just in time. Other days we're years too late

There is the Body Lying in State

There is the body lying in state,
there are the gifts, there are the flowers
that follow the form of poised
eartrumpets listening up to the air,
the carefulness that is the flowers' work.
(That is how they were arranged when
growing in some mercantile garden,
we have arranged them again
which is the work of the work.)
We are having trouble having a here.
There is the body lying in state,
the lying body many months late.
We are having trouble placing

our shoulders to the evening,
my sister, her sisters, the speaking one,
all the children of the body there.
There are the gifts at the bedside
which with their secret pattern
could cause something to happen,
there are the children of sisters arranged
around the bed in the form of a plot,
as carefully drawn as a plot which is
the form of what will happen inside
the stink, the veil of disinfectant & flowers,
there is the absolute body lying,
even the youngest child could cause
something to happen inside: a generation.
There is a carefulness in the air
around the body lying there,
this poised evening of 18 months,
we are having trouble having a night
without her, without the body,
having trouble placing ourselves
in the form of paired crucibles,
in the fetal self-involution,
we are not that desperate for her
body's body to work itself around,
surely it will happen as arranged,
we are not so faithless as to lapse
into that all-night gesture
of supplication known as sleep

LISA COFFMAN (b. 1963)

LIKELY

Magnolia bloom can sex the air
until one thinks for long blanknesses
only *magnolia, magnolia.*
The tree shakes with the climbing of two girls.
The taller, stretched among four branches
looks up, carrying a knife.
The other settles at a lesser place
and thinks of falling. Magnolia

withers if touched. The petals
spot where the fingers were, then darken,
spoiling the smell. A girl raised
to be her daddy's boy knows to reach,
slowing and slowing the hand until
it wavers with the flower.
She cuts the slight wood at the stem,
tips to her a color of things hidden—
skin at the lifted clothes, or the shining
averted face of a woman undressing.
The younger girl will run alongside with the news.
The flower floats all night in a glass,
the kitchen lit in other places by the moon.

GIRL/SPIT

She presses her dark lips
in a pleased way, as if she has said
the word *whiskey* again, or tucked
into a corner of her mouth a grass blade
which she briefly squatted and chose
before standing, and with a slap
to her back pockets, slouched
into the length of herself.

It's the hook-thinness of her smile
that draws something like the beaded
metallic chain of a lamp
down my spine and stomach, toward the pucker
her smile has pushed to its corner—
the flutter of that cheek
working down on itself, working spit,
and finding its own taste sweet.

CHEERLEADERS

Out of the American provinces
regarded by many as exile
one is born into—
evolves the oddity of a girl
to whom her own opinions pose a danger
yet able to shout, pinioned

in the execution of a complex-figured leap
before any number of audience, local, or from nearby towns.

Admitting "their attitude is like that of strippers,"
admit a scrubbed citric innocence to the sex.
No Venus grins here from the foam, curl ends tweaked water-dark:
the hair fanned across the inwardly groaning boy's fourth-period desk
has been ironed flat or flipped up,
the hairless lotioned calves end in sock folds,
the chest is topped demurely with a carpet letter.

As for the bruited away-bus escapades of sex:
these are more often exaggerations
in the nature of all town troubadours.
The intent is, rather, "to be kissproof:
put on lipstick, then have someone
powder your lips through a piece of tissue. Do
not inhale." Not admired by majestic-thighed women
passing in and out of steamroom steam
are the somnolent voices roused to staccato, single drawn word starting
low ending loud, childish bell still to *go OH go OH*
as the lead girl takes her hands from her hips
among all eight waiting in identical postures
and puts the bunny-ear shape of her sneaker to an in-place prancing
or strikes the wooden court boards hard
until the stands start ringing back.

Even admitting the ingenuity of their pleats
that allow the skirt to extend straight from the waist,
and the athletic rigor required for certain jumps,
no one accuses cheerleaders of usefulness:
they are discarded at the end of high schools
excluded from cabinet meetings and businesses,

yet, while it is known
"there are no women like that, anywhere!"
as the young photographer cried, home
from retouching hair and blemishes
on women already exemplary for beauty,

his girlfriend and sisters in the magazine-
littered living room
merely looked at him, then went on with their reading.

COURAGE, OR ONE OF GENE HORNER'S FIDDLES

After I write *My face burned and I wanted to cry*
I watch Catherine Osborn, who was on oxygen all winter,
walk slowly by the canal, with the jerking motions of a small boat
when the people in it move or change places on their knees.
You don't know nothing. Do you? Gene had said.
I had come to see about buying a fiddle.
Rainy day, the Cumberlands blunting any notion of future.
Well, I said. My face burned and I wanted to cry.
Then he played for me, he would have played for anyone,
a dark maple fiddle he'd made, such a pure sound
it could have belonged to either of us,
it seemed to rise from the frets of my wrists, my curled hands.
We are wrong about courage. It is closer to music.
It rises from us simply as we move in this life, or submit.

NICOLE COOLEY (b. 1966)

UNDINE

After she rose from the dark throat
of the sea, her voice, light
as a shell, calls along the water.
The fishermen wait on the shore
when she loosens her hair over wet white shoulders.
Their wives watch at the windows.

At dusk these women scrub supper fish
and set the frying pans to burn.
In their bowls of black wine
the men find Undine, arms open,
her body shearing through the ease of the dark.

She has come to land before.
She knows the urgency
of the fishermen's hands, that breath
in her ear. She leaves
an umbrella of hair on each pillow,
a shadow pale as a fish
in a cave of water. Then she will travel

through the night into the sea,
into a deeper, retrospective blue,
her mouth seeking only her own name.

DIANE ARBUS, NEW YORK

*To experience a thing as beautiful means:
to experience it necessarily wrongly.*
            —Friedrich Nietzsche

Russeks Fifth Avenue, 1933

My father arranges the window like a stage.
Tea-length gowns, Dior dresses, taffeta fanned
over driftwood. Faces back-lit by Chinese lanterns,
the wax women will draw crowds. He fastens a rose

to a mannequin's hair while in the Millinery Salon
Mother models the new collection, Joan Crawford coat
with a swing collar. Hand set on her hip, she poses
for the customers. The clerks are paid to watch and smile.

At home she hides my books and pushes me
outside to the street, the world of other children.
She locks the window eleven stories above the Park,
the ledge where I stand to look down at the reservoir.

In the evening the parlor is hung with smoke, cards
laid out next to the crystal glasses for gin. Mother took away
Alice in Wonderland, and I wait out the end of the night
in my parents' marble bathtub, wait in the dark.

When I step from my dress, I step outside my body.
I imagine men watching from windows all along the Avenue.

Coney Island, 1959

On the boardwalk Jack Dracula sits stiff
and straight like a Victorian child.
Twenty-eight stars are printed on his face.
An eagle flies across his chest past
the head of Christ. Inside his body the dye

will turn to poison in the sun.
At Hubert's Museum I photograph
the flea circus and the family of midgets,
but what I love most is the failed magic,
the box of mirrors holding the girl
the magician doesn't cut in half.
Congo the Jungle Creep swings
his grass skirt and swallows cigarettes,
dances on a row of kitchen knives.
On the boardwalk my camera
is my passport as I cross the boarder
from one world to another again and again.
I am crossing the boarder. Along Jack's wrist
I LOVE MONEY is written in curving script.
I hold the Rolleiflex waist-level to meet his eyes.

Central Park, 1971

Between the trees I watch a woman
holding a monkey in a snowsuit,
cradling its body like a child.
I am photographing people

with the objects they love.
I photograph myself with my camera.
I am studying attachment.
I print each image again and again.

On a blackboard beside my bed
I list objects to photograph: a pet
crematorium, a condemned hotel,

the ocean liner from my dream—
a world of women, gleaming and white
and stacked in layers like a wedding cake

where we drink and smoke and play
cards all night. No men are watching.
The white ship is on fire and sinking

slowly and I can photograph anything
I want. Because there is no hope
I can photograph anything.

All night I ride the train under the city,

studying the faces of the passengers.
I want to startle them from sleep.

I want to take them home with me
to lie in my bed beside me as I grow
smaller. No one is watching.

I want someone to cross over with me
as light stains the film silver and the image
turns dark, unrecognizable.

THE FAMILY HISTORY

In the sister's garden it is still winter
when the boy who will be my father follows her
between the spines of trees, down the dark path.

In his mother's house on the shore of Lake Michigan
where one room opens onto another with no place
to find refuge, his sister comes after him, chases

him from one closet to the next, drags him out
from under the bed. Their bodies knock together.
This is not an embrace. He is a trespasser

into her life. "My garden is my own garden."
On his arm the scab from last night opens like a bloom.
No one alive will tell me this story, you see, but I'm here,

hidden on the roof of the castle, behind the leaves
shaped like stars. I have come to help my father find
the way out of childhood, the long road that will lead

to oblivion. I never saw a photograph of this scene
but I know enough to tell the boy, if you find a cottage
in a clearing in the woods, it's not safe, don't stop.

My garden is my own garden. I know the day
she pushes his face under the ice of the lake
till his body stops shuddering, his hands float

to the surface. And I know his dreams about animals:
a frog waiting on a bed of damask roses, a centaur,
crocuses wound in its horns, who can rescue him

with the promise of Paradise where he'll be alone.
His sister wears flowers wound in her braids
and holds him down on her bed till he cries mercy.

Father come with me, I see the prints of two nails
on your palms, the prints of two nails on your feet.
The golden ball lies in the mud at the bottom

of the well. The single pea is buried under stacks
of counterpanes. You won't find it, but in the backyard
rows of red poppies will send you off to sleep.

My garden is my own garden. The trees aren't women
who lean toward you in the wind. There is no salvation.
Father, listen. You won't know the way back.

LESLEY DAUER (b. 1965)

FALLING

You're pressing your fingers against the sky,
asking Jesus if he sees how close those trees are.
You don't believe in Jesus. A stewardess takes everything
sharp that could hurt you: plastic cups, prayer beads.
All of her omelets are gone. You're watching your window
like television—a show about the suburbs, those stubborn lives.
Whole families relax and look lovely at home.
You're folding your hands around the armrests,
feeling the vague sadness of the stewardess's voice.
There are no clouds today above the boxwoods.
You could live in a world so solidly blue.

PHILIP THE STORE POLICEMAN

Philip has stolen a tie—
not his color or style.
I'm not polite, he tells a salesclerk.
Look, my eyes are slow and poisonous.
Philip sees that his fingers make prints

on the counter—little misshapen lungs.
He watches the salesclerk wipe them away.
I'm inappropriate, Philip tells the boy
he's bringing to the lost and found.
This tie is not mine.
He announces the child's name
again and again until he sees the shadow
of a woman's hat move towards them.
I'm not helpful, Philip tells her.
My father was a businessman while he breathed.
My mother wore a hat like yours—she told me
everyone we love will leave us
and we'll let them get away.
Philip says *Phil*, softly, out loud,
believing someone must find him.
The salesclerk, maybe.
She'll make him give the tie to her.
She'll keep him here.
I'm not kind, Philip tells a mannequin,
whose eyes are still and turned aside.

WILLIAM

William has whole buildings inside him,
open windows, someone waving hello.
There's a William no one knows
with Doris who is kind sometimes.
Their waitress says *stay with me*
to a customer who's leaving.
It's too late to take it back.
That's William driving by,
one side of his face lit by a streetlight.
Around the corner, William is a child.
He splashes colors, oiled and lovely,
on a lady's paisley coat.
Apologize, William, and William won't—
the city looks so soft beneath the water.
Elsewhere, William walks
beside a motel's blinking lights.
His reflection, gray in the office glass,
returns his momentary glance;
there's a vacancy here.
William sits inside a passing train.
He waits for it to stop somewhere.

Miles and miles of walls go by,
fire escapes, arbitrary spray paint.
William, where are you? What happened?

LOIS AT THE HAIR SALON

For Linda

Mrs. Nelson thinks there's no one left.
My hands look old, she says to Lois,
for the simple reassurance of sound.
Lois trims the hair behind her ears,
her scissors clicking slightly.
Mrs. Scott fears seduction
more than silence. *If he loved me,*
what would it mean? she asks Lois,
who sculpts the curls along her neck.
Lois would like her to look
like someone more content.
Life is not what I imagined,
says Mrs. Simpson. *That mirror*
is wrinkled, and I'm tired
of always going away.
Lois cuts the hair above her eyes.
She sweeps up what's left
and starts towards home, where life
is sharp and sometimes lovely.
Lois sees scissors skate on a frozen lake
while the silver afternoon recedes.

CHRISTOPHER DAVIS (b. 1960)

NOD

In this mind
beyond dry cornstalks
I come across
my patriarch's abandoned Cadillac

the door gapes
I crawl in

try turning the wheel
it does turn

I tease the radio's knob
twiddling it between pointer and thumb
clicking it on off
clicking it on off

turning it up all the way
hearing nothing
taking in the pain
singing in the pain

Enough. Enough. We interrupt this whining
to broadcast more cowboy yodeling,
the starting of your engines,
gentlemen.

Who'd jump this old thang?
Poisonous pokeweed prods through the bumper.
Why not kiss its dents, fate's public sculpture?
Let it rust out here a few more days.

It might yet get us
where we need to go
if there's no solid place to go
no world called home.

LITTLE CRISIS FRAMED IN MY WINDOW

Three men
laughing
around a boat's prow in her driveway, each man armed,
each shotgun broken in an arm's crook, all the men
wearing identical camouflage raincoats, each
making goose calls with a call clenched
in his fingers. She's behind them

and they know it. Leaning
relaxed in her doorway, letting
cigarette smoke rise from her two fingers
like a pistol, is she humming
nursery rhymes they half-remember
but can't name? The three seem

nervous, embarrassed. Air is sweat.
In the shadowy living room behind her back, a hidden TV's blue
    light throbs out toward two armchairs,
one empty; propped
in its twin's lap is a framed photo—
of a baby? She puffs out white smoke slowly.
She mouths something to the youngest, who just turned.

He seems so young, his raincoat gone. He pushes
his way past her. Into
her.

    He'd unbuttoned his shirt. His friends
shrug, and he's gone down a dark hall.
Probably it's work he'll have to do, lift
down some books.
They both doubt this. But not aloud.
Back to their cool, small cleanlinesses—
Loaded.
The two alone now.
Shy.

ANY NEST I CAN'T SLEEP IN SHOULD BE BURNED

These chaste
words go out
to you, rough ogress Mrs. Hardcastle trying
like hell to get me axed maybe
you think you really
ought to be the best maybe
answering the phones I come off
smarter? Your imagination
is it *stripped clean*
of love
the way mine is? Why's your
son always so late
picking you up? The disorganized
red pens on your desk do tell
the future Who do you think keeps dis-
connecting your son's
calls Your crossed
arms like luscious hams safe
at your breasts why can't
you
keep aiming that

glare back into this full-length mirror called our body
    staring
down. Moving gently these bare
hands. Moaning *Let me*
in
this ton of air torn out
cold lungs
I can't be helped Your stare trans-
fixed out onto the wind-washed
parking-lot I feel there won't be
any future
known or
blank
unless You hold me

OLENA KALYTIAK DAVIS (b. 1963)

MOORER DENIES HOLYFIELD IN TWELVE

Caesar's Palace.
The way life keeps splitting itself in two.

Twenty four hours later Florida
had pushed itself under
the wheels of our white Olds.
My father getting out
of the car. I'm squinting, his
shirt is that bright.

I was stunned for a minute
but was able to clear my head.

I'm on the phone now, trying to keep this front
from moving over his white cloud of a head,
because my father used to be two men,
but now he's old.

One minute you're talking weather. Then,
a nasty left-right in the second round.

I didn't mean to start talking obstacles, hooks,

comebacks.
But, suddenly, I'm going down, saying:

I've been holding on with my teeth.
I've developed this strange social stutter.

I had to let my cutman go.

THIRTY YEARS RISING

I needed to point to the buildings, as if they all stood
for something, as if Detroit could rise again
into its own skyline, filled in
as it always is inside me:
each cracked sidewalk, each
of the uniformed girls, braided
and quiet as weeds, each bicycled boy, each man
with a car and a wife, the ones I slept with
and arranged, neatly, like a newly laid
subdivision.

But I was driving with my brother
who doesn't like to think
of the thirty years rising
inside us, the leavened truth. He's arrived
at the heavy black X of destination
on the inside of his forehead
and he doesn't want to see me
looking like this: open-palmed
and childishly dressed, with hipbones
instead of children, aching
to put my sneakered feet on his new leather
dash.

He doesn't want to hear me
say something fucked-up, something like:
It's in my bones. My sternum
runs like Woodward Avenue,
it's pinnated, parked on, full
of dirt, holding women in wigs and cigarettes, bars
lit from the outside in, it's overflowing
with pooltables and ashtrays. My ribs
are holding up factories and breweries, two-bedroom
houses and multi-storied lives, this strip,
this city, these sidestreets,

a bony feather.

He's lived here all his life.
But I gave up these streets
for so many others. I hopped
turnstiles to ride the Metro,
memorized EL tracks and Muni stations
until I had a huge worn subway
map on the inside of my head, but couldn't get off at any stop,
couldn't begin to live in any city, and couldn't sleep
with anybody but myself. I gave up
this body for so many others. I've been both
an exaggeration of myself and someone
who looks just like me but sounds different.
But now I'm back
to visit both, and I need to point
to my first hotel room;
to the mortuary above which
my tall half-chinese half-german
punkrockboyfriend fingered me
like a book in his little bed;
and to the hospital where our bonemother
died so late or so early that
we were both sound asleep.

I didn't say it,
but: My sternum is breaking
with this, it's sinking
like Woodward as Detroit rises around
my brother's turn, rises and falls.
Falls not at all like this light summer rain
but hard, like someone else's memory,
insistent, unwanted, but suddenly,
and again, being claimed.

THE PANIC OF BIRDS

The moon is sick
Of pulling at the river, and the river
Fed up with swallowing the rain,
So, in my lukewarm coffee, in the bathroom
Mirror, there's a restlessness
As black as a raven
Landing heavily on the quiet lines of this house.

Again, the sun takes cover
And the morning is dead
Tired of itself, already, it's pelting and windy
As I lean into the pane
That proves this world is a cold smooth place.

Wind against window—let the words fight it out—
As I try to remember: What is it
That's so late in coming? What was it
I understood so well last night, so well it kissed me,
Sweetly, on the forehead?

Wind against window and my late flowering brain,
Heavy, gone to seed. Pacing
From room to room and in each window
A different version of a framed woman
Unable to rest, set against a sky
Full of beating wings and abandoned
Directions. Her five chambered heart
Filling with the panic of birds, asking: What?
What if not this?

CONNIE DEANOVICH (b. 1960)

AMERICAN AVALON

Knock the zoo out of your eye, the sand dollar with dried
babies or dried money inside. All along this beach the
view is the same. It's you waving from a pastel balcony,
and everyone *knows* you're the kind of woman who can
cook family chicken. A sparkling pan of vision with an
abundance of front and sides is an array reserved for the
moneyed, so here's a 1920s man on a postcard. They
always wore suits then even when the vision is of him
waving from a cart of grapes. In the American Avalon this
is the cart of conveyance and he is the dead I carry to the
paradise of my collections.

When the vision is of a society matron decked out for an
Arabian Nights charity function the ghosts that stomped her
grapes into wine dwell here. We don't want to waste cake

so the stripper pops out of a hat instead. At the party to
celebrate free speech and humor through flippancy you say
Listen, didn't mean to come off as a preachy pornographer,
and then we hug, our arms encircling like balletic islanders.
Why celebrate notions anyway, or achievements? Why
collapse onto the grass reading a book about the Kickapoo
Indians who lived in this very section of Illinois? Perhaps
exactly where the mailbox is they too set out tokens to
friends. That the tokens may've been dried squirrel kidneys
is excessively factual, and how can this addition to
knowledge substitute for a party anyway? The fact that
Brezhnev's widow admits she fell for him because of his
eyebrows is a better substitute, but won't there be a Day of
the Dead party or some kind of party some time in the
future? Our myths are about to stagnate like James
Baldwin, and our visions are contained in a drawer.

What you need is an infantry of desires to ransack your life,
to get you bloody before the grape cart comes to trundle
you off to the beach you'll never leave. Even in a dump
there is the mirage that saves you, the glass in the ugly
houses that can redden, the fresh new interesting piano and
flute music that can come out of some of them. Then a
voice suggesting a reputation built around a canopied bed
doles out the last shred of its Southern strength and you
hear it but then it's gone. Wanting is chronic. The ratio of
longing to actual splash in the pool. It's a conspiracy the
idea of beauty. The condition of the sky is distributed
unequally, but at least it's sky you can breathe. If this old
notion of beauty stopped being invisible and rotated around
you like a stranger doing the fire dance would you
collapse? Maybe one packet of splendor per day set onto
your lap like a puppy.

ZOMBIE JET

like the roofs of buildings
what's inside you
is beautiful and hard to reach
without the proper tools
the proper ukulele
the one Marilyn played
in *Some Like It Hot*

the one we all are sure
we too could play

and on Ukulele Mountain
many devotees
are presumably still doing so
waiting for jets to pass
to get a Shoestring Tempo

but the white dog in the window
across the street
hears this same jet and looks up
as if it could be a magnificent butterfly
or some other food
that's 10% treat
90% surprise

51% of today was walking
and 49% was laying down
exactly like a zombie
who must feed then rest
exactly like a pilgrimage
of zombies who must feed on a whole town
then rest in the field the town becomes
exactly like wandering hordes of zombies
who erase the rest of the world from
the light of day
but who cannot themselves
be erased

tonight there will be a quarter moon
a 10% promise and a 65% descent
into the section of the globe
that spins most magnificently

a night with a spiral staircase
echoing disintegrated chatter which
if you listen very hard
means squat
but if you listen loosely
is a cannonball of language
streaking across the sky like a zombie jet

My Favorite Monk Is

raking leaves
brown as his robe
and he's the kind

who speaks (most
eloquently about
the vow of silence)

Language he says
is the skeleton
of the spirit

It's nice
to think of a skeleton
the Halloween kind

with a patch over one eye
as the bony place
where words

can shimmy
Inside
he bakes a chicken

in honey
and his house
is like other houses

on a regular block
Surrounding it
like a halo is

a garden
never tortured
by lawn decoration

At times
while working
in his yard

a drawbridge goes up
unexpectedly
and he catches

faint whiffs
of the stinky
flowers of hell

REQUIREMENTS FOR SUGGESTING FATS WALLER

a stack of summer suits makes a better emblem than a piano
the sound of which lures a group of ambassadors to a tall fence

after opening the biggest brass door in Chicago
88 Girl Scouts celebrate overcoming obstacles
by wiping their brows in order of height

after combing her hair out to the ground
my grandmother sat very still
as if preparing to do The Carolina Shout or The Alligator Crawl
both of which end in frenzy but start in silence

put a few coins in
and a sweaty polka dotted neckerchief comes out

MARK DECARTERET (b. 1960)

COLORING

There's a horse on the fridge
done in blue crayon, a forecast of rain
and eleven more Crayolas—
with all of the animals, flowers,
and birds to choose from
he wants to draw me with
my cup, his old man, useless
after a night at the track.

THE TOWN CLERK

What do you want from me?
she concludes every evening
thrusting her body
in front of the mirror,

hummels lurking in the cracks
between her teeth and white lies.
What idol is this, she asks
dangling a girdle from her toe.
Each wisp of hair is the memento
of a ritual or catastrophe,
every twitch of her eye
the search for a ghost.

Recollection begins with a dirge
she has dredged from the pit
of her stomach, where the town
founders meet through the night.
Words she has engraved on the plates
to her hearse, and sings softly
as she sits on the toilet
smoking a cigarette, smacking
the funnies into place.

The first kiss wasn't good
nor were any that followed;
for memories like these a rubber stamp,
and an ink both transparent and cold.
If you looked under "loss" in the files
her life would be reduced to certain phobias,
heaped ashtrays and a clothesline
of shivering starlings hoping
for the leaves to catch fire.
Even with the added weight of dust
the clock's time is still hers.
When it's time to relieve yourself
of trash, declare the intentions
of your heart, you will answer to her.
When it comes time to die.
How can I help you? she is asking
everybody in the room, she is asking
someone in the mirror.

JUAN DELGADO (b. 1960)

CHUPAROSA

The feeder is red with sugared water.
A hummingbird's wings burn.

Behind a window with bars
a man lies face down on a cot;
his chest beats out a dream
while the hummingbird hovers.

The dreamer sips at what
his eyes offer him: the U.S. border.
Poking his face through
an opening in the chain-link fence,
he checks if it's safe to cross.

The possibility of work is his nectar.
He dashes into a ravine
and lies flat on the ground;
he has made it past the patrols.

His dream is the hummingbird's flight.
His eyes scan the night.
If he is not spotted, he will join the rest,
but the desert is a sweeping net.

CON LOS PÁJAROS

I sat under my father's clothesline,
a web of ropes tied to four-by-fours
jutting unevenly out of the ground.
I saw the sky in muddy puddles,
the dripping of sleeves and skirts.

Like a pot, our street simmered.
Our neighbor's face in the kitchen window
disappeared behind a raised pot lid.
Her girl peered, then moved to the table
once she saw her mother cool down
the spoon, the first taste of supper.
When father arrived, he untied the bandana

around his neck, the day's sweat.
He leaned on his truck, and I noticed
the line of clothes sagging, tired as limbs.

On Saturday we finished our house.
I mixed the stucco, shoveled it into a bucket,
carried it on my shoulder up a ladder
to where he dug in with his trowel and worked.
Pressing the stucco into the chicken wire
and smoothing it out, he stopped to recite:
"We're just a coat of stucco away."
I mixed until a coat finished the wall,
drying with the odor of moist soil.

Once his hands returned with the birds.
His song was a bundle of carrots caked
by dirt, dark as his palms at dusk.

DANDELION

He is going to stop thinking
about his crooked teeth,
about all the rattling his truck
makes circling the golf course
while passing her country club home.
So, she is rich, so he
is her gardener, so he is
the Mexican, so what
he says to himself—he will go
to her pool, get courage
from its mouth of light and wait for
her sign, the way crabgrass
hides its roots when it is weeded,
and he assures himself
endurance will be his beauty.
When the pool is shadows,
she waves him on from her window.
He rubs and cleans his teeth
with a dirty finger, then spits,
walking to her front door.
Only self-doubt can kill a weed.

I–5 INCIDENT

"Hit-run victim survives four days alone."

On the fourth day the phone wires talked,
replied like voices pressed to pillows,
trapped behind walls or dying in the wind,
then quiet as a priest who listens to sins.
All sorts of things I imagined; they kept me going.
No. I didn't see the car; I had my back to it.
I only heard its radio, you know,
American rock and roll. No.
I wasn't crossing; I stayed to the side.
When struck, I hit the rushing ground
and dragged myself toward the bushes
of an embankment, afraid they'd return.
In La Sagrada Familia, my neighborhood,
a man delivering Coke on his bike
fell at a corner and lifted his head
only to vanish under a city bus,
so I wasn't going near the road again.
Plus, I couldn't. Look at my legs.
My jeans were soaked in blood.
Dirt stuck to them. I patted my legs,
thinking they were part of the ground.
I was half dead, a lizard without a tail.
Luckily, I had the sprinkler's water;
its head was broken. I held its cool neck,
but my stomach groaned, all knotted up.
I shouted when I heard a car coming
and shook the bushes at the headlights.
Through the night I held on to a branch
and had a dream about a market place
where people drifted among the stalls.
Some glanced, keeping up with the crowd;
others haggled, then turned from the vendors,
walking away, seemingly losing interest.
I came upon a stall of toys: race cars,
dolls with eyes bright as hubcaps,
and puppets hooked, their limbs still
as if they had fallen through the sky.
A child stopped to tug the string of one
and tried to get his mother's attention
by having it dance and wave its arm,
but she was already several stalls ahead,

looking in front for him, shouting his name.
He ran, dodging strangers and yelling, "Wait!"
I heard his voice over the crowd's
and woke to a semi and the rush of wind
that made the oleander's leaves tremble.

TOM DEVANEY (b. 1969)

THE AMERICAN PRAGMATIST FELL IN LOVE

The American Pragmatist fell in love.
The dictionary became the embedded case of "I like you,"
Meaning—a button you sewed on my gray shirt with gray thread.
This wasn't the first time ever I saw your face
Or the first time ever I kissed your face.
Your face was facing everything useful and it said,
"You suck," and you did, and later, "You rule," and you did.

When the American Pragmatist fell in love
They stuck to their guns.
Their story was straight, with crooked lines;
It had God's handwriting written all over—it was sloppy as hell.
It made me feel religious in ten thousand places.
The error message read: "I'm bored," "you're too neat."
"It's not safe to turn off your computer now."

The year the American Pragmatist fell in love
They had a nightcap all night and in the morning called it a day;
They argued with everyone, all the time, that nothing is one, except one.
Wrote our baby talk in long hand, misquoting
Everything so you couldn't know what they were saying.
They had no way of knowing,   they knew everything
And knowing this, they knew it would ruin their friendship.
It had to, they were the American Pragmatist.

SONNET

For Joanna Rakoff

You know all those sonnets the ones where I said, "I love you," well
this time, I mean it, this time I'm talking about

your curly hair soaked black from October's frozen rain,
you reading Milton and eating BLT
our up-front lies about being vegetarians
(Milton's "I can not praise a cloistered virtue").
More really, all those times we never kept meeting,
till we finally never met—giving up,
till bacon, Milton and the rain were all we had.
Admit now I never wrote you sonnets,
and that this probably isn't a sonnet either,
tho' I'll call it one, and loud skies pour down
   to live on, back-of-the-brain with you
     Milton, bacon, your face in a year of rain.

ELIZABETH DODD (b. 1962)

LYRIC

It doesn't matter
     whether
          a tree falls
or doesn't on this hillside.
     I am here
          in this buoyant silence
lifting from snow cover.
     There is no story to tell
          about cause and effect,
no one to pull
     the stiff sheet of grammar
          over a scattered pattern
of bark and branches
     broken on the snow.
          I turn sideways
and the wind slips among us,
     so many vertical,
          dark shapes.

LIKE MEMORY, CAVERNS

Dry creekbeds littered with buckeyes, fallen
leaves, geodes—those stones you wrap
your hands around like ancient tools,

hold firm against a stronger rock and strike
until the round splits open, spilling dust
and bits of crystal.
                    To Rilke, perhaps,
solitude seemed a geode: that hidden
hollow where, in its slow,
unconscious time, the self could grow
and strengthen, mineral, elemental.
Think of him working, Paris, a rented room,
we are unutterably alone—

Floyd Collins liked to go alone. On his belly
in a cave he felt his presence fill the space
around him, damp breath hanging
over surfaces of clay, shale, the wet mineral crusts
from water seeping deeper beneath the surface.
He could be standing dappled in Kentucky sunlight,

then step into dark, stone, distant
sound of water dripping or rushing, the way, like memory,
caverns heighten sound beyond the archetypal.
Until the day he crawled some narrow passage—
elbows and hips inching him forward,
the shallow stream washing against his chest, his legs—

When the stone fell, he could neither kick free
nor turn around. The days he lay there, feeling
his body slowly cooling in the little current,
listening. Much later, the rescue party
tried to lift the stone that pinned him,
each time failing.

There is a moment when the soul confronts its own negation.
Once there was a man, once there was a woman:
the story repeats for us each. When he was two, my father's
father lay awake beside his mother, knew the minute
she was no longer alive. My mother died alone—
unconscious, the doctor guesses. Who knew
what she thought or believed? Sometimes
the little triumphs gleam their patterned facets;
sometimes we panic in the dark.

TOUCHED

In my home town we called them The Loonies.
Like images from Breughel, their faces
wore the great, tuberous weight
of the mentally retarded, and we knew them
with that safe amusement and affection

distance gives. Just after high school
I worked part time at Burger Chef,
where each Sunday a man would come
for black coffee and a dozen hamburgers.
His body curved toward me over the counter:
disformity, or years of medication

or rage; his spine hung like an obscene question
in the air. I remember how,
before I took his money, he'd count
those burgers into his shopping bag, lifting
each one cautiously, as if they all might

somehow change. At Woolworth's, I'd see two women
from the halfway house buying toiletries and candy.
They moved with that consuming
intimacy of girls in junior high, destructive,

reassuring, constant. And late afternoons
the fat man sat in the window of Bojangles,
having draft beer and baskets of peanuts.
His eyes, when someone walked in,
looked blandly toward the door, then

slid from focus, the way the mind slips inward
to remember, or forget. Those years
I gently starved myself, leaning
into hunger like a kind of slow
arousal, imagining my body in the windy dark,

pulling each cell
more nearly toward perfection.
In the back of the bar, the stage
stood by the restrooms, and nights
when a band played bluegrass I'd sit
and look at the musicians
and watch people come in and go out of the john,

the way we touch each other's lives in these
repeated but tangential rhythms.

SEAN THOMAS DOUGHERTY (b. 1965)

THE PUERTO RICAN GIRLS OF FRENCH HILL

The Puerto Rican girls
of French Hill
shine
like saints
like frescos
from cathedrals
freshly painted
Cadillacs
& chrome
plated silver dollars
melted gold
& emerald
crowns of Incan
Mayan Afro Spanish
grace they
walk
a walk so
thick
with slang
a machete
could not
slice away
the Samba
in their hips
that sway
to Latin beats
through city
streets they
shout at night
at passing cars
& point
at streetlight
matadors
& say
don't play like
you're
the man
you ain't.

Long Coats with Deep Pockets

Cigarettes snuffed down a sleeve, a candy bar slid to the hip, bags of chips, and even cans of corn beef hash, Spaghettios—it didn't matter what as much as the taking.

Only after the last bar was closed, would we saunter into a convenience store as another one of us stayed outside to pump the gas. If a man was working, Stevie paid with his straight ahead questions, asking directions.

But mostly it was best if a woman was working—Keester could flirt a street lamp into flickering on and off at will, though nothing felt right he said, after the night he talked that sad, middle-aged blonde into believing he really wanted her, while Brucie slithered sideways out the door so his body blended with a full case of beer.

Cocoons

Dead moths fell from the sky. Swirling swarms buried traffic lights. The blizzard breathed, but there were no angels on the lawns. Rocks sizzled in doorways, in houses where the door was gone, and the hallways lit by pipes.

I carried a bag of groceries from the corner bodega, slid my way along the sidewalk in smooth soled boots. "Are you set?" A hooded white kid wearing black—I could barely see him—shouted from behind a parked car; his high voice whistled past my hollow ears.

Buildings creaked at night a noise that meant forgetting. I dreamed a dream of Chinese silk, slave-factories, a million worms spinning threads into tiny, oval moons. Outside, the razor'd wind ripped the streets. At dawn, I work thirsty. The snow had stopped. In the watery light of the world, there was this silence: no one worked the block, no one asked, or begged or pleaded.

Double Helix

Through the screened window
a noise pierces our sleep—
some cat in heat howling, I think,
until I realize it is a baby's
cry—hunger or fear climbing
up from the bowels to the mouth
without thought or idea—instinct
filling the night's emptiness
with the noise of constant longing,

and us, eyes opening, awakened
by the call to come, awakened
from our shared sleep—Kundera's
notion of love, the twin hulls
of our bodies crossing the waters
together—we stare up at the ceiling's
shadows, flickering abstractions,
shapeless, as if at the edge of a cave,
the fire sending forth the resemblance
of living—leaves washed in the night
breeze, the streetlight's liquid
illumination, our toes barely touching—
the child's crying crescendos, shivers
our skin as the wind rises, the room clatters
with the patter of footsteps against the roof
of our hearts, swollen with the child's voice
now ebbing, as hands cradle its head,
stroke its legs, nuzzle its tiny mouth
to the mother's breast, the quietest
lullaby, the milky giving of light.

DENISE DUHAMEL (b. 1961)

YES

According to *Culture Shock:*
A Guide to Customs and Etiquette
of Filipinos, when my husband says yes,
he could also mean one of the following:
a.) I don't know.
b.) If you say so.
c.) If it will please you.
d.) I hope I have said yes unenthusiastically enough
for you to realize I mean no.
You can imagine the confusion
surrounding our movie dates, the laundry,
who will take out the garbage
and when. I remind him
I'm an American, that all his yeses sound alike to me.
I tell him here in America we have shrinks
who can help him to be less of a people-pleaser.

We have two-year-olds who love to scream "No!"
when they don't get their way. I tell him,
in America we have a popular book,
When I Say No I Feel Guilty.
"Should I get you a copy?" I ask.
He says yes, but I think he means
"If it will please you," i.e., "I won't read it."
"I'm trying," I tell him, "but you have to try too."
"Yes," he says, then makes *tampo,*
a sulking that the book *Culture Shock* describes as
"subliminal hostility . . . withdrawal of customary cheerfulness
in the presence of the one who has displeased" him.
The book says it's up to me to make things all right,
"to restore goodwill, not by talking the problem out,
but by showing concern about the wounded person's
well-being." Forget it, I think, even though I know
if I'm not nice, *tampo* can quickly escalate into *nagdadabog*—
foot stomping, grumbling, the slamming
of doors. Instead of talking to my husband, I storm off
to talk to my porcelain Kwan Yin,
the Chinese goddess of mercy
that I bought on Canal Street years before
my husband and I started dating.
"The real Kwan Yin is in Manila,"
he tells me. "She's called Nuestra Señora de Guia.
Her Asian features prove Christianity
was in the Philippines before the Spanish arrived."
My husband's telling me this
tells me he's sorry. Kwan Yin seems to wink,
congratulating me—my short prayer worked.
"Will you love me forever?" I ask,
then study his lips, wondering if I'll be able to decipher
what he means by his yes.

ART

Because I was brought up in a working class family
I used to resent poems with references to supposedly famous paintings
which I'd never heard of or seen. Not that working class people
are excluded from looking at paintings, it's just that my family never
        went
to a museum except for the Museum of Science after our jaunt
to the Boston Aquarium. Then one day after I'd been to college
and read a lot of books and went to the Southwest,
I wrote a poem about Georgia O'Keeffe

and I thought, well, that's not too bad, since you can buy O'Keeffe
calendars and postcards in Job Lot, a discount store
in the town I grew up in. I justified my poem since
Georgia was pretty famous by now. And Renoir was OK,
since everyone had heard of him even if they hadn't seen his work,
or Keith Haring since his paintings wound up on buttons and tee
    shirts
and advertisements for vodka. Or Andy Warhol
since there was a book about him in the window displays of mall
    bookstores
and, after he died, gossip on TV about the fights over his estate.
But I didn't think it was OK to write about El Greco or Velazquez or
    Goya
since you had to go to Madrid or Barcelona to see most of their
    paintings
and most poets write about their experience of seeing the real thing
as opposed to seeing reproductions in a book. But then I met my
    husband
who loved art and could name periods and influences and who
    studied under whom.
His life had been a fairy tale and he took me in without condition
like all Princes who marry Cinderellas do. He told me his story,
how he was dropped from his furry nest
near a rice plantation into the crib of a mansion
where his new parents were so happy to see him
they bought him a sombrero and a mini-guitar
and the maids fought over who would be the lucky one able to
    change his diaper
and powder his sweet rump. He took me to Spain and showed me
what his father had shown him on all his childhood trips
from the Philippines to Europe. All the men
in El Greco's paintings had small heads and long dark bodies,
his trademark the hands with middle fingers stuck together. And I
    knew
I could write a poem about "Las Meninas" because Velazquez
had ambivalence about the rich like I did and tried to show them
in a rather unflattering light. But who in my family would know "Las
    Meninas,"
the self-portrait with the trick of the mirror and innovations
in perspective? Who in my town had been to the Prado?
Who wanted to go even if they could? I stood near Goya's nightmares
and shadows, the tour guide speaking first in Spanish, then in English.
My husband had started out poorer than I had, before he was adopted,
but now he was confident, looking at the small details
of a witch's bloody teeth, contemplating each brush stroke and meaning.

Oh Velazquez, I want to go back to your work in the other wing,
the portraits of midgets and jesters painted with the same dignity as
    royalty.
You knew how so much about luck and money
are accidents of birth, how magical and unfair it all is.
I crumpled my admissions ticket then smoothed it out,
my ticket I'd press behind the plastic flap in my scrap book
not to show anyone in my family back home
but just for me, to remind myself that I was both, still
and no longer, who I once was.

BICENTENNIAL BARBIE

Because she is the most popular doll
of the twentieth century, Barbie
is buried in a time capsule in Philadelphia
on July 4, 1976. She is scrunched between an empty Kentucky
Fried Chicken bucket and a full Coca-Cola can.
She's become a cultural icon, and now she has to pay
the price. She remembers a time
when just a few girls knew her
and she didn't have to put on such airs.
Now a full-fledged collectible, she has to make sure
every hair is always in place. I've just been voted
Best Personality, a superlative category
in our junior high yearbook. I'm able to pose
for a picture with the cute Best Personality boy,
the first and only football player
to ever ask me on a date.
He says he wants to go steady with me
and another girl at the same time.
I don't think it's fair,
but being the Best Personality girl,
it takes me a long time to say that.
You see, it's turned out that, though I'm too old
to still play with fashion dolls, they've somehow become
implanted in my subconscious. I don't look
anything like Barbie so maybe I don't deserve
a boyfriend of my own. And to make things worse, in my mind,
my rival resembles Barbie quite a bit.
When I finally write the Best Personality boy
an angry note, flustered, I slip it between the slots
of the wrong locker. The nobody boy who finds it
won't give it back, even when I ask him politely.

Soon everyone will know I'm not always in a good mood.
Fearing a scandal, I ask advice
of the Best Dressed and Most Likely to Succeed.
They say they don't care what the masses think—
and though I sense they're not telling me the truth—
suddenly it doesn't matter if my class
takes my Best Personality honor away or not.
At least I know I'm better off
than that one repressed Bicentennial Barbie
who'll be stuck in that stuffy time capsule
until the year 2076. Maybe
when she finally comes out, the pressure
will have been too much. Maybe she'll be able, like me,
to express herself. Maybe she'll wink at the Coca-Cola can
before they both shake, explode, make a mess.

KINKY

They decide to exchange heads.
Barbie squeezes the small opening under her chin
over Ken's bulging neck socket. His wide jaw line jostles
atop his girlfriend's body, loosely,
like one of those nodding novelty dogs
destined to gaze from the back windows of cars.
The two dolls chase each other around the orange Country Camper
unsure what they'll do when they're within touching distance.
Ken wants to feel Barbie's toes between his lips,
take off one of her legs and force his whole arm inside her.
With only the vaguest suggestion of genitals,
all the alluring qualities they possess as fashion dolls,
up until now, have done neither of them much good.
But suddenly Barbie is excited looking at her own body
under the weight of Ken's face. He is part circus freak,
part thwarted hermaphrodite. And she is imagining
she is somebody else—maybe somebody middle class and ordinary,
maybe another teenage model being caught in a scandal.

The night had begun with Barbie getting angry
at finding Ken's blow-up doll, folded and stuffed
under the couch. He was defensive and ashamed, especially about
not having the breath to inflate her. But after a round
of pretend-tears, Barbie and Ken vowed to try
to make their relationship work. With their good memories
as sustaining as good food, they listened to late-night radio
talk shows, one featuring Doctor Ruth. *When all else fails,*

just hold each other, the small sex therapist crooned.
Barbie and Ken, on cue, groped in the dark,
their interchangeable skin glowing, the color of Band-Aids.
Then, they let themselves go—soon Barbie was begging Ken
to try on her spandex miniskirt. She showed him how
to pivot as though he were on a runway. Ken begged
to tie Barbie onto his yellow surfboard and spin her
on the kitchen table until she grew dizzy. *Anything,*
anything, they both said to the other's requests,
their mirrored desires bubbling from the most unlikely places.

THOMAS SAYERS ELLIS (b. 1963)

BEING THERE
Kennedy Playground, Washington, D.C.

We forced our faces
into the circular frame
a stringless hoop made,
hoping more than silence & light

would fall through.
We fought for position.
We fouled & shoved.
We high-fived God.

Our Converse All-Stars
burned enough rubber
to rival the devil and his mama.
Hoop, horseshoe, noose.

We aimed at a halo
hung at an angle we couldn't fit,
waiting for the camera
to record our unfocused

need to score.
We left earth.
We lost weight.
We disobeyed bone.

Our finger rolls

& reverse layups
were rejected by angels
guarding the rim,

same as prayers
returned to sinners.

TAPES

We got them the hard way,
Taking turns holding recorders
Blessed with the weight of D batteries

On our shoulders.
We pressed PLAY & RECORD,
Ready to release PAUSE

The moment the drummer
Flexed visible muscle
Or the synthesizer whined

Like a siren.
Weren't we lucky
A few clubs had balconies.

I remember the red lights,
How when they danced
We looked up.

We made copies,
Refusing to trade the ones
With our names on them,

Came to blows
When one was lost, stolen.
"Make me a copy,"

Carmichael said the day
After his brother's murder.
A way of remembering,

Holding on.
Ranked next to gold chains
& school clothes,

Our love for them
Was southern—the older ones
Getting the most

Attention.
Care.
Respect.

H EID E. E R D R I C H   (b. 1963)

FAT IN AMERICA

This is no joke. She is fat and happy in the U.S.A. The kind of woman who always has plenty of loving men—not just perverts either. You are thinking that she can't be all that fat. Well, she is. There are folds of flesh at the back of her neck—her half-moon cheeks swallow her eyes—her eyes are olives sunk in whole wheat dough—her chin doubles when she laughs, and wobbles when she talks—her shoulders are broad and solid as an XXL man's. Her breasts are vast. There is no other way to say it. Unless we say they are globes of warmth or that she would nurse nations. Oh, she has held a lover's head between them and covered all but his bald spot. And yet she has a waist, still obviously indented beneath a rich ring of belly—her hips rise biblically (mounds, doves, wheat, hills) nothing is fertile enough to describe them, except the Great Plains where she was born. Yes, her hips are like cropland. And the valley between? A gorgeous secret place, a gorge of ferns and falls—her thighs are sacks of grain, a harvest—her calves carved timbers, marble sculpture. And her feet? Ah! These are the platforms of faith—holy and round and strong.

HOPI PROPHET CHOOSES A POP

The light and air? They are mountain-perfect, here in Taos, near
some tennis courts, our conference room door open, all that clear
sun whisking in while we carry on our hot debate in a think-tank of
artists and healers.
            We are out to save the world.

My own insomniac clarity lets me see how powerfully ordinary he is,
that Hopi elder, who says humbly, simply, what we somehow knew

was true all along. How sweet his words, clear water rushing cold to
our lips, all the drink we'd ever need—
                              Until coffee break.

The foam cups lined up, the donuts piled like a stack of spare tires—
I go outside and find him there, nothing between us but bright air
and a tonal vending machine.

That junk's not for me, he says, glancing back to the foyer door, now
blocked by three stainless coffee urns.
                              No, I reply.

He pats his pockets for glasses. The vending machine sighs.
We approach it respectfully, as teens do juke boxes, as gamblers
do slots.

Read me what she's got, he squints through yellowed lenses, I will admit
it: I hope to divine what he'd like, that my right choice will somehow
reflect how much of his teaching I get—*There's sparkling water*, I try,
jingling my change.
                    No response but a slight, expectant shift.

There's apple juice, veggie cocktail? I ask, thinking he'd like something
natural. *Or Bubble Up, ginger ale, cream soda?*

I am on a roll call of beverages: *root beer, Crush, Nehi?* As if that
machine contains all the liquids ever canned by human hands.
I list *tonic, sarsaparilla, lemon-lime, Coco-yahoo soda, diet this, caffeine-free
that, and all your regular colas.*

I appeal to the horizon, source of inspiration, and make one last
certain offer: *Mountain Dew*.
                    A pause, but no, no response.

Finally, I feed in dimes. The coin slot gulps, my own favorite choice
rolls down. Just then the button flashes—machine's all out—And
then, of course, he cries: *That's right! That's right! That one I like.
                    I'll take that Doctor Pop.*

THE QUIET EARTH

Snow fills the leaves that haven't blown,
inverted umbrellas, they weigh trees down.
The tall elm leans almost into Helen's garden.

Out in her backyard, the winesap branches harden
in an icy armor that will snap those limbs.
In her barn, the auction goes on. Winter comes
too early, freezes the grass and blows away the birds,
blows faintly in the kitchen, in the attic overhead.
Helen's plates, white as eggs, tremble in a stack.
They say ghosts grow loud in hunger and must be fed,
but today she is silent when I want one word back,
an ordinary phrase or the way she shaped my name.

Snow turns to rain. Pools gather on the frozen ground.
The earth's so hard there's nothing it takes in.
Branches crack like lightning strikes: Helen's apple trees.
To her forgotten orchard of windfalls and blight,
we drove on dry dirt roads in the long light
of my childhood summer afternoons.
In exchange for seedlings, my father would prune
or graft a row of trees back into shape.
This was a lonely place, but loud with wind
and overgrown with a kind of ivy, a wild grape
that twined into the trees, tore them to the ground.

I've fixed Helen there forever, so old and light she shook,
her skin like powder and in her eyes a hard blue look—
With my forehead fit into the cup of my palms
I sit for hours, think of apples, think of Helen.
The wind rails, knocks leaves off the elm
whose bare arms hang sad as a willow leaning low.
I press my cheek along the crook of my elbow.
Snow turns to rain. Pools gather on the frozen ground.
The earth's so hard there's nothing it takes in.
Helen's plates, white as eggs, tremble in a stack.
The earth's so hard, there's nothing it gives back.

FUTURE DEBRIS

"The typical object up there is about the size of a filing cabinet."
— From *"Space Junk a Danger to Launches,"*
Johns Hopkins Gazette, *August 23, 1988*

Until he died we thought our neighbor dull.
Now he's a distant point of light.
His cremated body orbits low
in its reflectorized canister creating
what the space burial firm called

"a twinkling reminder of the loved one."
There's a wheel chart to map his course.
Nights we go around back of the house,
gaze at what little true sky winks
through the haze of debris.
It amazes me and is a relief, really,
not to have the whole universe
smack up against me like a wall.
All my life I've strained to comprehend
planets and motion, all the unending
that's been clouded, obscured
by the detritus humans seem to produce
naturally, ink to the squid, protective
cloak through which we cannot see
and therefore feel we are not seen.
Some night, a little girl, who will know
only tame animals, city trees, will listen
to my tales of wilderness and game.
I'll hold her up so she basks in the glint
of celestial jetsam. She will spread her hands,
reach for the bright flecks, ask if they are wild.
Lying to the child, I'll say they are. Then the filing
cabinets, ah, they'll glimmer like stars!

SASCHA FEINSTEIN (b. 1963)

SUMMERHOUSE PIANO

As though squeaks in the piano were not enough, a mouse
gave birth to her litter between the wooden center boards,

unreachable. Nothing could damage that ivory
upright, a yard-sale item dumped in my room by default,

but I had trouble sleeping with those high sounds. My step-
mother tried to drive them out with a few crippled strains

of "Maple Leaf Rag," and it left me with more admiration
for the mice: they could survive anything. That night,

the chirps more insistent, the life of their mother doubtful,
I wondered if perpetual noise would make them leave, a player

piano with an endless scroll, the ones played by four hands,
not two, though a boy can't tell by looking. It's like the story

of blind Art Tatum hearing those old scrolls before he knew
the instrument, and figuring, *That's the way it's got to sound.*

I tried humming his solo from "All God's Children Got Rhythm"
but it moved too fast, traveled into my head like a movie:

Art's round gut near the keys, how he'd lean back, flash
his Steinway-smile, roll through the fields, brushfire on dry

pine needles. I saw him sitting at our off-white piano, laughing
at keys that wouldn't come back up, but dealing with them:

special runs around the quirks, long lines driving the way
the force of a swollen river can push a fallen tree down—

stream, the massive trunk cascading forward in its current.

BLUES FOR ZOOT

They had crew cuts then, puffed cheeks like kids
spitting water: Al Cohn and Zoot Sims spouting tenor saxes
on the cover of *You 'n' Me*, my dad's original pressing;

I hoped they'd sign it. Zoot clouded the room,
smoke fading his face, milky freckles. In five years
he'd die of cancer, and maybe he knew, maybe I knew,

because instead of looking into his eyes, I stared
at his shoes, then thought of the Kenton band, Zoot forgetting
to wear socks one night, how Stan said he'd have to leave

if he couldn't dress right. Next gig: still no socks,
and Zoot—he rubbed shoe polish on his ankles. Backstage,
when I met him, his pant legs hung too high, and I could see

blue socks, even a hole, his striped pants thin and washed
out. Al put his horn down, scribbled his name, walked away.
But Zoot checked out the tunes and brushed his fingers

across the photograph. He said, *Man, this is old,*
and I thought he meant, *Where'd you get it, kid?* I told him
my father's name, Provincetown summers, the Fifties,

how they'd play softball. Zoot closed his eyes, hard
to think back so many years, until, looking up somewhere
in the room, he said, *Oh yeah*. I'm not sure what I wanted

to hear, perhaps just my father's one-liner, *Good tempered
stuff, and lousy playing*. He'd talk about artists, sculptors.
When Mulligan or Sims played the "A House,"

Dad would say, *they'd hit with us*, and I'd always ask for
the Zoot story. *Herman Cherry pitched that day*, he'd begin,
Franz Kline at first, Sims led off. From the bench,

*Mulligan yelled, "Give 'em Hell!" so Zoot smiled, and Herman
picked up a softball.* He'd pause as though he needed to,
ask if I wanted to hear it all again. *We had painted*

*this grapefruit with white acrylic, black scratches
for stitching. Herman lobbed it slow, a moon ball,
and you could see Zoot's eyes get big. Then he really*

connected—THWACK! We'd laugh, his hands rapping
the table. *There's this burst of fruit and juice,
little pieces of white paint sailing down the third base line!*

Zoot just dropped his bat and said, "Shit"—he rubs
his hands and laughs, glances at the liver spots
on his knuckles, and says, *You should have seen his face*.

When I met Zoot Sims twenty-six years later, I wanted to ask
if he remembered the sound from that day at the plate.
Or how it felt to be one of the Four Brothers. Instead,

I watched his pen sign the photograph, his fingers holding
the jacket for a last look. *Here*, he said, *collector's item*,
and before he turned, reached out for his yellow horn,

I shook his hand. Christ. What else was there to do?

SINGAPORE, JULY 4TH

Banyan roots almost reach
the river where small boats
putter to shore before dark.
The Red House,
best chili crab in town

and your friends reach for sweetness,
picking apart claws, hard shells,
sucking legs that burn the throat.
If Louis Armstrong were alive
we'd celebrate his 89th birthday,
his chili voice singing
Stars Fell On Alabama.
No reason to miss the States
but I do. Tonight, back home,
when the sun begins to set on Cranes Beach,
the old mansion in the dunes
will send off Roman candles.
To Dixieland and Southern blues
floating across the seascape,
men in tuxedos will put down their scotch,
hold theirs wives by the waist—
the way I'd want to be with you,
until my black suit faded into night,
your white dress only a vague glow
under chandeliers of bursting sky.

Blues Villanelle for Sonny Criss

A lunar eclipse, and your solos spread
across wild clover as I exhale
and try not to think of the gun at your head,
how we say but rarely believe, "You can't be dead

if you're on record." Your alto wails
to the moon's elision, the solo spread
against the splintering woodshed.
It's '57, one year before jail,

twenty before the gun's at your head
and you're my age playing "Calidad,"
"Willow Weep for Me," "Love for Sale,"
as the brief clips from your solo spreads

the graying moon like cigarettes
in walnut-paneled dives, overpriced cocktails
cold as the gun you'll hold to your head.
But I'm trying not to see that, trying instead

to let the bass and chromatic scales
eclipse you, solo, outspread.
I'm trying not to think. The gun's at your head.

Lisa Fishman (b. 1966)

Diagnosis: My Mother's Breast

Recalcitrant, the empire sleeves of her dress hold back
her arms, empty of all long-stemmed flowers now. More blue
enlivens what the wrist keeps track of: the hours
on their daily jaunt around the malls, just as what's ours is wanting
to stay true and earnestly regretting when the sun goes down.
We are pitched into dizziness if we look there, where the *vita* flees.

Her hands are still
behind her back, her mouth is stained with chokeberries.
She flew the coop when the fashion changed. Now our knees
are without hope, too visible for praying on or for the mad
professor to cup his hand around. She wants God sewn

in her hem like a stone in a valance,
like the lead in a bib,
so each time she lifts her dress for a lover He is there
wedged in the balance, accounting
for her breasts, her ribs, and the dress
falling radiant over her head.

Promiscuity

Tell me the stories of wanting are flowering
past engravings of the poets on the windowsill.
Past the sea that's shoring up its singers:
names and dates of birth and what hurt them
hurtling, now, toward the constant
vow, to listen. And to see
the paper boats go sailing when the body
peels back all its notebooks and its petals.
There are zinnias and anemones afloat.
They can barely hold their perfume in
their veins, they are the story
the earth tells of wanting
to be beautiful, and how it loves
what opens.

Tell me the future
is a border beginning

where the bones of the mind
shine early in the moon's
forsaking light when fullness
is everything and everything is
visible. To be seen is almost as good
as seeing, as the river
says, come in, come in. Tell me
the river.

If radiance can be beheld
then flesh is luminous with seeing.
But to touch is purest knowing
and the wind keening afterward. Both the becoming
and to be leaving. The song of the mind,
the body breathing.
Tell me why one can never be satisfied
though the other is.
Tell me the stories are true.

V's FARMHOUSE

He's at the window now,
at the foot of the bed looking out
to a full blue night the kind the clouds move fast in
and the color's in close as if the sky's right there and you could touch it.
She says she took the screens out, so he opens it
and he's pissing a long arc into the sumac and Queen Anne's lace,
didn't even have to leave the room.
She says he looks majestic
outlined in the window, we see
what we want to see.
To hear is more difficult, this discord
in the pact of things. What he said once before,
turned away from her in the dark
and she, climbing over him to ask so she could hear it.

No one ever died of desire.
They leave the window open
when they sleep, the essential
circumstances fly out: the adulteress
writing a letter, the reprieve
asked for, received
and who it is she loves
already falling past her—she wakes but has only
an opening window, unframed
sky moving faster than anyone could see.

NICK FLYNN (b. 1960)

BAG OF MICE

For my mother

I dreamt your suicide note
was scrawled in pencil on a brown paper bag,
& in the bag were six baby mice. The bag was
open to the darkness &
smoldering
from the top down. The mice,
huddled at the bottom, scurried the bag
across a shorn field. I stood over it
& as the burning reached each carbon letter
of what you'd written
your voice was released into the night
like a song, & the mice
grew wilder.

EMPTYING TOWN

After Provincetown

Each fall this town empties, leaving me
drained, standing on the dock, waving
bye bye, the white handkerchief
stuck in my throat. You know the way Jesus

rips open his shirt
to show us his heart, all flaming & thorny,
the way he points to it. I'm afraid
the way I miss you

will be this obvious. I have

a friend who everyone warns me
is dangerous, he hides
bloody images of Jesus around my house

for me to find when I come home—Jesus
behind the cupboard door, Jesus tucked

into the mirror. He wants to save me

but we disagree from what. My version of Hell
is someone ripping open his
shirt & saying,

look what I did for you.

GOD FORGOTTEN

God mercifully forgets us for a few hours.

A blind woman in a folding chair
rests in the sun on the sidewalk below
& doesn't think about heaven
for an afternoon. I put my hand

on yours & say, *show me,* and you begin
slowly, steadily, my hand

riding yours, a spidermonkey
holding on to its mother's back, until

your fingers disappear inside

& my fingers follow. I see myself reflected
in your face, you smile & I realize
I'm smiling also. There is so much

I want to tell you. Once I spoke to my mother
through a long cardboard tube,
put one end to her sleeping ear & the other
to my mouth & whispered,

can you hear me? She was younger
than I am now, now

she will always be younger. Another hour passes, we open
the shades. Outside
a man in a wheelchair crosses his legs. You show me

a photograph, a group of children beside a '60s
station wagon, you ask, *can you find me?* My fingers
tangle your hair, trace
your skull, your face so radiant

I can barely look into it.

Fragment (found inside my mother)

I kept it hidden, it was easy
to hide, behind my lingerie, a shoebox

above my boys' reach, swaddled alongside
my painkillers

in their childproof orange cups. I knew my kids,
curious, monkeys,

but did they know me? It was easy

to hide, it waited, the hard O of its mouth,
it was made of waiting, each bullet
with its soft hood of lead. Braced

solid against my thigh, I'd feed it
with my free hand, my robe open

as if nursing, practicing
my hour of lead, my letting go.

The youngest surprised me with a game,
held out his loose fists,
begging guess which hand, *but both*

were empty. Who taught him that?

Ruth Forman (b. 1968)

Abraham Got All the Stars n the Sand

Daddy 43 but look 40
35 when he laugh
ma family big n pretty

Bo
look like smooth onyx stone
Randy look like
Florida sand

Winnie
the breath of honeysuckle
Leesha
a redwood tree
Peaches
look like plums
n Momma
sweet coconut meat
next to Daddy color of baking chocolate

n Jojo
she buckwheat honey
in the mornin
when Daddy grease n part her hair
for the ready red ribbons
glow so next to her skin

he put twists in Leesha's
n Peaches get three thick braids
We always sing
different songs at the table

n Gramma let us do it
as she pour her coffee
watch them lil teeth shinin
thinkin
Abraham got all the stars n the sand
but she got all the rainbow.

SOMEONE

is in love with someone
not in love with her
someone sings to the sky
alone
someone walk home
rattlesnakes watching from the path
someone walk barefoot with stones
in her throat

he will love me someday I will grow my hair long
I will slim myself slimmer than an idea
I will walk like breath

and that's what she did

slipped through this world into a ghost
nobody could see
silent woman once in love changed herself
so much
we can no longer find her

KIN

Buffalo burned sage
steel jaws around the ankle
high prayers lowered foreheads high noon
these days gone
with my ancestors now long passed

who to carry them
when everyone claim his head too full
who to carry the story
of true things

we walk
empty armloads too full for treasure
thus the old winds must find a new way
into our children's ears.

WE ARE THE YOUNG MAGICIANS

Go sit yo ass down
we don't need no volunteers
to disappear
from a box trap door
a hole in the floor
we reappear
folks you never seen before
reach deep
behind black velvet curtains

we don't need no trick cane
to amaze
with a mere wave of the pen
we transform grey concrete
to yellow brick roads

we don't pull no rabbits
from a hat
we pull rainbows
from a trash can
we pull hope
from the dictionary
n teach it how to ride the subway

we don't guess the card in yo hand
we know it
aim to change it
yeah
we know magic
and don't be so sure that card in yo hand
is the Ace

KENNY FRIES (b. 1960)

FROM *The Healing Notebooks*

(5)

I bed next to you, I feel your heartbeat.
I follow your veins: the blood flowing

to each end of your body. I want to pour
all your blood from your body, to spill it

out of you, cleanse this invisible thing
from our lives. I want to wrap you in a blanket,

run with you far to the mountains, to the edge
of the sea. I want to find protection.

But the world is as it is. Blood is no longer
life. Positive, a different meaning now.

(15)

Who knows the precise moment when the stream
will overflow? You look for signs: white

on your tongue, a red blotch growing
on your thigh, fungus between your toes.

Who knows when it begins? The rituals
of the worried well. The fear of the common

cold. Wouldn't it be easier if it happened
now? The inevitable wasting away,

the delirium. But who is immune to hope?
On a night like this who would keep

the window closed? Open it and hear
the stream flowing all night long.

JOANNA FUHRMAN (b. 1972)

ATLANTIS

After the gods left, the trucks of evening
arrived. They were slow as a sunset filmed
but we loved them anyway. We smelled
their heat through our chlorine-soaked skin.

After the gods left, we took up digging.
Bought goggles to wear

when the sun turned red. We watched
the final airport close. So brave a tune
we played that night, fiddles burst into wings.
Grass refused growth.

I though a new city might rise:
built from our tunes. Instead, a sameness fell.
Gods left. Trucks stayed.

EVIDENCE

If you don't blink, nothing is funny or so
a scientist says, as he measures the wingspan
of an extinct Arctic hummingbird.

Similarly if you hear a sad story eating peanut butter
you will not cry out. This test has been replicated underwater
and out of earth's atmosphere. Nobody ever cries out.

Once a girl in Tuscaloosa wrote an evolution of beetles
in green ink. When she went swimming
a new story sprung up. She felt a loss like birth.

Reporters swarmed, snapped her picture
for cereal boxes. Asking, "could she blink?
Had she tried eating peanut butter in bliss

or mixed with honey in a submarine."
The girl laughed. With her plastic flower,
she shot the reporters wet

and left. Some speculate there were confounding factors
to her flight: the smell of southern wheat or
the warm touch of sun off apricot dashboards.

No one can quite grasp the cause.

O but what we can imagine:
the reporters and their subjects and us,
drinking ice tea under trees' lush canopies,
pollen flush from cut kudzu.

All evidence drifting away—

PERSONAL AD

A couple slumps on a veranda opening flat cokes.
The ex-girlfriend of the boyfriend and the boyfriend of the ex-
girlfriend play scrabble in mittens. It is that party again,
where I find the personal that reads,
Must be willing to whine and be whined at.

It is not a day for making sandwiches.
A potted shrub blooms a vermilion rash.
The guests are waiting for the spectacle
to denounce its departure.

Must avoid talk about work
when work matters.
Must look potential in-laws in the eye.

A marinated rabbit sizzles on a charcoal grill.
A woman applies lipstick to a Burmese cat.

Must answer telephone messages right away,
I stand on the picnic table to announce,
Must lie and tell me everything is great.

WATCHING TRAINS

A blue arm stuck out of the train's window
and a cat shaped figure wavered, suspended

over the moving ground.

You could see the figure shifting backward as the train went forward.

As the train went forward, you could see the figure shifting backward.

Somehow, you knew what you couldn't know:

that the arm protruding from the window was a man's arm,
not a woman's,

and the cat shaped figure, hanging in the air, was really a cat,
not a cat shaped toy.

There was no clatter from the tracks,

no sound of cat or man or train.

By your window, you drank cola from a long straw.
Wet hair clung to your scalp.

There was no clatter from the tracks,

no sound of cat or man or train.

A flute's crescendo challenged the radio's static.

The train rushed forward. The cat back.

HERE, I SAY

In my dream Pinocchio is six feet tall.
We are walking on the beach. His wooden palm

pulses in my hand. He says, *Gepetto was wrong,*
lying is the language of trees: a crab shell, sand,

his glass eye gleaming. *If lying is that,*
then what is truth? I want to ask. Instead, I say

I am cataloguing my life so I won't forget:
seashells, pebbles, a gull's feather, a swimmer

in a red cap on the horizon. What is the purpose
of *describe*? I long to ask. Pinocchio laughs.

The gulls glide east toward evening.
His tied-on limbs swing awkwardly in the breeze.

SUZANNE GARDINIER (b. 1961)

TO PEACE

All day I search for you without success
None of the benches dividing the north
and southbound sides of Broadway holds you
and none of the fouled snow surging in torrents
into the sewers will tell where you are
My soles are tired and the sun is setting
over New Jersey streaming along streets
empty of the ring of change in your pockets
you who walk before the light gives its direction
facing the trash-blowing river wind
At intersections the fractious traffic
pitches and steams In the markets oranges
lie under their winter blankets still
Below the wood water towers and bare
unsettled rooftops the shadows of rising
smoke against brick walls tiers of windows each
framing a woman alone who stares out
below the ladders for escape from fire

the light stays longer and I say your name Here
beside steel-rimmed curbs and the rush of pennies
shaken in cardboard cups here below
unblinking streetlights and the later dark
I fasten my coat and walk looking for you
Here between the cobbled seasons I wait
Here above the subway trembling I say your name

WHERE BLIND SORROW IS TAUGHT TO SEE

Near where I lived there was a fenced schoolyard
where at night the bloody ghost children played
calling in all the languages
I never saw them there again after
that night on the small curved street when you kissed me
Past the screen door where the late dishwashers
stood to smoke past the young woman sitting
on two overturned milk crates sorting roses
with bats of her fingers coaxing the curled buds
open you stood me against the dark bricks
and kissed me insisting your tongue quick and sweet
Why were you not afraid as I was
Why was there no forbidden place
You held me and opened my shirt and touched me
in the building's shadow where no one could see
All evening I had watched you lifting
wooden sticks over the plate of pods
and blossoms your eager reaching to open
oranges and folded futures What were
the words I whispered Your legs held
mine apart Did I tell you everything
You pushed your fingers inside me Sorrow
hovered and found no lighting place
its bruised cheeks healed with your lips' attention
its restless thirst watered and soothed to rest

AT WORK

You so sleepy baby Who you been
botherin all night Clarisse laughs She sets
on the green counter eggs triangles of bread
and a gleaming orange glass *She don't say*

nothin she tells her friend I don't answer
She ain't givin nothin away
You better eat up baby She aligns
a knife and fork on the napkin One hand
brushes mine *You hardly holdin up*
that sleepy head She crosses to the window
It's still too early for Saturday's thicket
of orders the row of tickets hung
by the kitchen portal the ache in her feet
She sits at a set table Winter roaring
through the village makes the plate glass tremble
Where your babies at Clarisse her friend calls
and her face changes The smile returns
to the place where she keeps it She rubs her eyes
and doesn't answer *Where your babies today*
her friend calls again They are three
Their photographs grin from the wall by the toasters
I have never met them but I know their names
Girl Clarisse starts She stands and gives me
her square back on the way to the kitchen
to answer *Clarisse Where your babies today*

BLUES

By this fire I still can feel the wind
By this fire I still can feel the wind
Stays by my shoulders like it's listenin

All night I hear somebody callin me
All night I hear somebody callin me
But I can't think what could the answer be

When I get home I'll lock the peaceful in
When I get home I'll lock the peaceful in
When I get home I'll tell you where I been

STEVE GEHRKE (b. 1971)

MOUTH TO MOUTH

Like trying to blow a feather
from the bottom of a hat,
the trickiest of negotiations.
What voice do we use
to call the freshly-dead back?

My mother brought one up once.
Weighted down with airplane tequila
and flopping from the after shocks
of a seizure, he was a real bottom-dweller,
bobbed in the battle, surfaced and dove.

She breathed into him with wind
from the tornado of three small children,
troubled-marriage wind. She pressed
the rhythm of her working-mother
days into his chest.

When the living mate with the dead
it's not charity, but a balance
and counterbalance that pilfers loss-heavy coins
from the purse of each chest.

So on a day that was not Easter,
it was Easter for an average man from Ohio:
tailor, divorcee, ordinary sinner. My mother
inhaled just enough of him
so they both hovered above the black rim
to the deep-hatted other world.

WALKING FIELDS AT NIGHT SOUTH OF HAMPTON, IOWA

The last of the wheat is drought-bruised, bending
to its toes. Hay knuckled under weeks ago.

In the ditches, the hens form rows. Above me,
stars burn away the edges of quiet.

Gulls nest in grain elevators, hollow as sky,
when clouds don't keep a dark horizon.

I've walked a very long time, waiting to connect
these things to my life. Waiting to say—

my heart burns in its great quiet, or *wheat bends
in its brittle body and I bend in mine.*

Whatever flattens these fields, though, has little
to do with grief. And I can't speak for hens,

to say—*hens think stars are the ghosts of grain.*
I say, if there never were stars, I would not miss them.

NEAR THE MISSISSIPPI

August stretches into fall. Clouds spread
rumors of a false frontier. Above you,
the moon raises a fist at the stars.

A shudder of dust blurs the highway
and you realize for the hundredth
time that you have never existed,

that the river braids two thousand hard
miles south and never breaks its spine,
that trees are the bones in the perfect

anatomy of a forest, and that stems,
goldenrod say, can stitch themselves
in the same pinholes of earth for years

and never need rain or shade.
They are complete in their delicate bodies.
And you, in a crude garment of skin, are not.

TIMOTHY GEIGER (b. 1966)

DISPROPORTIONATE

On some level everything in the universe is connected.
—Bell's theorem in physics

While half the globe away the highest peak of Everest
lifts an icicle another centimeter to compensate,
halfway down the block an old woman loses control
around an icy bend of Pheasant Road, goes through
the foggy windshield of her white Oldsmobile,
knocking over an old-growth tree where a squirrel
that raided my bird feeder all last August
sleeps in a mansion of sticks, acorns and mud.

I was one part of a crowd gathering in the cold,
looking for cause and effect in skid marks,
the twisted trap of chrome, and a fallen tree.
Pondering the accepted theories of probability,
I considered everything I knew about chaos—
the random possibility that nothing is set in stone.

My next-door-neighbor huddled to my side
to say something about a shame, to invite me over
to his place later and give me a slide-show
from his second honeymoon spent in a tourist-trap
four miles outside the city limits of Flagstaff.
He described the town's main attraction,
a boulder as big as an eighteen-wheeler, tracing
a thousand-year-old trail inch by inch in the sand,
carving a rutted path toward the Nevada border.

He explained that scientists have concluded
tectonics and seismic activity, but he doesn't believe
in fault lines, thinks the boulder's locomotion
is due to the patterns of prevailing winds—
thirty of his slides snapped during one strong gust.
He said if I looked close I would see it moving
frame by frame; I told him maybe some other time.

After the wreck was loaded onto a flat-bed,
and the sirens and fallen tree cleared from the road,

a paramedic pulled on a black cap, shaking his head
no. My neighbor sums up the day's events
saying there are no accidental deaths in his dreams,
everyone lives forever, or as long as he needs.
I should probably go home, back to bed,
but now I imagine taking him up on his offer.

Over coffee I'd explain the world's invisible states,
the gaping hole the size of Iowa opening the ozone,
no chance for a useless ice-plug to ever reach that high.
I'd tell him to forget about his time-lapse
photography, instead, let's consider the afternoon's
repercussions—the woman's dead weight kissing
the tree kissing the ground, causing a long monsoon
in Katmandu for years to come. I know all
about that boulder, I'd tell him we move it every day.

A DRY SPELL OF FAITH

Above a ceiling of emerald junipers
crows commit their weightlessness to the wind
and follow the slow pattern of nimbus clouds
against the indigo drain of sky. A dry breeze
carries with it the memory
                              of rain,
memories of another August—the day
my best friend and I traced the muddy banks
of the Antietam creek behind Union Fabric Mill,
following the steep path through the woods
all the way to Levine's farm.
                              There, in a field
of Pennsylvania wheat, he showed me the scar,
the gray rope running the knotted length
of his skinny back. In that dim light
the braid of his spine did not look strong enough
to hold the weight
                              of anyone's life together.
I couldn't see the bones filled with cancer,
or feel, as he must have, everything growing
lighter at the soft edges of his skin—
I only knew the hook of his scar, the voice
as dusk came on, asking if I was ready to go.

SOUNDTRACKS

I'm keeping to myself on my little porch
out front listening to the rocking chair's ribs
making music each time I push back and return

to my brother's eighth birthday party, 1972.
Spinning the small knobs of a new AM radio,
twisting the cord to the waxy plug in his ear,
my brother is holding a tune in a black plastic box
for the first time.
                        Now, I'm hearing that song
again, thinking someone redid it last year
and I still can't recall its name. I'm coming
to the conclusion it's the same music
all along the dial, the same stories wherever I go.

Everyone has a friend who knows someone
who, leaning over the gas stove to light
a cigarette, singed off both eyebrows and went
for three weeks looking oddly incomplete—
a house without shutters, a Cadillac missing
front hubcaps—
                        everyone has seen someone
go down for the count doing something stupid,
everyone has faced that music before.

Which is why I keep remembering my brother
after the birthday party where no one was hurt
when he leaned over to blow out the eight candles
and nearly set the top of his head on fire.

Later, alone outside, his singed blonde hair
swaying back and forth, foot tapping a rhythm
only he could follow—
                        the way he pretended
to raise a conductor's baton over his head
cross the wholly quiet air then bring it
down quick—it must have been a symphony.

Lisa Glatt (b. 1963)

Amanda

If I offered up my bell and bones to you, Boy,
and you offered up your body, dropped your guard
and brown corduroy pants in the foyer, and accepted,
we'd have trouble here in my apartment on the sand,
a hurricane or tornado named after some good girl

on the edge of Florida. A girl who's so good
that she can't understand why the dogs and adults
have grown afraid of her. On the six o'clock news
they warn that Amanda is coming, they say, *Bolt*

the doors, tie the babies to their cribs. They say,
Close the pantry, hold on to the roofs and boats,
pets and lamps. They suggest yellow tape,
demonstrate making X's on the windows.

I don't know what I'm most afraid of: natural disasters,
death, or you. My mother, in a thin and borrowed bed,
took one last gasp. You didn't know me then, but you
should have loved me. You should have rubbed my back.

I climbed into the bed and held her from behind
like a cocky fellow who knows a girl well enough
for that act. My fingers knitted under what was left of her
breasts, two scarred holes, and I whispered about love,

the books I'd write in her honor, and transportation. *Your car*
is here, I said, nonsensical and perfectly sane, and my mother,
my love, went speeding off without her girl or black felt hat.
I stood at the bed's curb, waving my hands, stomping

my feet on asphalt or tile or grass. Now, you're here,
at the door, silk and keys in your hand, threatening to fill
the hole she left in my body, and I can only shudder
and wince. I want to be a better girl for you, honest

and loyal. I want to offer up my bones and bell.
I want to rip the yellow tape from my skin's windows.
To hell with the dog and that annoying bird. Let the palms
tip and bend. Let the rain sweep the cat across the yard.
Let the roof fall, the stucco cling to our two valiant bodies.

What We Did After My Mother's Mastectomy

We didn't sleep.
Three nights we sat up
in her bed, watching bad talk shows,
the same news again and again. We stayed
there, our shoulders and twin hips
touching, the sheets twisted, four bare feet . . .

We could have been anyone: man and woman,
girlhood friends, lovers. We could have been
at any point in time, any age, her
in her thirties
with an Afro, a husband,
and hot pants, me
looking like a boy
at twelve, resenting
her body, her soft legs
and arms, hating the ease
with which she pinched off
her bra, and the breasts
set free then
for all the world.

But we were fifty-five
and thirty, mother
and daughter, two women
in bed, awake, three a.m.,
our eyes open, four a.m., our lips
parted, mouths dry, five a.m., staring
at the ceiling, and she said, *Your brother
was a better baby, funny*, and then
we stared in silence, at the ceiling,
at the yellow ceiling, paid attention,
watched the cracks, listened,
and waited.

One Night With a Stranger at 30

He moves his hips
and the lies we've told, the ring
he's hidden in his shirt pocket, that I've
never, these lies

and more
solidify, then go liquid,
and later, when sober
we will hold coffee cups
that do not match. We are not
anxious kids
who will curtsy politely
in the morning, our thirty years
here, the simple repetition
of this, what it doesn't
mean, our bold nudity,
a limited conversation, talk
about the map
above my bed, going
nowhere, his bright blue condom—
The fat girl moon
is meant to be romantic, he says.
If he were someone else, if I were,
I would tell him
how hot
these sheets are
with grief, how the dust
has crept back, how I wanted
to be someone else
by now, full of love, how I thought
I would be, how sometimes
making soup
or standing in the shower
I almost
believe I am.

DOUGLAS GOETSCH (b. 1963)

THE WALLS

In the suburbs our lives were separated
by sheetrock, which cracked like an egg
when you threw your brother into it.
The house was made entirely of chalk.
You'd walk through it, almost by accident
like a ghost. So when we heard the thump,

followed by the sound of falling chips,
we knew it was only Andy, who'd been poking
around the attic when the ceiling busted
through, depositing him in the bathtub
dusted white, confused, like a dumb idea
that couldn't even stay up in the head.

URBAN POEM

We are made of newspaper and smoke.
We dunk roses in vats of blue.
The birds don't call—pigeons play it close
to the vest. When the moon is full
we hear it in the sirens. The Pleiades
you could probably buy downtown. Gravity
is the receiver on the hook. Mortality
we smell on certain people as they pass.

THE BEACH

While they met with the real estate brokers,
Timmy Jones, the older boy next door,
took me down the slope. The sand was sharp
with stones and barnacles and vacant shells.
In tide pools hermit crabs lifted their
borrowed homes and dashed about like
old men caught in public in their underwear.
Sea gulls tore away at mussel beds,
hoisting them up, teetering on stiff wings,
then dropping and cracking shells on rock.
He pointed to the stripes of stiffened seaweed:
the high-water mark, receding.
In the salt stink of muck at low tide
I wondered why my parents wanted this.

Later, the beach was always good for hiding
when stores phoned to say I'd shoplifted.
Later, I went there for teenage brooding—
I though the incoming waves proved
something about time, how every moment
carries the next on its back. Timmy stole

our wood for bonfires. I spied on them
partying, drinking, getting to third base.
A month before he left, Dad sat down there
in the June sun, on a blanket, with a lady,
in plain sight of Mom, up at the house
drying dishes. She told us it was only
Mrs. Kaufman, Dad's new bridge partner.
They were going over bids, strategies.

NOBODY'S HELL

At the bus stop on the first frigid
morning in January I felt the prickle
of hairs freezing in the caves of my nostrils
each time I inhaled, and when Cathy
Stegbauer arrived having just showered,
I broke off pieces of her frozen curls.
Later in math class I studied her head
thawing into a ragged mop, the torn
curtain of bangs framing her face.
I pressed my reddened fingertips together
waiting for that warm tingle of feeling—
I was always petrified of frostbite,
of pieces of me never coming back,
like the brown zones in freezer-burned meat,
like a troubled memory where part
of the heart dies, like when Chris Paffle
dropped a penny on the locker room floor
and said to me, "Pick it up, Jew"—
I didn't believe this actually happened
because a piece of me froze right there.
It dangled in the center of me like a clapper
in a bell, like the diseased hamster
Dad put to sleep in the freezer; if it ever
defrosted it would smell like a murky river,
a place downwind of a nastier place.
In college, when I read Dante, I already
knew why the Inferno's core was frozen,
and why, coming up from that hole,
the first thing Dante gazed at was the stars—
someplace warm, someplace that is nobody's hell.

RIGOBERTO GONZÁLEZ (b. 1970)

PERLA AT THE MEXICAN BORDER ASSEMBLY LINE OF DOLLS

Her job was to sort through the eyes
of dolls. Snapping hollow limbs
into plastic torsos had been a soothing task
for Perla, like arranging the peas back into the pod

or picking up spilled grains of salt, one by one.
Since she was born without a womb
and her ears closed up because no infant's shrill
had kept them open, Perla's fingers had developed

sensitivities to dolls: she exchanged
her gentle touch for their rigidity,
which stiffened her bones to the wrists;
at rest, her hands shut down like clamps.

But she could not refuse this trade.
Sometimes she became too easily attached
to the hands, whose curvatures embraced
the crooked joint of her index finger.

She'd go home with her pocket full of arms
too often and would bury them in her garden
in pairs: a right arm with a right arm,
a left one with a left—the fingers always pointing

down like roots. After seasons, the only growth
was the ache inside her bones, while her arms
kept shrinking, narrowing like stalks.
Perla asked to be moved to heads.

Here she was appalled by how strands of hair
are jabbed in with pink hooks, how noses and ears
are pinched out, and with what brute force
the mouth hole is ice-picked through.

And for years she had equipped these dolls
with arms too short to massage themselves.
Sometimes she had sent them off
without arms at all, and she imagined

the limbs in her garden digging deeper
into earth, like split worms madly searching
to comfort their severed halves.
So Perla requested the task of sorting eyes,

eyes that sink into her thumbs
the way rosary beads cave in fingerprints.
Yet here she doesn't count or pray;
she only teaches how to dull the pain.

Her gift with a squeeze of her rigid fingers
is the luster of the callused tips,
their stoic gaze. The dolls give up
the sensibility in eyes that do not blink.

The eyes freeze over like the surfaces
of lakes, while Perla's fingers feel again,
though everything she touches slices
clean into her most afflicting nerves.

With the pupil locked in place as if in ice,
each eye stares up accusingly at Perla
as she's about to push it into place: a tack
threatening to thrust back the fury of its nail.

Day of the Dead

Before, it was a fascinating game
we played with our dead: a candy skull
wearing my abuelo's sugared name

across its front, a molasses-coffin full
of sweetened bones, a picnic on his grave
spread out on marble. Abuela, in her dull

black apron and rebozo (who saved
her best conversations for the tombstone)
said that joking with the dead will pave

a smoother, shorter path into their lone-
ly voyage. While women talked about the dying
and men toasted their tequila, I craved the bone

with its seven sweet letters winding
into my abuelo's name. I licked off the cursive O

and left the other six sticky with saliva, drying.

I would not remember that innocent theft
which transformed "Candido" into "Candid," until the day
I took my bottle to the tombs, bereft

of my own mother, her name written and displayed
on some ridiculous, purple-flowered head.
I could not reason anything to say,

thinking of that horrible truth spread
like honey, calling maggots to the dead.

DEATH OF THE FARM WORKERS' CAT

Locked up until next season's harvest,
the communal shack holds in its final draft.

Rolled-up mattresses lie stacked awkward as
spiral shells with the hollows squeezed shut. A forgotten

cigarette stays cramped inside the crack of a wall,
numb as a flower bud. And because it was her habit, the black

cat crouches on the windowsill, white whiskers twitching,
waiting for the double doors to split.

The men will recognize the carcass—
the animal that crawled between discarded boots to

stiffen like a muddy sock. *Negra*, one man
called her. Another, *Sombra*. Yet another named her

Cascabel, what his sweetheart called her cat in Tuxtla.
Murmuring that name reminded him of murmuring

inside his lover's ear, of the indiscreet meows
that made his lover whisper *ssshhh!* half

alarm, half pleasure. In the shack, purrings
fluttered, delicate as lullabies. Fur

charged the heart through an electrostatic touch.
The cat seeks out that touch, shifting day and night

from wooden sill to concrete floor. At once patient,
leaning on the boots with the memory of feet, at once

restless, trapped behind the window with
her wet nose drying up against the glass.

DEBRA GREGERMAN (b. 1962)

SILENT GLOBE

Third Avenue is a vacant lot with a Desert Air sign
and all the details I can think of.
My sister goes on about taxes long distance
until I have to hang up into oblivion and a long nap,
sleep off the vagueness of the afternoon
and the ends of the earth pulled close by the phone
and the unfaithful promise of who or what
I'm not quite sure of that has died away now.

I can take myself around the barrio
with the clouds blown out from the center of the sky
like a huge smoke ring overhead,
sit down on the curb in front of the OK Market
and be someone—without cashing this moment in
for a room full of people with jobs to hate,
comparing gripes and brownie points and affairs
with proper names in their hearts like acquaintance and ex.—
names for we're just friends and what is sometimes called a fling.

No. I can sit here with my knees showing
for as long as I want, in the face of girls staring
at what is none of their business, sporting combs
in their pockets like guns, and not care
if the tattoo man hits on me today about my eyes
or what he likes. I'm as still as I feel and it becomes me to wait
with my ass on the damp ground for the sun to turn away
as if just then someone I loved
would throw the screen door open wide and call me in.

HIGH SPEED

This man measures my waste like substance abuse
and I'm willing to be anyone he wants for now.
My friends at the bar untie their hands
from each others' hair at the juncture of a beer

and what comes next to wash it down.
And I would not care to have my letters saved,
bound by a rubber-band, stuffed under an old boyfriend's
bed, where his wife wants her back rubbed
and wishes I wouldn't stare at their boxspring anymore.

I look out where freighters shift and fart,
mouths of litter and paint—
and I'm not really lit yet.

For this stranger I move away from talk,
hip to hip in the backseat of his voice, driven
at high speed across the sprawl of the city below
to a place where nothing is gentle enough

once you arrive—
to a place where the happy hour
of a kiss wrecks you for a stranger,
this far on the other side of yourself,
this close to him breathing.

LULLABY

My fan is preaching abstinence but I want a miracle
from Richard downstairs—a catastrophe of wrestlers
on his late-night t.v. screen, confessing what is my pleasure
is my pain, while the neighbor's son sits gassed on music
in the passenger's seat—a malaise like a faith
across his lips. I can hear his music, metal on metal,

a revival in my sleep and wake myself up kicking
the sheets. His chalk voice is glory above
the flushing sound through the wall when I kneel
at the receiver and say my prayers—words that sound
together like nothing I've said out loud all day.

Your mouth is so empty of words, repeat after me:

Are you my enemy, memory, are you my country?
Like this flawed and tractable kiss on borrowed time,
electricity rocks the Plymouth out front

where a boy sits wagging his head saying yes, yes
to a rhythm so deep he doesn't dare to mention it.

STRICTLY SPEAKING

Rather, cars will honk as if to say it's easier
than you think, when we stand at the street corner and kiss,
and perfectly clear to us driving no place fast,
what exactly you people are doing. It's no mystery at all.

I am more than willing to appease the facts
for one more devastating look at your torso in the light—
for memory which is indiscreet.
All you can say is sorry, these hands could be anyone's.

The movie was not memorable but true enough to life.
The stain around the moon refused to dissipate at all.
The parking lot after the show taking on immense
proportion and your groping, imagine that.

If these hands could remember the half of it
they might go on and on like a couple of fools.

MAURICE KILWEIN GUEVARA (b. 1961)

ONCE WHEN I WAS IN THE EIGHTH GRADE

I got caught staring out the window when the bells were ringing
Maybe you want to tell everybody what's so interesting
There's a man with a bottle of wine walking toward the mill
He's wearing rags and the rags are burning blue
In one of his palms there is a green bird
hatchling of the sewing box   She breathes once
every time the earth walks around the sun   I heard her sing
before they used her soft green body in the mines

After that he let me stare out the window the rest of the year

Doña Josefina Counsels Doña Concepción Before Entering Sears

Conchita debemos to speak totalmente in English
cuando we go into Sears okay   Por qué
Porque didn't you hear lo que pasó   It say
on the eleven o'clock news anoche que two robbers
was caught in Sears and now this is the part
I'm not completely segura que I got everything
porque channel 2 tiene tú sabes that big fat guy
that's hard to understand porque his nose sit on his lip
like a elefante pues the point es que the robbers the police say
was two young men pretty big y one have a hairy face
and the other is calvo that's right he's baldy and okay
believe me qué barbaridad porque Hairy Face
and Mister Baldy goes right into the underwear department
takes all the money from the caja yeah uh-huh the cash register
and mira Mister Baldy goes to this poor Italian woman that I
guess would be like us sixty o sixty-five who is in the section
of the back-support brassieres and he makes her put a big bra
over her head para que she can't see nothing and kneel
like she's talking to God to save her poor life
and other things horrible pero the point como dije
es que there was two of them and both was speaking Spanish
y por eso is a good thing Conchita so the people at Sears
don't confuse us with Hairy and Baldy that we speak English only
okay ready
                    Oh what a nice day to be aquí en Sears Miss Conception

The Miniaturist

I make tiny, tiny huts,
the hills, too, are tiny,
small hills, small trees,
a silver river, a forge with smoke,
a little blue water tower.

To work on such a minute scale,
I use magnifying lenses,
jeweler's goggles,
sometimes even the instruments of microsurgery.

Perhaps you have seen some of my pieces?
The Sun of Copernicus. The Ferris Wheel.

The Funeral Parlor (how difficult it was to glue the greenbottle fly
onto the right index finger of the corpse.) Or
the one for which I am famous: *The Lovers of Late Afternoon*.
Her hair falling back, the red at the tip of his ear,
the universe of heated molecules, just above their bodies.

POSTMORTEM

Even the corpse has its own beauty.
                              —Emerson

These lips of Mr. Tunis Flood are cornflower
Blue. I have a set of cups like that.
I bring my ear to his heart but hear no murmur,
No vibrato, no baroque flutter of blood.
I love Pathology because there's never any rush.
I sip my coffee. Think. Write, "Nipples the color of avocados."
(How beautiful they are in the fluorescent light.)

Time to open and discover now the exquisite
Essence of Tunis Flood. Syringe: prick—
Vitreous humor for the fellows in the lab.
On my little radio Scarlatti plays, and when my door
Hinge creaks, it speaks. "Hello," it says. I

Concentrate. Write, "Tardieu's spots
Bruise the livid skin. Like violets in a shade."
With my favorite knife I trace a line from heart
To chin. From sternum to pubis. I watch a man bloom,
And remove, remove. Each organ I weigh and record.
Perhaps I should have been a postman
To send my friends and lovers away,

Boxed, in parts. Why is there wind
In this windowless room? Where is my mallet,
My chisel? There: crack.
The calivarium slides out
Like a baby. I hold your brain,
Mr. Flood, and wonder what matter
Holds back the rush of memories.
And in what soft ridge lies the vision of your death?

BETH GYLYS (b. 1964)

FAT CHANCE

Every day another broken heart.
We try, but fail, to find our perfect match.
We'd never get involved if we were smart.

The woman thought she'd have a second start.
She'd loved a married man for years, a lech,
who didn't give a damn about her heart.

"I'm mad," she told her shrink, "I'd fall apart
without him in my life—I'm too attached.
I wouldn't be involved if I were smart."

Working in Maine, she met a man named Bart,
who called her "hon" and wore a diamond watch.
She told him all about her broken heart,

her father fix, her need to put the cart
before the horse. She warned, "I'm such a wretch.
You wouldn't get involved if you were smart."

Still, he proposed. They planned to wed in March.
He died before that, at a tennis match.
"Cracked and chronic" defines a broken heart.
We'd never get involved if we were smart.

BALLOON HEART

For days after the wedding,
she left the balloon heart
hanging on her car's antenna.
She liked the way the limp
bubble drooped and bounced
each day becoming emptier,
heavier, less like a celebration.
After three weeks it snowed,
By then the heart had slid down
until it touched the hood,
and as she drove, the thing,

now frozen, knocked and knocked
like knuckles on a hard wood desk,
like an ice pick chipping away.

FAMILY REUNION—AUNT VERN'S TWO CENTS

"So, Dear, your mother says you got a divorce.
How could this happen? You seemed so much in love
when you got married. I saw you walking down
that aisle—you were floating. Anyway,
I said to your mother: I hope she's dating.
A shame to be alone—a girl your age—

so pretty too. When I was your age,
I had two babies, no time to think of divorce.
It wouldn't matter today. When I was dating,
things were different. We still believed in love
for life. Together, couples found a way.
I tell my kids they better not head down

that aisle until they're sure. My oldest, down
in Texas, his girlfriend's nearly half his age.
I've prayed that they'll break up, but now the way
it's going I'm sure they'll marry. 'Headed for divorce,'
I tell my husband. 'But, Verna, they're in love,'
he says. (He's such a romantic.) They're only dating

now, thank God. Of course, even dating
is scary these days, with AIDS, date rape. Just down
our street a woman's son got AIDS. You love
your kids as best you can, but . . . I've seen her age
ten years since he moved home. His whole divorce
was bad enough, but carrying on that way

and then to get so sick. Things aren't the way
they used to be. I'm probably dating
myself to say so, but I can't believe divorce
is any answer. It comes right down
to making a commitment. Kids your age
you think it's easy. You marry out of love,

and when that first glow fades, believe the love
is gone. There's got to be a better way
to make things work. You think a marriage

is fun and games—you want it just like dating.
In forty years, we've had our ups and downs,
but I never once considered divorce.

Down the road you'll see: love isn't dating.
There's a rhythm to the way a marriage
works. Divorce destroys the best of love."

JAMES HARMS (b. 1960)

FROM NOW ON

When Ron and Lisa split up, she took a job
at her brother's bar, while he went
upstate to a place like Frank Martin's
in "Where I'm Calling From,"
to "gain a few pounds," he said,
though what he meant was that he'd lost
everything and wanted some of it back.

I don't think I've lost as much,
though some mornings I sit with coffee
at a window facing the harbor
and watch the tide fall beneath the boats all day;
it puts me closer to the friends I don't see anymore.
Toby used to drive from San Clemente
to Malibu on an average Saturday

looking for waves, and I'm almost certain
he's alive somewhere. And Tod I bet
is sailing, always sailing. I guess hope
is a swallow building its nest near the window,
winter on the wind, the storms shifting from
south to north, every omen saying *leave* . . .
but here comes the waitress with more coffee.

Ron came back and Lisa simply opened the door
and shut it behind him, no big deal, a few shrugs.
Her brother gave him work, and now Ron
is another alcoholic bartender, which is how
I met him. We can see the waves from

his window as he sets out the drinks
for the regulars, who leave before three

and return after ten, when the tourists
have taken their sandy bathing suits
and burned skin home to the wide valleys
filled with smog. Ron pours us each
a cup of decaf, which we sip
as we watch the parking lot empty, the beach
beyond empty, as we watch the surfers

paddle out for the next big set.
Ron and I retired our longboards a few years ago.
What we like now is the burnished look of a wave
at sunset, how the water streaks with black
as the crest trembles and pitches forward,
the ocean at the horizon a spill of Rose's
grenadine, a bottle of which sits behind Ron

on the shelf. Every once in a while he fixes us
Shirley Temples, sticks the little umbrellas in,
and we toast another day done well.
It's not that I've lost all that much.
Or that I want back what I've given away.
I just "need to get used to the changes,"
is what Ron says. He should know.

AFTER YES

There's nothing over there
behind the sacks of old newspaper.
There's nothing in the cigarette box.

In the glass bowl, no apples.
No peaches or late bananas.
In the well outside, water

but no bucket. No phone calls
flashing on the answering machine,
no hang-ups or warnings, no tired message

that ends, "Oh, hell, just call."
Outside, a breeze: no clouds, no moon.
No dew on the rye, no frost,

no shadow in the pocket of night.
No ghost behind the river oak, whispering,
"No sense worrying about it."

And in between dreams, she kicks
the blankets off, rolls toward
the open window, and there is

no one between her and the edge
of the bed, no soft collision
to save her from falling.

MY OWN LITTLE PIECE OF HOLLYWOOD

Maybe it's always Saturday in heaven.
—The Jazz Butcher

I hate that particular dream
where she walks out of the hardware store
holding a rake and a sack of rye seed
and attempts to hug me—
I wake up scratching myself.
Worse yet is remembering
that she doesn't live here anymore,
not that she ever did with regularity.
But when we used to run into each other
now and then, there was a peculiar sort of
futility to our conversations that I miss;
I think it's because they so often
led to wistfulness, which is a derivation
of loneliness that I find companionable.
And in the other dream I hate
I'm back in the Roxy on Sunset Boulevard
watching the Replacements mangle
their last few songs, closing with
the theme from Gilligan's Island.
Bob Stinson's on guitar—
he throws up behind a speaker
without missing a note
while I pocket an ashtray and turn
to see a woman I used to go out with
pour her drink in her purse and walk away
without her wallet. And I'm trying
to move toward her table

to retrieve the wallet or yell or
something but there are all these people
between us and my voice sounds like
the wind behind a flock of
pigeons lifting off the pavement.
Then the band decides to keep playing.
I hear Paul Westerberg
start my favorite song in the middle
so he's singing.
"I'm so, I'm so, I'm so. . ."
and now he's screaming it,
the rest of the band gone on
with the song as it's written
but Paul stuck on that line,
screaming it over and over
like some pre-Altamont mantra,
until I know it's me singing
and I wake up sweating.
Sometimes there's someone
with me, someone looking at me,
and usually she's afraid.

TOMORROW, WE'LL DANCE IN AMERICA

In America, there is an answer for everything,
though little has been asked.
We stand around the water cooler comparing notes.
If it is Friday, we discuss hope.

In America, in a bar, I sit beside. . .
well, her, for instance.
I expect the shadow boys in satin jackets
to emerge any moment from their rented corners,
distribute the bruised carnations.
Flowers are only a dollar, sometimes more.
It hurts to sit this close to someone
I will never know.

In America, I would be the first to say
someone has lied to us. Oh well.
Last year my lung turned black with empathy.
Please believe me when I say
all of this is a ruse for honesty.
In America, I can propose marriage to a pool of guppies.

In America I stand around wondering how to say
I love you, until she asks, Coffee?
I think I could live my whole life
waiting for someone to say the word
Love, knowing a cup of coffee was on its way.

TERRANCE HAYES (b. 1971)

GOLIATH POEM

I am always sorry for the big ape falling
from the Empire for love. Or Esau, a big man,
begging his father for even a breadcrumb
of thy Grace—sly brother-Jacob scampering
off to seed a nation. Dudes like that.
All muscle and hands weeping on the shoulder

of regret, which is a kind of blindness,
a recognition come too late. Sometimes I am sorry
for Rick, whom I love, where ever he may be,
six-foot eight hurling stones through the window
of another woman who's turned him away,
and I too far this time to drive him in the night.

Who will save the big men of this world?
Earlier I watched *King Kong* and was sorry again
for those building-size fuckers we see falling
from miles away. Those we thought invincible,
almost permanent like the sun which burns,
truthfully, only a few hours each day.

Once when his girlfriend called me, I drove in the rain
from college to his house. Nintendo cords roped
his shoes, a bottle of pills between his thighs, he sat
on the couch. In the darkness we could have been the same.
Perhaps I thought of holding him, my twin,
or thought of another door and my father weeping

beyond it a month before. I could have talked
about the horse on its carousel; how each man lowers
his head to circle, blindly, his life. But we said nothing.

We listened to rain like the sound of a big man's tears,
the sound God made before the Word or Light,
And the moon curved above us like an ear.

BOXCAR

For John & Miles, together

Black as snow & ice as cool/ Miles stood horn-handed while
John so&soloed/ I mean mad but mute like you be when you
got five minutes/ to be somewhere ten minutes away & a train
outta nowhere stops you/ boxcarboxcarboxcar & tracknoise/
that might out shout your radio if you had your windows
down/ boxcarboxcar & hotcars lined up around you/this is
how mad Miles was/ Impatient like his dentist daddy/ listenin
to a badmouth whine about some aching pain / *See, Doc I was
tryin to blow down my old lady's door/* Theres Miles listenin/ to
Johns long song about sufferin & loss/ & hes heard it all before
in a club in the village/ He standin horn-handed but the
jazzfolk sit lovin it / cause it all sounds new as Sunday
shoes/ / Ticked Miles checks his watch/ tickles his trumpet/
& listens to a muscular music that wont stop/ & he loves it or
maybe he scared nobody will ever hear him again/ or maybe he
hungry & want to get/ home to silence/John got nowhere but
here/ got nothin but this/ cause his wifes asleep/ & she cant
give him this kind of love/ his lips swoll as carolina clay/
almost bleedin on the reed & its just what he wants/ Blood/ / &
when he finally hush/ dead years later/ his liver rotten as corn
& Naimas gone/ Miles aint even glad its over/ His ears full of
whats left him/ & he thinkin of black hands dancin like
crowswings/ & he thinkin of a lovesupreme a lovesupreme a
lovesupreme/& this too is what Im thinkin/ as I drive to see my
diva/ with old jazz in my speakers & the only thing between us
these boxcars pullin & pullin & pullin past

AT PEGASUS

They are like those crazy women
        who tore Orpheus
                when he refused to sing,

these men grinding
        in the strobe & black lights
                of Pegasus. All shadow & sound.

"I'm just here for the music,"
    I tell the man who asks me
        to the floor. But I have held

a boy on my back before.
    Curtis & I used to leap
        barefoot into the creek; dance

among maggots & piss,
    beer bottles & tadpoles
        slippery as sperm;

we used to pull off our shirts,
    & slap music into our skin.
        He wouldn't know me now

at the edge of these lovers' gyre,
    glitter & steam, fire,
        bodies blurred sexless

by the music's spinning light.
    A young man slips his thumb
        into the mouth of an old one,

& I am not that far away.
    The whole scene raw & delicate
        as Curtis's foot gashed

on a sunken bottle shard.
    They press hip to hip,
        each breathless as a boy

carrying a friend on his back.
    The foot swelling green
        as the sewage in that creek.

We never went back.
    But I remember his weight
        better than I remember

my first kiss.
    These men know something
        I used to know.

How could I not find them
    beautiful, the way they dive & spill
        into each other,

the way the dance floor
    takes them,
        wet & holy in its mouth.

BRIAN HENRY (b. 1972)

DISCOVERY

Of course no one sets out to discover
artificial insemination, natural selection, wooden dentures
while removing the garbage or paying the cleaner
or adhering to the missionary like an upright quaker:
no one is adequately prepared for the sight of the unfamiliar
for the unfamiliar sight precludes preparation (not to over-
emphasize vision's importance, being the faultiest of our
senses, open to trickery at every global corner:
instances of vision's failures dwell everywhere,
as do instances of failures caused by those failures—
the veteran vacationer who neglects to remember
that abandoning one's spot is always a risky venture
(why someone recommended in some handbook or other
to slip some kid a fiver to sit by the meter
and say he's waiting for his father)—
others' fortunes have been made while some of us rehearse:
cases have been settled, fines levied, and the town's coffers
topped off while we earnest myopians squint into the future,
on the verge of deciding to settle a colony or further
wander, unable to see beyond the third row in the theatre,
if the woman on the screen is laughing or dry-heaving: how much
   richer
our home movies and moving patterns would be if we relied on
   another
to show us to our seats—if we let the tongue be our usher).

SKIN

Never mind the fantasy about the tweezers and the tongue,
the one about the bicycle pump and the twisted rim.
Never mind the angle of penetration, or the number
of blessed repetitions in the series of withdrawals and givings-in.

Never mind the dream about the bean-bag chair and the virgin,
the one about the tree and the bull terrier off its chain.
Never mind the song the words will not attach to,
the visions that arrive with the noises next door,

when a sneeze, or a sob, is mistaken for something else
and someone finds himself clinging to the wall,
perhaps with a glass to his ear, or his glasses on,
hoping something dark and old-fashioned has pulled him

from sleep this close to dawn. Never mind the crack
between the blinds and the sill, where a single moan
will keep him waiting an hour for another, his face pressed
against the pane, one eye open, half-blinded but guided.

And never mind the woman in the grass beneath the statue.
Her palms are cupping her head, her skirt an inch off-center,
glasses gleaming as the sun hums on the monument
of the general, the skin of her arms slowly going red.

GARAGE SALE

They all came by today.
Passersby, browsers, neck-craners.
Big Wheel riders, circus goers. Small time hustlers,
phone tappers, check bouncers, rear enders.
Tattle talers, crank callers, nose pickers.
Water bearers, moped wreckers, trash compactors,
furniture refinishers. Stroller pushers, leaf rakers,
windshield wipers, trash talkers, diaper changers.
Backstabbers, manure shovelers, gem inspectors,
toy breakers. Left-turn-on-red takers.
Baby killers, fortune tellers, right wingers,
bumper stickerers. Neck wringers, forgotten drifters.
Seat belt fasteners, shape shifters. Dizzy spinners,
plain clothes snoopers, house sitters, baby sitters,
couch sitters. They came by. Reckless drivers,
ancient mariners, natural fooders, kindergarten teachers.

Lounge singers, artificial colorers, dog trainers,
spaghetti strainers. Marriage counselors, bargain shoppers.
Lottery losers, hair receders, hair croppers.
Loot stashers, wave riders, wishbone breakers,
wish makers. Drink downers, bet takers,
fat watchers, purse snatchers. Pork barrelers,
farewellers, racetrack gawkers, foreskin snippers.
Butt pinchers, crotch grabbers. They all came by.
Door knockers, shot blockers, mailbox bashers,
fulsome praisers. Nostalgia waxers, coke snorters,
streetwalkers, penny pinchers, orgasm fakers.
Movers and shakers. Cussers, chain smokers,
court jesters. Paddy wagon passengers.
Raggedy Ann clutchers. Belly button pokers,
pipe dreamers. Car bombers, cat nappers,
gun toters, bong hitters. Sword wielders,
sword swallowers, dirty dancers, last chancers.
Dixie whistlers, middle finger givers. Allegiance pledgers,
carpet deodorizers, crap shooters, paper shredders.
Natural selectors, conversation makers. Bread bakers,
contagious yawners, butt kissers, baby kissers,
tree huggers, tree climbers. All of them,
they all came by: so much paint flaking from these walls.

BOB HICOK (b. 1960)

ALZHEIMER'S

Chairs move by themselves, and books.
Grandchildren visit, stand
new and nameless, their faces' puzzles
missing pieces. She's like a fish

in deep ocean, its body made of light.
She floats through rooms, through
my eyes, an old woman bereft
of chronicle, the parable of her life.

And though she's almost a child
there's still blood between us:
I passed through her to arrive.
So I protect her from knives,

stairs, from the street that calls
as rivers do, a summons to walk away,
to follow. And dress her,
demonstrate how buttons work,

when she sometimes looks up
and says my name, the sound arriving
like the trill of a bird so rare
it's rumored no longer to exist.

OVER COFFEE

What you mean to say about the film is that
it moved you, the woman alone at the end
beside a burning field of cane, her brother
carried off in a covered truck to be tortured/
shot. That you're not sure but think
it wasn't about politics but bedrooms
and kitchens. Hands and eyes. The light of dusk
because it stops us on the stairs and makes us
bless a child earnestly chiding her doll
or cherish a crow lifting from an oak, charcoal
smearing blue, when we feel tender and vast
and brittle because the emotions that are hybrids
of anguish and elation are the mediums for spirit's
binding to flesh. But your husband and friends,
up on genres and the lineage of dictators,
wielding jargon like the clipped
phrases of birds who know what the trills signify,
speak of fades, Marxist insinuations,
the opening scene's allegory of whore as El Salvador,
fought over, pierced, beaten by men. They travel
staunchly in the other direction, away from sentiment,
from the image of the woman on her knees
at the edge of a field turning orange, into history,
they abandon the facts of smoke, the muslin dress
given by her husband, her stare as the truck
zippers-up horizon, gets lost in the distance
with its appetite for souls. By the time
they ask your opinion you don't want to talk,
knowing faith dissipates through words,
sure you'll passionately refer to our indebtedness
to memory, suggest that by imagining
the vanished flower, repeating the name

of the lost cat, we retain our lives, webbed
by what we've touched and needed,
the persistence of love despite death an act
of vengeance, a refusal to diminish, you'll swear
the film was about the failure of every good-bye.
All of this you try not to say but do in a clumsy rush
as if the words are falling down, then a pause,
the surrounding chatter coming in like the slurrings
of waves as you hold your breath on a seawall,
then the shift, their eyes dilating in recognition
of conviction, finally the stammers, the rush to be
the first to address this exhilarating stranger.

Heroin

Imagine spring's thaw, your brother said,
each house a small rain, the eaves muttering
like rivers and you the white skin
the world sheds, your flesh unfolded

and absorbed. You walked Newark together,
tie loosened, a silk rainbow undone,
his fatigues the flat green of summer's end,
all blood drained from the horizon.

It would have been easier had you music
to discuss, a common love for one
of the brutal sports, if you shared
his faith that breath and sumac are more

alike than distinct, mutations of the same
tenacity. You almost tried it for him,
cinched a belt around your arm, aimed
a needle at the bloated vein, your window

open to July's gaunt wind and the radio
dispersing its chatty somnolence. When
he grabbed your wrist, his rightful face
came back for a moment: he was fifteen

and standing above Albert Ramos, fists
clenched, telling the boy in a voice
from the Old Testament what he'd do if certain
cruelties happened again. Loosening the belt,

you walked out, each straight and shaking,
into the hammering sun, talked of the past
as if it were a painting of a harvested field,
two men leaning against dusk and pitchforks.

That night he curled up and began to die,
his body a pile of ants and you on the floor
ripping magazines into a mound of words
and faces, touching his forehead with the back

of your hand in a ritual of distress, fading
into the crickets' metered hallucination.
When in two days he was human again, when
his eyes registered the scriptures of light,

when he tried to stand but fell and tried
again, you were proud but immediately
began counting days, began thinking
his name were written in a book

locked in the safe of a sunken ship,
a sound belonging to water, to history,
and let him go, relinquished him
to the strenuous work of vanishing.

MARY CROCKETT HILL (b. 1969)

RUTH

You want this world, smudge of oil on the feather
we found beside the river—
its luster, a warning to other crows.
You want the trout's grey mouth
like a ring snug on your finger, your hair
a clutch of river weed, your pale blue knees two stones.
On the bank wild radish blooms early into seed,
a patch of chickweed babbles in the grass.
You want to be the radish, white muscle
growing downward, the tiny spray of flowers
another word for *soon*.

BAD KARMA

I could be a heart patient in my forties, waiting out winter
dreaming of buds as carnal as broccoli, begging
some anonymous woman to lick my feet.

The laws are simple and clear:
Five minutes, I'd groan in the seashell of her ear,
just five minutes please . . .

SLEEP

    I'm looking for a blue door,
        the knob palmed smooth, the rug
     woven with an old woman's hair,
          and in the corner something new
  —a jar spilling cattail and wheat.

Here our sleeps become confused
        like moths in a room too full of light.

       What my palm dreams
    pours into your hip—your murmurings
      sap my shoulder
     until the arm is stiff
    and gold all the way through.

This drowse, our tongues
  as soft and rasped as mulberries;

     this sleep, a child's
    hazed breath on the window,
    her finger following
      the arc of her own name.

I know what your body says
in the raglush of morning:
     it wants, and is owned
by what it wants.
    But here
     in this room of wan-light and dream

  there is a blue door opening,

   the body says *palm, shoulder, yes.*

ABOMINATION

I could go seeking some secret part of nature, the bulbous tumor
in the heart of an elderberry tree, or better—a rot of bark, glazed
    with slime mold,
moist and airy as pumice. A treacherous stone. A limb with
    bad intent.
The femur of a cow or miscreant, splintered at one end,
sharp enough to pierce a lung. Now quiet in your palm.

I only go to the woods anymore in my mind, the shallow
    between trees
where wet abominations are buried under leaves.
That one year, I knew what it was to walk all day on someone
    else's land.
The light around me, soft cathedral glass, and turning
like a warm cup in a cold hand.

Now the t.v. and toaster and poems about beavers
and two Christmas trees.
My breasts all the while yearn unwittingly
toward some unborn baby, the baby to be mine, the beavers
    to be golden, the wanting
does not stop here—quiet on your tongue.

ELLEN HINSEY (b. 1960)

Planisféria, MAP OF THE WORLD, LISBON, 1554

Space was easier then, and time slower—
One faced the white of distance with purpose.
        The unknown beckoned, like the polar caps,
        or stilled one, like an awkward moment:

beyond the horizon, trees stirred like birds;
heedless of latitude, temperatures rose,
        fir trees bent, their needles uncalculated.
        This desire to possess, to flatten space

was dwarfed by waves that the astrolabe could
not settle. Yet, the mapmaker took sides:

Africa would be veined with great water
arteries, but the Amazon would diminish

halfway cross the *Mundus Novus.*
Other rivers were silenced, though needed:
>to be known, land must be entered
>by those green arched passageways

above which birds in formal plumage
led the way to inland knowledge. Still,
>whole continents slid off: passed up and cast
>into the corner of the mapmaker's dark.

THE ART OF MEASURING LIGHT
From the Pont-Neuf, Paris

The light here has begun to pass and as it passes
it will bend down to the Seine in the last of its
winter gymnastics: unwrapping its hands from
the white crevices of Saint-Germain-des-Prés,

giving a last honor to Sacré-Coeur. One will
turn one's eyes to the horizon, but there only
shadows lie, and the beams of cars that follow
the Seine northward toward Le Havre, their lamps

yellow like the pleasure boats that illuminate
the shores with serpentine eyes. But standing
in half-light, the mind devises a method,
and knows that distance is an arc, not a line;

it will follow light as it curves past the river
to meet its welcome in woods, distant from
the sphere of the thinker, yet distant only as
a pair of hands, clasping a tool in a far-off field.

The body in its accuracy cannot close the calipers
of space, but knows just the same that light
that has passed here is light that will contrive
to touch the white of wood on maple-lined streets,

deep in New Hampshire, where snow is piling
high, in the unbroken shadow of a new day.
Where for the difference of six hours, the hands
of the clock are unlocked, and Puritans progress

with morning. They will carve out a day, wrapped
in time, envisaged in the silence of apple and pine,
and of light curving to where it will break in the
suddenness of a windfall. Perhaps there one will

measure a quantum leap, where from pasture post,
to the end of the road, light will seize the form
of an animal breathless beneath the carcass
of a rusted frame; or watch as it breaks stride

at crossroads, finding figures passing surrounded
by the wreath of their breath. They sky is not a narrow
passage, and light is there to flex the ample arm of it.
On the side, the Pont-Neuf is dark, and the mind,

that lone traveler, comes back to rest like a cast
shuttle to a waiting palm. Across the bridges
night figures come, their loads weighted like
lanterns—swinging slowly in narrow arcs.

THE APPROACH OF WAR

That morning, daylight was the same.
            Everyday rituals, observed by no one,
      left the bedroom door open as a jaw in sleep.
      The faucet's three-four time went unnoticed.

At midday, a ragged curtain shifted in the breeze.
            The paper's checkered voice quietly yellowed.
      When afternoon arrived, there was soot in the air,
      and birds stayed nested in the dark, thatched groves.

Across an open field, a querulous voice called once
            and received its answer.
      The road was empty. A car, wrapped in dust,
      swept the lane, vanished.

The willows were still. A door mated a latch.
            At dusk the smell of pears rose,
      and a mist trawled the lake.
      A match was cupped under the dome of a palm.

Night, not yet soiled, made its way across
            the lake and into the arms of branches.

CHRISTINE HUME (b. 1968)

VARIOUS READINGS OF AN ILLEGIBLE POSTCARD

Horny or Harm seems an ordinary home.
Or Having seen the orchard and hives,
I'm satisfied I've picked the dark pocket
pink or satisfied, pickled larks protect the jinx.
You know I'm trouble with Dixie cups, croquet
and wicker or humble with desire for (cough)
the wicked. Ago? A queer little dog grazing
or gazing lives in my room or ivies my noun.
They have a saying here about your duct-taped boots
or They keep savvy bees in case the butcher balks
which is not cool is nautical is nonsensical.
Attention trick eye! A tension trickles
or After swimming we found the housekeeper dead.
I sing or swing, Let's keep her dear!
All day an unmade bed. One day I'll be young or
going as he who homesteads in foreign castles
deserves or whose domain feigns, casts designs
say, like shadows on the outhouse door or
the outskirts humoring me or out-skirting rumors
last as long as keeping honey
                    or homey
                    or phone me, money?—Yours

BIRTHDAY

Steam was what she thought
we should be—
fatherless, scented, cataracting air
where the windows cultivate
mean and simple shadows,
not a scattered applause,
not the fat panic of fading
the way old soldiers go home.
Because we are happy we eat cake.
We eat cake because we are happy.
And the body listens
to the rising sugar's resolve.
Punch my stomach
hard as you can. That flat,

it should be that smooth.
She pulls out the knife
not quite clean from golden center.
There the eye will be born
solidly within the skin, the eye
as sunken as it will be angry,
wise in the wake of appetite.

DIALOGUE OF THUNDER

Dropped off the tip of the tongue
Or the mind's muddy backslide, a place called
Forgot keeps her listening to downflights,
Laundered lightning's tuning-
Fork-hum of parents still at work on her.

Rubber gloves poised for recondite
Ransacks, their yellow, crooked fingers pass,
Counterpass, stunning her nimble senses.
Fat chance of catching their alarm
And high-toned gravy running with the news.

Their leisure is all industry to her.
Humdrum, they flex near her crooked chimney;
God-eaten spaces spring with experience and
Know-how, singing *Likewise-Likewise. Child,
Don't look at us through your dirty bangs.*

What purview she has stutters.
See how confusing her one body is,
See-sawing on the hinge of house and home.

DIRTY MONEY

Came buffalo heads
To crowd the slick nickel cliffs
Came everything warm,
Rank, shorter than prairie grass
Dashing for one narrow ray

Came his fullest eye
And scalded hand rising from
Gift sack, front pocket.

Our from his benign whistling:
"I like the big-headed ones."

"One buffalo, Two . . ."
Became his sight-seeing song,
His motion sickness.
Came a fly caught in his beard:
This light petting, that dark pet.

Austin Hummell (b. 1963)

Salt Longing

Inland far though and away
from the cursive coast that bore us
under smaller village roofs, where
the rain was stranger to the earth
than our voices to the sea.

Farther than the gratitude
of hands that touch us or don't,
no landlocked drawl reaches
deltas into our salt birth.

What state can hide the sea like this,
in sharkless gardens and rain, where
the owls are not what they seem
beneath their nervous rhetoric
and the quail speak only their names?

Where in this land split
by rivers of big canoes
is the blowsy shade of willows,
the oak hammocks where ferns and ivy lie?

Maybe I'm lost in a stand of loblollies
and Missouri is a sugared dream.
Maybe I'm thirty in a coil of banyans
dipping limbs into origins like Florida—

its spongy, sinking soil—
its scorched, ashen soil.

SARABAND

We must remember again the tribal pride
of dance bound to time, the local ode
fat as fishnets of roe-plugged
salmon. We must think lyrically
about the death of the receptionist.

This is what the calendar says:
Step wildly into March, scatter
folders from her desk, burn
the blank miscellany of memos.
This is how the calendar turns.

Take this dance, what the calendar says,
swing her in triple time, croon
the news gently, that we've danced the old
saraband on desktops since she came;
this is no time for a vacation.

I NEVER SAW A GODDESS GO

My girlfriend's eyes are nothing like the Sun
sessions of Elvis or the rock ledge end
above the tiger cage at Grant Park Zoo
from which a man in khakis and a general's grip
drops raw meat. The sun is always too bright,
her pupils pinned, and her eyelids wave lazily
at all meat and most advances by men
waving it or newspapers or sonnets
or anything that's been done one hundred
and thirty times and bores her more than rain,
dope, or downtown, or any name she might
assign to heaven or sleep or the morning
scent of poppy that drops her there. She nods
at everyone but the man in sandals with china white
skin and allergies, who never knocks and grinning says:
    Cover your face with newsprint;
    I am the rain today.

SCULPTURE GARDEN

The kiln-charred children in the yard
are breathless, laughing with a noon eclipse
which taunts them in shadows,
bears them the life the midday sun
denies. They writhe as they writhed
by the sight of a sculptor's hands,
as he coaxed them from the earth,
from the beat rhythm of dewy dirt
and the redolent behavior of the day's dream.

As usual they don't sleep today—
issue of a man who cast his yield
in his own infernal gaze.
They have never slept in the garden's
awkward bedding, further charged by eager springs
and the hysteria cast in a dead man's eclipse.

BRUCE JACKSON (b. 1963)

IN EXCHANGE FOR FORTY ACRES

I own nigger, I purchased it with the blood of my fathers. I stole it
from the lips of my masters. I created it in the soul of my sons. It is
mine. I am its god. I own nigger, every letter, every syllable. Don't
touch it. Don't whisper it. Don't speak it. It is mine.

I own nigger. It defines you now. It reveals you now. It will beat
your motherfucking ass now. I own nigger. It don't chain me anymore. It
don't beat me anymore. It don't rape me anymore.

I own nigger. It's in me. It is me. I say it. I scream it. I listen for it.
I hear it when you look at me. I hear it when the sirens flash, I feel it in
the anger of your fist. You want to take this from me. But I own nigger,
and I'm holding on tightly. You'll never get it back from me.

SHOOTING, KILLING, DRUG BUSTS, COVER-UPS,
FUCK-UPS, LIGHTER SIDES, WEATHER, AND SPORTS

"Wake me up at eleven," she says. "I want to watch the news," she
says. I let her sleep all night. She asks me why.

"You know," I say, "you need a better reason to wake up," I say.

Another Impostor

"I'm an African," that's what he said. He was standing on the corner of 95th and Broadway screaming, "I'm an African," to anybody who could hear, the cars passing by could hear, the lady with the cats and the plants could hear. The kid with the rock wrapped in foil under his tongue, he could hear. The cops rolling up and down Broadway, they could hear.

"I'm an African. I'm an African," he was screaming. And the john in the alley busted a nut. The john he was with asked for a napkin. And the Johnson kids turned up the volume, so they could hear every word the TV said. And the old man across the street took a hit from his bottle of Cisco making sure he kept it in the bag.

"I'm an African. I'm an African," screamed that nigger. And he'd listen, then scream again. And no one questioned him. No one sniffed him for the odor of fresh elephant. No one asked him who Mandela was. No one pointed him in the direction of home. And if they didn't have to, no one even bothered to look at that nigger.

"I'm an African," was the scream. And no one opened their doors. And no one missed a step. And no one made it a point to hear that noise. He was on 95th and Broadway now. 95th and Broadway. He looked like he was home.

Riot at Winchell's

I want his doughnut. He was eating that fucking donut the first time he kicked my ass. He's gonna be eating that doughnut again. I want his doughnut. I used to walk by wanting that doughnut. I used to walk by wanting a taste. Now I'm gonna have a taste. I want his doughnut. I want what makes him stay here. I want his jellies. I want his glazed. I want his chocolate caked, and anything, anything that makes him stay. I want his doughnut. I know there's gonna be trouble. I know there's gonna be a fight. I may put fresh bakery items at risk when I get my ass kicked this time, but I want his doughnut. I see his gun. There are little white frosting prints on the trigger. I see his badge. There's a drop of custard staining the metal. I see blue. I see black. I see white. They're a striking contrast to the pink box full of fantasies he's been teasing me with. I want his doughnut. He's waiting for me, powdered sugar stains on his lips and fingertips, my flesh, my bloodstains at the ends of his billy club. I'm gonna get my ass kicked again, but I want his doughnut, and he won't give it to me.

J. L. JACOBS (b. 1967)

TWO VARIETIES OF THE BITTER ORANGE

I.

These hollow truncated cones of wicker into mud:
    The promise, even more.   And birds scattered.
And field. And pond. (I found the name and place of
burial in sealed papers, the hawthorn before me.)
Two distinctive trees. The drink itself. And minor
notes of old melodies beginning and re-beginning to fall.
    Now the orange grows everywhere. . .even in the
        heart of the forest.
    We enter front rooms.   This way of drinking it
to pass.   The tea is prepared by pouring boiling water
over a spoonful of leaves.
Old women sing.
    A landscape in these upper reaches.

II.

A waterfall and a forest, natives of this countryside.
The flamingo-tinted dawn when we watched for jaguars to
    swim the hour.
    Not to wake in it.
    Asleep in a land of heavy rainfalls.   And not years of
here or our.   A girl.   And so on.
    I sing the rain.
    I sing to you.
    And I wear these fingers out on the edges waiting for
the mud to dry in your ears.

III.

Gods in multi-color across the sky.   The stranger
whom he worshipped.   With bird-life, blue mist,
the very waters   you are.
    And yet remain.
    She barefoot and sounding far—
    across the field.   Spring, the second
daughter, a foothold.
    Take her hand.   Branches from cold thinly
against this storm.   Cold more cold, but green against
Autumn.   Stripped orchard branches.   The stairs made

even here, as if put in order.   Half open blurred out
with tea leaves.
        A girl.
        And so on.
        Low hills.   (hill\ I remember) variegated
purple-blue.   Hanging back over dreaming and waking
        strand by strand into darkness.   I remember
their boats.   The edges frayed out in favorable rain.   She
barefoot and sounding far.   To be sent forth backward to
walk the finer row.   A world history prepared in bends.

IV.

Read out the names.
Her face (still voice) answered in heavier water.

One hand.   A small bridge eroded
into archways
beginning and re-beginning
to fall.

I walk paths cold but green against Autumn.
Someone must find the papers.   Someone must work
out the music.
(Tall drinks are on an opaque bar in the attic.)

Think of places: The longbow, the highland jonquil on black soil.

And the moonless reach.   Listening.

NEARING LONG MOONS

To look up slowly,
as they moved Northward.
(White triangles of birds.)

"They leave with the moon," she said.
"It's still half wild out here."

There are clusters of weeds   yellow
as the memory of houses at a certain distance.

Late that night I watched from the balcony,
working compost into black soil.

I remember the sunset coming through
the dark from July to October.

(What is left will gather.)

(She placed the leaves in her shoes, as a remedy,
and sang to hear her voice echo in the well.)

Some would walk barefoot
and men scatter out into fields, or
under trees.
She   half carried to a row of chairs.

(A new moon will rise on the river floor.)

SNAKEROOT

At sun-up, inside,
she stretched fabric
three chair lengths.

It is a bird of the mountains:
in summer it is widely spread
found in foothills
or   again in groves.
"There is a legend," she said.

Three rivers arise out of the peat bogs
of one Welsh mountain.
They reach the sea together.

We entered barefoot,
forward,
a screened off sleeping area.
Her fingers dark
        of purple hulls
before the storm.

The raw smell of snakeroot,
(it was as much as in our bodies)
standing in a shadow
and gathering fruit
when the moon is full.

JONATHAN JOHNSON (b. 1967)

ECLIPSE

I love to drive women's cars.
I honestly don't mean one
specific car, although the woman
is often a friend of my wife's
from work. She's often
in the human services field,
a social worker for the county,
or a speech therapist
at the General Hospital, in her twenties,
with her Masters Degree,
confident, getting used to
that adult feel of her first job,
on the phone in her
airy upstairs apartment, say,
ordering a burgundy sofa
from the *Spiegel Catalogue*.

But her car. It's wide
and low to the ground,
with a wishbone suspension,
somebody's *Unplugged* CD
clean and bright through new speakers.
It's fast and sure over wet pavement,
forest green and stealthy.
But not a Stealth. No,
something more like an Eclipse
or a Grand Am,
a *Consumer Reports* "smart buy,"
and she keeps it immaculate,
my wife's friend does.

The car's a reward for herself.
She can feel the pull
of that zippy turbo through
the soft leather steering wheel
when she turns out
from the parking garage
into afternoon traffic. And,
driving that clean,

neat, new car of hers, I am
genuinely happy for my wife's friend.

I am afraid now
of what you're thinking, that
you think you know
just what kind of guy I am,
and you don't much care for
what you think is my dubious
and transparent car/woman analogy.

But damn it, it's an act of trust.
This is a relatively expensive car
we're talking about,
her first big purchase,

and she's put the keys in *my* hand.
She is single and smarter
than the undergrad guy in the polo shirt
she's finally given up on. We're all
driving up the coast north of town—
my wife, the woman from work,
all of us heading up to hear a band.

They're both a little drunk already
so it's me at the wheel.

Or my wife and her friend
send me down to Safeway for
birthday candles and a video.
That's the sort of night I mean
when I tell you about
the new Firestones slashing wet pavement,
the stickshift dropping into fifth,
the glow of instrument light,
clean guitar music filling her car.

If you're still with me,
I think you know exactly how her car smells,
how you could ride in that smell
to every Safeway in the state
and back.

The View Café

Stream of rain off metal awning,
rain like sparks on the *Spokesman Review* box,
rivulets down the dirt lot.

A blue pickup crosses left.
A silver Honda crosses right.

Their mist trails swirl and cross.

A drop, clear a convex moment, falls
and the shrub branch recoils then bends again.

Hum of wet semi tires, then the semi,
amber running lights on.

The head waitress' husband is
six days into his suicide.

Everywhere, in here, prayers multiply like silverware
tossed in a plastic bin.

Through an opening in the jackpine across 95
there is a slate lake. *Henery's* in blue neon,
Draught in red neon, backwards on the glass
on the dusk above the water.

Past the lake, three ridges.
The first is evergreen peppered yellow
with tamarack,
the second a single,
more distant green, the third
a mere shade of the water of sky.

Midnight Run

When the ice fell through, there was plenty of time,
a solid chance to regain control. The dogs sank,
dazed and silent. He knew it was neither act
nor accident. The ice had no opinion,
no targets. In fog they'd veered off course, away
from the orange cones—the barks from other teams
dissolving with the lights of town and solid crust,

a record thaw flooding the race with slush and risk—
and had fallen into open water where the lake
rebuilds itself. What remains, once we survive
our names, is guesswork and paranoia that ruins us
for this world we've made. We cultivate
the obedient clues to salvage an epitaph. No one will
use the washing machine tools in his truck.
Everything else is dog related, even his five acres,
littered with sleds and doghouses made from dryer shells.
So it's come down to this. He's fallen through before,
on the last leg of the Yukon Quest, slush up
over the skids, soaking the team and his feet
in river water cold enough to burn flesh...
we have no way of knowing how cold. In the morning,
the Coast Guard pilot will spot three huskies
wandering the edgeless floes and pass the word
to the rest of us who will perfect our impatient,
vague despair. But now the private gesture.
Tonight, all that remains is to unharness the lead
and wheeldogs from the rest, a doomed gang chained
to each other's drowning. Their grey eyes panic
for surface light then fix to a man's headlamp
still burning through the water all the way down.

UNMARKED STOP IN FRONT OF WESTMOND GENERAL STORE, WESTMOND, IDAHO

I have a life. I stand abandoned,
the bus two miles downroad and upshifting,
by now, past acres of white cattle,
past an aluminum house trailer that
sends up woodsmoke like the last bubbles
from a sunken steamer. Forget the trailer,
with its hopeful, broken cedar-shake porch,
everyone else does. Forget the rim
of soft mountains. I admit the naked sound
of cracking gravel. I admit it is bright
here, and cold. The pine shadows reach across
the oily road ... but what do I know of reaching?
I have never looked here from above,
from the few square fields of long cleared woods
on the mountain behind this little store. No,
I only look out, or up, afraid—despite
myself—to die. But fear or none,

it waits, clear as the constellation
of words it takes to say *a wall of birch*,
clear as the wall of birch itself.
A muddy Kenworth rolls by, overstacked
with mill logs. I can't hear any chain saw
in them, they're just dead. Even the few
small branches with tufts of fur left to whip
in the highway wind are dead.
And they'll be no less dead when I stop looking.
Once, pages of sunlight fell across bawling sheep
in the hollows of the Vandersloot barn,
and the sheer head rattled away,
nicking bloody an occasional teat or vulva
beneath of stack of bodiless fleeces
caked in gold lanolin, blood and shit.
End of the day, the door swung back,
they funneled out, heads straining above
a river of stubble and fuzz, these alluvial
sheep scattering in the last glow. Kicking,
and acting up a little when they knew
they were free. Unrepentant and pure,
they were already forgetting. I start over,
lift my bag to my back and walk, remembering
low clouds moving in these woods, the rain
off the mountain again and down my face, here
or somewhere else. Here, I could almost endure.

JUDY JORDAN (b. 1961)

THROUGH THESE HALLS

Of course it's all over the morning news
so the school bus buzzes with it
and my classmates look at me

with that wide silence, interminable as the inch of mildew
board by board through the guinea shed,
then their eyes drop, as if crumbling with a groan to rust and rot.

Worse than the few who openly stare
after the sixth grade teacher sends me
with a note to the principal's office.

Walking that hall noticing the paper shows
no shadows of ink-slants and lines, I unfold
my own dread in the blank sheet,

knowing somewhere the news announcer
again drones on about the father shooting his son,
as my cousin is sponged by the undertaker's assistant

and my uncle shuffles to a damp cell,
maybe already thinking of the ripped shirt,
the slug-sweat of the bar he'll tie it to.

It doesn't matter whether I pocket that paper
and turn back to the now quiet class
or continue toward the office—

there's always the teacher hushing the students
and my slip through the wink of each window
carrying my pretext down that long sun-slashed hall.

WINTER

(In memory: CNHJ)

First light shook with ax blows to the frozen pond
and the geese calling in guttural distress
as I chopped through to the still, black water.
All day the land gave over to thaw and snow released the cabin,

softened and eased off the ridged tin roof in foundation shaking crashes
until night when Orion whistled his dogs
behind clouds mottled like weathered rock,
then the farm sighed under the new storm
and silence returned like an old sorrow.

I wish that silence held some answer or passage
to forgetting. I would go to it
with its hesitant and dangerous tacks,
its seepage into night like shadows slipping into bodies,
where it hangs like smoke,
drifts into itself as smoke will,
rises slow above trees
to the flat of the sky, rises and hangs,
and like sorrow, waits and will not fade.

SANDBAR AT MOORE'S CREEK

Here where the creek culls sand and silt
and rises against itself

to become something else entire...
                     here I bring my sorrows
like the delft blue mussel shells,
finger-tip tiny most beautiful when strewn wide with loss.

If I ask anything of them, if I search for an opening
                            as if they were stars
                            in a sand-sky
which fade each night when the real stars
descend to drink the mirror of water,

what does the creek care?

It's day yet:
the light shaking down
through the hackberry branches,

the sky colored raw bone,
                     caught on the water's unbroken surface.

ALLISON JOSEPH (b. 1967)

SOUL TRAIN

Oh how I wanted to be a dancer
those Saturday mornings in the
living room, neglecting chores

to gape at the whirling people
on our television: the shapely
and self-knowing brownskinned

women who dared stare straight
at the camera, the men strong,
athletically gifted as they

leaped, landed in full splits.

No black people I knew lived
like this—dressed in sequins,

make-up, men's hair slicked
back like 40's gangsters,
women in skin-tight, merciless

Spandex, daring heels higher
than I could imagine walking in,
much less dancing. And that

dancing!—full of sex, swagger,
life—a communal rite where
everyone arched, swayed, shimmered

and shimmied, hands overhead
in celebration, bodies moving
to their own influences, lithe

under music pumping from studio
speakers, beneath the neon letters
that spelled out SOUL TRAIN—

the hippest trip in America.
I'd try to dance, to keep up,
moving like the figures on

the screen, hoping the rhythm
could hit me in that same
hard way, that same mission

of shake and groove, leaving
my dust rag behind, ignoring
the furniture and the polish

to step and turn as they did,
my approximation nowhere near
as clever or seductive, faking

it as best I knew how, shaking
my 12 year old self as if something
deep depended upon the right move,

the righteous step, the insistent
groove I followed, yearning to get
it right, to move like those dancers—

blessed by funk, touched with rhythm,
confident in their motions, clothes,
their spinning and experienced bodies.

ADOLESCENCE

No one calls you beautiful
at 14, or knows the longings
that fill your body, except
the other girls who lurk late
with you, the awkward emerging
women you are becoming
fragile as the puff
you powder yourselves with,
the mirrored compact.
Too early to love
any man, though you're learning
the trappings: leather heels,
lipstick, tight hose dark
around legs that tremble
beneath cold street lights.
Too early for breasts,
for the full flesh that marks
your passage from one another
into the arms of lovers.
In clear night air,
all you have is the silence
of waiting together,
of learning the rules
of attraction: the walk,
the talk, the hair,
the perfume you spray
on each wrist,
behind each ear,
along the vulnerable throat.

WEDDING PARTY

I wanted to have a wedding
where a band called Sexual Chocolate
would play cover versions
of "Turn the Beat Around"
and "Got To Be Real," tunes

so disco everyone's forsaken them
in the oh-so-cynical '90's.
I wanted my bridesmaids
in orange tulle, groomsmen
in light green, their cummerbunds
so wide their waists became
some thick, enticing region,
regal as an alleyway.
I wanted folks to glide
onto the dance floor,
doing quaint, antiquated dances
like the funky chicken, Latin hustle,
polyester divas doing moves so fine
even Shaft himself would have
to stop, grin his approval.
I wanted finger foods
in snack sizes, a wedding cake
piled so high in gumdrops
and coconut that no one's
blood sugar level would be safe.
I wanted it crass, and big,
and ugly, bad enough
to make relatives shudder
whenever they remembered
my denim patchwork gown,
platform heels. Instead,
I'm here at the city clerk's office,
an ordinary woman in an
ordinary dress, marrying
an ordinary man in ordinary
shoes. Still, I know that party
is going on somewhere, if only
in the strange regions of my mind:
music and costumes
by Earth, Wind, and Fire,
catering by Momma and Company,
and the m.c., of course,
is a dapper black man
who wishes us *love, peace, and soul*,
our lives one everlasting ride
on the Soul Train bound
for Boogie Wonderland,
li'l Stevie's harmonica
blowin' us one last tune
in the key of life.

JULIA KASDORF (b. 1962)

WHAT I LEARNED FROM MY MOTHER

I learned from my mother how to love
the living, to have plenty of vases on hand
in case you have to rush to the hospital
with peonies cut from the lawn, black ants
still stuck to the buds. I learned to save jars
large enough to hold fruit salad for a whole
grieving household, to cube home-canned pears
and peaches, to slice through maroon grape skins
and flick out the sexual seeds with a knife point.
I learned to attend viewings even if I didn't know
the deceased, to press the moist hands
of the living, to look in their eyes and offer
sympathy, as though I understood loss even then.
I learned that whatever we say means nothing,
what anyone will remember is that we came.
I learned to believe I had the power to ease
awful pains materially like an angel.
Like a doctor, I learned to create
from another's suffering my own usefulness, and once
you know how to do this, you can never refuse.
To every house you enter, you must offer
healing: a chocolate cake you baked yourself,
the blessing of your voice, your chaste touch.

FIRST TV IN A MENNONITE FAMILY

1968

The lid of the Chevy trunk couldn't close
on that wooden console with a jade screen
and gold flecks in the fabric over the speaker.

They sent us to bed then set it up
in the basement, as far from our rooms
and the dinner table as they could get,

out of sight for grandparents' visits.
The first morning, Mother studied the guide
and chose Captain Kangaroo for me,

but when we turned it on, the point of light
on the screen grew into black-and-white men
lifting a stretcher into the back of an ambulance.

Each click of the huge, plastic knob
flashed the same men, the same ambulance door
propped back like a broken wing.

After that, we were forbidden to watch everything
except the Captain and "I Love Lucy."
Yet, when Dad returned from business in Chicago,

I heard him tell Mom how police beat the kids
under his hotel window, and I knew whatever it was,
that vague, distant war had finally come.

EVE'S STRIPTEASE

Lingerie shopping with Mom, I braced myself
for the wedding night advice. Would I seem
curious enough, sufficiently afraid? Yet
when we sat together on the bed, her words
were surprisingly wise:
              Whatever happens, remember this—
              it keeps getting better and better.
She had to be telling the truth. At ten,
I found a jar of Vaseline in her nightstand,
its creamy grease gouged deep, and dusting
their room each week, I marked the decline
of bedside candles. But she didn't say lust
is a bird of prey or tell me the passion
she passed on to me is no protector of borders.
She'd warned me only about the urges men get
and how to save myself from them. Though
she'd flirt with any greenhouse man
for the best cabbage flats, any grease monkey
under the hood, she never kissed anyone but Dad.
How could she guess that with *Jesus Loves Me*
on my tongue, constantly suffering crushes
on uncles, I would come to find that
almost everything gets better and better?
The tiny bird she set loving in me must
keep on, batting the bars of its cage
in a rage only matched by my cravings

for an ample pantry and golden anniversary.
She let me learn for myself all the desires
to accept resurrection. I knew that marriage
is just a trick cooked up by the grownups
to keep me from screaming my head off.

THE STREAK

A boy hammers a piece of lead pipe
against the lip of a watering trough
until it is thin and flat as a coin
then cuts it into slender strips
his sister will pinch on her snake-black
braids. In this, the boy learns
even heavy, hard things can be beaten
into other things, transformed entirely,
the way milkweed's translucent parachutes
become the stuffing for a soldier's coat.
Collecting the pods along a field lane,
the boy hums, thinking of a man in his coat
drifting under a white, silk scallop
somewhere above Europe, cold up there,
silent, so far from any place where
farmers must save even corn husks
to stuff their children's mattress ticks.
How his mattress rustles each time he shifts,
dreaming, the way dry cornfields scuff
in the wind. One day this boy will turn
from sleep to rouse a woman, then
turn back, the streak on her thigh,
a slug's bright leaving, and I,
his only daughter, will come of that.

LAURA KASISCHKE (b. 1961)

FATIMA

God exists. Instead
we are a group of teenage girls, drunk
at one of those awful

carnivals in a field, out
between the airport and the mall.
It's raining, and this
has become a festival
of mud, which is just
fine with us. A man

with hundreds of tattoos
has taken a fancy to Heidi
and is slipping her extra darts
to lob at the balloons. There are sirens
every time she misses, and she wins
nothing. Why

is there straw in the mud, why
is it plastered now to the wet
sleeves of our leather jackets? Something
cruises into the air
with its light bulbs zapping
and when we turn around, the man

has disappeared with Heidi. Am I wrong
or has every teenage girl been
at this same carnival in rain, in 19–
78, with four wild friends and a fifth of peach
schnapps in her purse with its bit
of rawhide fringe? Music

spins at us and away from us
as the Octopus starts up
its scrambling disco dance. Am I

the one who says *Don't worry*
she'll be back or have I
gone to the Port-o-Potty
to barf again by now? Imagine

hours later
when we are terrified and sober and
still waiting, when she
re-appears with her hand
tucked into the back
pocket of the tattooed man
who has no T-shirt on now under
his black vinyl vest
so we can see all

his swastikas and naked
ladies—imagine

that we are just
a few peasant girls
on a hill in Portugal. It's night, but the sun's

swung out of the sky
like a wrecking ball on fire
and even the skinny whores

in their ice-cold brothel smile
while the Fascists are gripped
with cramps
and shudder in their shiny
uniforms with tassels. Imagine
when we see Heidi:

her blurred blue robes
in the distance, her soft
virgin voice, and the way
it knocks us to our knees
like a crate of fruit, tossed
off a truck
and smashing into the street.

PALL

Because my mother was too beautiful
as a girl   she died young and made
a horrible corpse. Her female friends backed

off from the coffin
which was quilted in satin and flashed
its glamorous hinges at them. Frost

scarved the pallbearers   their
gasps and sighs turned
to shreds of white chiffon across her grave. The one

who'd made love to her   once
or twice   took
my hand in his after
he lowered her into the dirt. *She
was lovely* he said   and his hand

wasn't warm   but I wanted
to kneel down and let him push

my all-wrong face to his belt   gentle   until
my teeth knocked the cold brass   which
would taste like rust   and blood   to be found later
that same day by her thin

hopeless friends
who were so afraid to die   a white
unlikely foot of a daughter   born
young and plain to a dead

sexy woman   pale
jailbait in a ripped slip
with that man   both of us
smoking in bed: a glass of gin in my hand.

MY HEART

When August was finally done, his
wife never mailed the dark
card to me that said, "Hon

he's all yours now, good
luck and happy Labor Day," and still
I *loved* that man, the way

magnolias go
sloppy and wet as pneumonia
on front lawns when summer's over, the way

a cool moon might appear on a bright September afternoon
to the naked eye to be
just a blind blue infant face

hovering in space. Those
human trees: Listen
to them wheeze all night in sleep while

the washing machine churns blood
and whiskey out of your sheets. I
loved that man, whatever that means.

Whatever you need, I thought.
Whatever you eat. GOTCHA

he wrote one morning   .

in red pen above my breast. Bull's-eye
where my heart was, and the earth
bobbed a bit

on the little string that holds it
over a whoosh of air
and emptiness, the way

when I was a child a magician pulled
a long silk scarf
from my ear. I could hear

red wind when it passed
out of me into his hands. All
the other children at this party

gasped, but I
knew where he'd gotten it from, and felt
my heart spin in me like a sparking

toy when he was done.

DAVID KEPLINGER (b. 1968)

INSIDE: GEORGE GAINES AT GRATERFORD PRISON, 1981

A point of moonlight
anchored through the barred window, and beyond that,
the field, the far-away, not-yet-created, or wholly-unearned world.

Night, a wall on four sides.
The smell of urine at the john. The shouting below.
From a piece of piping, he's sawed an edge to jab in the dark:

it has taken this long to find the means and the hours,
but at the center he comes back
always to himself, this cell, gravity pouring through his hands.

ANOTHER CENTURY

The women who fan
their skirts before the stove,
they live in another century,

where, along the river
the columns of blackbirds
don't mind that we walk near them.

When the pig is cut from neck to belly,
the river freezes.
The slabs are cooked.

Smoke fills the kitchen. Nothing changes,
January comes with police and hard bread.
With January passes a hundred years.

THE DISTANCE BETWEEN ZERO AND ONE

In April the carnival came.
The ice and the factory lot,
the carnival rides huffing black stripes of smoke ...

Pig slaughter music.
My great love stirring the blood with her hands.
Others cleaning the long blue
intestines in snowdrifts
filled with tiny stones.

GER KILLEEN (b. 1960)

TRISTIA

There is no science of separation
to console us with inevitable ends.
Each parting makes its own lamentation.

I've stood in a dozen crowded stations
where crowds dissolved the faces of lovers, friends.
There never was a science of separation

to let me know the final destinations
of those trains: That open distance will not mend.
Each parting sings its own lamentation—

heart-splitting whistle, dark silence, passion
of tongue and touch, emptiness no emptiness portends.
There is no science of separation,

only things to clutch in desperation—
a tune, a certain look; it's always different:
Each parting spins its own lamentation,

and the stars in their inhuman isolation
don't burn with the fires our tattered hearts expend.
There is no science of separation.
Each parting flares its own lamentation.

MY FATHER'S ANGELS

My father's angels
dropped to earth
like those of Tintoretto, heavy-limbed
and muscular as farm boys
saving the summer hay. And in his tales
they needed to be that way,
rescuing saints and ships at sea
and Spanish nuns from the Communists
in 'thirty-three. My father's angels
kept the world
on course for Paradise, and when
the gutters gushed with blood
in Derry and Belfast his angels
came and fell down on their knees,
rifles levelled and faces masked.
My father's angels
were angels through and through;
everything happened
like his favorite saint, Augustine,
says: When angels turn
their attention to the world of man
the nighttime falls. I heard
the darkness slam.

WISHES

A wish that I can get it true for you—

Snow bared the black lines of hedges in thorn.
The river stiffened like a swan's white neck
and every sound was like a bone splintering
through the thick silence and the long skinless
fingers of the reeds, though it was only
ribbon flickering back against a door.

And I know that deep in your city you
have felt this too: the hard echoing
of the bell, and church voice wavering with
the slow candle; shuffle of feet on stone.

And perhaps within us too is harshness
of hill and monument, for pain only
brings our wishes that we can get it true.

REWIND

Wing and thorn remain, etched into my mind;
images I choose for a leavetaking
in memory's montage. I rewind
the scenes we made when our lives were breaking.

Meeting you now, I take your offered hand,
forget the stark simplicity of pain,
buy you a drink, as a friend, you understand,
and after goodbyes wing and thorn remain.

Expecting too much, the expectation
projects the darkness of a tree bloomed bare.
How absence flits through the recreation
of such a photogenic, small affair.

AT THE BLACK EDGE

Our arms have grown
deep and wide as snowfields,
covering everything, drawing the trees, the stars,
the deer and the tall cities around us.
It is too much

for them to bear, and we
who demand such close knowing
we approach the atom
to explain the mountain. Already we see
the gods taking flight like a cloud of swallows,
their homes which are horses, and fish, and fish-
hooks becoming hard and pale as jewels
in our embrace. At the black edge
of the world two or three flowers are tossing
in the approaching blizzard of our words.
We cannot hear them singing
above our exquisite howl.

JAMES KIMBRELL (b. 1967)

TRUE DESCENDERS

> —*After Luca Signorelli's* The Damned Cast into Hell
> *(remembered from a high school text)*

No matter how thunderous the chorus
    of their damnation, surely the wine-veined,
gold-tipped fornicators must relish
some pleasure in the last hurling spiral
    down the spines of all the bat-winged devils.

Like the star-shaped sugar maple leaves
    plummeting toward the thick asylum
of my own backyard, that warped infinity
of roots, it's impossible that their descent,
    whether here or from the constellations

over Orvieto, could ever be anything
    other than beautiful, their harshly bronzed
breasts and buttocks growing more luscious
with every imaginable sin. And what's
    to be made of Saint Michael and his flock,

drawing their cloud-glazed swords,
    torsos wrapped in steel? Especially now,
when the landscape's flustered, it's difficult
not to begrudge the high archangel
    his stock of feathers, his cosmic lock

of windblown hair, his breastplate, cool
    to the touch. It's a point the leaves
don't have to argue, whether to give in
to the pull of a soon-to-be-iced
    patch of autumnal earth, or to resist and so hang

perpetually rigid, heavy-legged traitors
    to lust. Suppose our own innocence,
in that red November dusk at the end
of the world, should remain that righteous,
    should take up its silver armor against

the quicker passions ready to tumble
    in any celestial bed, we'd see how it is
that we've always lived in the house
of at least two Gods, one of nipples and random
    erections, one of devotion to the virtuous

invisible, and that to truly worship either
    is to finally love the other. If
the swollen, cartwheeling transgressors
of desire begin to desire once more,
    who'd not let the blue-with-death demons

untie their hands and follow their
    laughing down the hall? Who could
not feel their own body going holy?
Who would not take a lover then
    and guiltlessly watch the wrist-ropes fall?

My Father at the North Street Boarding House

The white brick steps were steep and off-level
Beneath the door which led to the door
Of his room. The half-hooked padlock knocked
As I knocked. A shuffling, then he led me
Into the curtained sunlight. The word
May not be flesh, but the voice is, and his
Had been marked and removed to keep cancer
From more than it had. We sat on his bed
With pen and pad. Through the window
I could see a window across from his, the high
Branches budding, the power lines and sky.

***

To not look at the cloth which covered his throat,
To not think of his voice, slurred or manic,
In summer mornings or late at night, in steady
Counterpoint with my mother, or with no one.
I'd driven two days rehearsing how I might say
That I loved him in a way that would not
Sound like I loved him despite miles of rivers,
Miles of towns where I was a kid without him.
He wrote and I spoke of daily things, the weather,
People he knew. There was the sound of a radio
Down the hall. One door, then another, closing.

***

The slight tap and scrawl of his pen across
The unlined paper. The room with gloam
Easing in, the lamp turned on in the corner.
I spoke, paused, spoke once more and said
Nothing I had wanted to. I stood there
Holding him. No sound then. No crickets.
No drunks stumbling in. Two grown men
Standing in a silence that did not fall apart
In the door's hinges, in the weeds beneath
My shoes, nor even when I heard it again
And again driving home through the April dark.

ROOFTOP

Above the corner of Water and Seventeenth, when pigeons
Tapped the window and the mid-dusk light drew us out,
There was huge industry in the oncoming silence, in the print
Of darkness between low flight antennas and scattered
Cable dishes. The first quarter of moon over the bridge,
The last bend of river, and farther back, the trestle's web-work
Like an elbow above the trees, the entire town a foreground
For whatever we were after, something so close
We could see it disappear. . .
                              But more than we cared
For the weedy mimosas or the bras on the lines or the iron
Gutter grates, more than the diesely tops of log trucks
Or the newspaper sheets stuttering through weeds in the field
Behind the school, it was the view above ourselves
That we wanted most to remember, and how easily we fell
Into feeling half-visible, level with the birds on the ladder
Of the silver water tower, with their angular winging away.

GERRY LAFEMINA (b. 1968)

HER ROSE TATTOO

I leave the English Department for my second life,
a paycheck chock full of alcoholics, musicians,
sex fiends and none of the above. Some nights
I don't know which of these I am.
Some nights the dissonance of hard rock gets interrupted
by the desperate howl of a squad car, another
violent deed. Who doesn't understand
desperation? Some nights
consolation and seduction consolidate.
I keep hearing about acquaintances dying
and I feel no grief. Almost every morning
in the third pew of St. Andrew's Roman Catholic
the church crones count the small deaths in decades,
chcking them together between their weathered fingers.
This isn't supposed to be elegiac.
This isn't about the dead. Nor is this about the minors
I bounce from the bar who learn to despise me
and watch for me. We adapt—I change outfits
about midnight; Christopher laughs but we both know
it works. Some nights
I can't help but summon my own adolescence of punk bands
and illicit whiskey, the first time I chanced a fake ID;
other nights I walk the parks of downtown
and inhale the solitude of blossoms. Once I went home
with a woman who had a rose tattooed above her
left breast and, I can't explain this, it made her more
fragile, or at least tender. When I held her thin shoulders
they shuddered, unless I felt my own hands
shaking at that moment. Come morning I turned away from home
as St. Andrew's summoned another service of mourners
whose growing chant of *Hail Mary full of grace. . .*
reverberated like an orgasm: another
little death. She wished her mother
had named her Rose although it would be difficult
to live up to something so elegant and resilient.
The residue of our love making still surrounds me
some nights, but I've forgotten the details.
I know she was young, I know Christopher marked her hand
with the bold-faced X reserved for minors

and the match light for a smoke changed her cheekbones to petals.
I can pray decades on the lit cigarettes at the bar.
As a kid I once wriggled a Rosary over my head
and couldn't get it off my neck later. It glowed
in the dark, and my mother had to cut its string
which scattered phosphorescent beads everywhere.
Some nights I'd see one burning green
under the dresser or in a tumbleweed of dust:
an easy luminescence—the glow of street lights
when morning is still
embryonic, that time of day Christopher strikes
the snooze button hoping for ten more minutes away
from the guitar grit on his teeth and in his ear,
and the cop cars streak back to the precinct, and the undertaker
wraps a Rosary in a corpse's hands,
its beads perfectly spaced like the thorns
of a barbed wire fence we're not sure is there
to prevent us from leaving
or to keep us from getting in.

WHITE DWARF

> *And I just stood there, struck for the first time in my life*
> *by how far away the sky is,*
> *how blue*
> *and how wide.*
> —Nazim Hikmet

That morning the sun trespassed
between the joint where the curtains meet
and stretched a limb of light along the length of her body
as I lay beside her, restless—

                    a citizen in a country of want
broad as this continent.

And let's say Charles Wright is right:
this is the world of the ten thousand things. Then my desire for her
is one of them. And my love.
And the casual caress of the sun on her thigh.
And the parameciums of dust

                    parachuting in that light—

all of it imprisoned within the walls of this room
and this sluice of minutes.

226

And to follow that light beyond the glass:
yesterday's mown grass growing like the fingernails
of a corpse; a gang of trees hanging out
across the street: scruffy jack pine,
gangly birch, the body-building mass of an oak,
its plumage rippling in the dawn's wind

and scratching the embroidered blue underbelly of the absolute.
Trellises of mist:

the morning so breathtaking
the moon still stands at the west, unwilling
its orbit
            and the usual breakfast quarrel of the jays
has been hushed. . . .

                    We're torn between two beauties—
the landscapes of the body
and of the spirit

I trace the ivory tusk of scar tissue
along her tan shoulder
                    which catches the light and shines
for a brief moment
like a white dwarf star imploding, finally—

its rays swept millions of years across this ever-expanding universe
so we all may see its brilliance
right before dawn, be startled,
                    and draw in our breath.

LANCE LARSEN (b. 1961)

RED

Because it might hurt, and because looseness
in a baby tooth, especially an eye tooth
bleeding a little, is its own virtue, my son

refuses to let me pull it, though he's happy
to let it bleed slowly and exquisitely
onto the unbuttered roll he holds to his mouth,

so that a tiny blossom forms, which he bites off
and chews, all the time staring at the ceiling light
and counting breaths or ghosts or dead moths maybe,

until his chewing gathers this quiet into a kind
of questioning, which makes me think of Jacqui
waking in Recovery after her first miscarriage

and the possum-faced nurse who brought in a tray
of cherry Jell-o and cranberry juice, and said,
Eat up, Sister, eat up, as if it was a color

she had lost, and Jacqui laughed, and I lay
down beside her and I laughed, and she gulped
the juice, then started in on the Jell-o, but slowly,

taking tiny bites to make it last, this red,
like my son eating blood in the kitchen's murky
half-darkness, and me watching, half hungry.

LIPS

Our cars were used and named after singers,
our cats always Siamese and dying.
Which fails as zen or science, but helps
explain why Ethel, our '58 Fairlane,
was stalled on a muddy road overlooking
Pocatello, and why my mother in a whatever
shade of lipstick was holding a dead cat
wrapped in Visqueen. She had errands
to run, and Dead Pet Hill was on the way.
I dug, she watched. Deep lipstick, suggesting
what—aloofness and downtown commerce?
Or maybe a lighter shade, to go with
the inside-out smell of rain and too much
sage brush. I don't know the color.
But wet looking and waxy and a favorite
kind of candy all at once. She dabbed
her mouth with her hanky. It was April first,
her birthday. Which meant blue omelets
for breakfast, and later that night, noodles
and the whole fam-damily at the Shanghai.
But for now just me, my mother turning 47,
and a cat to bury. Easy digging, on account

of the rain and I'd already done my crying
over the weekend. Except for a few roots
and chopped worms, the sides chiseled
clean, as if I were uncovering a hole
already there. Her mouth was smeared.
Nothing like her practice lips—blotted
on a pane of tissue each morning and floating
wet and flat before she flushed them.
That impeccable smile. She was waiting
for me. We had the car to start, then errands.
Bakery, library, the florist, a utilities bill. . .
Me running the easy ones, the car idling
and warm. I wanted to save all that, and her.
The hole deep enough but making it deeper,
bending sometimes to touch the clean sides.

PEACH

Call it treason, but I'm eating my way
south. Chilean peaches, swaddled in green
tissue. I buy them $1.79 a pound.
In Kalamazoo, in the teeth of winter.
Tart enough they bite back. By the shape,
this one could be Allende's heart.
I palm it, I lick its seams. Each day
I feel a little more Marxist. The fuzz
part is obscene, so I peel it with my teeth.
I take a long time. Think of peaches
trundled to market on a scooter, peaches
filling a maid's mesh handbag. I once saw
a girl in a catechism dress sliver off
a piece for her brother. Her mouth to his.
I never should have quit the Peace Corps.
I happen to be dragging the wet part
slowly across my cheek. If Congress
would try this, if the President of CBS. . .
I'm ready to donate everything to La Leche
League. I'm taking my first big bite.
I wish I was mestizo and uncircumcised.
I wish I could cozy up beside those sad
Easter Island faces. I want book titles
running up the spine, not down, whirlpools
in the toilet spinning the wrong way.
It's firm, this peach flesh—with threads

of blood and history running through it.
Sometimes I think I'm a she. I want Reagan
to remember everything he never was.
Go ahead, count the letters in his name.
Ronald Wilson Reagan. 666. All the U.S.
can offer. South is always better.
Chickens in bed with you, a llama watchdog.
I'm dribbling peach juice and learning
to disembowel with a toothbrush. I wish
San Martín could heal in English, that penguins
would teach me how to carry eggs. I'm
investing in copper futures and madly
trilling my r's. On my taxes I claim
children named María de la Purísima and Jesús.
And now I'm down to the pit, which I'm
biting. An entire hemisphere in my mouth,
Pablo Neruda between my teeth. I'm listening
with the ear of a Mapuche Indian. Closing
my eyes to speak. *Hetcha batgutcha sitza.*
Rough translation: eat bat guano, America.
All made up, I admit. But I *want* their talk.
I *want* those tough SOBs on my side. I blow
my nose and whole soccer teams fly out.
I will show this to every kind of doctor.
I wish Gabriela Mistral had nursed me.
When I marry, it will be for exquisite
black eyebrows and wide hips. When I
conceive, I'll burn white, then red,
then redder. This peach sweet as seven Edens
and a peasant virgin. Sweet as Chilean
cowboys. Already, it's churning inside me.

DANA LEVIN (b. 1965)

RED WATER

When the door between the worlds opened
I ceased to be a ghost, I became
the blood in my fingers in the veins of my hands
I felt the world under my feet
with its nails and its splinters I felt

the salt the red water in the loam of my chest I was

no longer a ghost, the vapors were gone,
I was solid, I hurt, my wings could be broken,
it was joy, I was living in it,
I bled, I cried.

WIND

My house was a house of winds
and my father was of the wind
and we were of the earth

and we were torn by him,
we were stripped by him,
by the bellows of his body,

by the twisting of his voice
coming shaking, elemental, before the kitchen table
where we sat like stones and he stood

like a hammer over the rocks
of our faces, and threw down the glasses
and threw down the plates, the hail of him

scattering across the tiled floor
as he whirled in his fury out the back door,
slamming into the air—

He was gone, he was gone
and the storm was coming, I could hear it
on the radio crackling in the kitchen

as we ran out the door and headed
for the cellar, the dirty wind gusting
and stinging our eyes as my mother

bent down and hurried with the lock—
When she opened the cellar doors
I thought I saw him coming, the grass

bowing down, bowing down, bowed flat
by the black clouds bearing down
like fists, so I ran out to the field

and opened my arms, the flayed skin of my coat
rippling behind me, the voice of my sister
calling my name, as I streamed out like a flag

into the currents and felt the wind slam
into all of my sockets, and stood like a stick
and was whittled to pieces,

flying off with the twigs
that kept pelting my face—
I was in the air

but in the arms of my mother,
clutching me and running us back
towards the cellar, and I held her, looking back,

and saw the tornado twisting down from the sky,
coming for us as we ran on the earth,
and I stretched out my arms because I wanted

to touch it, I stretched out my arms
because I wanted to fly with the fence-posts
in that furious rapture—

And then we were in the cellar,
in the darkness with the jam jars,
while he roared and tore past our doors.

FIELD

The antelope white against the charred hills
        eaten by fire,
the golden trees, the upstairs window,
        something

is running across the field,
        can you see it coming
through the yellow grass, can you see it coming
        from the windowpane,
are you closing the shutters, do you think it is rain?

        The wind banging the shutters back, the antelope,
the golden trees, the skirt of your dress

caught on the wire, the trampled grass,
the barbed fence, something

    is running over the field,
do you think it is crows, do you think it is dust,
    are you huddled
under the window-frame, are your legs cold,
    are your eyes shut?

Something is running across the field—
    The wind hurling the shutters back—
The antelope, the charred hills. The yellow trees,
    the parted field.

MARK LEVINE (b. 1965)

WORK SONG

My name is Henri. Listen. It's morning.
I pull my head from my scissors, I pull
the light bulb from my mouth—Boss comes at me
while I'm still blinking.
Pastes the pink slip on my collarbone.
It's OK, I say, I was a lazy worker, and I stole.
I wipe my feet on his skullcap on the way out.

I am Henri, mouth full of soda crackers.
I live in Toulouse, which is a piece of cardboard.
Summers the Mayor paints it blue, we fish in it.
Winters we skate on it. Children are always
drowning or falling through cracks. Parents are distraught
but get over it. It's easy to replace a child.
Like my parents' child, Henri.

I stuff my hands in my shoes
and crawl through the snow on all fours.
Animals fear me. I smell so good.
I have two sets of footprints, I confuse the police.
When I reach the highway I unzip my head.

I am a zipper. A paper cut.
I fed myself so many times

through the shredder I am confetti,
I am a ticker-tape parade, I am an astronaut
waving from my convertible at Henri.

Henri from Toulouse, is that you?
Why the unhappy face? I should shoot you
for spoiling my parade. Come on, man,
put yourself together! You want so much to die
that you don't want to die.

My name is Henri. I am Toulouse. I am scraps
of bleached parchment, I am the standing militia,
a quill, the Red Cross, I am the feather
in my cap, the Hebrew Testament, I am the World Court.
An electric fan blows
beneath my black robe. I am dignity itself.

I am an ice machine.
I am an Alp.
I stuff myself in the refrigerator
wrapped in newsprint. With salt in my heart
I stay good for days.

EVERYBODY

Today is everybody's favorite day of the week.
Everybody is rubbing ice across their necks and chests.
Everybody is visiting the gravesite of the President
leaving plastic cups filled with wine and chocolates.
Everybody is holding their breath as the song approaches its end.

And beneath the old rail bridge I run into a girl
I haven't seen in yours, in a beautiful sun dress
stitched colorful beads. It's a pregnancy dress: she says.
And we make love until the purple dusks on a pile of old tires
as the song-birds flutter above our heads.

This is the happiest moment of my life, I say.
And she says: this is the happiest moment
of everybody's life. And as we drift
down the river on a fallen log, others join us, drifting, singing,
and soon the dead and the sick and the poor are singing too.

And the stars begin to fall, and though everybody is waiting
for a terrible surprise, it hasn't come yet, not just yet.

WEDDING DAY

1.

I have an appointment with elsewhere
I told the crater
which was filling with water and fragrant debris.
But that's just me.

All the impatient green bottles were pairing off,
a few stuffed with dainty Spanish galleons.
I doused my rag in silvery butane.
I had a picnic to attack: lamb chops; childhood.

Mine was a wedding of pipeline and pomp.
My bride pranced barefoot in the rime-dusted marsh.
She who sold me her eventual surrender
before losing herself in the blades.

She was a pristine evasive gesture.
She was a prissy evasive jester.
Troubled by a prolonged fondling
at the construction bin she called home.

2.

A confidential grimace in the ditch.
A brass band with its mouthpieces removed.

She in dejection
swung in one hand her broken heels
at the stone altar and in the other
tugged her ringlets.

The turbulent breeze had found me
and asked me to slumber in its physicist's truck.
I had trucks. And this one's treads
had been scooped of sand with a sparkling trowel.

3.

One of the emotions not included
showed up on my fruit plate
like a seed but more like a listening
device. You've swallowed all

the mints, whispered my mate to me.
The mint with the imprint of a slave ship

and its masts and its slaves floundering at sea,
oh never to be reproduced.

Home: the chaff of stereotypical daylight,
potatoes in the closet, the waxy floor;
and squatting in shadows beneath the fuse box,
distracted by trumpets, my only lonely bride.

4.

It was solstice inside the atom
and I took a stroll
to the sandy atoll
where I hired a girl for a whirl.

There was room for me inside her and her family.
She was swollen with particles of Emerson.
She had a packet of locomotive stamps
that she longed to sell me in the future.

This is the future I said and she with longing replied:
You sir have bought yourself a shiny train.

KATE LIGHT (b. 1960)

MY WORST NIGHTMARE

My worst nightmare was to be the couple
that arrived separately and pecked sideways
and then glided by each other, supple
as snakes. Those are the ones whose eyes glaze
over what's close by, and yearn for the prize
out there somewhere. I told you at the first
party we went to: *This is who I do not
want to be.* Maybe it's my fault. Maybe I cursed
us, jinxed us, put our angel on the spot.
That was the target I wanted to steer
clear of, my greatest fear; what did I do?
Maybe I drew our attention, so new, too near
a nightmare so accurate as to have been rehearsed.
How does one make a dream come true?
I had a dream. It was to be with you.

From *Five Urban Love Songs*

IV. SAFE-T-MAN

*"This unique security product looks incredibly
real, with moveable latex head and hands, and
airbrushed facial highlights."* — Advertisement

If safety can be had from hollow men
whom one can place to fill the empty chair,
let's leave them to their task of sitting, then,
while I'll these blow-up men to you compare:
    Far off you pose, endangered, rare—
    and, coated as you are with scent and skin,
    you are surely filled with hotter air;
    still, neither heart can quite admit me in.
    Though Safe-T-Man can dress for many roles—
    wearing hats for winter or for tropic breezes—
    in commuter lanes, the *real* men can count tolls;
    yet . . . do not fold to fit precisely in valises.
To buy or not to buy the button-on legs—?
Can anyone be safe? The question begs.

THE IDEA OF LOVE BETWEEN US

It was a vision he had, a candle he lit,
something he cupped his hand around and held
gently, then gave to me: *"Here, you hold it
a while"*; and it flickered, and was frail, and smelled
wonderful. But it was like having a child
with no pregnancy, no time to prepare,
no clothes or ready bed, no room built,
no house. Where to put the child? Where?
No, it wasn't a child, it was a lit
vision. *"Here, you hold it,"* he said, and split.

BECAUSE

Because we love, this day, this age, more times than once;
because we enter our new love's rooms
with fear and wonder held out like candles; and in our guts'
casement all forms of grief and hope are stored perfumes,
which by sudden thoughts will be dispelled, unsealed;
because we want exactly what we do not want
(e.g., to be disturbed, unstopped, revealed);

because inside the timid wren's a cormorant;
because a heart will rise again from ash and effigy
knowing what it already knew but more;
logic and discouragement can't override its ecstasy
and so it goes after what it was looking for. . .
What strange perfumes will make a dream tonight—?
What candle ever burned so low and still gave light?

FATIMA LIM-WILSON (b. 1961)

THE WAVE

That night, the roof flew, singing.
Father rose from the dead, glowing
In the bedsheets that Mother
Embroidered with his initials.
The rain fell and fell.
I caught the drops in my mouth.
And I sang, clear as the bell
On Easter morning. Mother waded
In the kitchen, mixing rain
With the dough. We would look
For Father later, she said.
Meanwhile, watch your manners,
And wave from the window.
The neighbors floated by,
And the parish priest paddled
From the back of the life-sized
Crucifix. Could I play outside,
Please? I would bring back
Noah's dove and the latest map
To our underwater city.
I sealed my heart with a cross
And kissed Mother's hand.
How sure I was then
Of the way home. Somewhere,
Bread continues to rise.
Bedsheets snag on a bare branch.
I then did not realize
How drowning in knowing
Takes many, slow-motioned years.

Upon Overhearing Tagalog

Isn't it sweet to hear one's language lift
From the ordered streets? The sparrow
Chatter flies you home, home
To the lullaby din of traffic, the call
Of ripe scents rising from the open markets,
And the sweat's seduction, flesh upon flesh.
Stock-still, you take on that "lost-but-
About-to-be-found" look, sniffing the air,
Tracking down the much missed flock.
Should you rush to them, garlands
Of tears in your eyes, bubbling gratitude
For the singsong signals, the happy
Discord of trivialities overlapping intimacies?
No, you know only too well the scorching
Glare when instant recognition segues
Swiftly into oblivion. Do not dare pass
The parameters of privacy so carefully
Staked out in this territory of strangers.
What you share commands severance.
Avoid the lock of a familiar glance.
Look down, look past, look through,
Masks mouthing a monotone:
Panicked birds retreating, disappearing
Into the manicured orchards of English.

Explaining the Origin of My Name

I.

Curiosity, it means. Woman peeking
Through bullet holes, diamond pattern
Of half-shut hands. Woman unknotting
Men's talk, that nurtured sense
Of following history's affairs,
Through the din of kitchen pans.
She sits as if caught in the web
Of her own stitches, so still,
As if she has turned into another
Leg or armrest of the hardbacked
Chair. Her husband, hunting outdoors,
And her children, imagining themselves
Explorers in another land,
Raise hands to mouths, hearing

Themselves respond. She commands,
Silently, through the veil
Of vegetable-brained questions.
They stop in their tracks,
Seeing always, ahead of their own,
Her slippers' shufflings, and the wake
Of her chastising broom.

II.

Almost apologetically, I disclaim
All rights of the Prophet's daughter.
And the life with only my eyes
To show, squirming in the cocoon
Of loose black veils. My name
Is "Fa-tima" without the peacock's
Tail of an *h*, with the stress
Falling on the wrong accent,
Too eagerly, like a bare-kneed
Servant girl leaning heavily upon
Half-shut doors. My mother,
Carrying the crucifix
Of her unborn child, climbed the steps
To the other Fatima, a windswept cove
In Portugal, shielding her dripping
Candle as she unlinked bead after
Dark bead, mystery upon mystery,
Of her life's Joys turned to Sorrows
Cycling back to Glories. She knelt
Where the three kerchiefed children,
Behind the armature of fingers
Vainly netting their eyes, witnessed
The burning bush and the sad-faced
Woman under the heavy crown,
Crushing snakes with her bare feet.
And so I was named after a miracle.
And a prophecy. They share a secret:
Lucia, aging nun counting shadows
Falling across grilled windows,
And my mother, disappearing
Into the clouds of dust
Rising from her grandchildren's
Thundering feet. Two women
Wait in Lisbon and in Manila,
Wait for the cleansing fire
Of the beginning and end

Of the world while I fret,
Bruising myself
Against the gentle bonds
Of sacred syllables,
Fighting against the fears
Which have no names.

BETH LISICK (b. 1968)

PANTOUMSTONE FOR A DYING BREED

Until you change your mind
I'll watch you chew the olive from the toothpick
When I told you I finally got my teeth cleaned
I didn't really expect you to reply

I'll watch you chew the olive from the toothpick
as you continue talking about your wife
I didn't really expect you to reply
Nothing lies still long

As you continue talking about your wife
on the side of the interstate
nothing lies still long
and nothing makes you happier

On the side of the interstate
I told you I finally got my teeth cleaned
and nothing makes you happier
until you change your mind

EMPRESS OF SIGHS

Mom and Dad have abandoned the family home and retired to Palm
Desert. They moved into one of those gated communities of steel framed
homes on Gerald Ford between Date Palm and Bob Hope. Just cross the
intersection of Frank Sinatra and the Gene Autry Trail near the corner of
Fred Waring and Phil Harris, who for all the kids under 50 was a big
bandleader married to a big movie star whose name no one can quite
remember anymore, except she used to drink with Lucille Ball in her pjs

at Fletcher's and died a mess. Who doesn't anymore?

Mom says getting there is a snap, as easy as a cake falling off a log. Just take a left on Palm Canyon until you reach Desert Falls, bear left at the fork of Indian Canyon and Canyon Plaza taking Desert Canyon to Canyon Sands. This is where you find Rancho La Paz. Click on 2 for the gate, the guard waves you past and you're on Avenida del Sol where you continue on crossing Vista del Sol, Plaza del Sol, Vista del Monte, Sunny Dunes, Camino Parocela—make sure you heed the golf cart crossing—and then Thousand Palms, Emerald Desert, Desert Isle and Palm Desert Greens. Left on Sagewood, right on Sungate, left on Palo Verde, and ending in the cul de sac of Casa La Paz.

"I just love it," Mom says.

"You love it?" I say.

"Yes. I love it!" Then she calls to dad who's enjoying himself on the eighteen-hole putting green located just three feet outside the kitchen sliding glass door, "Don't we love it, hon?"

He tips the brim of his white cap, a cap he would have seen on someone a year ago and called them a fag, and says, "Love it! Another crappy day in paradise! Ha! Ha! Ha!"

Mom clears her throat a little and sighs. She is the Empress of Sighs. "Well, yes, it's still a little funny."

Same funny tax bracket, same funny year round tans, same funny cathedral ceilings. Same cars, same stocks, same paranoia and medication. Same politics and annoying anal polyps.

The same leather interior, glossy exterior and liposuctioned posterior.

Here comes the neighbor driving up in a luxury sedan just like your luxury sedan except he paid extra for the little headlight wipers and the gold linked license plate frame—and you didn't. You thought they were useless, extraneous, a little much . . . and now your neighbor comes rubbernecking by, waving real slow, doing the grown-up equivalent of "Ha-ha!" which is basically "Ha-ha! I am worth more than you."

And Mom sighs and admits it doesn't feel like home yet. This mom, Empress of Sighs, empress of afterschool treats and frumpy sweaters and marathon tickling and the *52 Casseroles* cookbook, doesn't feel at home.

So I map out a plan. I make a list on how one feels at home here. I say, you need to play bridge, throw a party, plan on some tennis, and it'll feel like home. Polish the silver, throw out old photos, balance your checkbook, it'll feel like home. Start eating more fresh fruit. Get your armpits waxed. Drink six 8 oz. glasses of water each day. It'll feel like home. Squeeze all your blackheads, clip your toenails in bed, watch thirteen straight hours of television. Complain about what trash they show on television and start writing a letter. Stop writing the letter cause it makes you think about yourself, yell at your mother instead, quit drinking, go on a crying jag, threaten to deport the gardener.

Consider rhinoplasty, blepharoplasty, and tummy tuck. Forget to water the plants. Buy plastic plants and forget to dust them. Buy bananas and watch them rot. Buy books and pretend you read them. Start a collection. Start a collection of something that might be worth something someday.

Now turn off the lights, sprawl out on one of the matching earthtoned leather sofas and pick a very high number. Start counting backwards. You're in the middle of the desert, the wind picks up and when you run out of numbers, you will find that it feels a lot like home.

TIMOTHY LIU (b. 1965)

HIGHWAY 6

A caravan heading east on Highway 6
with muscled men whose eyes are flashing
neon in a world of vacancy signs—
a Day-Glo decal shining on the window of a car
pulled off the side of the road, buzzards
lodged in pines with evening in their wings.
To love the moon in Provincetown as salt
glistens on the skin of shirtless men
cruising down Commercial Street, hand in hand,
as if death were merely some erotic aftertaste.
We are tethered to what we own, a ring
of keys with a different name engraved on each,
the doors we have locked now creaking open
not fifty miles from here. How memory's brake
locks up like a car spinning out on ice
while thirty birds on a wire all fly up at once.
Already I can hear the tow trucks revving up
their engines, trash bags in a moonlit ditch
filled with genitals, a full set of fingertips
last seen on a man who was leaving town
in the plush interior of a stranger's car—
guesthouse lights floating near the water line
where dead fish wash ashore, a cloud of birds
turning in to roost at the deserted harbor.
What would it matter now if a pair of headlights
suddenly swerved—and the world vanished.

POEM

If I held back each word, perhaps
there would be peace instead
of an open suitcase on the bed.
Or a broken bottle of gin
pooling on the kitchen floor.
Things as they were. No thought
of a silver wedding knife
buried somewhere in the yard.
Or was that just another lie
my mother told as grief hovered
over us—not a jet engine
so high we could barely hear it
but a thin trail of exhaust
dissolving across the evening sky.

THOREAU

My father and I have no place to go.
His wife will not let us in the house—
afraid of catching AIDS. She thinks
sleeping with men is more than a sin,
my father says, as we sit on the curb
in front of someone else's house.
Sixty-four years have made my father
impotent. Silver roots, faded black
dye mottling his hair make him look
almost comical, as if his shame
belonged to me. Last night we read
Thoreau in a steak house down the road
and wept: *If a man does not keep pace*
with his companions, let him travel
to the music that he hears, however
measured or far away. The orchards
are gone, his village near Shanghai
bombed by the Japanese, the groves
I have known in Almaden—apricot,
walnut, peach and plum—hacked down.

WELLFLEET

Our last resort. Lovers wading back to shore
with ankles garlanded in ropes of kelp,
my hand poised over notebooks that refuse
to close. On the horizon, a single sail
blazes late into the afternoon, the hours
receding without a sound. Wild rosehips
scattered along the beach while sandwiches
on sterile trays are wheeled past rooms
for the sick. Mother, no more mattresses
floating out to sea, nor ashes in urns,
the waves all sliding in well-oiled grooves
that heave up wakes of trash—shrieking
gulls circling above those watery graves.

M. LONCAR (b. 1968)

INSOMNIA

it starts
   inevitably
as something
      small:
the suicide of a friend
your team's loss in
   the World Series   a
         chipped tooth

first the cackle
of the echolaliac
in the bath and

then

above the din of
her heaving chest
when you're about to
close your eyes

you hear it:

a nest of thin
itchy trigger fingers
rustling at the end
of your arm

for me

it starts as
something

small

THERE GOES THE BRIDE

   a woman fresh off the train
and already i get orders   *so you're*
                the new caretaker?

          after all   it's an easy country
           to lose your way in

                what
with all those snakecharmers
      (in the bicarbonate belt)
             wailing

like a sinner on revival day
            (aww
       it's not the sex
      that's killing me

         it's
    the sentimentalism)

PICASSO SHAG

  sad?
  (admit it)
 you liked her (blue) kitchen
smoking all night and drinking coffee
     (she'd place a raisin in each cup)

        admit it
    you liked her (sad)
    way of ransacking the place
        best (how 'bout a cigarette
                babe?)

JOEL LONG (b. 1964)

BERMUDA TRIANGLE

I went to this party and all the ones who had disappeared
in the Bermuda Triangle were there, getting drunk.
There was First Sergeant Walter Smith who commanded
the twenty-seventh squadron into the sun, four planes
whose radios all went dead at once, and the last thing
he said to the air was "It is beautiful." There he was, swilling rum
and Coke, holding an unlit cigarette between his thumb
and forefinger, gesturing wildly to some middle-aged gal
in sunglasses. She told him she had been on a cruise with her husband
whom she had grown not to love, especially when he crooned
and played the guitar in the back of the boat as they drifted
over the base of the triangle, and his tropical shirt exerted the fire
of its colors. And behind her, Daniel Malkovich sat
in the corner with a look on his face as though he were
pulling one over on all of us, his black bangs forced
into a curl above his forehead with shining Brylcreem.
I felt like telling him his mother is dead,
that his wife had children with another man and died herself.
And then I felt like telling the Spanish explorer Ernesto Tortosa,
who disappeared with his crew and Spanish Galleon
in 1510 when a soft breeze lifted the boat from the water,
that half a continent is dead, that there is no more wilderness.
I felt like shouting to them all—as they sucked booze from ice,
as they told stories from the great war, as they bragged
about seeing Lincoln in Chicago and leaned toward
one another as though they actually had the bodies
through which desire could have some meaning—
I wanted to tell them that we left the questions of missing things
behind us, that we went on without them.

Music's Wife

For Wayne Shorter

Might there have been an echo of self,
blue after-image that lasted, a phrase,
the moment the plane exploded over sea?
Might she have slowly faded like a china bell
rung in the dark, lights visible from shore?
On the other coast he held the soprano sax
in his hands like a Midas-tamed snake,
sustained one note hard against happiness.
The chord resisted until he pulled his lip
from the reed. He looked out on the crowd
as though he could read in the multitude
a sorrow peculiar as flames on a saint,
the fish scattering, the water rising as steam.
To him this new silence sounded like applause.

PETER MARKUS (b. 1966)

Black Light

    For years he had heard his father talk about work, about carbon
boils, tap holes, skulls of frozen steel. And he had spent many nights
lying in bed awake—nights his father worked the graveyard shift—
wondering what it all meant, as if the mill—and the life that went on
inside it—was a part of some other world: a world to which he and
his mother did not belong. But one day all of this changed. One day
he decided to ask his father if he could come inside, if he could go
with his father to work, to see what it was like. And his father said he
did not see why not, though he would have to clear it first with the
plant manager, a tie-and-shirt type of guy by the name of Russell
Prescott. Which he did. And a date was set for that following
Monday. And so, instead of getting ready to go to bed like he usually
did at eleven o'clock, listening to the final innings of the Detroit Tiger
game, the voice of Ernie Harwell drawling through the dime-sized
speaker on his transistor radio, he found himself walking the quarter of
a mile upriver with his father, step by step in the darkness of this mid-
July night, the sky frosted fly-ash gray with a haze that hung over in
the wake of the day's ninety-degree heat. His father did not say

anything the whole way there, though as they passed through the black-grated entry gates of Great Lakes Steel, he pushed his hand down into his front trouser pocket and pulled out two tiny tablets of salt: white like plain aspirin. "You think it's hot out here," his father warned. "Just wait until we get inside." And then his father dropped the pills into his hand. And it was true. Inside, the heat made it hard for him to breathe. The hot metal was so bright—it was so black with light—he could barely stand to watch as it drained from the blast furnace down to the thermo ladle waiting below. He closed his eyes, held in his breath. But still he could see the sudden flash of molten sparks showering down, could taste the burn of cooked limestone slag, could feel the callused hand of his father reaching out toward him, taking hold of him, turning him away from the light.

LIGHT

When he wasn't working, on his days off, his father liked to spend his day outside, in the shingle-bricked, single-car garage, tinkering with his '52 Chevy Bel Air: a stoop-roofed, two-toned junker he bought off a drunk buddy of his, a fellow hot metal man by the name of Lester Litwaski, for a fifth of whiskey and a scrunched-up dollar bill. There were days when his father wouldn't take five minutes to come into the house to eat a hot lunch. Days like these his mother'd send him outside into the garage with a cold corned beef sandwich and an apple, and his father'd stop working only long enough to wolf down this food, his hands gloved with grease and dust, before ducking back under the Chevy's jacked-up back-axle. Sometimes his father would fiddle around past midnight, his bent-over body half-swallowed by the open mouth of the hood, his stubby, bloodcrusted fingers guided by the halogen glow of a single bare light-bulb hanging down like a cartoon thought above his hunchbacked silhouette. Sometimes he would stay up late and watch his father's shadow stretch like a yawn across the walls of the garage. And in the darkness of his room he would sit, silently, on the edge of the bed, by the window, and wait for that moment when his father raised up his hand, as if he were waving, as if he were saying good-bye, and turned off the light.

SHOOTING CROWS

In winter, when he was out of work and it was too cold outside to work on his car, his father would climb in his pickup truck and drive, downriver all the way down West Jefferson until it turned into a pot-holed Highway 85. Sometimes when his mood was lifted high with whiskey, his father might ask him to tag along. "Feel like shooting some crows," his father'd say. An hour later he'd be standing, his hands stuffed inside his pockets, in a cornfield standing dead for the winter, the sky alive and humming with the beating of wings. Once in a while, when his father shot with his 30-06, a bird might only get winged: wounded, not killed. But when his father drew out his Army-issued .45, and slipped in its six-bullet clip, and clicked back the trigger till the chamber ran empty, there was never any doubt the crows were dead. Afterwards, when his father said it was time to go home, he would stoop down by where his father had stood and pick up the six brass casings, as if each copper-capped shell was a penny that could bring him good luck.

DAVID MARLATT (b. 1963)

THE SUMMER OF THE NEW WELL

The summer I killed my pet chicken
my sister milked cows

at Lockshores and my brother drove
a rusted-out truck for Terminix.

It was the summer I lit
a rolled-up newspaper to see the lock

on the upper hayloft door. My friend
Jeff said *This looks like a good place*

to piss and arched out the hatch
onto a dead lawn mower. That summer,

I sold squash alone, and my uncle started
a cough that didn't stop until January.

Nobody slept the week of his funeral.
Katie Teppe took a drink and said,

That's a damn nice looking coffin.
I dreamed of him lying in the coffin

wearing my father's hat and buckle galoshes.
The summer I killed my pet chicken

I swam a mile with my sister. She said,
Nothing lasts forever. Let's go fishing.

Jeff stole me a bottle of beer.
My grandmother put her hand on her hip

and said, *Get inside, your dinner's getting cold.*
The summer I broke that chicken's neck

my hair went curling in the rain, and a man came
to drill the well about 20 feet deeper.

BRUCE AND THE BLUEGILLS

Bruce did–in 24 bluegills with a big spoon
from the kitchen drawer that night.
I said, "How do you know if you're hitting them hard enough
        to kill them?"
"Just give them a good thump," said Bruce.
He snapped his elbow out of the
five gallon bucket to avoid a fin pricker.
And he showed me how to fillet
a bluegill. I started cutting carefully
and thought about the bluegill feeding frenzy
not two hours ago. Near dark, they'd bite
at anything. We lost track of just how many.
There was a heron dipping its bill and blackbirds
lining the high tension wires across the highway
drainage ponds, and greenhouses. I snagged one
by the white of its eye. So I learned
how to fillet a bluegill.
Not much meat when you finish,
but they looked good swimming around in the big
milky pot of chowder, corn and onions floating by.
I sat there at the table drinking a Pabst,
and some of the fish heads on the newspapers jawed at me,
lined up as they were, gills down,
mouth up, talking to the ceiling's bare bulb.
"What's he saying, Bruce?"
Bruce lit up a smoke.
"He's saying, 'Stop hitting me with the spoon.'"

WORKING GIRL

If I said I once loved a girl who stacked
firewood close under her chin, I would say more.
That it was the deftness of her steps over
uncut branches and chips
to stack each piece of stovewood
that drew me close.
Her father cut stove-lengths
across a circular blade.
She turned her head away
from sawdust blowing in the near-winter wind,
settling on her wool hat and lashes.
They knew it was too late in the year to be
cutting stovewood from fallen old-growth,
but her father cuts while the gasoline holds out
and her own untiring hands curl at the wrist to carry
every new length to pile against the snow.
If I said that I loved her,
I would say that I loved her from that moment
I saw her sweating in the oversize
of her brother's worn workcoat.

KATHERINE'S HAIR

I once saw my grandma with her hair undone.
It was long, white and wild.
Wind blew it about as she leaned on a dying elm.
I'd seen her first communion picture,
dark brown pipe curls
overflowing her shoulder
onto the white, gathered dress
Aunt Kate made.
Her eyes are the same.
"Oh, don't look at me," she said.
The wind blew from the East
shooting maple seeds,
pulling long strands
across her face.
With both hands,
she gathered her hair
from the wind,
caught it up
with Ceylonese combs
carved from ivory

VALERIE MARTíNEZ (b. 1961)

INTO THE NEXT ONE

Eucalyptus, his mouth
on hers, on his. The taste.
The arch, the ankle—

the woman wearing a white sheet
and screaming, laughter.
She isn't a movie, a lover.
Is a loved woman forming a chasm
between her teeth. It's today
and what's important is the sheet,
brilliantly draped. It fell that way.

On a trip in Nevada there was a spot.
A trailer. A flower etched
against the desert. No time.
The heat and one flower, the desert.
It was the subject, it had to be,

and when a flower, a fuchsia
so penetrating frightens me,
I remember.

Cotton, damask, like the husk
of some creature
where the body is implied.
I fossil-gather. Besides,
it's the end of the century,
the globe is warming,
forests are vanishing,
cultures are dying. . .

But the woman (I'd forgotten)
in the black chair, reeling.
The sheet exquisitely draped,
the blessed femurs
making their indentations.

Later, the body cloaking hers

for an hour.

What happens on this earth,
this time, next time, is implied.
Prophesied by these imprints
on our eyes. I'm thinking
of that flower in the desert,
shapes of carcasses and flowers
draped by the desert, thinking
gather your robes,
gather the wide robes my god
we're going there.

COASTAL

Toward what force on the beach
where the girl goes with fingernails
so white it hurts.

The sea is round, and moves in.
The clouds wax shadows, and wet.

Near thin waves at the edge
the girl feels such dizziness—
who is moving?

Away on a cliff there is a figure
so small it becomes a beacon
for the sea to swell to.

And a string could suspend them both
like two glassy beads above the surf.

Creatures emerge from the sand
and the sun remakes them.

The figure moves and breaks
the absolute stillness.
It's turbulent.

See the girl's white body half-
submerged, making a bridge
between elements. See the figure
meet sky meet earth.

How they rose, millenniums ago,
moving headlong—breathed
water, breathing air.

A tumult of creatures,
so much here, so much there.

KHALED MATTAWA (b. 1964)

HISTORY OF MY FACE

My lips came with a caravan of slaves
That belonged to the Grand Sanussi.
In Al-Jaghbub he freed them.
They still live in the poor section of Benghazi
Near the hospital where I was born.

They never meant to settle
In Tokara those Greeks
Whose eyebrows I wear
—then they smelled the wild sage
And declared my country their birthplace.

The Knights of St. John invaded Tripoli.
The residents of the city
Sought help from Istanbul. In 1531
The Turks brought along my nose.

My hair stretches back
To a concubine of Septimus Severus.
She made his breakfast,
Bore four of his sons.

Uqba took my city
In the name of God.
We sit by his grave
And I sing to you:
    Sweet lashes, arrow-sharp,
    Is that my face I see
    Reflected in your eyes?

THE BUS DRIVER POEM

I wasn't driving
just crossing a street
with trees, leaves mustard
yellow and ketchup red,
when a low-ranking employee
of an insignificant bureaucracy
gave me the finger.
Did my face foretell
seven years of drought?
Did I remind him of
Don Kirshner, The Bee
Gees, the Cold War?
As usual I was lost
between the stuffed
tomatoes of my youth
and a future that says tick
tock boom boom.
Lost because I was living
the now of hurried afternoons,
the present that makes me bark
"No, I don't need help"
to the teenager bagging
my groceries at Mr. D's.
So when the bus driver
gave me the finger,
I gave him the Italian arm.
Brakes screeched, people inside
jerked around like carcasses
in a hot dog plant. He stepped
out shouting, big mouth
flashing. I couldn't hear
a sound. Still
I screamed fuck you,
fuck you, and the present
became a rabbit searching
for its severed head.
I mean the now was Reba
McEntire crooning to Sid
Vicious biting on a slide guitar.
Then the present burned
a heap of old calendars—
June 23, 91,
March 4, 92, the smoke

of all those days!
I didn't look back
but watched my life
from a helicopter
or a sewer hole, my heart
pounding 140 fists a minute.
Look at me, look at me
fling hours at the universe,
headbutt my old friend fear,
knee the wide skirts of hope.

LETTER TO IBRAHIM

You remember the joke, right?
About the guy who wanted
to build a future
but ran out of cement,
ran out of bricks, tossed around
by the wheels of fortune,
crushed under the concrete of neglect
like the bird we found
in the middle of a street
downtown, head nodding,
wings barely flapping,
drowning in automobile exhaust.
I held it, felt the warm clay
cooling in my hands.
I could almost see all its flights
returning to nest forever
in the grayness of its down.
You watched me make
a place for it under a tree.
At least it'll die
in the shade, you said.
And death will come
slowly riding the coattails
of a breeze.

It's morning where you live now.
In your room in Leiden,
you're calling friends
in London, Cairo and D.C.
There's a windmill
in the distance. The old woman

whose basement you rent
plants tulips because they,
like the Turk cycling to deliver
fresh milk and cheese,
are predictable, on time.
Your notebooks are crowded
with cob webs and pigeons
and the angels for whom you wait
build houses on the ocean floor.
Half drunk in Tennessee,
I think of you. I'm happy here
laughing at white lies and curses,
running out of bricks, but not embraces.
Listen brother, it's the same everywhere.
We all raise memories like trees
to live under their shadows,
to be sheltered by their magnificent,
leaking roofs.

ELLYN MAYBE (b. 1964)

UMBILICAL CORD

I feel like your umbilical cord
    must be dancing in a seashell
    somewhere off the
    island of lake michigan
    where the coast is clear
    except for memory and icebergs
    and dinosaurs
    who love to walk on water.

you go back to an old time
ancient is the tongue
    that sips lemonade and encyclopedia
    copper and snake
    within the radius
    of architecture and sea.

you know the difference
    between hero and sandwich

between orchards and carmen miranda
between tonsils and gramophone
between spark and scarecrow.

you know where
　　the world's tallest thermometer is
　　and where it isn't.

you know where
　　the singing telegram
　　got a lump in its throat.

you know where
　　the slot machines are
　　that screech with all levers
　　in a permanent outstretched volume.

humans are as dispensable
　　as oranges and cherries
　　in a las vegas of the mindset.

you know the keys to the cities
　　are in the bookstores and the trees.

you know most people
　　threw away their vocal cords
　　along with their butterflies
　　the first time the net was dangled
　　in their cereal and it looked
　　like a mirage above the t.v. trays.

all the dreams of the world
　　get chased around
　　like dogs circling their tales
　　like wedding trains
　　dragging the stomp of idea
　　the clang of blues
　　and the registry
　　of the store of open eyes.

somewhere in the place
　　where goggles protect
　　the pupil from chlorine,
　　where the vision is spared
　　the splinters from flying interference

there should be an eyelid
as big as a heartbeat,
with your wink
and your refusal to sleep.

SHARA MCCALLUM (b. 1972)

CALYPSO

Dese days, I doh even bada combing out mi locks.
Is dread I gone dread now.
Mi nuh stay like dem oda ones, mi luv—
wid mirra an comb,
sunnin demself pon every rock,
lookin man up and down de North Coast.
Tourist season, dem cotch up demself whole time in Negril,
waitin for some fool-fool American,
wid belly white like fish,
fi get lickle rum inna him system an jump in.
An lawd yu should see de grin.
But man can stupid bad, eeh?
I don learn mi lesson long ago
when I was young and craven.
Keep one Greek boy call Odysseus
inna mi cave. Seven years
him croonin in mi ear an him wife nuh see him face.
The two a we was a sight fi envy. I thought
I was goin die in Constant Spring at last
till the day him come to me—
as all men finally do—seyin him tired a play.
Start talkin picknie an home an wife
who can cook an clean. *Hmph.*
Well yu done know how I stay arready, mi love.
I did pack up him bag and sen him back
to dat oda woman same time.
I hear from Mildred down de way
dat de gal did tek him back, too;
him tell her is farce I did farce him fi stay
an she believe the fool. But lawd,
woman can also bline when she please.
Mi fren, I tell yu,

I is too ole for all dis bangarang.
I hear ova Trini way, young man is beatin steel drum,
meking sweet rhyme an callin music by mi name.
Well, dat the only romance I goin give de time a day.
Hmph.

JAMAICA, OCTOBER 18, 1972

You tell me about the rickety truck:
your ride in back among goats or cows—
some animal I can't name now—

the water coming down your legs,
my father beside you, strumming
a slow melody of darkened skies

and winter trees he only dreamed
on his guitar. The night was cool.
That detail you rely on each time

the story is told: the one story
your memory serves us better
than my own. I doubt even that night

you considered me, as I lay inside you,
preparing to be born. So many nights
after it would be the same.

You do not remember anything,
you say, so clearly as that trip:
animal smells, guitar straining for sound,

the water between us becoming a river.

THE PERFECT HEART

I am alone in the garden, separated
from my class. This is what comes
of trying to make the perfect heart.

Scissors: silvery cold and slipping
through my four-year-old fingers.
I did not know and took the harder route,

tried to carve a mirrored mountain top
from each center of the page
after page of red construction paper.

Now, I am counting the frangipani
in bloom. Teacher's words still shriller
than the mockingbird's. My cheeks,

wet and hot from more than heat.
If I had been taught, if
once I had been shown the way,

I would have obeyed—not been
a *spoiled, rude, wasteful little girl.*
Folding the paper in two,
I would have cut away the crescent moon.

IN MY OTHER LIFE,

I was born with a stone in my hand.
My first word was not *muma.*
I learned from early on that *duppy know who to frighten*
and chose carefully.
I learned to *tell the truth an shame the devil,*
to be seen when not heard,
to spell names of places I would someday know
more than my home:
knife an a fork an a bottle and a cork
dats de way yu spell New York;
chicken in de caar and de car caan go,
dats de way yu spell Chicago.
I took cod liver oil with orange juice each morn.
I ate green mangoes and drank peppermint tea for the bellyache.
I stole otahite apples from the market.
My hands would not listen and often took licks.
I showed the boys my panty because they said I wouldn't.
I ate stinkintoe on a dare.
I knelt down in the dirt and made mudpies.
I climbed tamarind trees, banyan trees, even palms.
I walked barefoot and was not afraid to *ketch cold.*
I tried to catch hummingbirds.
I made bracelets, earrings, and rings from flowers.
I was a queen.
I was a mongoose stealing chicks.
I was a goat on a hillside,
sure of the path.

Jeffrey McDaniel (b. 1967)

The Obvious

We didn't deny the obvious,
but we didn't entirely accept it either.
I mean, we said hello to it each morning
in the foyer. We patted its little head
as it made a mess in the backyard,
but we never nurtured it.

Many nights the obvious showed up
at our bedroom door, in its pajamas,
unable to sleep, in need of a hug,
and we just stared at it like an Armenian,
or even worse—hid beneath the covers
and pretended not to hear its tiny sobs.

Leonard

The boy was bright, like the retarded girl
he set on fire. No one predicted
she'd ever be so understood. Death
has a way of making sense out of everything.
Take that mother in New York City
who dragged her daughter down
Avenue B from a '78 Buick's
back fender. Didn't the whole block agree
this was no way to celebrate a birthday?

But who hasn't gotten mad and dreamed
of shining a lit cigarette into someone's ear?
Who hasn't been lonely and fantasized
about covering couples kissing in public
with blankets of kerosene? Like I said,
the boy was bright—perfect scores
on thirty-seven consecutive math tests,
a national chess champ at thirteen—
and Columbus Junior High bored him,

so one Christmas Eve, he set a retarded girl
named Rachel Cleaves on fire
and watched Delancey Street fill with people,
amazed at what they'd done.

PLAY IT AGAIN, SALMONELLA

Watching a man vomit on the sidewalk
is like going back to my alma mater,

where I was voted most likely to secede.

I carried white lies so far they changed
colors. I held tantrums in my pocket

a long time, before I actually threw them.

I was born with dynamite in my chest.
Some days I wish the real me would stand up

and shout *table for ten, por favor!*

I'm an emotional cripple, putting
his best crutch forward. My heart is a child

clutching his breath underwater. I know

these buttons don't control anything,
but I push them anyway and pretend.

I'm a card-carrying member of a canceled party.

The sound of my own head being shaved
is my all-time favorite song.

LOGIC IN THE HOUSE OF SAWED-OFF TELESCOPES

I want to sniff the glue that holds families together.
I was a good boy once.
I listened with three ears.
When I didn't get what I wanted, I never cried.
I banged my head over and over on the kitchen floor.
I sat on a man's lap.
I took his words that tasted like candy.
I want to break something now.

I am the purple lips of a child throwing snowballs at a taxi.
There is an alligator in my closet.
If you make me mad, it will eat you.

I was a good boy once.
I had the most stars in the classroom.
My cheeks erupted with rubies.
I want to break something now.

My bedroom is so dark I feel like an astronaut.
I wish someone would come in and kiss me.
I was a good boy once.
The sweet smelling woman used to say that she loved me
and swing me in her arms like a chandelier.
I want to break something now.

My heart beats like the meanest kid on the school bus.
My brain tightens like a fist.
I was a good boy once.
I didn't steal that kid's homework.
I left a clump of spirit in its place.
I want to break something now.

I can multiply big numbers faster than you can.
I can beat men who smoke cigars at chess.
I was a good boy once.
I brushed my teeth and looked in the mirror.
My mouth was a brilliant wound.
Now it only feels good when it bleeds.

CAMPBELL McGRATH (b. 1962)

SHRIMP BOATS, BILOXI

These wings, these lights, this shoal of angels
sieved against the gulf, gull-bent
arks of the high dusk
waters, arm in arm, rippled and linked
in their slow patrol
and orbit, the fleet, the nets,
the numerals
from which our days evolve,
wave-battered, moon-betrayed, fluid
as silk. Still
the moment

impends. A father and son
are trolling the shallows
for mullet, knee-deep beneath the pillared
dream of the interstate engineers
at neap tide. The black-
jacketed Baptists down from the convention
center for coffee and fried
oysters preach amazing
grace the gospel of life hereafter
as they distribute
refrigerator
magnets, but those who attend
the keening dorsals
are none so
certain, I mean the dolphins'
jeremiad, milky tiger
lilies speaking in tongues, wind-shuck
of the exhausted flocks, oil
rigs and pelicans and harbor-craft
on Mobile Bay, shiver
and rock
of the voyage out,
the journey
in, I mean
the rage of faith,
I mean the light-storm, blind
drunk on the oceanic
surge, I mean
the jerks, the shakes, the waves'
Lupercalia,
the blue seizures
of noon. Sweet
sugar of life
deliver me the means
to fix, grant me the music,
the salt, the song. Vast rapture of this world
bear me with the wings and candles
of your chosen
vessels, number me
among that company,
raise me high upon your darkening
harmony. Tide, wind, spirit
take me up
in these rags of twilight.

AT THE FREUD HILTON

Sturm und Drang narcissus, loose petals
in the windstorm of love: thus the anonymous
supplicants at the bus stop
across from the zoo

wait to see their analysts before work,
patient as jonquils beneath yellow umbrellas,
these brothers and sisters
in loneliness. In tranquil offices they will recall

the stuff of dreams, read the palm
of memory's hand, explore the polar regions
with a rush of self-realization
and the grace to give way

to warmer currents. This is how
the city was built: blueprints and jackhammers,
hard hats eating tuna sandwiches
exist, but only as so much flotsam in the backwash,

it is these galoshes-wearing islands
that form the more than token
archipelago of the resident, grief-stricken
here and now. Egrets,

dawn visions from some wild-eyed goddess of the Euphrates,
rise dimly from the heron house.
Reptiles, small mammals, the greater and lesser
numberings of the swarm.

Commuters gearing up for the day's multifarious
faces, ranks of polished coins, reflections
tossed from window to window
of a passing bus.

LESLIE ANNE MCILROY (b. 1965)

GOOD-BYE, VALENTINE

I have begged the angels
to appear, calling
out through fevered
skies, sins revisited
and halos half-cocked—
I can hear them whispering
that this is only practice.

I have asked them
to come on Sundays
when loneliness
takes its bath,
emerging clean
and vital. Naked,
a little girl, she drips
and picks the scab
from her knee;
like last week
and next week
it bleeds again.

Today Michelangelo
says a prayer,
alone on the scaffolding
high in the air:
when the angels rise—
flushed cheeks
and open jackets—
that he might put away
his red paint
having finished the heart.

HOW TO CHANGE A FLAT

The weather left me raw—
freezing sleet and leaning
wind icing my enthusiasm
for waving someone down.
Someone with a CB or a cell

phone, a jack and solid
work boots; someone
with a hard-on to do
something good,
to get on his knees
and apply his weight
till the lug nuts give
and let go the grip.

I could've faced the storm,
the winter bearing down
like an avalanche of wet
mean dreams; stood out there
with my arms spread wide,
my head bowed against the gusts,
or at least I could've read
the manual, found a flare,
jammed a white rag
in the door. But I'm thinking
it's got to let up soon and what's
the worst that can happen?

It's only 7:00 and I can catch
the news; I can flash my lights
from inside where it's warm,
where just now a shameless
version of Sweet Jane begins
to play, my hand drifting in response—
the slight resistance of the tangled
skirt peeled beneath my coat,
the heel of my palm pressed
flat against my stomach, the first
touch of fingers brushing bare thighs
warm and wet under the frosted,
highway lights. And I have half a tank
of gas—enough to write a letter,
enough to imagine telling you
about sex alone in the front seat,
headlights passing smoothly
across the windshield, the frigid
breath of January melting
from the inside out. How
when the flurry's spent,
mechanics mean so little
and the drive
is only the half of it.

Siesta

I do errands early
on a day this hot,
putting the groceries
away before noon
cutting lemons,
arranged on a
plate like a sun
burst. I wear my wide-
brimmed hat and tip
it back with the first
shot of Cuervo.

In this wooden
chair I read thin
books, the flat boards
of the porch
scorched and dry,
the way I imagine
it is in Arizona
or New Mexico—
there, the heat is un-
beatable and young
men grow skin
like leather to protect,
squinting occasionally
at the horizon
between swallows
of beer.

Now it is two,
and three lemons
are left. The line
of sun cuts the tips
of my toes, makes
my eyes crackle
like thin leaves;
turning the page
(I have finished a chapter)
I find a note
I made in the margin
about forgiving
and rise to brush
the salt from my lap.

PAULA MCLAIN (b. 1965)

RESIDUE

Not such a sad story: the woman wakes to an observation.
She's become a clear needle; thin enough, finally, to pick her own lock.
She takes with her one pair of tight shoes, a light bulb,
a line on her brow for every time she's given birth.
There will be moments of guilt in gas station bathrooms,
but no postcards from Omaha or Orange County: *Wish you were.*
Her daughters still have the polestar, their own freckled noses.
If pressed she would describe the long door closing with a cough
of dust and feathers. Not the seventeen blocks to the station,
strap of her bag spelling a new fate; not the way the fire escapes
sagged with their own weight as if to say *just jump.*
If she's learned anything it's that specifics stir everyone up. Exhaust
leaves enough residue for a sketch of her general shape
in a back window. The bus shifts into full groan, vanishing messily.

BEAUTY, THAT LYING BITCH

Of course what called you was lovely. A girl gone
milky with rain. You could show me now, couldn't you,
just where her glory of hair teased your belly into brushfire?
Or was it evening and her ass the lit crystal of the living moon?
Don't worry, you weren't the first or most foolish. She smiled
(porcelain curl of calla lily) as she told you the rocks
that would slit you like a herring were worth the song,
the fuck so slow and wrung with stars it would scatter you.
Do your research. The siren is bird and beautiful, but also a sea-cow,
a salamander with lungs on its back—wings shriveled as spent sex.
And here you were thinking ugly only got as loud as you let it.

CONNOR IN THE WIND AND RAIN WITH HIS COAT ON

Connor is four and every day brings a clutch
of clouds that shift when we say *elephant, wolf dancing
in a stand of trees, rabbit unpinning his tail again.*
Mornings begin several times before breakfast.
Numbers are still malleable enough to describe
the perfect stick, the way rocks find one another for balance.
His mother wants to blow him words like *Pakistan* and *chamomile*

and *gosling*. His father can become anyone at all. They are able
to forget everything but the way Connor clung to her belly
minutes after he was born, rooting like a sweet newt,
craning to display the small "c" of his marvelous ear,
and they knew they could stop waiting for their lives.

FISHING
Don Palos, California 1979

Two girls on a ditch bank
hang spark plugs with hogfat
and wait—for crawfish, suckerfish,
something to take hold. Brown water
tugs a fist of tarweed downstream. The soil
pebbles under and between them.
Bait stiffens at their feet.

They have touched each other and later
touch themselves thinking of this.
One will marry because she never
knew her mother and cannot believe
she is beautiful. She clutches bitterness
like a dream of missing teeth, does not forgive
even the sky for its slow faults.

The other will find herself lost
in the underside of the tongue
of the first boy who will kiss her,
the way some can never recover
from kindness. But now, see how
her sweet skin could break even the moon's
concentration. Ruin is the evening star
bobbing like a cast hook, the echo
of their earliest question.

WILLING

He says you're a blackberry, dropped into his mouth
by a crow, says *Sweet, sweet girl* to the damp of your neck.
It's afternoon. Through your squint, foxtail splinters,
blonde as the half-slip we fight over in the catalogue,
the demi-cup bra, satin-strapped and less candid
than this boy's hands. He'd wear you like skin if you'd let him.

He says locusts told him where to find you,
that your blue dress is plenty deep for two;
and you're starting to trust the muscle
all this wanting gives you. Your shoulders come back
when a car full of boys rockets by on the two-lane, pulling dust
and a long howl. All the way out to the interstate,
they talk about turning around.

Now your arm is beside you, bent, like a page you'll return to.
He says *Listen*, then stops talking. What comes next isn't news:
his sudden flush and bloom. Then the cell-like splitting
of this day into two, four, eight identical others.

I pass the shape you've tamped into the grass.
It looks like an animal has circled before sleeping. I lie down,
willing anything: a ripple, rain. I lick my hand.
There is no tinge of blackberry, no hint of what's coming.

MARK McMORRIS (b. 1960)

THE NEAR SPEECH

Fingers over the hedge, you move around
the countryside like a breeze pushing a kite
or leaves rolling or grass spit back from
a mower's walk during the spring months.
Thus, in small glimpses, the phonemes
change over from mouth to exist, as I
listen to your talk in one shelter
and you receive words like a seed or a thread
the yard comes clear in which we stand
and meaning goes up goes down like a rumor
to give blood and sanctuary out of itself:
consubstantial face of speech and delivery
a nothing til it voices, nothing to decipher,
relatives of source taking over the country
under buds of the tongue at the inside of words
that issue in us, now recognized, now sent
obscurely to earth or under to the roots of pulse,
the beat of a drum making sense with the masks
of hair, oil paint, and wood, of the grimace
that means our shock. More to come in figures

elsewhere stored and brought up on charges
arranged to divide as one from another
the chapter begins with once upon a word
how you come to me from the coast
to the gap by using our speech like a wave
and what you say means just that signal
of a string drawn tight, erased to be reformed,
a place for me to breathe in the way
that I breathed from your mouth, and then again,
the rumor comes to an end, at the hedge.

EVENING

The pictures come striding into the room.
The girls wear dresses; boys in the plum trees.
The men ride horses deep into the woods
That circle the field like a child's promise.

The women do not pick flowers. They beat
Wet clothes on flat stones by the river.
At times these women sing, and their voices
Flow with the gleaming river to the bend.

An old man ties his mule to the hillside
And wedges each rubber boot to the earth
And climbs the track with the sun behind him.
The boys run barefoot, tumbling down the slope.

Candle shadows on teak mantels at dusk.
The lanterns hung beneath the lignum eaves
Will glow like beacons across the valley.
The river grows loud in the fading light.

And comes a wake: the valley is mourning.
And comes a cry: the valley is ringing.
Tomorrow has its own rows, like a field.
Night passes like Sundays and evening breeze.

CONSTANCE MERRITT (b. 1966)

THE MUTE SWAN

White silence on the water pulls me in and under. And I know it
is a lady.

The impossibility of naming her desire has kept her white and
beautiful, while she has kept our secrets. She holds them deep within
the throat of her graceful neck, and it is hard to say whether, when she
bows her head, she is praying to take voice or to go on giving silence.

It is also hard to say whether hers is the silence of before speaking
or after. Almost as hard as saying nothing.

WOMAN OF COLOR

The splendid coat that wrapped the favored son
In fevered dreams of adulation
And turned his brothers' hearts from jealousy
To rage (*Behold, this dreamer comes.*)—though long
Since rent and soaked in blood, dried and decomposed—
Arrives through the long centuries over
Sea and land, the unexpected birthright
Of this particular girl. Its separate
Magic beads and threads spill onto the floor
Indistinguishable from alphabet
Blocks, the many pieces of her country,
And its citizens loud and teeming from
Their cramped Crayola crayon box. Each state,
Each letter has a color, a shape, its own,
Soft curves and sharp angles, compassionate
Contours promising something not hers to keep,
An abundance utterly unasked for and
Nearly impossible to give. *What is*
This dream that thou hast dreamed? Shall I and thy
Mother and thy brethren indeed come
To bow down ourselves to thee to the earth?

It is loneliness that bows her head, that breaks
Her free from silence's sweet spell, spilling
Her voice onto the brittle air, breathless
In its rush: green of sea, pine, forest, spring;
Blue of midnight, cerulean, cornflower;
Sky, navy, cadet, and royal blue; blue

Violet, turquoise, aquamarine; teal blue,
Blue green, periwinkle; burnt and raw
Sienna, bittersweet, brick and in-
Dian red, goldenrod and thistle, white.
And exile enters here, the lull and pull
Of distance between the voice's deepest source
And its unmappable destinations.
And they sat down to eat bread and they lifted
Up their eyes and looked, and, behold, a company
Of Ishmaelites came from Gilead with
Their camels bearing spicery and balm
And myrrh going to carry it down to
Egypt. And Judah said, what profit is it
If we slay our brother and conceal his blood?
Let us sell him for he is our brother and our flesh.

For her there is no Egypt to seduce
With strange, mad song, no famished countrymen
Falling to their knees and near enough
To make her tremble afraid she will be tender
Instead of stern. Instead there is only
This brilliant coat, a gift of love, that leaves
Her vulnerable to cold and knowing eyes
Until it seems she has no skin at all
Except for silence, except the weave of words:
Hound's-tooth, gingham, tulle, eyelet, chambray;
Broad-cloth, denim, paisley, linen, wool.
Her dreams grow full of birdsong; each bird says
Its name: Cardinalis Cardinalis,
Anas Carolinensis, Cyanthus
Latirostris, Mimus Polyglottos,
Cyanocitta Stelleri, Agelaius
Phoenecius—over and over,
Until finally, sure it's meant for her,
She gently stirs the waters' smooth bright skin,
And bursting from the deep into the world,
Its fear, its hurt, its roar; she tries her tongue.

LULLABY

Say to me: out there are only streets, and cars
Are only cars, and childhood lessons of
Both ways will never fail you now. I'd listen
Even if you whispered, strain my ears to hear

The way I silence other voices.
Random ones. I told you of the child.
How when she slept in her crib I could hear
Her crying everywhere—in noises the
House made, in heat and running water, even
Inside the breath of early morning,
My breath, the crying of this child not even
Mine, and she so peacefully asleep.

I can shut my lids on angels, bite my tongue,
Withhold my breath, swallow unbidden words
Before they form. But how to stop my ears?
I can't resist the charm that distance holds:
The silence of a street minutes before
I cross into the constant flow of traffic,
Or sobs that I hear buried in the laughter
Of a girl that make me wait above my book
In terror. As if she had no friends, had need
Of my concern. What is this love I'd heap
Upon the world like blankets unasked for?
And by what right do I stand eavesdropping here?

MALENA MÖRLING (b. 1965)

IN A MOTEL ROOM AT DAWN

Now the air is visible again, floating
through the room
like a liquid, like water
washing over the ruined furniture.
And washing also over my head
here on this pillow, here where many
other heads have rested
their orbits of thoughts
and slept or stayed awake listening
to the motorcycle riders rev their engines.
But now they are silent.
Now I hear only the wind suffering
in some shaft. When we die
will the thoughts stop coming,
stop telling us what to do
next? Before you took

your own life, did you think
"now I will never see the sky"
or "now I have done all the dishes
I will ever do?"
Did you say "now my shoes will forget
how heavy I was" or "now. . . ?"
Now everything is where it was left.
On the front desk the ledger lies open
showing the names of the guests
in the elaborate handwriting
of the clerk, and what it costs to sleep.
And now the maps of the earth
are resting folded
in the darkness of glove compartments,
all the arbitrary borders touching.

FOR THE WOMAN WITH THE RADIO

Everywhere we are either moving away from
        or toward one another,
in cars, on buses or bicycles.

        We are either moving
or not moving. But yesterday in one
        of the interminable hallways of the hospital

I suddenly heard Bach
        and when I looked up
the music was arcing

    about the paralyzed, middle-aged body
of a woman rolling face first toward me
        on a bed with wheels

The soprano was endlessly falling
    into the well
of her voice and we were on the earth

        and this was this life
when we would meet
    and depart there in the hall

where the hectic dust particles were mixing
        in the sunlight
in the air, between the green tiles on the walls.

For F.M. Who Did Not Get Killed Yesterday on 57th Street

When they shot you,
you did not become a stone or a tree,
you did not become lake water
or the unwieldy shadow of a cloud.
You darted like a fish
through the hole the bullet made in the air.
You became air,
refusing to thicken, refusing to talk back
or move unless the wind moved
as it does now through the elms
and the ailanthus. Today I can hear
the ocean at the end of the block
tossing itself up on the beach,
the sound of it has entered everything in the house,
even the thimbles in the drawers.

Three-Card Monte

It is Easter.
The last flurries
fall on the ink tongue
of the river;
behind Horatio street,
the hookers freeze
in their mini-skirts.

"To purify the spirit
we must mortify the flesh."
That is why
alone in the pre-dawn-dark
of the pantry
you poured the hot wax
on your skin.

I saw the Three-
Card Monte dealer
shot
through the heart.
The quick hands,
the entire sneaky body
collapsed

on the sidewalk
though the traffic
continued
uptown
and crosstown,
and the mannequins
grinned above him
in their long
urine-colored coats.

JULIE MOULDS (b. 1962)

WHEN BAD ANGELS LOVE WOMEN

When the bad angel loves
the woman next door,
the motion wakes me.
The tip of one of his
purple-veined wings
moves right through our walls.
It lifts and falls
as the two of them, a wind
like blue leather pulsing
through this house.
She packs cartons
of eggs like I do, during days,
with other women and boys
on a line. But home,
there is this angel.
His kiss, like a scorpion's,
marks her now, and suddenly
I have seen her tilting
out of time. When her
night voice winds
like a blue leather wind,
I know he is there.
she goes to him now
and he eats her
like a young apple,
the way men eat a woman

in a dark alley
until she is gone.
One day, he is with her always
his windy presence
rolling the eggs
from our cartons.
The ladies and I are tired
of all this breaking;
tired of seeing dollar-sized
bites disappear
from her neck. She
is the color of blueberries
on cheesecloth.
Antlers or the bones
of wings break her back.
Luminescent, like blue neon,
she tries to fill her cartons,
but the eggs
slip through her hands.
I could hear him each night
eat her soul,
I say to the ladies on the line
the day she disappears.
The whole house could hear
while we stacked
our wet plates,
his giant wings spreading
like a fan.

LATE SUMMER LITANY

My neighbor's almost ex-husband, an auto salesman with a different car each week, is over to visit his son, a lively bear cub of a boy. The man only comes over with electric prodding, to his son's delight. In the former's defense, the man cannot help that he enjoys golf more than small boys. His two daughters from another marriage live in Maine and do not demand much of him. He says marriage has bit him in the ass two times and he has learned his lesson. My neighbor upstairs grieves, as anyone would, at their failure. She remembers the charm he had ten percent of the time. I sit on my concrete steps, drinking cold rum, watching the boy enter another new car. The crickets and the birds keep repeating, *we don't change, we don't change,* and the fireflies turn on and off like love.

Renoir's Bathers

What is it about women in water
that almost makes them part of the landscape?
Renoir's bathers, pink and mustard
and vaguely nippled; their ample thighs
rising from a purple river in a scene
centered by one brown tree. What is it
about women, painted by men,
that they become landscapes, creamy roses
in a garden? In another age,
when people could still sleep
with almost anyone, my sister and I dipped
ourselves naked in a Michigan lake, both of us,
still, miraculously, virgins.
I suppose some painter in that art colony
where Brenda washed dishes
could have captured us, like Renoir,
two flowers with leafy thighs and brown
daisy faces. Perhaps he would accent
our round hymens with petals. I want to be
the woman, with her brush, sitting in an oak
above a pond where twelve nude men are frolicking.
She is painting a landscape of men:
lying flat with grapes above their open mouths;
men, with buttocks turned towards her; men,
with arms arched behind their long necks.
She would call it *The Dozen Adonae*. Pink
chrysanthemum men; dark, magnolia men;
legs spread, organs rising or fallen,
depending on your eyes. In another time,
in a deserted field, I lay naked as a lover
wrapped me in oil. I must have even walked
through high grass, and, knowing me, worried
about where bugs could enter.
Insects never crawl up the legs
in the paintings of the three Graces.
In those landscapes of the masculine
dream, men want to paint us perfect,
from a distance, then break petals,
like a cloud or a swan.

RICK MULKEY (b. 1963)

BLIND-SIDED

> *"Only one person is known to have been hit by*
> *a meteorite. On November 30, 1954, Mrs. E. H. Hodges*
> *of Sylacauga, Alabama, was sitting in her house after*
> *lunch when a 9-pound stone crashed through the roof*
> *and hit her on the thigh."*

> —Walter Sullivan, *We Are Not Alone*

Nine years and three days later I drop to the earth
with considerably less speed, but with as great
an impact (and don't we all want to believe
we've made some mark, a crater of significance
we call our own), or at least that's how my mother tells it.
And she lived to tell about it, as did Mrs. Hodges,
once she recovered from the shock, the thrill
of coming as close to the eternal universe, eternally,
as a few inches. But isn't that always the way.
One moment we are minding our own business,
wandering about in our lives, no apparent course,
the next we're changing diapers, rolling them into
a meteoric knot and hurling them into the pail.
Or, as with my friend J., we're finishing
our lunch when out of nowhere a wife stiffens in her seat
and looks across the room. There's nothing there,
but still she looks, hoping that the words will fall
from the heavens. There is no easy way
to say it, so she leans into the table
and without apology says she's had enough,
that it's her turn to find herself, that the monotonous
orbit she's been forced into won't do. Her tight, stony fists
hang in her lap. Silences stretch light years,
and all the feeble attempts at reconciliation
will never reach her now. It's all the same feeling
as when Mark Preston blind-sided me,
stone-hard knuckles snapped the ridge of my nose,
a stream of blood flared into the parking lot.
Some other kid might have swung back, but I was horrified
at the pool filling my palm. My blood,
I repeated to myself as I sat there
quietly while a friend finished off the guy I believed
was trying to finish me. He never knew what hit him.
Nor did Mrs. Hodges until they calmed her, medicated

her from a pain that wouldn't end. Years later she'd wake
to the fiery ache in her leg, a reminder of what she'd
been and what she'd become, survival's gravity
twisting her life into one deep breath, like the first breath
that coughs up the phlegm of another world and deposits
it right here in this one where all around us stars
flare into bits of battered stone, and the universe
leaves each of us alone to explode in all directions.

Why I Believe in Angels

Because I've seen their musculature joined
hip to hip in parked cars, their bones,
under the glisten of skin, twisting into flight.
Because I've seen them rock through one another
in that oldest of nights, in that moonless hour of clarity
when the field mouse briefly turns its head from danger
and only a wingbeat marks its passing.

Because I've heard them speak in tongues
in late night bars as their bodies writhed
in the stage's strobed light. Because I've seen
their breasts encircled in the incense of cigarette,
and I've held their heart's beating planchette and deciphered
scribbled prophecies on back-alley walls and discovered
their words, like ours, are mere ticks on a clock.

Because I believe the quark and lepton that leap from lovers' mouths
were once part of a rotting branch on Centauri Prime,
and because I wake at night full of a past compressed beside me,
and voices of friends whose wives left or husbands cheated,
who, faced with such truths, are certain they didn't know:
"I stood there," they confess, "though someone else possessed my body."
Then all I can imagine are the unpaid bills a life accumulates,
the voracious guilts and minor misdemeanors, the interpenetration
of morphogenetic fields that allows the rat in Seattle to convey
the way through the maze to a rat in Boston to the rat inside my head,
and because I can't ignore these signs, because I can't ignore,
I find, without looking or understanding, my wife's hands,
or my son's hands, crossed upon my chest,
and there like two wings they've ended their journey.

MAGGIE NELSON (b. 1973)

56 WESTERVELT

We sat
in big
chairs
in front
of the
steeple
and the
sodden
street
curled
up in
morning
and in
love.

Before
character
sealed
fate,
magic
was simply
the un–
shakeable
belief
that
magic
would
happen
to us.

SHINER

I wake up growling apples and dirt
naked and stretched under a barn sky
I cannot recall how I hurt my right eye

Arch of vessels gone grape under the lid
An army of red ants, a cast of shadows.
Good God. My eye has gone weak. Simply

put, I walked into an opening door.
The world is constantly changing shape
very dangerous. Two desert tortoises

duke it out on Arizona soil. By morning
one's always left belly-up to boil.
Now you roll around with a rock

and see what kind of bruise *you* can muster
Dolefulness, caprice, regret, trauma
My bicycle has two seats get on

WISH

What kind of pain is it
that has nothing to teach?

I sit around all day
burning things.

Then ask you kindly
Lay me down among the persimmons

and fear itself.

MOTEL STORY

We were in the middle of something big.
The United States, for example. I
was in a new bed in a new room. We
had a key, something to misplace and find.
All night we had heard a banging next door,
of intimacy or imprisonment.
You coughed and I ripped psalms from the Bible.
We bled all over. The blood did not move
far. It clung to the drain, towels, tissues.
In the morning I watched you in the lot
pulling a suitcase from the trunk, half-dressed.
In my dream we stay alive. In my dream
we stay together. Outside in the lot
your half-dressed flesh moves like weather.

RICK NOGUCHI (b. 1967)

THE TURN OF PRIVACY

Kenji Takezo feels everybody
Watching him,
It is the biggest wave all day.
On a shortboard, he stands,
Cuts left.
Instead of doing the quick
Vertical maneuvers
Expected of him,
He borrows an old trick,
Makes it his.

He drops around his ankles
The trunks
His mother bought him
Last year for his birthday,
Exposing his private
Skin tone, the same color
Under his wristwatch.

The trunks at his ankles
Lose their purpose and become
Something else. Cuffs, binders,
Keeping his feet
Together, Siamese twins.
He cannot take the stance
Which would give him
The balance,
Enough to ride the wave's length.
He falls.

During the tumble, the wash of ocean,
The trunks are lost,
His feet twisting out of them,
Talents of an escape artist
He never practiced, never dreamed.
A sleight of the hand, a sleight of foot,
That surprises him.

The crowd, laughing,

Waits to cheer him.
But Kenji stays in the shallows
Planning his next trick.
He makes the best of it,
Paddles back out,
Catches another wave, then another,
Until the crowd grows
Tired of him and forgets.

His Wave

The retired man showed the town
The perfect wave
He kept
Inside a bottle.
He turned it continually
Back on itself so the water
Broke over and again, never resting.
He told also
The story
How it was captured.
All at no cost.
With each telling the wave
Grew big then bigger
Until finally it no longer fit.
He had to buy large and larger
Bottles that would hold
His growing wave.
When it became too big
And he could find no bottle
To store it, he had a tank
Installed in the yard.
Now when he tells of its capture
Nobody believes him.
Now he is the town's
Crazy man
Who spends too much time,
Gets too much sun
Next to the swimming pool
He never swims in.

NOT SURFING SOME DAYS

Inside the empty chamber of a wave is the same
Sound a child memorizes
Hiding, dusk, in the green heaven above
His house. Madness calming
The sky while a slight offshore breeze gives
Breath to a paper wind carp.
Hungry, its aperture is round, the letter O,
Open the way a folding comber forms a mouth.

The parents of that child sip a bitter tea.
Their lips tight, they wonder why
He sits so often in the puzzle elm—
Never fitting the pieces together.
He's lost in concentration
Riding the ocean he remembers, feels
Surging through his veins,
Currents from a ground swell miles away.

Through a back window, he sees
The two in the living room watching television.
Silence resting between them.
Their thoughts washed by the drone of voices.
When the streetlamps flicker on
The son climbs out of the tree,
Returns home. His mother has fixed for him
A scoop of orange sorbet.

He lets it stay in the blue ceramic bowl.

JENNIFER O'GRADY (b. 1963)

POEM FOR THE WOMB

A room sometimes vacant, sometimes engaged. A red-light district, just
before the flood. *Cinnabar, cherry, post-office red.* He wore her like a glove;
she fitted him like a shoe. In the spill of lamplight he laid her down: it
was touch and go, no sooner said than done. *Moonstone, ruby, incarnadine.*
She'd consult her pillow; sleep on it. *Red lake, madder, flame red, rust.* Red
leaves mean change, little flares of loss. *Ink, tape, blood cell, breast.* A
flowing confession signed in haste. Loose fist; used envelope; abandoned
nest.

Anonymous Wedding Photo

First, Plaintiff contracted with Defendant

    in the beginning there was light

Within several weeks, numerous
defects began to emerge

    fixed and unwavering
    frozen forever on this surface

Defendant agreed to replace

    the woman positioned on a wooden chair

Plaintiff attempted to arrange delivery
on numerous occasions

    the man upright beside her, his hands
    hidden behind his back

Defendant chose to ignore

    the paper still clean, uncreased
    like a bed no one has slept in

These representations constituted
representations of fact

    despite the fidelity of detail
    dense wings of mustache

Plaintiff reasonably relied on Defendant's
misrepresentations and omissions

    the constant eclipse of her shawl

Plaintiff agreed to pay

    the shared silence that will always suggest
    failure or refusal

In the apparent belief that Plaintiff
would abandon hope of obtaining

all we can know about them is that
this moment, like each other, passed

As a direct or proximate result of
such breaches, Plaintiff has suffered damage

lost yet undissolvable
as figures caught beneath ice

Again, none of these messages
was ever returned

someone told them to look at the light
someone told them to smile

BUSTER'S LAST HAND

He spent the last afternoon of his life playing bridge.
—Mrs. Buster Keaton

It's '66 and Keaton's playing
bridge with his wife and a young couple
who look like anyone's neighbors, but are really
quite famous. Now he's forgotten
their names, and he's tired and bored from so much
coughing that shakes him like laughter.
In the kitchen, his wife makes a kettle scream.

Somebody deals. Keaton orders his cards—
a shifting of thumb-worn frames from which
the one-eyed jack stares blankly out.
Keaton leads and he lays down a heart,
pretending it's stuck to his palm. Pale
starlets titter politely. His wife smiles.
As usual, Keaton says nothing.

Outside the picture window, the weightless
snow falls, white and useless, creating
a spectacle of itself—ageless
brilliance without color or sound.
But it's California. It won't last.
Small buds scrape the sky, and already
the boy next door is out there with a shovel.

JOE OSTERHAUS (b. 1960)

GAMBIER

A thought about *my* place in the long war
the intellectuals and poets fought
to a standstill in 1944;

the shooting war continuing full force,
life as we all know it half on hold;
gas, sugar, eggs, and butter scarce,

wardens pacing the alleyways at night
checking for escaping light, their cards
showing the blue silhouettes of airplanes;

who had to bear the possibility
of dying in the street, and at all costs avoid
being seen against the grey wash of the Thames.

Against this backdrop the new critics fought
for subjects not respected up till then;
one sees it in their pictures, the tense nights

spent poring over Tennyson or Donne,
mayflies buzzing at the copper lamp,
the pocked moon shining over a field

in Iowa, Ohio, Michigan.
And if indeed they won, what was the yield;
a way of living deep within the line?

When I look at one old picture, taken
in Gambier one summer night, my only thought
is God, that Nancy Tate was beautiful;

if I'd been there, I surely would have been
flirting over the potato salad,
knowing yet again that I'd confused

the beautiful with something like success,
yet unable to stop; my awkwardness
my only contribution to the night.

And there, in the dusk beneath the catalpa,
Berryman looking sly, Lowell assured,
while Tate recites the catalog of ships.

New York Minute

Save that the curtains, drawn
and held by jagged darts
arrest the light with flecks of gold
the music, when it starts,

pours through our hero's penthouse suite
so unexpectedly
he starts to tap dance, while, downstairs,
creased, but fresh and coy,

our heroine sits up in bed
and glares into the dark,
still not prepared to talk to him,
but angered by his joke.

Our hero slows mid-step in thought,
dashes into the hall,
and, lifting an ashtray in his arms,
both bowl and pedestal,

swings it back into his room
where, cued at the end of the bar,
he pours its cache of fine white sand
across the polished floor,

then does a soft-shoe, carefully
sweeping his outstretched feet
through the fine white sand, that brush and glide
freshening the beat

until, downstairs, she smiles; the notes,
diminishing, converge;
and she falls back on her pillow, launched
on sleep's transparent barge.

FRANKIE PAINO (b. 1960)

THE TRUTH

My father died near evening, having spent
most of the day straining towards that closure.
In the end, I watched the monitor count down
the beats of his heart's surrender, his eyes
fixed on nothing I could see, though I'd like to believe
he was looking *at* something, his own father, say,
coming to show him the path into a different world.

I never knew dying could take such effort, as if Death,
at the last, pulls back his outstretched hand
and we must chase after the shroud of his dark wings.
All day I'd held my father's hand, leaned over
his thin form the way I remember he'd leaned over my bed
when I was a child. I ran my fingers through his fine, black
hair, matching my breath to the respirator's hiss—

as if desire alone could save him. The truth is,
I wanted nothing more than a flat line on the screen,
the steady hum which means the heart has lost its music,
blood going cool and blue in the veins. I wanted
it to be the way that cliché goes, the one which says
we don't die, really, we just go to sleep. But his heart
refused romantic notions, hammering an unsteady beat

hours after I told the doctor to disengage the machine
which kept the pulse constant against his body's will.
I started to write how his muscles, deprived of oxygen,
rippled like the smooth flanks of horses in the home stretch,
that graceful and sure, but it's a lie—the truth is,
the spasms were strong enough to make our own hearts
quicken, our arms strain as his head slipped over the pillow,

his legs quivering, pitiful. I wanted to tell you I saw
a boy, slight and beautiful, leaning against the waiting room
door, his right shoulder transparent, half in, half out
of the dark oak grain, as if he wanted me to see there is a life
beyond the one we know. But that, too, would be a lie.
The truth is, that room was empty except for the boys on t.v.,
the ones in Soweto who doused a man with gasoline, set him

alight, his head engulfed in flame like an infernal nimbus,
fire folding its terrible arms around him as he fell
to the ground, silent as snow. When my father died
the sun was just beginning to set. Friday. High summer.
Though I couldn't see them from the tight, dim room, I knew
cars crowded the streets, everyone anxious to get home where,
perhaps, someone else waited. Or maybe it was just solitude

they rushed toward. I didn't begrudge them such happiness,
but blessed their ignorance as they squinted against the light,
cursed the grass, too long to be ignored, and the mailbox
with its freight of bills, news, catalogues which promised
to satisfy any desire. Standing by my father's bed, I needed
him to live because my own heart was breaking. The truth is,
we never have all we need. I came to understand how my hand

grasping his must have made him hesitate between two
worlds, the way a child learning to swim glances from
a parent's hand to the pool's blue-green shimmer, then back
again, or maybe the way I hope those boys in Soweto paused
before they turned toward their neighbor, small fires
in their palms fingering air. My father moved his head
against his shoulder as if, already, he were looking back

at us from some vast distance. Perhaps Death is more timid than we
imagine, slipping off the soul the way love might begin
with the shy undoing of an evening gown. I held on to my
father's feet—how elegant they were, even then, like the feet
of a Bernini seraph, sleek, cool, too perfect to believe
they'd carried him through the world so long, and finally,
to that bed. I didn't want to hold him back but, if

such a thing is possible, to push his spirit out
through the crown of his head, give him the power to rise
from that body, its twisted spine, thighs thin, hollow, ready
for flight, and the cancer we'd measured in the deliberate
spreading of red, mottled skin like a map being drawn in front
of our eyes. What world, I wonder, did it describe?
We talked about the times my sister and I went with him

after bluegill, grayling, bass—the week in Canada
we didn't catch a thing, the evenings loons would cry
across still water while we sat around a fire,
our faces amber, otherworldly in that light. It must have
been those memories which gave him strength to move
towards that other shore which only the dead can know,
where perhaps he rose from dark waters deep as sleep

and remembered this life as a dream. In his room the monitor
pushed an incandescent line across its screen as if to
underscore morality. A nurse removed the needles, the tube
which ran like a tap root into the sweet cave of my father's
chest. His mouth, open, filled with the machine's emerald glow,
as if the tongue he now spoke were a language of light. Sometimes
we have nothing to grasp but such implausible fire. Just that.

A MATTER OF DIVISION

At the last moment, they said, my cousin held
    her arms out to emptiness, whispered something
        like *Thank you.* The leaves were falling,

still green enough to bruise with the crescents
    of my nails. And it was warm. I don't remember
        much more about that day. I'd spent the morning

on our front steps, my father's magnifying glass
    a weapon I used to incinerate ants, leaves, the delicate
        web of flesh between thumb and index finger.

I'd watched Angela's body devour itself
    for years, hollow stomach pushing toward the spine,
        her eyes iridescent from fever. They pumped radiation

into her until hair fell out in handfuls
    and her voice was nothing but sawdust and sand.
        I might not have remembered this, except for

the magnifying glass, how it shattered in my hand
    perhaps at the instant my cousin was swallowed
        by whatever light or darkness takes the dead.

I couldn't say. I held, a moment, web,
    sun, burning leaf—fragments of fragile mosaic
        which crumbled when I squeezed the metal frame,

buried slivers like secrets in my palm.
    And though I can't be certain, I believe
        in the end it's simply a matter of division,

what we leave and what goes with us, which is us,
    rising toward a light that beautiful.

1965

(For Gerrie)

Those mornings were thick with Benedictine incense,
the priest's movements languid in the heat,
better than a dream, his robes incongruously fluid,
airy in their bright embroidery. The sun set fire
to the stained glass of my favourite window,
Lucifer's proud falling, and washed the walls in crimson,
violet and gold. Sr. Jerome would sit between us,
her black serge habit a curtain meant to divide
us, twin sisters, and force our eyes towards the altar
where a ruby arc of wine spilled into the chalice
and figures of saints wavered in shadows
like spirits taking form from darkness.

Jesus hung before us in cold white marble,
so peaceful in death he could have been any man
stretching after a long sleep except for the nails
in his hands and feet. His eyes were sealed,
as if God meant to turn away from this handful of children
shifting in the pews, bored with his familiar miracle.
I was more interested in the candlelight
flashing off your crystal rosary,
the way your hands fluttered through smoky air,

and the window where Lucifer shook his fist,
toes breaking the surface of a smouldering lake
while St. Michael sheathed his sword of flames.
And Sr. Jerome would be clucking, a nervous sound
she made with her tongue when the two of us would glimpse
each other and laugh. It was as if she understood the mystery
in our mirror faces, knew about the game we'd play at night,
our pajamas scattered across the bedroom floor.

I was always Lucifer, and you'd be one of God's
faithful, your hair a helmet of wings. We'd hurl
our bodies, shapeless as boys', against each other
in the amber glow of the nightlight. Our battles
were fiercely sexual, though we wanted only the pleasure
of skin on skin as night pulled toward morning,

toward the brick walls of St. Angela's
sweating in the heat, Sr. Jerome's eyes dull with panic
when you fainted, your head thudding against terrazzo,

a hairline of blood unsmoothing your cheek,
while the priest raised the wafer and I smiled, knelt
beside you, pressed my lips to that warmth,
taste of blood on my tongue tangy as salt, sweet as sin.

ALAN MICHAEL PARKER (b. 1961)

LULLABY

Sleep and rain, two gangsters.
The day lined up, a murder of crows
on a telephone wire and still
the current runs. I would sleep
but dream of waking; rise
to walk the feed-corn field,
lashed by wind, stalk and silk
leaning as if to listen.
Listen. Sleep and rain,
two moles. Nose to nose
in the city of the mad plumber,
where each has the right of way.
Tomorrow's in the trees, an air-
brawl of starlings, a riot of leaves,
the sun in its music box where it sings
to itself. Sleep and rain,
two ladies in a hat store. And home
to tea in the library, to read
the novel of each other's palm
and dress for dinner. Night
steeps in the flower vase, succulent
in the lilac's hundred fists.
Sleep and rain, two dancers on a cliff.
I would sleep but for the rain.

MAGPIE

I.
So terrible a scold above the squat adobe,
the borrowed house and bed, the preposterous
bulimic cats. Ugly bird on the roof
above the blue Mexican water glass

rocking on the rickety nightstand.
Magpie, clamor and kin, the world lolls
upended, for the woman I love
is sad, and showering again.

II.
Cut into a mesa sits the little soul's hut:
little table, plastic plate, bag lunch,
and Sunday's news. Where possession of
the good takes a form of beauty,

and the hermit who can bend the light
around his shimmering hand
sleeps in a chair. Magpie, stubborn
as a muse, where do you hide?

III.
Particle and wave, ball and chain,
the body tethered to the body.
A magpie flies in the empty, crooked
palace of the sky, as everything

falls west with everything we say,
sliding into hieroglyph
sidelong as a coachwhip snake,
sibilant and obsolete.

IV.
Of appetite, and what I know
cannot be mine. Of indiscriminance.
Of the magpie on the roof, who will eat
what there is, and in whose call

our lives are satirized.
The woman I love dries her hair,
leaning into a towel, persistent
as a wish, in this borrowed house.

ALCHEMY

On the first good day of yard work
winter pours from my body,
soaks my shirt with its brine.

Out of storage, window screens fleck the lawn

like great farms seen from the air.
My fingers wriggle in new workgloves,
itching to do a little digging, to join
the earthworm's long, dark translation of the world.

On the stoop by the porch, a locust has left
a carapace intact, a good idea of himself.
In his kingdom, what's done
in the name of introspection
can often be a curse.

A lone toad hops on into town, passes Big Man,
knocks back a gnat, and goes underground.

Here for a moment, mine
is a small lot: I only
turn the soil, and often
fail to recognize what I uncover.

In light of the crocuses,
in their still-blooms,
the garden begins as
a patch of dirt:
anything can happen.

ABOVE THE TIMBERLINE

The impossible truth: I asked God
for a pair of gloves
and there they were, proving
nothing. In the immense emptiness.
The horizon in my head.

We need new rules. Waiter,
some new rules please.
I clap my hands
and the air claps back.

Life is furious. Thin breath
whistles in my chest.
The body knows another language
altogether; we embarrass each other
with our own ideas.

There are no trees here,
nothing against the sky.
I believe
but I don't know how.

G. E. PATTERSON (b. 1960)

LETTER FROM HOME

Aside from rain, the weather stays the same.
The sky is never anything but blue
or gray. The dogs in the yard of the house
on the corner still bark at everyone
who goes by. Mrs. Jones' high yellow boy,
you remember, barks back, when folks are out.

If you're missing quiet, this is the place
where it's resting. You're sure welcome to come
join it. It's been so long since you've been home
you'd be surprised at what's changed, what hasn't.
You could pretend it's someplace new. You could
pretend you were a stranger, just passing.
I'd play along, treat you like some nice man
who got lost and needed new directions.
I'd let you in so you could use the phone,
fix you some lemonade and a sandwich.

If you visit we can play that game. (Smile.)

AUTOBIOGRAPHY OF A BLACK MAN

> *Who has not*
> *On occasion entertained the presence*
> *Of a blackman?*
> — Raymond Patterson

All the ladies feeling lucky at love
ask me if I like jazz, want to go out
and kick it at some club they know. I nod,
being a man who never disappoints.
Every white man I've known has wanted me
to join his basketball team, softball league

or book-discussion group. They invite me
on week-long, fly-fishing trips to Montana.
One day I might say yes. They think
they admire my superb athletic skills
and my broad education, but it's nothing
more than my color. I am The Black Man
the whole world mythologizes and envies.
I can get cats to march like boot-camp soldiers.
No dog ever dares ignore what I say—
sit up, fetch, play dead—the whole fucking routine.
Even New York roaches know to behave,
scurrying and hiding when I say, *Scat!*
I'm big and too damn powerful. The boss
on the job gulps hard and fast while I piss
into the cracked urinal. His hand shakes
as he follows me out, making small talk.
I will appear in his dreams 'til he's dead.
Black brothers, too, hurt themselves to get near me,
like crabs trying to climb out of a bucket.
The Latinos up in Harlem yell, *Jesus!*
when they see me. They fall down on their knees.
Am I the Messiah? Might be. Might be.
Koreans behind fruit stands bow their heads,
treating me like a Buddha. That's alright. Let 'em.
My father wants us to be better friends
as if father and son weren't close enough.
My mother loves me more now than before,
since I grew up and became a Black man.
I'm twenty-three, and I'm king of this world.
Everyone fears and worships me. I know
I'm the motherfucking object of envy.
I'm the be-all and end-all of this world.

LAMENT
Hades

I would like to undo it, to take back
The flower, the red seeds, the words I said—
Alter time in an instant—if I could,
If that would put an end to all the talk.

The talk is mostly women laying blame,
Telling the world how badly I behaved,
Telling lies, claiming the woman I loved
Was wronged the moment I whispered her name.

As if mistakes are not always how things end,
As if anyone could stop things going wrong.
As if I made more trouble than love that spring,
Made a new misery and unleashed an old.

I carried her happy into my home
—Such an ordinary start to my shame.

V. Penelope Pelizzon (b. 1967)

Clever and Poor

She has always been clever and poor,
      especially here off the Yugoslav train

on a crowded platform of dust. Clever was
      her breakfast of nutmeg ground in water

in place of rationed tea. Poor was the cracked
      cup, the missing bread. Clever are the six

handkerchiefs stitched to the size of a scarf
      and knotted at her throat. Poor is the thin coat

patched with cloth from the pockets
      she then sewed shut. Clever is the lipstick,

Petunia Pink, she rubbed with a rag on her nails.
      Poor nails, blue with the cold. Posed

in a cape to hide her waist, her photograph
      was clever. Poor then was what she called

the last bills twisted in her wallet. Letter
      after letter she was clever and more

clever, for months she wrote a newspaper man
      who liked her in the picture. The poor

saved spoons of sugar, she traded them
      for stamps. He wanted a clever wife. She was poor

so he sent a ticket: now she could come to her wedding
            by train. Poor, the baby left with the nuns.

Because she is clever, on the platform to meet him
            she thinks *Be generous with your eyes.* What is poor

is what she sees. Cracks stop the station clock,
            girls with candle grease to sell. Clever, poor,

clever and poor, her husband, more nervous
            than his picture, his shined shoes tied with twine.

A LATE APOSTASY

For D.

Roaming the Via degli Alfani
late each night, I pass Saint Sebastian
swooning in arrow-stricken ecstasy
from his quattrocento niche. Christ's passion
sweetened the pricks so their piercings ached like lips
against his beating skin. My charismatic
apostle of more secular erotic trips,
you've grown apocryphal as this fantastic
martyr who wrecks me with his brimming eyes.
Half-jesting, I drew hearts transfixed by arrows
across my first envelopes to you. Jokes die
like saints, we found: they leave hard-to-swallow
legends, illuminating our naive
supplication to a god we once believed.

THE WEDDING DAY

They drove to Grado in a borrowed car,
in borrowed clothes and borrowed shoes. She drove,
pink scarf instead of flowers in her hair
while he peeled blood oranges to prove
No voice cries out, and fed each segment to
The solemn child behind, whose tiny gloves
stayed folded in her lap. His daughter, new
to him and still unsure if this is love
he offers in the form of oranges.
Who wins the mother wins the child, he croons

falsetto. *Hey, you know what stubborn is?*
It's going on your parents' honeymoon
refusing Dad a grin. He mocks a scowl—success!
His wife's smile ghosted on the smaller face.

THE FEAST OF SAN SILVESTRO

All week, the explosions have increased.
      On Monday, three or four
            startled the afternoon,

sending up a piazza-
      ful of pigeons, their wings
            clattering like water on stone.

Every car alarm
      within fifty yards went off.
            Tuesday, they gathered steam.

Rapid clusters seemed
      normal by Wednesday,
            and though lunchtime was sunny

we kept the windows shut,
      afraid an ascending rocket would
            sent the curtains aflame.

After three, just when
      a siesta beckoned to
            freshen us for the feast,

some back-alley wits
      blew up the metal
            trashcans outside our

bedroom wall. God
      bless mankind! Whose
            youthful spirit, head

bowed in the temple of
      the festive muse, hath found
            toy elements—

thunder in a paper cup,

gun-powder perihelions
           eclipsing with a

shriek. Listen, sweet,
           early tomorrow, while the
                      infant deities

still sleep, we'll walk
           the river's edge to greet
                      the year's first, foggy light

come stumbling over
           the celestial
                      shards sodden in the street.

TRACY PHILPOT (b. 1961)

WILDLIFE

I warn you to remain velvet and motionless on whatever
freshweeds resemble you   dreaming against awareness   a
salmon-colored answer to the barking stars   an older bride 30
years ago   the caged bird spends its last hard day in the wild
a windfall   and the sexy gravity pulls it down into a world
that makes the Bible soloist disappear   the clouds stranding
the mountains   the smell of hair   to find you by the water
so popular with mirrors   I've never been so proud of you
sleeping in the sun   the length of your fingers a truly private
window   I want to be the best scar on your body

LOUISA'S WEDDING

A week after her wedding I watch the Kentucky Derby
And pick the winner as usual; I'm alone
Drinking bourbon and have wagered nothing.

Do you understand the lateness of the twentieth century?
Is your marriage holding up to the strains
Of neighbors cutting grass? Raising children? Watching?

This part is not her future but mine,
I mean my lovers' and mine,
Participating only in the ritual of love
And separating, moving to a new house
Just down the street, sleeping in the sun with books.
The idea of you, Louisa, is most beautiful.

At the last minute, someone needs new shoes.
Not the neighbors, whose weekends wear the same clothes.
Not the actors in Paris writing the same sweater of memory.
In this late race, a horse needs new shoes.

And because we all have to wait
I catch a glimpse of a black horse,
Crested and unproved,
And bet on him
Whose only children will be horses.

How to Live in the Elegy

What started out as a study in naturalism
ended as a rescue mission—
I stole this, as after you died
I drove you in a cab to the hospital,
riding with the violent medicine
of dark in a cab.

The breath initiates a ghost between us,
see it married already
wanting to relove
another expensive meal.
How to live in the elegy,
the day of mountains we tended
and were honored to destroy it, the choice.

"I have no pictures of my ex-"
he told me. "They hang in museums.
I crumbled away from them
the same year we bridged over water
bordering an attempt."

When I visit her in the museum,
her almost real fingers in front of my eyes,

she reminds me of the times of Vesuvius
when lovers upheld their dark color
against the gold, when big operations of the heart
required three drinks a day,
a half a bottle of what got us here.

We have overdone the past
but O what great evenings of sacrifice.

We want to emulate that experience, the fermentation
of late autumn, the couple dining.
The man scoops up his wife like snow in a fur coat,
stumbling with the months he stood at the door,
singing the blues, tripping toward her in flight
all of eight stories down.

Out-of-season angels dot the walls
looking toward the fugitive and weaker songs,
heralding a quieter, more sincere ceremony.
We left behind a few sprained words,
the introduction of a wedding.

Do you drive past her house at night?
How do I look from afar?

I sang to him.
Cooked him breakfast in the nude.
Named each tent after him.

Because you are great I can say this:
The last part always has to do with posturing,
the difference between lovers who look at you for you
and the ones who look at you so you'll see their want.

Dancing
convulsing in it a fur coat
but I hear all the major custodians do.

D. A. POWELL (b. 1963)

[TALL AND THIN AND YOUNG AND LOVELY THE MICHAEL WITH KAPOSI'S SARCOMA GOES WALKING]

tall and thin *and young and lovely the* michael with kaposi's sarcoma
                                    goes walking
and when he passes each one he passes goes "whisperwhisperwhisper."
                                    star of beach blanket babylon

the sea washes his ankles with its white hair.   he sambas past the
                                    empty lifeguard tower
days like these who wouldn't swim at own risk: the horizon smiles
                                    like a karaoke drag queen
broad shoulders of surf shimmy forth as if to say "aw baby, sell it, sell
                                    it."   he's working again

towels lie farther apart.   the final stages: he can still do a dazzling
                                    turn *but each day*
smiles grow a little sharper.   he blames it on the bossanova.   he
                                    writes his own new arrangements

[A LONG LINE OF BOHUNKS AND HUNYAKS: WE SETTLED IN PODUNK. THIRTEEN CONSONANTS]

a long line of bohunks and hunyaks: we settled in podunk.   thirteen
                                    consonants
surrounding a vowel with an umlaut.   that was the name we carried
                                    from ____ tz ___ tz
into the new world.   in the grainbelt smackdab plopping down with
                                    our oxen and hogs

a cedar trunk in the junk-cluttered attic of a maiden aunt   [her name
                                    forgotten]
[so many ellipses in the tale of our begats]   keeper of tintypes.
                                    christening gowns
the quilt patched out of hand-me-downs: scraps from grands and
                                    great-grands

difficult to say who we are in the present.   broadcast across farms
                                    like so many other seeds
threads of familiarity gradually unraveled.   whole generations
                                    apparently eaten by moths

KEVIN POWELL (b. 1966)

GENIUS CHILD

For Langston Hughes

simple ain't it?
the words flow
like a river
winding
your smile

a thumb snaps
an eighth note
bebop!
a horn's lips curl
at a girl
in a red dress

you, too, fragment
a dark vein
it sings
it sags
like a blues bag
weighing dreams
on lenox avenue

HARLEM: NEO-IMAGE

sunset nails the lip of a building:
a shadow eyes
            an ashy windowpane.
an old man sits on his cane
regurgitating cups of lenox
and the savoy:
i drink his face   it burps
southern clay and city welts

SOUTHERN BIRTH

For Lottie Bur(r)ison Powell
(February 23, 1912 - May 16, 1988)

a procession. southern wails. a yellow
face emerges specked with black moles.
two pennies slit the eyes where the dirt road
used to be. those thick glasses
distract from the tobacco-stained
teeth. tingling carolina stench braid
coarse charcoal hair.

i ache until it is wet, naked,
full of bounce: a gushing wind
corners a heart; puffy cotton veins
snap the way grandma lottie
broke string beans in the front yard.
a moist sound spills onto
the dirty plywood. reverend wilson's
eulogy fogs the church. homemade
syrup and cornbread descend. my mouth
plummets into an emotional abyss: a lover
flees the outhouse and a baby inherits the pain.

ROHAN B. PRESTON (b. 1966)

CHICAGO BLUES

For Kel

The forest is crowded and a wounded
animal drags entrails across rocks and
thickets, tumbling over branches
and grinding gravel, and all
around spinning and turning
clearing spider-webs from
the face, the sound of
breeze and trees and
rattling and high-
pitched bawling,
dragging and
lagging and

finally, out
into a
clearing,
solo,
a wailing solo.

* June 8, 1990: Chicago, Illinois

MAMA

For Lucy, that's what they call her

They have been gone so long now, your
children, that they do not recognize you.
Are these your children that laugh
at your cataracts? Are these your children
the ones who strike at you and bid you run
after them? The ones to whom your fingers
gave charge to stand, to sit on their stools?
Are these the babes to whom you read
the psalms and proverbs? They do not know
you now—scrawny hands, cotton hair and all.

After missiles, missives, fired your way
their glee gives way (slightly) to faint
resemblances. A pause. Then, poor orphans
finding biological parents, orphans grown
among the wildebeest and other hosts,
they come home with even more vengeful hands,
plucking at your bosom, stealing your food
and cursing you (the early manners worn off).
Your hands clasp tight in genuflection,
they already know about the Phoenix,
what lessons can you teach them, now?

* June 14, 1991: Chicago, Illinois

DEEP-SEA BATHING (INNA REGGAE DANCEHALL)

Deep-sea bathing (inna reggae dancehall),
mish-mash, swoosh-splash, filling up
not only in a dead fish fashion.

Between each bass-blast

the woofers inhale like cartoon gods
ready to deliver one more blow.

The boomers gasp and pant with the plop
of a bobbing person every time
she pushes up, up, up, above the waves,

so the bass dubs and dubs, body-batting
as if the wind were filling out hung clothes.
Deep-sea bathing, my round, settling

stomach makes hollows as if sweat
were peeling off of lovers' bellies
my concentric rings fold over each other

like dewlap; and I begin to shake
them out, one by one, the way Mum taught
me when she ironed clothes.

* June 8, 1991: Chicago Illinois

KEVIN PRUFER (b. 1969)

MY FATHER RECOUNTS A STORY FROM HIS YOUTH

He who discovered
three tektites along the sheer banks
of Crater Lake, mounted them
above the fish tank,
who unearthed four hundred flint
ceremonial blades from the muck
of a Neolithic lake,
in central Ohio, photographed them,
put them in a book,
this is the story as he told it
to me:
        He was just eighteen, younger
than I am now, beardless,
his father vanished
to Switzerland, his mother
dying in Baden Baden.
The Brazilian summer had stained him

brown as the village boys who played
on the ancient cistern wall below.
At his feet were pottery shards
painted in green whorls.
The day he spent in the quiet
sun, piecing them together
for the older archaeologists.
The water was clear and deep—
the village boys raced
along its edge, raced and fell.
From the hill above, my father
could hear them laughing,
shouting their foreign
exclamations.

        It was their cries
rising, faint, distorted
on the wind, that caught his attention.
Those shimmering figures,
six of them, each alike,
black-haired, child-like—
and the first leaped into the still water.
My father counted the seconds, but the boy
did not resurface. The second jumped
laughing, and did not reappear. So it went
with the other four, each leaping
from the stone wall, vanishing
into the green water.

        In my family
we are all susceptible.
My sister often wakes
to see our dead grandmother
standing over her bed with a cup
of tea, smiling in the dark.
My cousin imagined his room
filling with water. He climbed
onto the window ledge fifteen stories high
to save himself. Even I
have seen figures disappearing
into the curtains, or the red-faced
old man crying on the street corner,
nowhere in sight when
I look again.

        My father
draws this conclusion:
You could vanish like that, he says,

into the green waters of wherever
you go. He holds onto me then,
or he takes me to his study
in the back of the house. This,
he says, holding a round black stone,
is a tektite, four billion years old.
This is a projectile point, white quartz,
quite rare.
                    Sometimes he tells me
about the six Brazilian boys.
We're all going that way, he says.
Outside, it is raining, drops splattering
on the skylights. There is nothing
permanent in this world, he says—
and he is surrounded by everything that is.

THE BABYSITTER'S DEVOTION

Ears like a walnut's broken shell,
my duffle, my zero, my worm's cocoon—
how you startle at the phone's unthinking cry.

See the cribside clock spin its orange finger?
I'll tell you about airplanes that curve
and curve above too-stormy cities.

As your parents sip their egg drop soup,
I'll read to you from *The New York Times*,
rub your back until you sing.

Don't you know pigeons ascend in flocks for you?
Don't you know the radio towers wink
their consistent red eyes in your direction?

For you, all the doorbells in the city are ringing.

ON FINDING A SWASTIKA CARVED ON A TREE
IN THE HILLS ABOVE HEIDELBERG

Later, on the Neckar's oil-slick banks,
I fed a two-headed swan a stale bread crust.
The healthy head ate;
the other, featherless, eyes closed or undeveloped,

dragged from the end of its garden-hose neck
in the mud on the shore.

Meanwhile, all along Schwartz Strasse,
as they do every day, the citizens sat
in pairs at their outdoor cafe tables
swallowing schnitzel, sighing at the sun's descent.
They shredded their napkins
then rubbed the rims of their wine glasses
until the evening was filled
with a crystal air-raid siren sound.

The night floated down like a thousand allies
lashed to black parachutes.

FOR THE DEAD

The memory of childhood, of stooping
above the drain grate, dropping pebbles
one by one between the metal bars,
imagining they would never hit bottom,

reminds me that you, too, have fallen
away, tumbled between the teeth
of another sort of grate,
into a different darkness none of us

knows a thing about. So now,
the rest of us hunched around this beach
fire, spilling our stories
into the night, and you not here,

brings the wish back with the memory:
that each bright pebble might spin and fall
through all the airy dark, the water's
unbroken surface endlessly below.

CHARLES RAFFERTY (b. 1965)

THE MAN ON THE TOWER

No one in the Arrowhead Pub believed
I had the guts to climb that tower
across the highway. So I tottered to it
at rush hour, waltzing past the men
who sped to their wives
and rented lives. When I gripped them

the rungs were hot
from a sun that kept us
crouched at our beers. I climbed up anyway,
and the cops arrived quicker than I thought
and began to ricochet
like blue marbles from car to car.

I didn't think
a man's desire to ascend
could shock them all into action.
But they were shocked
and pointed their voices toward me,
rerouted the traffic

to clear the road. I'll bet they thought
that I would fall, drowning myself
in someone's windshield.
But they were wrong. I clung to that tower
as if it were a woman
and inched my way toward contact.

The faces in the cars grew indistinct.
The horizon spread with every step
till I could see
where the sun fell down. I didn't stop.
I worked with deaf ears
against gravity and the shouts

of their bullhorn. The tower tapered
and I was pinned against the sky,
pricked with a notion to fly.
I had never been above our town,
had never seemed the focus

of so much pure attention.

Why I clambered down
with the care one takes when stooping
for keys in an unlit room,
I cannot say. But I did.
And the whole pub cheered.
And the traffic began again.

THE ARSONIST TELLS HIS STORY
TO THE ATTORNEY

It got so bad I never saw
the same girl twice.
When I told one about the barn
I burned—how the flames
slid across the rafters,
exciting the whole frame
into a frenzy it hadn't felt
since it was trees on a stormy night—
she made me stop the car.
And her unkissed thighs
walked back to town, leaving me
my hands, a hot silence
that had to touch everything.
I eventually stopped dating.
I spent my Saturday afternoons
scouting out buildings
that reminded me of girls—ugly girls
who had asked their mothers
for makeup and been refused.
That's where I came in,
like some big-hearted Avon lady,
moistening the floorboards
with gasoline, touching a match
to some place appropriate.
I did it for the beauty
and for the fire that came,
transforming a shack
to a red-haired woman
in an orange dress—
who kicked her hem above her head
to the crackling of castanets.

STORY OF THE MAN WHOSE TASTES
WERE TOO REFINED

Once there was a man
whose tastes were so refined
that nothing could please him.
He would detect the flaws
in the finest bourbon
and declare it undrinkable,
and the women he met
were always out of proportion—
too much here, too little there,
the wrong color hair
for a particular handbag.
His tastes eventually reduced him
to a mixture of scowls
and uproarious guffaws.
Of course, he considered
suicide—leaving his life
the way he'd left so many movies,
before the repulsively blonde
protagonist was saved—
but there was also the hint
of cowardice to consider,
the carpets he might ruin,
the inherent inability
to revise a bullet's path.

HEATHER RAMSDELL (b. 1968)

BRIGHT RECEDING

For Roy

With speed the prior body
of the tree could not have foreseen

in orange flakes rising from safety
of, this its release from,
the locus of fire into mossy night,

an imaginary fire in actual night.
Amongst blacknesses, that star already

imploded now is the size of

a rose window, actually
I made that fact up. The sun
came through the window again

by such light, some
burnt trees—such
trees in the yard *make sense*

having incongruities which
occlude both, dread numbs
both—both
include part-answers.
And no research gels.

In being numbers, the shadow faces
turn, locate
one end first, one part, color

of orange and red and black, black
as the black of an eye, please
find me my coat, it says.

It says, you cannot prefer both
the image and itself, you cannot reside
in the possible, henceforth,
resolving to climb inside the solid mound, not see.

NEARLY CIRCLE

Sad, to shut
to shut other
things into the space left
the space that I left
the space in skewed perspective twisting
foregrounds, sags in glass—*this is your conscience
speaking.* Frontal laughter even
politely refuses the antidote, the closing stroke

later to be fixed, fudged
in memoriam, during the naming of names when you finally show in
    the picture.

And you know who you are. Hold still
just for a moment. Now move. You move
the cloth away from your face. And the face

is vague particles twisting
into thin air, is dust. (Don't I know you?
      I must, I recognize your face in all things and all things must fit
      together as all stars once did, as all sands did so that sand on the
      floor made sense until we looked closely at it and it spread.)

CLAUDIA RANKINE (b. 1963)

ELSEWHERE, THINGS TEND

★

Viewed in this way,
                          . . . her voice
at any distance cannot be
heavier than her eyes. Listen, among the missing
is what interrupts, stops her short
far from here in ways that break to splinter.

Until the sense that put her here is forced
to look
before remembering the towel that wiped sweat
and wet face and dust from each mirror:

she cleans her glasses with that. So in the end
is this defeat?
She thinks in it we are
as washed-out road, as burnt-down, ash.

Dismiss the air and after her gesture, there,
the thrown off—

★

This then is—

It remains as dusk with the hour, feeling looted
in the body

though every shadow is accounted for.

Who to tell,   I am nothing and without you,
when good comes, every hand in greeting. There is
no reasoning with need.

I coach myself, speak to my open mouth,
but whatever abandons, whatever leaves me sick,
a rock in each hand, on the shoulder of some road,

its nights unmediated, its dogs expected,
knows its nakedness unseduced:

                              (cruelty that says, cut loose

                                        —its voice keeps on,

meaning empty, the mood reproachful, faint. Don't think.
Don't argue. Surfaced again: This
plummeting, pulled back, sudden *no*—

which cannot be given up as though one never hears back,
as though all the seats are taken. This

                              —drawn out of bounds
without advantage and knowing, my God, what is probable is

this coming to the end, not desperate for, not enraged.
At first, embarrassed, lumbering beneath the formal poses,
the well-cuffed, the combed hairs, the could-not-be-faulted
statement of ease, though utterly
and depleted, closing the door behind, for in

this, the distance—wanting and the body losing, all the time
losing, beforehand, inside.

★

Similar also,

each gesture offering a hand to the atmosphere, like a wave,
until it's realized the one I'm waving to can't see me anymore.
Or is it my back turned? Me who leaves?
If I remind myself all of us weep, wake, whisper
in the same dark, and the sudden footfall or the longer silence
separates us beyond each locked door, I am returned

only to my own. And am reluctant to complain as if
exaggerated is the high water, as if it didn't swallow thousands,
these fossils, this bone, as if between us are not many
extremes: the taste of blood in our mouths though the blows
are seldom physical. What I wish to communicate is that
it can be too late: this life offering sorrow as voice, leaving
nothing to shadow. I want to say, a life can take a life away.

THE QUOTIDIAN

                              What we live
before the light is turned off
is what prevents the light from being turned off.
In the marrow, in the nerve, in nightgowned exhaustion,
to secure the heart,
hoping my intention whole, I leave nothing
behind, drag nakedness to the brisker air of the garden.

What the sweeper has not swept gathers
to delay all my striving. But here I arrive
with the first stars: the flame in each
hanging like a trophy in the lull just before
the hours, those antagonists
that haunt and confiscate
what the hardware of slumber draws below.

★

Night sky,

all day the light,

responding without proof, vigorously
embraced blue,
lavender-sucking bees,
a stone mouth spewing water to golden carp.

Light piled on indisputable light rekindled bits of garden
until bare-shouldered, coherent, each root, its stem,
each petal and leaf
regained its original name
just as your door opened and we had to go through.

Which is to know your returned darkness was born first
with all its knowledge—

routine in the settling down, little thumps
like someone knocking at the temple—arriving

within each soul growing old
begging, impatient
for these nights to end, wanting
never darkness—

its murmurous mirror:

*

its drained tongue

as dead driftwood soaking the vein
as these words float up
out of body

in a joke sharpened in or sharpening
each myopic minute
met

and now dirtied up, or far too beautiful
for this

and now desperate for
the never would or could
or at least had not meant to mean).   Pity the stirred.

So stormed out, as in exhausted, my eardrums left watching.
Each nerve, in the mood exhumed,
hissing, *go away*,

go away,   night sky, did we come this far together?

I am cold. And in this next breath,
the same waking,

the same hauling of debris. I am
here in the skin of . . . otherwise) shoveling out, dryly

JOANNA RAWSON (b. 1964)

THE BORDER
Negev Desert, Israel

Leaping from the eucalyptus branch, the wild desert pigs
practice flight,

while salt mines flaunt their electric necklaces—
an empire of runways
for the suicide squads in bedeviled outdated double-wingers,

those sporadic Arab pilots gliding, noiseless,
off the serrated dark bluffs of the valley,

blown to smithereens
by the fixed gunners stashed in secret folds of
sandstone and nightchill.

The moon was a gaping
beckoning eye, a charm on the desert

that caused men to sail the air, silver, wicked,
toward the flat saltplain,

though no one admitted the sea had sunk
back into the planet, leaving a white crescent scar
long as a myth.

What water was left, they could not crash or drown in,
so saline its remains.

They floated
those black motorless birds toward the appointed border
as if already underwater.

By day, we worked the fields—eggplants, dates,
the technological fruits unfolding under veils of plastic.

Beside us their dark-eyed clobbered women
imported over the border on ramshackle buses at dawn,

with spines like roaming slopes
and toddlers flocking their skirt hems,

dirt labor who mumbled in a tongue odd to me,

they suffered the barren clay-hot late afternoon
hours like soldiers themselves.

We did not dream their dreams—fuselage, petrol, that clutch of fury
that propels the antics of heroism.

I knew even then that by night
they swaddled the bodies of their lovers and sons
in black gauze and hoods

and oiled up the wheels of some discarded creaking glider
for flight.

It aroused suspicion on my part,
like locusts on a rose, spiders on a fresh white wall.

What I knew was the conspiring way
they assailed the air with betel juice spit

and struck with precision
the nail on the sheltershack door

though no one spoke of it.

MAP BURNT THROUGH

Of our chosen place,
nothing but instructions toward ending.
Even without desire
the barbed hickory grove ignites upwind.
Mares flee their stalls through crackling mash,
their black figures frothing toward the banks.
Beyond tent poles, beyond the stable's eave, under a gorged sky
reeking snakegrass and clay
that will not, not ever
burst, the silos and shacks in the back lot
suffer the blast in a splattering rust.
Old women thread needles by its light.
Dead ants fry in the wiring.
The crew returns at dawn, blackened.
Two crows in the burnt branches
scatter the roses below with scat.

Their ripped stems spit up a carpet of scarlet.
Suddenly paradise is not ours.
And so we get up and are running
for the annihilated river.
And we are flying for the ruined sky.

WILLIAM REICHARD (b. 1963)

THE MONSTER'S DREAM

Remarkable that the skin has such resiliency,
that the mechanics of tendon and bone
bend to this extent.
Where is the magic of breath?
On winter mornings, I've watched people
breathe, and their breath pours
from their mouths in a solid cloud;
these people wake the air, the heavens
issue out of them in white vapors.
Once, a man was dipping water from a pool.
I crept behind him and looked
over his golden shoulder;
it was the symmetry that startled me,
the color of his eyes, blue
as if the sky had nested inside.
When my face rested in his
on the silver surface of the water,
the way it only can in water, he screamed.
I had never stood so close to a man before.
What I remember now is the way his mouth
moved as he spoke, the scent of his breath
like sweet fruit and soil, the surface of the pond
as our twin faces shattered,
the way his blue eyes spread out and out
as the ripples sought the farther shore.

THE CLOUD GAME

The clouds carry in another of June's remonstrances. Last week
the wind blew so hard a single strand of straw was driven
through a window without breaking the glass. We take

our meanings where we find them: eyes in the sky; the face of God
in the clouds; the visage of Christ in a hand towel or the bark
of a tree. On the hill, in Medjugorje, where the sun dances

and the Virgin speaks, not one rock or pebble remains.
Pilgrims have carried them off, hoping to be healed or at least
reminded of faith. When I was ten, the sky turned gray, then green,

and the wind screamed in the trees. When I emerged
from the basement, I found an apple tree sitting in a garden
where none grew. In those few minutes under the stairs,

I prayed, and God or something spared the house that is today
fallen into ruin. Perhaps I didn't pray hard enough, and only delayed,
but not denied, that final destruction. In the ceiling of the room

where I grew from child to man, I play the cloud game, searching
in the water stains that daily grow for some report from heaven,
a face in the plaster which comforts as it collapses, a guarantee

for anyone under that roof that she or he will sleep safe,
that the worst of what the heavens offer will be stayed,
the sternest of salvation's sky spared them.

REBECCA REYNOLDS (b. 1962)

THE OBJECT OF BURIAL IS INTENT

Accretion,
     dispossession

in the parlor of breath. A thing
refuses to resonate (I'm thinking
of the object lost from its threads)

as if I could make it signify
"in the beginning" despite
this death-log of nature. Not like this—

when something you love turns to this dialogue
between birth and death:
in the beginning was the end—

and in the end, the starship
stumbling on this loop between
past and future

infinitely repairs
its history. To alter
so no alteration finds.

And here I was digging and undigging
to fix an awkwardness, a clutter
that runs in the genes

like diabetes or mood swings;
why the self
is a description of the body,

why we must hope
that love is blind:
so that someone will take us.

PERIDOT

The mattress loved the explicit. She would find
two coins: the plum coin of blood
hatched in its navel, and the semen, blued
with some relative's
distorted permanence. These

she scrubbed into ink, blurring
the proof of their bodies before the surface blanched
below the snowy window. She closed her eyes.
A man would call from a National Poll;
a map would unfold before the mailbox. She preferred
the loss of a line to the presence of a wall.
The bedstains

shot under her lids. Her body
wooed them back, within
membranes, tea-colored membranes, as an exercise
in perspective, in keeping things.
"Choose your focal point," they addled.
It was the same scenery
but phosphorescent
and rude, as if she slaved and labored
in coupling. These

were the obdurate words, others' versions
of the covenant, "be fruitful and multiply," and worse,
what comes with age (which she foresaw)
the slow deflations, urine maps, what children
leave in the nest, what liberates the mind
from order—the obscure
peridot. She seeps

out of herself in spots, a true creator,
pregnantly, but not
rehearsed in the logic of lying
within bounds. O cradle of my soul, the crumbs
that Gretel scatters on the stumps are not
for her to find her way back, but for others.

SURPLUS

The heart—
a canned tulip—
cannot bear itself. And the mind's light masonry
houses a crap shoot, waterlit, below
the level of the dark. Here is the C-note
slapped on the table's jade block,
the insufferable jukebox that keeps the outfit tapping
as long as anyone survives: in smoke,
war-issue tables and chairs, the pale-faced clock, the body's
motor of wounds. A veteran
lifts his beer like a feather. A light breeze
unpins the curtains on the moon, a threshing blade, to a song
that dabbles among their ears (lady, moon, and veteran),
below the level of the Good. Outside,
an air of nostalgia brushes the wheat, the landscape
rigged with pie sills and holly, the scene
carved out of a headboard like flowers—
or out of the head—
either with the crooked stalks of a battlefield in the moonlight, or,
in some parody of a perfectly normal town,
where loved ones lie sleeping, without
any sense of the world.

KIM ROBERTS (b. 1961)

FROM *The Constellation Frigidaire*

I. THE TILT

Sitting shoulder to shoulder,
leaning heads together until they touch,
two lovers make an isosceles triangle
in the blank space at their necks.
I know all about blank space.

Somewhere, a moon shines on two lovers.
It is not my moon;
it is not yours. A light breeze
ruffles their hair as if playing
at the strings of a harp.

The whole world seems ready
to fly off its axis, gravity's
ready to give up the ghost,
ions crackle and explode.

But not for us. You are gone
and I am planted firmly
in one place, my shoes
glued to the alluvial soil.

I'm glad that no sparks fly.
I'm glad I don't have to worry
about a sudden freefall through space,
the Milky Way reflected in my eyes.
I'm glad:

The moon shines, but not for me.
The breeze blows, but not for you.
The planet continues its soft
turning, tipped at twenty-three degrees,
everything going slightly askew.

I sat by the edge of the field
looking up, looking anywhere but in,
the moon above me the slimmest of crescents
and the dark portion glowing faintly,
reflected in Earthshine.
My grandmother had a name for it:

"the old moon in the new moon's arms."
My grandmother never took a measure of her love
to dole it out cup by cup.
Later, tangled in my sheets,
I dreamed about a boyfriend long ago,
from high school, one I never think of anymore.

But when I awoke, I knew he represented
my last boyfriend instead of himself,
the most recent half-measure;
that's the way our minds transpose the world.
Nothing's the way it appears to be.
Science confirms this again and again.

The seas of the moon never held water
(Mare Imbrium, Sea of Showers,
Oceanus Procellarum, Ocean of Storms)
and Venus, coy deceiver,
the planet that symbolizes love,
is covered with volcanoes and deadly rain.

THE PLASTIC CUP

So it's one of those bars, see,
where everything is painted black:
the walls, the windows, the crowd,
and the music itself, banging
loud and black. We're all drinking
beer from these clear plastic cups,
they don't trust us with glass
and the band's tuneless and it's too loud
to speak, though what is there to say?
The scene, the people, everything's
clouded, and the music everyone

keeps thinking they might come to like.
We could be anywhere,
Detroit or Houston, with these
spotlights shining their circles
randomly on our heads, until this girl,
she puts her empty cup down
right in the middle of a circle
and it glows, it glows like God
right there on the floor.
And it's got you, the kind of light
you wish could blaze inside you, solid
enough to hurt. It's got you.
You're sure it's not just the booze,
and that cup is not a cup. It's larger.
Its light could locate you, stop
the banging, could change, could slow,
you're sure, you don't know how, the thing
that makes your standing still here
a flight.

NIGHT TUMBLES INTO TOWN BY RAIL

"Everything you want a train to do, it does."
　　　—overheard in a Chinese restaurant in Phoenix

Night tumbles into town, bruised
and swearing. I look at you,
the way you connect to me: arms and legs—
and slowly the word forms on my lips:
Boxcars.

We settle small details—
what to wear, who to call,
getting there on time—
by the exercise
of our own deliberation.
It is all scenery:
trestle bridges, depot houses.

More important matters,
such as the curve of our bodies
and the bodies of those we love:
a hazy shoreline seen from a train window
as we pass—who can tell where
water ends and sky begins?

ELIZABETH ROBINSON (b. 1961)

SALISBURY PLAIN

Bones in a sand cliff. So I could say frigidity prevails
through a full moon. The light retracts, but this does not signal
gentleness. Absent movement of hand over bleached hair.

And other, artifactual, evidence. I stand by an abrupt hill.

I stand by a large upright rock. I turn to it and embrace
it. It falls and crushes me.

Later, the visitor can assess my profession by the fall of
the stone.

But nothing follows from the origin of mass and its placement.
Daylight propped. The shore caving in my history. Barrows,
cattle.

The gorgeous light falling back for caution's sake.

So this is what the humidity partakes of. Careful statement. The
highway appended to a series of boulders, or finally, a number of
quick movements through the floodlight that washed the close.

FOUNTAIN

Below its floor, mint,
the startle of each, a mason
would alliterate.

Rutilant, he forgets
the turn to count, counts aside,
the funnel limits.

But more, the tile clicks:
scent of cover, of hapless
conviction. The fit.

Bed of lists. The membrane
a cluster of white pulls down
round, too hard to toss.

For Karen

As a child, I could never sleep.

I would wake up in the middle of the stairs
and say,
"I want to go home."

My mother would say,
"Lift up your white nightgown and let out the wakeful air."

I say that I can't sleep because my body is too small
and the shift

falls in a breeze to the ground.

I say that I am not tired.

I say that the air rushes both ways through the fabric.

Shatter

Some marring in the glass of the body

has the wound placed as more voluptuous
than its field

Now the field is losing its sturdy terminology

The wife beckons

nakedly to say

One modification before another

losing its orderly being   The smear

in the heart of the divination

The spouse as he sails past
saying   locked and unlocked   saying
unlocked and locked

Now in the childish field

the collar simply slackens

MESHES

What a mouth has to do with the opening in a door. I hid a
stolen book of stories in the lining of my coat.

And waded knee-deep into a river, only later rolling up my pant legs.

You see I was a boy. I stole my orthodoxy from that flat
incident. Or smoked cigarettes surreptitiously as an adult.

Or was still a mouth around a key. However one does it, deleting
the score. Other appropriations seem better.

There's too much talk about drowning when it's really just rinsing
your hands through your hair.

Preacher, bat and ball hitting together. I fell into the trough.
I scared the other boys. Smoke came out of my nose when I forgot to
exhale through my mouth.

MATTHEW ROHRER (b. 1970)

A SHORT HISTORY OF ILLUMINATION

Concerning a nun, composer and herbalist,
and the miracles she concocts on her travels,
at the end of which she is to be investigated.

Aren't all plants sacred, she asks along the way,
especially the poisonous ones?
The tinker under his enormous hat grins
as she hands him the red vial.

In her chamber after midnight
she is engulfed in fire
and after she's put it out by rolling on the tiles
there is a new song in her mouth.

She performs her songs from the tops of steeples.
They are said to bring peace to the village.
Of a woman who wears a smock that was hung out to dry

during this performance, it is said that no man can resist her,
that cats follow her into the bedroom.

Safest to say the nun's songs were given to her by God.
Safest to say, "I should write holy words to this."

Best not to think of the curtain that speaks.
Best not to send down the singed gown.
Best not to admit composing while in flames.

HOTEL DE L'ETOILE

The long thin window to the stars holds up the tenement.
The column is bent in thought. The floor underneath the window
cries out when someone stands there to look out at the night,
unless it is the young girl with her lemons.

She watches for skiffs avoiding the stars.
Her feathered brother is on one knee, calling down to the shore.
In his backpack are three goats. He's on the lookout
for shipwrecked sailors, who have been seen
checking into other hotels, who have been seen
spending their dark gold on wine without opening their eyes.

QUICK SELL THE PIG

All sorts of plants were beautiful
and seemed worthy of description.
The trees, for instance, fingered low clouds suggestively.
Construction awaited an impressive building.
Teachers led their classes to the flowerbeds,
to write in their notebooks.
One particular flower—the rose—
attracted the most attention.
They wrote "It is very red"
then chased the girl who smelled.
From an open window: timpani.
From a passing car: a thin rainbow on the damp streets.
From the farms outside town: the unmistakable smell.
The fog rolled down every street alphabetically,
while small groups of people strolled by the river
pretending to listen to each other.
One man worried he would be asked which part of dusk

he liked best.
The part at the beginning when the bats come out
and everything seems possible,
or the part at the end when all that can be seen
in the moon is bright mud.

A Hummock in the Malookas

For Jennifer Kitchell

From a hummock in the Malookas
I have a clear view of heaven.

It is the stars pinpricking the grass
through a hole.

It is the blue snow we awaken to.

From a hummock in the Malookas,
where the women run topless
until they have worn a dirt path around
the island, I have a clear view of heaven.

It is the glidepaths of satellites blinking over pizzerias.

It is the spindly Southern Cross I have yet to see.

It is our nearest star anointing
the heads of all the flowers equally
and the green roofs of terrariums.

A Last Look at the Mutineers

What can the mutineers hear from the hold?

    The thrum of fingers on drums
    and the popping of fat in the fire
    and the insides of the forest saying *All of you, just go away.*

What else can they smell besides themselves and the salted meat?

    The oil on the freshly sharpened knives on shore.

★

In the stillness one of the mutineers confesses his love
for the Mother Superior who raised him,

one of them cries for the gull endlessly circling the mast
of the ship,

one of them swallows a poisoned tooth
worn on a chain for just this occasion,

and one of them listens carefully enough to envision
the exact size of each drum.

*

The captain is just the tapping of two heels
on the boards above their heads.

The jury is just the occasional nervous laugh from the rigging,

and as for Fate, they have been listening to the sea for days.

LEE ANN RORIPAUGH (b. 1965)

PEARLS

Mother eats seaweed and plum pickles,
and when the Mormons come knocking
she does bird-talk. I've never seen
an ocean, but I'd swim in one to look
for secrets. She has a big pearl
from my oji-san, says it will be mine
when she's dead. It's in a drawer
hidden with silver dollars. I hope
she doesn't buy a ticket, go back
to her sisters and leave me.

With stinging strokes, she brushes
my hair, pulls it into pigtails
that stretch my face flat. I walk
to school across sagebrush while
she watches from her bedroom window.
Once I found a prairie dog curled

sleeping on the ground and I brushed
away ants on his eyes. Mother
saw me dilly-dally, told me not
to touch dead things.

I have a red box in my desk
with a dragon lid that screws on
and off. It smells sweet from face
cream and I keep a kokeishi doll
inside for good luck. Wishing
for more colors in my crayon pail,
I make up stories about mermaids
and want a gold crayon to draw hair,
silver for their tails. But
we can't afford lots of kid junk.
I have piano lessons. She says
I'll be a doctor someday
but I think I'd like to be a fireman
or maybe a roller derby queen.

One day when I was walking home
some boys on bikes flew down
around me like noisy crows.
They kept yelling *Kill the Jap!*
I ran fast as I could but fell
in the dirt, got up and fell.
My mother came running to me.
She carried me home, picked out
the gravel, washed off blood,
tucked me into her bed and let
me wear the ring for awhile.

I wish I had long, white skinny
fingers, gold hair and a silver
tail. I'd gather baskets
of pearls. But my hair is black,
my fingers stubby. Mother
tells me they're not found just
floating underwater. She says
oysters make them, when there's
sand or gravel under their shells.
It hurts. And the more it hurts,
the bigger the pearl.

PEONY LOVER

A thinnest sliver of moon, and caterpillars
gather in their bodies
with the wiry, circular precision

of a rice-paper lantern
folding back down on itself, colored
patterns collapsing into

denser, indecipherable forms. Rabbits
leave lacy teethmarks
rimming the ragged edges of lettuce,

and I am like the opossum
who stares up with glowing, hungry eyes
waiting for persimmons to fall.

All night tree frogs throb and thrum
with the numbing pulse
of a discotheque, and fat, lacquer-backed

cockroaches creep in shiny,
bumper-to-bumper lines toward the promise
of food, drawing a zigzag

connect-a-dot from garbage can to can,
hub to hub, the way your flight
now circles another city, talons outstretched,

like a blinking, red-eyed
bird, while the damp of your sweat fades
from my pillowcase.

Because I let your hands undo me
like an origami crane,
fold by fold, fingers easing out creases,

because I let the ink
of your brushstrokes seep the whiteness
of my paper-thin skin

and mark me, I could call this love,
or maybe delusion.
And when I creep barefoot in moonlight

with my hair undone,
reach into the sky to pull you back down,
there is nothing

but heat, and sound, and dizziness,
only a handful
of peony petals crumpling in my fists.

CATIE ROSEMURGY (b. 1969)

HARD PUT

Spite made the architects put the front desk of the hotel
right next to the exit so that people in clean uniforms
could watch me sneak by. The devil and the combined weight
of me and, good Lord, a sailor put these creases
in my clothes. There's no telling who or what
put the voice of Mary and the designs of Jezebel
in my drink last night. I watch the bedspread,
make sure he doesn't move, put on my jeans,
but I don't zip them, don't risk waking him
with that spiteful roar until I'm halfway
down the hall. I push open the front door. I put myself
in the middle of a clash between the hoods of cars
and sunlight. While I stand blinking, I pray for his hands,
for his calluses, for no one to speak to me.
Of course the hill puts me high enough to glimpse
the harbor. Other people invade, smuggle, yacht,
and brood over landscapes. The world runs on bad habits.
I continue to sneak, past two, three houses at a time.
I didn't put out last night. I put up with every song
the band played. I put my finger on a line or two
about crossing the water and extrapolated.
I pat my pockets and wish
I was the kind of person who always puts
her keys in the same place. I almost don't notice
that an angel put a geranium in her window
between her lace curtain and the glass,
a young mother put a gold barrette
in her daughter's dark hair. I can't put all
the acts of kindness on this street into words.

Why God Invented the Cold

To give the people a break
from repositioning their lawn chairs.
To tease us with a glimpse of life
without bugs. Without weeping welts,
the odd fever, and yellow guts on our shoes.

To confuse young boys.
To force them to ask, why do teenage girls
smoke outside in January
until their nipples get stiff?
And why do they stand around

with their coats undone
and life smacked onto their cheeks?
Am I that promising?
To caution the men that the boys grow into
against following their semi-aroused girlfriends

into May lake water. Seasonal Affective Disorder.
To break up those pesky highways
into manageable chunks. To make it
clear just how stupid it is to climb
the highest mountain. To encourage

cuddling and mittens. The powerful
sleep lobby. To give drunks a dreamy,
snow-plowed alternative to liver failure.
Blue lips and frosted eyelashes. Ski pants,
for Christ's sake. Dark roads, tight sweaters,

no boots, and stalled cars. Country love.
Wanna ride, need a lift. Homespun
complex legal issues. His word pressed
firmly against her word. Zero degrees
and fourteen snowmobiles missing.

Natural selection. Two feet of fodder
for made for TV movies and more expected.
No fiber, calories, vitamins, hallucinogenic
properties, or nicotine without the tar.
Just pain in your membranes, unexpected

falls, sprained ankles, and hyperextended
thumbs. To see if you can
catch yourself. To put you down. You thought
you were mean and hard to figure out until
you found out about wind chill.

To give us a way to understand
people who won't give us sex,
meter maids, Siamese cats, what it's like to kiss
your best friend's lover. To distinguish the sweat of euphoria
from the sweat of shock. To up the ante.

Because he could. Because he's lonely and it leaked
out of him. Because he wants attention
and a fluffy blanket that's big enough to cover his toes
and reach his chin. To create melting. To give us
another hint that the body is dead.

To add ice. To let him come as close as he can
to holding some of the glittering water he made.
To let us skate where we couldn't two weeks ago.
To let us glide on top of darkness.
To show us what it means to break through.

AN ANGEL FINALLY ADMITS WHAT SHE KNOWS
TO LOU BINKLER OF BETHANY, MISSOURI

Some people weren't meant to eat a New York Strip.
Some people weren't meant to actually touch
the amniotic ocean. Some people, Lou,

weren't meant to wiggle their ten toes
in the sand and say, *Hey!*
Those waves are nibbling everything away

besides me! Some people weren't ever ever meant
to fall from the sky. Some people,
ya gotta have faith there's a reason for them. They don't even try

to defy gravity, no matter how see-through
your dress or how long

you float, blonde and stiff-nippled, right over them.

Still you whisper *I'm not the moon, you fool.*
But some people just weren't meant
to understand English. Or time and space.

Some people weren't meant to know the rush of stars
past their terribly bone-encased heads.
But never mind heaven.

Let's start from the beginning.
Some people weren't meant to be born
with two legs. Some people weren't meant to go to college

and then keep a clean house. Some people weren't meant to perfect
their vibrato in a spotlight or to shake when they kill
a fourteen point buck. Some people were not meant

to be let outside. Ever. Some people,
it sounds silly, weren't meant to own pets.
Some people weren't meant to be touched

or inhaled or lifted off the ground.
Or penetrated. Or believed. Or fed.
Or lived with. Some people

weren't meant to sleep well or to put up
with this world past age twenty five. Some people
weren't meant to see their own blood. Or to give any away.

To save any rare babies. Do you see the golden plan, Lou?
Some people weren't meant to walk
into the pasture reflected in a wild mustang's eyes.

Some people weren't meant to shoot a pop can
off a fence post and feel good about it.
Some people weren't meant to nurse

a pigeon with a broken beak. Some people weren't meant
to look at the sun and blink as slowly
as other people pull a blanket over a sleeping baby.

Some people weren't meant to
be alone. Some people weren't meant to ever stop
smiling, sleeping, and holding the sticky baby fingers

that pull their mouths down
into a terrible drool. Some people
weren't meant to stop kissing long enough to thank god.

Some people, let me try to touch you
where you've never been touched before while I say this.
Some people, I'm sorry Lou, my touch must feel

just like your own familiar ache plus a little warm air.
Some people, come here Lou,
weren't meant to ever fall in love in the first place.

SARAH ROSENBLATT (b. 1962)

LEAVING HOME

The five-thirty light fell onto the dining room table,
pushed through the juice in our glasses
and slid bright orange along our forks.

We talked and laughed at dinner
losing our faces in mouthfuls.

Later, my mother curled up in the purple chair;
my father lugged his laundry up the stairs;
And I remembered I was waiting for a train.

Our faces fell to their borders
like cakes in the oven
when someone has jumped.

VISITING NEW YORK

It's a wandering kind of crazy way I'm taken
out of one place I always am and put into another place
I rarely am. And rare faces stare at me in rare spaces.
And eyes wander over the surface of my skin and then land
on the billboard or band playing behind me. And it's behind me
the eyes linger as I linger within
gasping at the emphasis placed on other things

but nothing emphasized here is emphasized there.
And emphasis is a matter of extremes
that evens out. And the street cleaner drives by
and the light from the pink and blue sign hits
the white table and runs along its surface
until it hits bigger and better things.

SHOULD I STAY OR SHOULD I GO?

I wonder where it is we belong
when daybreak wrinkles your new coat,
and pleasant is a word that rhymes with buckle.
I've been more or less unbuckling
into the late afternoon.
I've been hurt by your excursions,
not knowing the Chinese word for go.
There are stuffed animals with words written
along their bodies, torn and desiccating in the closet.
And men whose microphones reach further
into the afternoon than my shoes.

THE SECOND HALF OF OUR LIVES

We are all friends who have lived our childhood
way into adulthood.

Childless, we go out for dinner.
There are no compromises.
Each limb is its own.

There's only the commotion of living
the second half of our lives
in the bulk of the first.

THE PROCESSION

The hardships of tomorrow are put off
as we make our way to the grocery.

The living go to cafes
and discuss their injuries.

The dead keep their places

underfoot, marinating.

Meanwhile the procession of carts slows
in the paper towel aisle.

Those walking down the street with groceries
are indisputably of this time
properly devoted to this century.

Tin foil radiates off a windshield
wrinkling the reflections of the passersby.

Humbling those who
are already humbled.

MOM AND DAD GETTING OLDER

She went back to her hometown.
The recesses between her parents
teeth were growing wider
but love still shined through the holes
in their knit sweaters
and kept things at a warm familiar pace
with lunch preceding dinner.

SARAH RUDEN (b. 1962)

A BEGGAR OUTSIDE CAPE TOWN STATION

Not lichen, not yet here when this began,
Not cold, not river water, but a man;

Not sand, not weeds belonging to the place,
Not posters, not cement, but a dark face;

Not with me as my friend once was, a leaf
Thin with my pity, veined through with my grief;

But like him now, gone out beyond the grace
Of grit and noise and sunlight in this place.

LETTER

Try to see the spring here
Beyond my words:
The iron thickets breaking,
Releasing birds;

The boards and straw dust dark
And damp again;
The age and anguish of the barn
In the new rain;

The rainlight in a field
No talk has blurred;
The hollow wind retreating
Without my words.

THE STUBBLE BURNING

I have lost my friend. The semi trucks out there,
Their far sound in the desert of the air.

The field, the smoke dissolving in the clear
Evening above the refuse of the year.

The house, the children shouting on the lawn,
Their rhyming menaces. My friend is gone.

JOHN RYBICKI (b. 1961)

BROTHER BEN

They call him the Dog,
Ben Dog, because
he slings numbers
in his three-piece suit,

throws money out
his bedroom window
to the poor in our yard,
his family. The red hot

engines of our bodies
sputter on dollar bills,
gulp down the last fumes.
My brother Benny, wild,

slaps your hand
like all America
is in line behind him
to greet you.

In Directions

I roll awake on the carpet over
the bones of last night's words.
Outside, kite-tail children whip
against the air, and the day
lifts its cages off of my blood.

Yesterday I hugged my old man,
as always, for the last time,
slapping his back
as we let go, not crying
until my half-blind Charlie dog
stopped chasing my car.
He swung his nose to some shrubs,
then scratched his back against them,
letting go of me entirely.

For Daniel Beels,
Third Generation Bricklayer

The dawn birds on Somerset
bark in the late night air.
Someone has drawn us to that wound
in us we avoid. We soften,
notice my dog's keen ears
glinting in the street light's neon:
as if the world could reclaim its wildness,
as if the initials in the sidewalk
could turn back into children.

THIS SUN

I train my train into this city of mud and brick and collide
with my sis, her friends clanging their blood bells around me,

the city itself smeared in Rybicki rouge—all those bricks
humming their energy fields inside each mason's palm.

God how this city necks my neck with its fur coat of bricks;
those red hot dawns I dip my bushel basket

into heaven's own fire and drench it down over rooftops
and power lines and steaming beds; pouring that fire

across the grass and concrete grids of streets.
I flick my smitten fingers over the flaming beds,

lift in one palm what we call *sun*, tow it in
my oxen's cart slowly out over the world, my hand

to my own mouth blowing kisses back at those red bombs,
blowing kisses back at all those hearts exploding in my nest.

MARY ANN SAMYN (b. 1970)

POEM WITH LIGHT ON ITS SHOULDER

For Ellen

—And on hers.
Though she doesn't know it,
brushing up against the private hurt:

little spur, little asterisk—

She is thinking x'd out:
smudge smudge.

She remembers someone's thumb—

And earlier, *x x o o* —
short for *I would touch you*
if I could—

Such a small idea and gone:
her hands in the air at dusk,

        the sun—just a click now in the trees—

THE ART OF KISSING

The first lesson is electricity.
The second, *Attention, gentlemen*—

Or at least it was in 1936
in the book of *How*.

Unless of course you were *the girl*
in question—
                (unless you were hedging)
But the truth was I wanted him to.

Even though kisses shouldn't be free.

          (my mother told me)
Even though love is dirty.

          (she yelled when I was ten)
But he possessed *the same gentleness*
as would a cat
lifting her precious kittens
and touched my face
just like the book said.

        (mew mew)
This was what she never once mentioned: the *sex-hunger*,

never said white space
        fish mouth
           which way please please—
But gradually—

So pretext was unnecessary:

      After all we were not the book's shy couple
      and not hers either.

Though, yes, we sat on the sofa.

          (yes, there was a quiver—)

TROMPE L'OEIL IN WINTER

Everything white, the lake's cheek, turns
whiter, birds like hands at its sad mouth.

Snow at the edges, my body, trees' black
pale into blank landscape, then less, a vanishing

text gone like my name in breath against
the glass, the window flown off, its shuttered

wings beating. For mirrors now, only ice,
a tongueless mouth, entire alphabets swallowed,

the verb for dusk, the cold and foreign sky.
Shadows kneel in the dark boat of night,

its thick voice like deep rowing overhead,
beyond the moon and past the frigid stars.

MARGOT SCHILPP (b. 1962)

DEVOTIONS IN CONFIDENCE

There's a word for what we do
when a moment passes, when
the incidentals of traffic

and mayhem don't bother us at all.
Aren't you willing to be blown an inch
or two into what the winds inspire?

I believe everything you will never say.
I'm holding my ticket and the spectrum
is reversed: sweet green

a red glow, sirens of moss,
bruise-leaves and hematoma grass.
My ribcage flutters under its negligee

of skin, breath falling hard

and entering another mouth.
All it would take would be this

strange colloquy of fur
and carapace and wing. Try thinking
of sidewinders and a sloe gin fizz,

or the gentleness of persimmons:
there is always a secret
that won't bear telling.

Under the Scorpion's Heart

What I was reaching for
was a handle, a brick,

or a gun, so I didn't notice
the sky darken to black canvas.

I didn't notice the rain.
I sat on the steps

and let the light obscure me.
There are places

I'll remember as kindling,
where centrifugal force

drives everything from the center,
and nothing I've ever heard

is true. What if the mud dries
to mirage, and there is no door

by which to leave?
The surf entangles

the logic of the sun,
but sadness is no answer.

Take into my mouth
the constellations of lemons,

and—as feathers presume water
and wind—make up my mind to rise.

Non Sequitur

These days, what comes from your mouth
often surprises. This afternoon I am
reading to you the biography
of Teddy Roosevelt, condensed
by *Reader's Digest,* yet expanded,
too, the light banking off the large print,

the pages glaring. My voice
keeps coming out hard, loud,
almost falling against itself.
I continue. I explain.
As though your childhood had come after
mine, as though the light
in this room had always bounced

off plastic liners and catheters.
I am angry how age is romanticized.
Angry that people don't talk
about incontinence or skin
that erases itself from
the constant weight of the body.

You are in bed, but I ask,
this third time, if you want to get up.
You're satisfied to know
you're already there, again.
It's some time later when you crook a finger.
You ask me to come closer. You whisper,
You could kill me in my sleep.

Triage

It is a kind of triage, a setting
of priorities, this loving the bud
and hating the wilted flower: the red
of geraniums, another siren, another
little death resting in a bush, where
the air is different, the light
is different, the very molecules

we are, are different. All the stars
are out tonight, and I am spilling

salt, watching its crystals fall
into the patterns of stars, into
beautiful sadnesses. Vega, Sirius,
Alpha Centauri: I am wishing
on them until I run out of names.

It is the month of buds
and the vines begin their strangulations.
This life is a falling-away,
a discarding, though we collect
many things—our supplies of helium
and laughter are not in danger.
Still the end of winter turns

into itself: we must stay
in our own bodies, and though
we may leave cells on the pages
or on doorknobs we turn,
the stars keep turning out to be
only the idea of stars
before their light can reach us.

RUTH L. SCHWARTZ (b. 1962)

WHEN THEY KNOW

FOR H., WHO TESTED POSITIVE

> *"The man sitting next to Susan just disappeared,"*
> *said one passenger.*
>
>   *—News item, February 25, 1989*

We are talking about the plane:
the nine who followed the fuselage,
the sky which sucked them up lit by the jet's parts going up,
debris storming the hole—
the three hundred and forty-six who remained,
firmly buckled in their seats,
bolted to the floor, fused
to the wings and frame.

And it is not surprising that I think mostly of
the three hundred and forty-six:

their lives gleaming ahead of them,
some of them turning to religion, others finally able to love,
how they will continue belting themselves
into their seats, as if it keeps them safe,
how they will think there is some reason they survived—

while you can't stop thinking about the nine:
those few, randomly plucked from their lives,
radiance hurtling into dark—
you are with them in that instant,
just when they know they are leaving

GRIEF

Tonight a man with AIDS called,
threatened to set himself on fire
in front of our office next week
unless somebody does something.
Goddamnit, someone
do
something.

Sometimes I want to kill you
before the virus can.

★

I'm getting tired of loving people
who are someday going to die. I'd like
another kind of love—angels maybe,
starched and virtuous. All those gauzy wings!
Or maybe the already-dead,
    no surprises there . . .

★

I want to take you to the airport,
wave to a blurred face, a tiny hand
while the huge plane roars.
At least that one goodbye would be distinct,
    comprehensible

★

There is nothing now which death does not enter

Sex, the unnamed forest fire
That hour between us like a lit match

*

Yet how joy surges, sometimes, at death's lip
when there are no more reasons *not* to live

Late Summer

Walking the earth in all the changing
weather of our bodies
Days like Indian corn, their kernels
amber, ruby, jade

Lugging around these bodies, awkward as potato sacks,
a giant's boots, stumbling through the fields
picking raspberries

The fruits fall whole into our hands
They do not grieve

The sugars in your body, rising like a tide
Your baby skin, your old woman's breasts
The wild vanilla of your breath
Your blood's jewel on the white slide
of the glucometer

I think the soul must love the flesh
like we love fireworks,
for brief extravagance, for lighting up the sky
with their disappearing: rubies everywhere

LISA SEWELL (b. 1960)

The Denied

Often I return to that room—abject,
mortified—where after weeks of quiet,
an occasional moan or singing, something fell
hard and I opened the door to find my grandmother

collapsed. All the shades were drawn and the air
had that hospital scent of medicine
and stale urine. When I tried to move her back
onto the bed, I felt her thick
frightened weight, our shared weariness
and panic but mostly fury at my parents
who had left for the day. I can't forget
how I wished I hadn't heard, how I knew even then
if I had passed her in a diner, her hair in a net,
the left lens of her glasses shattered, with her sweet roll
and black coffee and Parliament cigarettes, muttering
in Yiddish and trying to catch my eye, I would have denied
that I knew her. For years I have offered up this scene
as the touchstone of my nature, evidence
that I lack the portion of chromosome
that carries the genes for courage, human decency.
But recently, I have begun to practice
another kind of compassion and have looked back,
full of tenderness, for the girl I was, especially
for the moments when we lay on the damp
grainy floor exhausted, and with my arms
still wrapped around her impossible, mortal shape,
both of us rested, the only sound our labored breathing
and my weeping, as we waited
with a faith I have not felt again, for me
to find the strength to lift her.

EXPULSION

Then I finally understood that the angel
when it comes will not be mild, but horrible
like Raphael who came down to paradise
with his warning and had six wings, not two—
one pair that covered his face, and one that wrapped
around his feet while a third flapped the air
behind his shoulders.

He must have seemed more gargoyle than cherub
with unnatural appetites and words that undid her, a beauty
that promised certainty not comfort. And after feeding an angel,
how could Adam—mere clay, God's handyman—appease her?
Their shared history, the familiar gestures
and syllables of his love-making would seem
a kind of suffocation beneath the roar
of those wings and even his explanation of her dream

must appear limited.

When the serpent opened his mouth, Eve might have seen
that pink flickering tongue and known enough.
Instead she closed the door on day
after day of the same. The second angel
came to lead them out of paradise and Eve
was ready. Holding up her binoculars
to drink in the terror of his slow approach, she smiled
despite her fear and regret, and felt
somewhat like a god herself to have called
such a thing forward, those wings coming toward her.

RELEASE

I have been the woman on the subway
who cannot keep, whose forehead
bears the mark of bewilderment,
the one you turn from to grant relief
from the searing self-loathing self-spectacle.
And I have recognized her crying
on the treadmill and looked away
or looked too long, become entangled.
One year almost every night I woke unnaturally
to the sound blood makes
as it streams from heart to brain and thrums
inside the capillaries. I wore my weariness
and could not abide the coloring book's instructions:
reserve red for the arteries, blue for veins
and green for the bile ducts. Every vessel
colored green against the ones
whose loves remained, for the man
who woke satisfied with morning,
even for one who suffered
not the failure of love
but of the loved one's much loved body.
I agree that grief can make the world expand
and stretch your skin to a dazzling luster, but today
I was glad to be the one to turn away
or look on in silence, that the heaviness
that entered the room was an inexact fit
and my own was elsewhere,
biding its time, that during those moments
sorrow smoothed my tousled hair
but did not linger.

PERSUASION

In the evening, an animated salesman, a cartoon version of a man,
	Mel Farr, flew into the firmament,
		leisure suit topped by a cape, a vast, gold "M"
across his chest, prepared to offer deals on the full line of Fords and
                                                                Lincolns,
	prices slashed like evil
		in my wayward metropolis, Detroit.

I waited for my mother's footsteps as Mel Farr soared and promoted
	his wares. A boy's deft hand
		found the clasp of my bra and dismissed it
with a flick. He whispered, "my dad and Mel Farr are 'like this'"
	marrying two fingers, that hand
		distraction, the other wandering in nervous circles.

His desire and mine, curiosity, my father's metronomic snoring—
	that's what it takes: balance
		of elements and humours, all good planets
in line, Mel Farr in the stratosphere—unwitting cupid, his salespitch
	background music to a static
		seduction. I imagined Mel in the showroom,

navigating straits between cars named for horses and mythical heroes,
	foreign words for speed, light, and wind,
		then flying into a sky-blue backdrop, his telegenic
image indelible, spondaic name impressed upon that night's
	constellation. The boy's name
		has dimmed, replaced by clusters of memory

dense as inky nights flush with stars, far from that city, any city,
	far from intervening light.
		I let him think that he could talk his way
in and under, the way a good salesman can—perhaps now
	he would rather be known
		for some other talent, but then, that was enough.

GOOD WATER

For C. V.

When the fires found their way up over the Laguna hills
soon to meet the nothingness left by good-guy fires,
backfires officially set to deprive the wild ones

of bounty, to starve them of fodder, we moved in closer
to watch, eye level to hell, a place where destruction
is so beautiful, you can't help staring. Told that rage

must exhaust itself, that flailing water wouldn't help
until the fire stopped to breathe, we sat on our heels
outside our frangible houses and saw what burns,

which is almost everything natural, as is the burning
itself. And we knew we were faster than the fires,
that some things that hurt us are slow, or seem slow,

or if truly fast, envelop the time before and after,
claiming their turf the way death dog-ears its place.
Where the fire began has long been abandoned,

though we're not sure where that is—the sun always
first to be questioned when some flame gets loose,
as if every fire was borne of a magnifying glass

and we spend our time trying to impress our symbol
on a dead leaf that ends up a smolder, or wanting
to prove that with a lone prop, we could survive

a cold night in the wilderness, though nights
are no longer cold that way, the coolness
one of indifference: Old God tired of pacts,

New One of healing, and now the sky bleeds
with dogs, bugs, warriors, ladies and ladders flung
by Olympians. But you and I can outrun the hour,

the flame's detour around the charred hills, away
from the numbing sea that would shock your limbs
into forgetting how to save themselves, erasing

memory and its pain, pain and its memory: help
we do not need. Our footprints indent the grass.
We watch. Then run. Why not? While we are fast.

You and Them

When a guy calls your jazz show
at 2 a.m. and asks for "Kiss Kiss Kiss"
by Yoko Ono, lock the doors.
You're there for two more hours,
and your home Studio A is
the best-lit room for miles
of sleeping suburbs. Studio B
looks like a space-ship,
all knobs, buttons, consoles
and their eerie green lights
that signal go, keep going,
one looks like your heartbeat,
scraggly neon cliffs that repeat
at your pulse's even meter.
A vat of black coffee,
a leaning stack of vinyl,
your microphone, suspended
from a robot's metal arm,
and big, padded earphones
cradling your head.
"It's 2:15 a.m.," you tell
your listeners, reading them
a lullaby of names off the back
of an album. You tell them
a story, the last time you went to
the Blue Note, on your birthday,
Carmen McCrae's 11:30 show.
You held your goblet's stem,
it was glistening and thin,
the barest glass skin around
dark red wine. Your date's
hand alit at the small
of your back. You don't
tell them that, that
would bring the crazies out,
the other insomniacs who want
to be wooed, already so
lonely and a sigh would make them
think you understood. Your voice
has sunk to its lowest pitch,
cadences that barely rise and fall,
you can picture undulations
in the air around your mouth,
they take you farther and farther

out into the darkness where
this sound that represents you
doesn't need you at all.

BRENDA SHAUGHNESSY (b. 1970)

RISE

I can't believe you've come back,
like the train I missed so badly, barely,
which stopped & returned for me. It scared me,
humming backwards along the track.

I rise to make a supper succulent
for the cut of your mouth, your bite of wine
so sharp, you remember you were mine.
You may resist, you will relent.

At home in fire, desire is bread
whose flour, water, salt and yeast,
not yet confused, are still, at least,
in the soil, the sea, the mine, the dead.

I have all I longed for, you
in pleasure. You missed me, your body swelling.
Once more, you lie with me, smelling
of almonds, as the poisoned do.

YOUR ONE GOOD DRESS

should never be light. That kind of thing feels
like a hundred shiny-headed waifs backlit
and skeletal, approaching. Dripping and in
unison, murmuring, "We *are* you."

No. And the red dress (think about it,
redress) is all neckhole. The brown
is a big wet beard with, of course, a backslit.
You're only as sick as your secrets.

There is an argument for the dull-chic,
the dirty olive and the Cinderelly. But those
who exhort it are only part of the conspiracy:
"Shimmer, shmimmer," they'll say. "Lush, shmush."

Do not listen. It's a part of the anti-obvious
movement and it's sheer matricide. Ask your mum.
It would kill her if you were ewe gee el why.
And is it a crime to wonder, am I. In the dark a dare,

Am I now. You put on your Niña, your Pinta, your
Santa María. Make it simple to last your whole
life long. Make it black. Glassy or deep.
Your body is opium and you are its only true smoker.

This black dress is your one good dress.
Bury your children in it. Visit your pokey
hometown friends in it. Go missing for days.
Taking it off never matters. That just wears you down.

POSTFEMINISM

There are two kinds of people, soldiers and women,
as Virginia Woolf said. Both for decoration only.

Now that is too kind. It's technical: virgins and wolves.
We have choices now. Two little girls walk into a bar,

one orders a shirley temple. Shirley Temple's pimp
comes over and says you won't be sorry. She's a fine

piece of work but she don't come cheap. Myself, I'm
in less fear of predators than of walking around

in my mother's body. That's sneaky, that's more
than naked. Let's even it up: you go on fuming in your

gray room. I am voracious alone. Blank and loose,
metallic lingerie. And rare black-tipped cigarettes

in a handmade basket case. Which of us weaves
the world together with a quicker blur of armed

seduction: your war-on-thugs, my body stockings.
Ascetic or carnivore. Men will crack your glaze

even if you leave them before morning. Pigs
ride the sirens in packs. Ah, flesh, technoflesh,

there are two kinds of people. Hot with mixed
light, drunk with insult. You and me.

R EGINALD S HEPHERD (b. 1963)

West Willow

For Christopher Cutrone

Morning traffic murmurs like an ocean
out my open window. Now it looks like rain, whatever rain
that hasn't fallen looks like, scrawled over the illegible,
sky moving south from Evanston with thunder in its gray
felt pockets. Happiness, I've heard, is easy, joy written
on earth, russet and sorrel leaves, fruit
fallen past ripeness darkest where the rot has set in.
And who wouldn't wish to live forever in the sensual
world, but not just yet? In bed at ten A.M.,
I asked for the authenticity of forms and the day
gave me this twig twisted from its branch, this broken bracelet
stripped of charms, a tear shaped like September
in the yellowed shade. Who wouldn't wish this sky
on anyone, clouds squandering their slate-gray
on potential weather? I walked out into the street
where life resumes its absorbing routines (I admit now
they mean nothing to me, people hurrying
to labor, people hurrying to leisure), crushed cochineal
small berries into the sidewalk. Even crows and starlings
wouldn't eat them. *If the fruit lasts long enough to fall, it's bitter*
through and through. I picked one up and crushed its globe
between two well intentioned fingers, it smelled of nothing
at all. These are my hands, these are love, that fails
and tries again tomorrow afternoon, as clumsy, as incapable
of making any single thing whole. These are my hands,
that have no power to hurt anyone, that wake
each day with no memory and begin again, lightly touching
this thing, touching inaccurately that. Rain shivers
in its several voices all night long, the scenery's submerged

in liquid air, white atmosphere awash in generalities.
How clean I can become. Now the trees lining the parking lot
are bending over solicitously, everything the wind moves through
is whispering *now, now*, and patting me on the shoulder
like small rain. It looks like this. Wherever love is found
(bent penny cured to ruddle, rust, raw chestnut
half cracked open), my hands are stained with it.

MARITIME

For Jocelyn Emerson

There's always been this dream that reason has, shearing off
from the conceivable like pollen or Sahara dust: a windy day
along Lake Michigan, cold water, cold war won. The ferroconcrete
lakefront where yuppies jog with dogs and clouds of midges
hover mating is a second nature, like the city it defines
by exclusion. People sun themselves on yellow
terry cloth across cement, water too clear
to be clean. The mind, unable to rest in such fragments
capital has shored up or left behind (man-made rock
fissured to exposed steel rods, absence filled in with lichen
and a sudden fear of heights: the undertow
of Lincoln Park a marsh, contradiction
buried in an unstable foundation), would be an inland gull or kite
convenient to the lowest clouds, flat roofs
of residential high rises across Lake Shore Drive
and lunchtime traffic: crippled by a rising wind,
untimely car: tethered or tangled there. Would be a sign, NO DIVING
SHALLOW WATER SUBMERGED ROCKS. Enlightenment
comes later, or not at all, lampposts flaring on in orderly rows
in summer, when days are long and promise
stalls like a gull against prevailing currents and falling
barometric pressures: every third bulb dead, burned
out. Would be anywhere, almost. Over there, the real
world of elevated trains and the Chicago school
of architecture rises into the sphere of possession,
claims the view south: the Carbide and Carbon Building
or U.S. Gypsum tower. Market fluctuations and assorted
human rights violations are duly noted in the ledger, cement
that holds society together, the concrete world
of what's smashed in order to make other things
whole. That's what this afternoon America tastes of, floating
tar particles and pulverized quartz on the tongue, wet sand
trucked in from building sites to make a beach, closer to mud

without the salt to desiccate and keep it fresh: glass silicates
and contained local conflicts, the debris disposed of
carelessly (a rusting corrugated breakwater, collapsed causeway
green-yellow algae plashes over, a drifting Fritos bag
or this old woman asking if anyone can spare some
coffee), also called the Third World here at home, but not in this
neighborhood. The wind employs each cardinal point
in turn, or pushes a low-pressure zone across the Great Divide:
of which I thought I caught a whisper, echo, or response,
anchor, answerer, or worse. Also, you figure.

WHO OWNS THE NIGHT AND LEASES STARS

I wanted to be touched, so I went walking
at four a.m., looking for cars. (I could have
written *loved*, lake wind that late a glove

that kept my body cold, so it would keep.) Blue
was the color I chose, because of the visible
sky even then, inside the black and under

purple; occluding streetlights ticked
off every half a block or so. I walked more
than half an hour, no one was scouring

cold streets *(they are all gone into the world
of good-nights)*, looking for a light or wrist
-watch. No one stopped and offered me

a ride to some room I've never been
before, or wait, I have, some neighbor
-hood, apartment, studio, some other part

of town where no one remembers my name, naked
when the lights go out. Harm is in us, and power
to harm, a stranger's hands staining my body

until I can't be found again. No one picked me
up or put me back in place, no one asked me
the time, and I told him the truth. At four a.m.

I went out walking, waiting to be touched.

Martha Silano (b. 1961)

In Henry Carlile's *Writing 213*

there were many *don'ts*: pirates, maidens, deer
resembling Bambi. And we were urged to be ourselves,
or selves, that is, who knew birds.
And if we had the nerve to begin
with a peer through a key-hole
we knew what couldn't follow. Trees

had names, in other words—
Texas mulberry, one-seed juniper—
it was time to learn them. To steal
from cormorants, admire our shadows, sing.
To make sure, if our speaker drives a Kharman Ghia
a semi destroys it. Pay attention

to your neighbor's yard. Juncos
plump in the rain. Beware of what you hate: the reddest
redneck loves. Listen

to chirping (rooms of industrious
typists, deep-pitched *jug-o-rums*, fingernails
running the teeth of combs). Observe the slowly
opening tulip (once it reveals its mysterious black,
it's over).

Rip the ring from your ear, the parrot
from your shoulder, unveil
the innocent, dismantle the fawn.
Find the bird that drums its wings
like a car that won't turn over,
spend a year with Richard Preston's *Trees*.

There is a toad, Henry, distant chorus
a diesel engine, engine you taught us
runs on compression. There is a bird,
ten years after the mill shut down,
still whirring like a circular saw.

On a warm night in early March, lost
in a maze of gray apartments, fooled you're far

from what sings, strain your ears.
This increases the odds.

But I hear them, Henry,
and you're right: it isn't a *ribit*,
any more than a creeper's a *seeseelookatme*.

You will fail most of the time.
Mostly, you will fail.
You will find yourself driving
in circles, buildings: A, B, C ...
you will long to knock on a door.
Always there will be singing you can't
put a name to—petals so perfect they drop.

SWEET RED PEPPERS, SUN-DRIEDS,
THE HEARTS OF ARTICHOKES

Pagliacci Pizza wants me
and lying in bed on a Sunday morning

I could almost want them back.
The trick, a deliverer said,

is learning to hesitate. Not in the car
or walking to the door, but just

inside, when they've paid
and wait for change.

Or I could manage a bingo hall,
dance behind glass at the Lusty Lady,
hone my knowledge of protocol.

Once it was a cornfield,
sixteen hours a day in a moving cage, reaching

for tassels. And I've picked cherries, scooped
pickles, sold knives and rakes and

rolls that fell to the floor
while my bosses took up flying.

Maybe Pagliacci's wouldn't be bad.
Evenings. A car. The minor streets

of Queen Anne. And I could settle in,
at the end of my shift, to eating
what got sent back.

The Moon

Though its map is drenched with watery names—
Lake of Dreams, Sea of Clouds, Bay of Dew—
the moon is waterless. Temperatures range
from three hundred above to three-hundred below.
Rising 15,000 feet, the Apennines
stood up long before Galileo.

To sleep in the light of the moon is to weaken
your sight. The moon, the bushmen say,
is a man who angered the sun. "Bloody" moons,
red because the earth is in the way,
portend catastrophe. To wax and wane
in Tierra del Fuego, the moon adds and loses weight.

Evil, fickle, noble, ruler of Monday,
giver of dreams and home of broken vows,
mirror, silver candle, assembler of stars:
only astronauts have seen your dark,
mysterious side. Though in pictures it looks like more,
Aldrin's footprint didn't sink an inch.

Once, in Kansas, on a golf course white
with snow, I saw you through a telescope.
Your brightness sent Orion to bed. When a rock
arrived at the Trenton Museum, I skipped school
to stand in line. In the Wallowas and the Bitterroots,
through the lace of urban curtains, I've watched you rise.

O place of lunacy, wasted treasures, squandered
time. Confuser of noodles, poppy, sad guitar.
Think of oceans, what something far away can guide,
think of the taste of tears.

Such a Way to Go

But that's how it is in this world. One minute battling traffic. Next, head
in an oven, inner kingdom hospital blue—cool and soothing glacier,
                                              what a baby boy

comes home in. With a sparkling silver toothbrush, the blanket's
                                                        unsinged.
De-ashed. Daisy Marble, Butter Sponge removed. And

what satisfaction! Such blue brilliance—spent comets, star cinders—
                                                        loosened
with Ajax. With force. No wonder she chose this: rising

crescents, soft braids, perfect white. Left her children (bread and milk).
The pan too large. Under. Over. Not quite done. Tick and bang of
                                                        a cold place

heating. Head where flour, water, salt. Peaks before they fell. . .

ROSE SOLARI (b. 1960)

CURRENTS

                    By the second
night of the storm, the ground had grown
so soft that whole trees were wrenched and thrown
against the unforgiving concrete, mangled cars.
I watched the T.V. newsman showing the height
of the river, and film of a woman wading hip-deep
into filthy water to save her belongings.
For no reason the storm was gentle where
I live: though the afternoon sky turned black,
the leaves turning over with anticipation,
what followed was only more hard rain,
over long before morning.

                    In the house
I grew up in, the basement flooded
every time it rained. I remember
a doll's house lifted an inch off the floor
by the current, the cold tiles that even
in summer kept the damp, leaf-rotten smell
of autumn. And I remember the gray,
stained couch my mother kept down there—losing
its threads and stuffing, lumpy with broken springs—
where Kevin McGuire for the first time slipped
his fingers inside my jeans.

                                    We lay there
together for most of a rainy, dim
October afternoon, my parents at work
and Kevin working to get me entirely
out of my clothes, and his hands did something
I'd only done alone and for myself
and we tried to breathe quietly, trembling,
touching each other's legs, hearing
the water build up in the window wells,
inside the gutters, outside the door.

DECEMBER 25, 1991

Where you are it will not be snowing.
Where you are the sun will be warm and wet
on your skin, and if it rains it will only
be beach rain. Sweet, but not actual. Not like
the absolute sand. You lie there now,
I think, on your back, a margarita
by your right hand, and though your eyes
are closed the outline of the horizon
is burned in—beauty too sharply focused,
like postcards, though something beneath
the surface is off. Inside your body,

a boy is ready to take his sled
down the hill one more time. He is ready
to steer straight for the icy patches,
the bumps that send him up, then back down
on the wood with a smack. Speed is his first
infatuation—a way to cut through the visible
world—and he looks in one direction, the rest
a blue-white blur at the corners of his eyes.
This is repeatable magic, how angels might fall
out of heaven, his muscles recalling, later,
the perfect exhilaration of near flight. Afterward,

there is always cocoa in front of a fire.
The strings of his hood, unlaced, release
a new tumble of snow that inside the house
turns wet, turns ordinary. Spilled water.
But his face in the mirror retains the stolen world—
he realizes he's beautiful, not like a movie star,
but the loveliness of a body falling in love
with itself, for itself. And inside that mirror

I see your face. I give it back to you now,
the day, the boy, the storm. Wherever you are,
however the heat unfolds, I am opening up a door
to a room that is only what it appears
to be, only for you. Go ahead. Go in.

TRURO

If I could be still
there would be a beach,
not too-difficult waves
and your jeans wet and crusted
with salt at the ankles.

The conch fishers go out
as I head back to the cabin,
my head full of beer and Cuervo.
I can tell the couple next door
are worried about me.

A fourteen-year-old boy
tried to pick me up tonight,
rollerskating out of the shadows.
He threw me a joint,
said *have a good weekend.*

I was standing, at the time,
in a liquor store parking lot,
trying to get up the nerve
to buy a bottle of champagne
to drink alone later.

I know I am going
to lose you—the facts
are in. If you could see
yourself, running like a boy
up the dunes.

ANGELA SORBY (b. 1965)

SYNCHRONIZED SWIMMING

How did decay work its way into the theater of water,
the Green Lake Aqua Stadium that was clear as chlorine
all through the fifties when Marilyns, Sues, and Doreens

formed a human hula hoop of blues and greens?
The past is a bag of Wonder Bread: bright dots, trapped air,
a place that suffocates. Still, I think the sky rose like yeast

when my mother, age twelve, broke the surface of the pool
as one-tenth of an opening rose. Her legs were firm fish:
all muscle, nothing to jiggle or squish. If I could visit her

in 1956, I would brush by like a cat, my eyes fixed
on some blah boy with a buzz cut. I would ignore
her spectacular kicks. I would not betray her with a kiss.

THE MAN WITHOUT A MIDDLE
After a painting by René Magritte

"Monsieur, your ribcage
    is a birdcage."

"Yes, well, my heart felt imprisoned
in my ribs, so I cut it out,
like a zealous saint,
and buried it at Père Lachiase,
where it sprouted a maze of foxgloves.
Since then, I have taken in boarders:
pigeons, and the occasional hen.
I once had a teenage nightingale,
but he was worse than my erstwhile heart:
demanded six worms a day!
These pigeons, by contrast, ask nothing.
They gurgle, like water at Lourdes,
or blood from a Muslim martyr's font.
They cannot be bothered with words.
They swallow for me,
and breathe for me,

and their eyes have become my eyes.
I see a blunt world, based on food,
and I wouldn't accept my heart again:
it's poisoned with petals, it's bad for the head.
So many things are more central than love:
shiny bottle caps, for instance,
or the woman in the park near the Gare St–Lazare
(God bless her!) who scatters the bread."

GOSSIP

People open up like doors
onto the blowing prairie

with its gorse, its fever ticks,
and the tricks a twister plays:

setting a child in a buffalo wallow
and her crib in a willow upriver.

People open up and the whoosh
of their weather untethers

dark lilies, a moon so full
it splits in two, a cold spell

that drives mice into the heart
of the hay. Maps map zip

on this frontier. The world
is aswirl in Wile E. Coyote

fake roads. Sunflowers
spin like Ezekiel's wheels,

like doorknobs on portals
swinging to let in Lord

knows what: a dangerous
pollen count, airborne toads,

the sense of being stunned
and swept off your own land.

LAND OF LINCOLN

That's where Lyle Wilson went, wearing his Mariners
baseball cap. In 1979 he was drinking tequila by a paper shack
near Bothell, Washington, when he got killed by a car
that didn't stop. The driver drove right into the Reagan
revolution, leaving Lyle Wilson, a boy who was no longer
human, to escape like smoke wafting out of a stovepipe
hat. The afterlife is bare as Illinois: the Land of Lincoln,

south of Chicago, where farms flatten to grey as if a spray
of ash has fallen. I'm loath to drive through,
even with the windows rolled up, but I did it once,
en route to St. Louis. The towns were not true towns:
just Burger Kings, and houses with their doors nailed shut.
No wrestling teams were practicing in the dark
and windowless gyms. In the Land of Lincoln, everything
turns into him: he's a tow truck, a tire store,
a bank, a school, a canister of logs, and a national park.

There is no heartland except in the heart: it is a single
apple, the red start of two or three trees. It is not Illinois,
where the prairie root systems are uprooted. Is it weird to lust
after the dead? Sometimes I picture Lyle, luminous in his skin.
I wait for his pulse until it beats in my wrist. In American
gothic novels the heroines aren't really afraid of ghosts.
No, they're afraid of ironing: the board, the sheets
and pillowcases, the flatness, the Midwestern

flatness.

PHILIP STEPHENS (b. 1966)

HANGMAN

Snow falls so hard the neighbors' windows seem
To stare at me through viscid cataracts,
And so I feel like I'm watched but unseen.
She's gone. The strokes took her away piecemeal:
Her reasoning failed, her left side lost all feeling,
But on the good days she'd ask where I was.
"Right here," I'd say. That answer didn't suit her,

So I'd ask her where I was: "Hunting quail,"
She'd say, or "playing poker," things I did
Before we married. Sometimes she'd mistake me
For suitors I'd contended with in school,
Or she'd hallucinate events from childhood:
A grassfire down the street, the shell-shocked soldier
Who swept the floor each night in Dunstan's Drugs,
Leeches she scraped barehanded from her shins
After she'd skinny-dipped in Francis Branch.
So quickly she regressed I thought of dolls
One twists apart to find another doll,
Another and another, until what's left
Is nothing, the last piece lost some years ago.
Each day, though, I remain at my routine:
The morning paper's crossword, cups of coffee,
Then errands, supper, reading, and to bed.
But with this snow, the streets have disappeared.
It seems too soon for snow. I set out bowls
Of candy last night, like she always did,
But was disturbed when children rang the bell.
Swaddled in sheets, baring plastic fangs,
Laden with besoms, they cried trick or treat
As if the night were some uproarious joke.
It started snowing harder, and they vanished.
My neighbors turned their porch lights out, but still,
Teenagers from the run-down neighborhood
Just blocks from here kept knocking at the doors.
They wore jeans, hooded sweatshirts, and they stared
Through me unless I asked, "Where are your costumes?"
One of them always said: "These are our costumes."
This morning, thumbing to the crossword puzzle,
I read that in that neighborhood, a man
Fashioned a noose from an extension cord
Then climbed up in a tree in his front yard
And hanged himself. The corpse remained for days.
The neighbors thought it was a decoration,
Bound straw or newsprint dressed to scare the kids.
Without her, I've not finished many crosswords.
She'd putter in the kitchen while I called
For answers to the clues I couldn't get:
Eight letters, for example, river islands;
Or seven letters, pardon; or nine letters,
Ends with an N, a system of I.D.
And thus, in turn, we'd fill the empty spaces,
Which is what pleased me, grids laid down like maps,

Lone letters as mysterious as runes,
Until each word or phrase we had to link
With ordinary human life was formed:
Sandbars or amnesty or Bertillon.
But I've been thinking of that children's game
Which takes two players. One knows the solution,
Draws lines for every letter of the phrase
And then a bare-boned scaffold and a rope.
The other chooses letters that might fill
The blanks; however, with the first wrong choice,
A circle's drawn below the rope, the next
Wrong choice, a line, and then more lines, until
A human figure hangs, just as some nights
Like this, while snow erases all the streets,
A spindling dark form dangles from a branch—
A lower case *l* scratched inside a square,
Hinting at words like *life* or *loan* or *loss*.
No. It's an effigy in casual clothes
And at each gust, it kicks. What's it made of?
Old straw bound up with twine, the *Times*, the wind?

THE SIGNALMEN

Our gang dug down two feet. With two feet left,
Our shovels scratched at oblong cobblestones,
The remnant of some streets to Sunnyvale.
We strained our backs, heaving out stones by hand,
Then where we could, we dug deep, laying pipe
In which we'd run the wire to each new signal.
That was the day that Paul Gonzales drove
Too fast along the main line to our ditch
And told us that he'd seen a girl struck dead
By a commuter on the eastbound main
Near milepost 36. He'd been called out
To check a switch and saw some schoolgirls cut
Across the tracks. But one girl wouldn't cross
Until the others teased her. The bike she pushed
Caught on the rails. "Worked more than forty years,"
Gonzales said. "Got two months left to go.
I tell you. I don't need to see that shit."
Our foreman kicked a clod off a stone
And said, "When I worked down in San Jose,
There was this woman hid between the rails.
Nobody saw her. Then a freight came on,

And she sat up as straight as Lazarus.
Wasn't a goddamn thing we could have done."
He shook his head then looked up from the stone.
"Hot rail," he said. We climbed out of the ditch
And watched the train approach. From far away,
We saw the black cowcatcher where the cops
Had marked the girl's form—trunk, arms, legs—with tape.
We smelled the diesel smoke. We felt the heat.
Wheels squalled, cars clamored, the commuters stared
Down through the dusty windows. We stared back.
The dirt we'd dug kicked up and danced around us
Then settled when the final car wailed past.

GOD SHED HIS GRACE

I struggled to read Homer in translation
And keep my hands from trembling with the jolt
Of the commuter back to San Francisco.
I reeked of diesel smoke and creosote.
Sweat rings had stained the ankles of my boots.
Eleven hours and I would rise again
At 4 a.m., just barely able to make
A fist or hold a cup or grip a shovel.
The reading was a ruse. I craved no knowledge.
I wanted coffee, sleep, tobacco, supper,
And I'd grown tired of reading how that culture
Reveled in glories past and failures coming.
I dozed and woke, dozed. The *Iliad* fell.
I woke, head slick against the rattling pane,
And saw we'd passed Bay Meadows racetrack where
Retirees tottered on; they stunk of beer
And griped about their kids they never saw.
We'd passed Hillsdale; the pretty girls who worked
The shopping mall, offering up perfumes,
Sat still and straight in seats along the aisle.
We'd passed Bayshore; the Vietnamese man
Who each day wavered through the car, his workshirt
Gleaming with sweat and grease, his forearms bright
With metal filings from some tool and die,
Sat with his tiny daughter near the front.
He slept, his head swaying away and back
So that he sometimes brushed against her sleeve.
She didn't care. She stood up in her seat

And sang "America the Beautiful."
Two women back of me said she was "darling"
And "precious" and "an angel." Storm clouds churned
Across the bay. All day, our gang had watched
Them rise but roll no closer to the ditch
We dug by hand. But they came as again
She sang "O beautiful for spacious skies. . .
For amber. . . For purple mountain majesties. . .
America, America, God shed. . . ."
Maybe she sang it when her day began
After she'd pledged allegiance in her class.
Or maybe she was proud to learn it through
And sang it once again, not to forget.
One of the women shouted, "Look. Out there.
How the sun's shining on that cloud."
                                   "How lovely,"
The other said. "It's like the sky's on fire."
Then hard rain beat the thin walls of the train.
The girl sang louder, battling with the clatter
Of rain and wheels on tracks across the flat
That ran to Tunnel Three. Her father stood
And yelled at her, "Goddammit, you shut up.
I want to sleep. Shut up," and sat back down.
She sobbed and clutched the seat. We hit the tunnel,
Each rider's profile captured in the windows—
Retirees, pretty girls, and worn-out men,
The backs of heads like barley in a breeze.
But faintly, I could hear a woman humming.

ADRIENNE SU (b. 1967)

ADDRESS

There are many ways of saying Chinese
in American. One means restaurant.
Others mean comprador, coolie, green army.

I've been practicing
how to walk and talk,
how to dress, what to do in a silk shop.

How to talk. America: *Meiguo,*

second tone and third.
The beautiful country.

In second grade we watched films
on King in Atlanta.
How our nation was mistaken:

They said we had hidden the Japanese
in California.
Everyone apologized to me.

But I am from Eldorado Drive
in the suburbs. Sara Lee's
pound cake thaws in the heart

of the home, the parakeet bobs on a dowel,
night doesn't move. The slumber party
teems in its spot in the dark

summer; the swimming pool gleams.
Somewhere an inherited teapot is smashed
by a baseball. There may be spaces

in the wrong parts of the face,
but America bursts with things it was never meant
to have: the intent to outlast

the centerless acres,
the wedding cake tiered to heaven.
Every season a new crop of names,

like mine. It's different
because it fits on a typewriter,
because it's first in its line,

because it is Adrienne.
It's French.
It means *artful*.

ANTIDEPRESSANT

The purple pill rattles
out of its tinted bottle,

makes my hands therefore my pen
shake, cloaks me in thirteen

layers of delusionary fur,
stunts my walk, and blurs

each stark moment so it won't
be so stark. At last I don't

know what time it is
sometimes. I like this

effect all right, although
I'm still sad. Night goes

too fast, bringing sun,
whose brash light comes

unwanted into each crevice
of the apartment. This

could be a matter of life
circumstance and pills might

be the wrong fix, but I know
things won't change if I go

to Spain or take up fencing.
I'd be the same wincing

Adrienne, only armed
or in Spain. What harm

in staying by the window
to think, wish, swallow

pellets of hope, and not eat?
I'm not unrequited, don't need

company, haven't lost friend
or family. I just tend

to be a sick plant,
and no antidepressant

can shield me from the sun's
burning; leaves drop one

by one to the sill. I'll win
my war yet. My angel isn't

dead, just lost on the moon
or snowed in, gone but soon

to come, nudged out of sight
by another sleep's night.

VIRGIL SUÁREZ (b. 1962)

SONG FOR THE SUGAR CANE

today at the Publix with my daughters
I spotted the stalks of sugar cane,

there under the boxed Holland tomatoes,
98 cents a stalk. I grabbed the three

stalks left & brought them home.
My daughters, born in the U.S.,

unlike me, stand in the kitchen
in awe as I take the serrated knife

and peel away the hard green
of the stalks for the fibrous white,

pure slices. "Here," I say,
"nothing is ever as sweet as this."

We stand in the kitchen & chew
on the pieces of sugar cane,

I tell them this was my candy
when I was a kid growing up

in Havana, this was the only
constant sweetness in my childhood.

This delicious stalk. You chew
on a piece & remember how to love

what you cannot have all the time.

Song to the Banyan

the wind frustrates itself held
in the thin leaves, sifted

through the tendril, rope-like
roots of the mighty banyan

stumps of elephant feet, tough
grey skin, of a tree that doesn't bend

against strong wind or hurricane
this one survived Andrew

in Coral Gables, where the Cubans
live now, they grow backwards

into the ground and sprout
more roots. How like exile

to leave such marks on those spots,
the places where life continues

in exile, the hand clutches
any dirt the heart can call its own.

Cuban-American Gothic

My father stands next to my mother,
both in the simple stained work clothes

they wore to their factory jobs,
instead of sitting next to the Singer

overlap sewing machine, zippers
snaking all around her, she bends

in the background; beyond her storm
rages, lightning fractures opaque skies,

while my father, instead of cutting denim
for pattern jeans, cradles an armful

of mason jars filled with blue fractal
light, bolts of lightning captured

for all time—in the distance, the bad weather
so absolute, this rite of passage from their

immigrant lives —*la vida dura*, my father
calls it—this skeletal American landscape

exposed by lightning, this flash of longing,
as if by x-ray, in this new foreign town,

against the ravages of time and forgetting.

DONATILIA'S UNREQUITED LOVE REMEDY

a brewed *tacita* of espresso
dark & bitter
some crushed leaves
of *yerba buena*
cobwebs
plucked from a vacant room
pillow hair (from the subject)
& one whole *colibrí*
feathers & all
stir over intense fire
bring to a boil
let simmer
once cooled
the trick then is to get
the person to drink it

RICE COMES TO EL VOLCÁN

the corner *bodega* run by El Chino Chan
where when the food rations arrived

the people in Arroyo Naranjo, Cuba,
lined up and waited and listened as Chan

called out "*alo, alo*" Spanish-Chinese
for *arroz*. Rice. I, six or seven, stood

in line with my mother in the shade
of the guayaba trees, watched as people

moved in and out of the sun and heat.
Women fanned their faces. Talk & gossip

buzzed like the horse flies that flew up
from the fields and brook. Chan told

stories of when the great Poet jumped
into the river and the villagers, to keep

the fish from eating the poet, tossed in
rice dumplings wrapped in bamboo leaves.

Rice. The blessing at weddings. Constant
staple with its richness of spirit. Sustenance.

Slowly the rations are filled and the line
moves and my mother and I reach the counter.

Behind it hang *papalotes*, kites made
of colorful rice paper, next to them

the countless oriental prints of carp,
dragons, tigers and egrets. Chan talks

about the grain of rice kept in the glass
case at El Capitolio in the city, a love poem

written on it in print so small one needs
more than a magnifying glass to read

what it says. Chan, rice, magic—the gift
of something different to pass the time.

Now, so many miles and years from this life,
in the new place called home, rice,

like potatoes, goes unnoticed when served.
Often my daughters ignore it and I won't

permit it. Rice, I say, to them, needs respect,
their full attention, for blessed is that which

        carries so many so far.

LARISSA SZPORLUK (b. 1967)

THE GRASS AND THE SIN

They are waiting for it, waiting all their lives.
They are question marks, changing into feathers.
They are lost between their legs. *Desire hath no rest.*
When grass is blowing, it lives twice, as grass and waves.
When they're in love, they give themselves to prophecies
and tongues, clouds that come with clear instructions.
Forty days and forty nights. . . . There is soundness in it,
soundness in her thighs, scrape, grind. They are waiting
to run down. They are hot. There are brilliant colors
in the sea, so deep no one sees them; air hides even more.
Two of every sort. . . . If he is not her husband, but divine,
if they are found, will they be punished? With no aroma,
who will know, if he's divine. . . . If Noah's water never
came, who would know how bad the land had been. . .

LIBIDO

A hand has her hair.
Don't move, don't cry out—
The odd foliage is shining in the light.

With the stealth of a wheel,
he rams against her knees
from behind. She falls

back into his purpose,
which is hers: to be provided for,
to find her insides altered

and grow huge.
But he runs off, done with her mouth,
leaving her dazed by the waste

of that kind of love.
She asks around, asks how,
where do we feel to find who we are,

watches some poppies freeze
in an orgy of plants,
their cold red gaze grown sideways.

She listens to parrots,
true inner birds, never at rest,
into whose breasts the world

blows pleasure,
shaking like nests full of Indian bees—
To scream is to sing.

DURESSOR

In darkness, crabs are believed to rest.
It is nobody's world. It is even less
theirs when they touch that first
inch of beach and the stunning blow
of elastic fire that is nobody's star
knocks them out of existence,
knocking them out like knees
in a murderous arena of tungsten lamps
and questioners. Of tables and pounding
fists. Of the decision of tide
to rebel against attraction, flattening out,
the moon looking up in surprise
from the underside of the stagnant water,
twisted and sad, like a coroner's eye
scrambled in a dearth of time,
the faraway body's insomnia, the crabs
combing the sand without minds.

RICHARD TAYSON (b. 1962)

NIGHTSWEATS

When I hear the guttural throatcall,
I tie the line around you, pull it
so you float toward me
like an unconscious swimmer.
I feel the wetness on my arm,

and think you are pissing or I am
sixteen and sleepwalking with a hard-on,
waking in time to see the arc
sluicing against Mother's new rug.
But I am twenty-eight and think you are
peeing on me, I turn to let it
douse my back but feel
the sheets wet and wake
fully and see
the sweat forcing its way
out, your whole skin
coming apart. You shudder
as if your bones have loosened,
I shake you, but you don't want to
leave the underwater lair of sleep,
I pull the blankets
down, remember
how I had lain before sleep
in the hollow bowl of your pelvis
and ribcage, cradled in the black
slime of pubic hairs, deep-sea flora
floating, how we fell asleep like that.
Now the horror in the dark
is the leak, the sweat
greasing your whole
torso, you don't wake
and I turn on the light,
shout, *wake up, it's a bad*
dream, you cry,
it hurts I'm scared, and I go
fill the tub because I don't know
what else to do, begging you
to climb into the cool water
before you catch fire, the whole ocean
a burning oil slick, the sweat
spilling on me
like gasoline, hot
wax, the sun
coming up as you climb in
to your chin, I keep
lifting your mouth above water,
crying as you sleep.

THE CHASE

I don't remember where he was taking us
but the radio was on,
Father tapped his wedding ring
against the steering wheel
and whistled like he always did
when he was away from my mother.
Maybe we were going to get a fifth
of something or other,
up Telephone Road, I wasn't fighting
with my brother, I was lulled
by the even keel of the engine, the car
so full of sun you would have thought
life was bliss, narcotic, I was
numb when the red sports car
pulled in front of us. Father hit
the brakes, my seat belt
tightened as if someone had reached
his hands up through the chassis
and was pulling me by the waist,
but my body lurched out of his grip
and we stopped before we smashed
into that car. The couple inside
didn't know they'd pulled in front
of us, they were drugged by the smell
of the ocean on a clear day,
I think they even kissed, and Father
pounded his fist against the horn
and said, *goddamn guy's drivin' worse
than a woman.* I looked
at my brother, and the Porsche
pulled away, but Father couldn't
stand it, he leaned out his window
and yelled, *whose ol' lady taught you
to drive*, and the guy
heard, his arm appeared, he flipped
my father the finger and that was it,
Father gunned it
and the guy saw us coming so he
gunned it, we flew
up the on ramp to Highway 101 doing
sixty, the Porsche darted easily
in and out of traffic, we were
losing him but I was proud
to be on the racetrack

with such a competent driver.
I remembered Father saying
when you hit a guy
you have to lean your weight into it,
so he floored it, we almost hit
a school bus, Father smiled
as if anger made him happy, his eyes
lit up bright as radar in the pupils
of the Six Million Dollar Man, I was
staring at a hole in the seat cover
where Mother's shoulder usually was
when my brother spotted the Porsche
turning into the J. C. Penney Center
where Mother liked to shop.
Father cut off two cars
and made a quick right, I thought
he would fly through the plate
glass store front or smash
that car to pieces, but he slammed
the station wagon into park
and jumped out like Clark Kent
bounding up through the phone booth
to show his two young boys how
to treat people in public, he grabbed
the driver's door and raised
his fist and reached in
to pull the guy out, when his face
turned blood red, his mouth
slackened, his body
went limp, as if he'd never seen
a woman before.

J. TARIN TOWERS (b. 1972)

MISSION POEM

When she dreams, she dreams
Of Mission Street, her body a bus (men ride)
Men get on and off, get on and get off.
Her face is as open as a vacant lot,
Walled in and fenced in and empty
Of all but the dirt, garbage sprinkled

In piles soft enough to curl up in—
But for the broken glass.
Her hands make the shape of a Styrofoam cup
Reaching for something to fill it.
Her eyes expand into oceans
Oceans the way they look at night
Cold and wet and black and oh,
They don't stop, they just rush in and out
Like the men from the check cashing shop,
Like the men from the barber shop,
Like the men from the bar,
Like the men from the Triple–Dash–X Theatre.
And her mouth, it is something to dance to,
A soft music escaping the dark,
Lips folding and unfolding, teeth seen
(but rarely) as glimmers of hope.
And when she smiles, if she smiles,
You will feel she has snatched a part of you,
You will feel that something is missing,
You will call her a thief, when you call her.
You will marry that mouth in your mind.

THREE OBSERVATIONS ON BELIEF

She believed she was cursed. She believed her guardian angel had
been detained at a flea market by someone selling tarnished halos.
Her halo was not tarnished. Kahlua's halo was spun from the finest
fiberglass and no one else could see it, but no one else had ever looked
for it, she figured. She believed she was cursed, and she knew you
were following her.

The boy's father found it easier to make schemes about selling disaster
than selling talent. "If you had a horrible skin disease," he said, "We
could make so much money. We could walk around saying we were
too poor to take care of your awful skin disease, your terrible skin
disease, and people would give us money to fix it. We would keep the
money, and your skin would get worse. They'd give us more money,
and I'd say, 'I've bought everything.' And they'd develop a cure. And
when we were really rich, and no one knew about it, they'd cure you,
and we'd move to another country."

I could have believed that your girlfriend died. I could have believed
you were on the rebound. I could have believed you got even more
depressed when I fell in love with someone else. I could have believed
you failed a class because of me. I could have believed you slept on a

couch in a trailer park. I could have believed you smoked crack. I could
have believed you got over me that quickly. But when you did,
I didn't believe you at all. Not at all.

ANN TOWNSEND (b. 1962)

FIRST QUILT

Her hands feed striped cloth into the machine.
Against her needle, cotton surrenders
while the first snows cascade outside,
silent in darkness. Her whole room hums
like a motor in the cold. By morning
she has stitched together the first stages,
light and shapely, the many pieced squares
of a simple quilt, baby-sized. Cars slide sideways

to the stop sign and the ash trucks murmur
uphill, sifting their weight to the ground.
She cannot tell what else she has begun,
though she knows each piece must keep the least
perfection and mistake in the pattern.
It all depends on the scissors' first cut.

AFTER THE END

Because I left him there so you could see
        his body, broken by the fall, the hawk's

small relatives hopped from higher branches
        and called a kind of glee that he was dead.
                By afternoon, the ground around him dusted

with feathers and gravel kicked up, he looked
        like a bundle of rags tossed

from a car and tumbled there, but still
        graceful, neck flung back in the moss and dirt,
                and the yellow claws curled to question marks.

Then the trees were quiet, the other voices
      gone. When a car turned into the driveway,

I knew it wasn't you. They sat a while,
      four men, the same dark suits, carefully
            tended hair. Missionaries: I could tell

from the window where I stood beyond
      their line of sight. All their doors opened

as if by a common feeling, something
      unseen and insistent in the air.
            They did not see the hawk lying there, dead

from its long fall, or age, or driven down
      by the crows that nest in the pines above.

They did not see me. I stepped back, behind
      the curtain, and wished you home, who could see
            these things and know what is beloved, what is dead.

EIGHTEENTH-CENTURY MEDICAL ILLUSTRATION: THE INFANT IN ITS LITTLE ROOM

Little sympathy, who kicks beneath my ribs
      for comfort, the clock reads 5:10
            and I am awake. Even held inside,

lightly under water, you hear everything
      and answer back to laughing voices, high music
            and the heartbeat, unceasing:

insistent baby, whose hands press out,
      who wakes me before light,
            the house is quiet except for us.

I don't know the moment I turned
      from one to two, when I began
            to think in plural. But long ago,

before sonograms and the x-ray's touch,
      before the Doppler monitor, one man drew
            what he thought was there, cupped inside

the cradle of the pelvis: another man,
        arms outstretched, a gold ring
                on each tiny finger.

Eyes raised, he looked
        for the place where music calls,
                where he might find a new world unfolding,

all glittering candlelight,
        graceful girls and bobbing flowers.
                Little one, we have this body

to ourselves, its ticks, its murmurs.
        We have a pulse, a subtle pressure.
                It drives us forward now, in time,

a late, insistent rhythm
        that plays as background
                for the waltz you've learned to dance.

The Bicycle Racers

Daredevil riding on the concrete lip
of an unfilled swimming pool, my brother
cartwheeled into the deep end,
tumbling twelve feet onto blue tile:

1969. Our parents disappeared.
We wandered loose, mining the woods
for the snake coiled underfoot,
lost dog shot between the eyes, for the farmer

who loved an audience while he beheaded
chickens for the church dinner.
Where were they when his birds fell
in a shower of blood, slavering their spattered wings

into the dust of the farmyard? Where were they
when I grew up wild?
I trust the blanket of solitude.
Now, when my daughter

prefers my company over her books
and a thousand piecemeal plastic toys,

I set her on her bike and push her free,
toward the narrow gravel road.

Ten stitches to the lip and a mangled
front tire: my brother lay there
for an hour moaning before the dogs
found him, and set to barking.

PIMONE TRIPLETT (b. 1965)

SPECTRAL DUES

In the lens of memory, that smudged bungler,
I can see a bed set below a picture
window, one rectangle reflecting the other
in a room which might stay with me for the rest
of my life. Most often, I'd wake before him,
coming up fitfully from sleep, from the mind's
floor, its dull grains of sand, all separate.

A runt of a room, uncurtained, water
in a glass stolen from some restaurant,
early light slicing through it, making
small cuts on the blue wall, on his skin. What I
couldn't know yet: how this was the year of wanting
someone so much that his body, that other room
he owned, was also a limit. Didn't know how

my caught attention—a thought snagged on the two
aureoles of his chest—rising and falling
those mornings, was a wish to reach *beneath*
the skin, to pierce, like one eye into another,
glints below the surface. Maybe I just wanted
to break his breath in two with my own. Or find
the measure of the corner that resists,

as if the soul could be found out, fixed at last,
made to turn, made to look at me. As if place
could be the remedy for place. Once, as he slept,
I stepped into his closet, wanting to find
his scent inside, something more to keep. And if
there is shame in this, it's that now I can recall
nothing of what I found there, past dark clothes,

jagged hangers. Who wouldn't like to know
whether the greed, or grace, of desire
is simply the coin you have to pay, turning
the face up? Outside, the neighbor I don't know
turns his face up, wheeling the unearthed azalea
as though it matters where a plant can belong,
its underside a black heart, roots exposed,

fibril veins trembling a bit in the barrel.
The world is too bright. And he looks up at me,
waving, until I am waving back now, caught
with nothing—ears ringing, eyes blurred—falling
with nothing here but that other sunlight,
just once, branding skin and bones, two bodies
burning, burnt, through the stolen glass.

STUDIES IN DESIRE

1

More than eager to rid himself of a father—
that pragmatic mandate to "take only snaps"—
Edward Weston migrated from Illinois
to Mexico, marriage to mistress, driven
by a lust for purity that made him raid
surfaces and skins, finding, at first go,
the pleats of crepe de chine in a cabbage leaf.

After that, a door in a wall opening
behind a door in a wall. And beyond,
the slow spread of blond rocks mirroring,
mimicking the lintel from a wrecked house,
or the soft inner bank of a woman's thigh.
All the while scale starting to fall away
like an old attachment, the motive and motif,

as always, to move, to travel west. Intent
on anchoring the flesh, then finding a dead
man in the Colorado desert, that skull,
enlarged, up close, lapsed into fractured lines,
strands of separate hair just echoing
the cracked enamel of an abandoned car
he'd seen miles earlier. Still, the pairings

were random, bodies broken on a spine
of bad circumstance. For days his real art
was in warding off the cold, ice fronds
branding the lens at night, crystals forming
in a basin of fixer. Until one morning,
waking to sand dunes fingered by a night's wind,
he thought he saw the perfect inscription,

a new language of lift and bend, as suddenly
the waves took on just the look of her rib cage
when she arched the small of her back in the moment
he'd told her *don't stop breathing*. Now he could
step back, owning the likeness he'd chosen,
saying to her, *stay with it, stay long enough,
and the exposure, love, won't let you go.*

2

Then in the doctor's office, story of a man,
his equipment and cravings, as he made her step
first into the exquisite light of the x-ray,
watched as it burnt past the ladder of her ribs,
finding the tubed heart in its hiding place,

the liver plump and radiant. The room itself
radiated in shortened wavelengths, a beam stripped
to the less than visible. Something like what
we used to call "soul," its measure unable to be
reflected or diffracted in time. From the new

science, a magnetics so frankly astral
as to pierce through flesh, muscle, any old
tabernacle of the solid, stopping
briefly at marrow to find a pin lodged
in the hand, a bullet taken to the head.

The morning Weston let the light take him too,
looking down to see his own torso fixed
in the picture, lungs revealed simply
as stacked caverns, veined chambers of tissue
as yet unwrecked, in the second he thought

he could see his own wet throttles built
for the inner and outer weavings of air,
suddenly—the ears rang, the eyes blurred—
another step and down he went. She propped
him against the machine to recover.

A wooden cabinet, a coil and rotary.
As for the body's sway of targets and breakers,
in that moment she knew there was no cut deep—
skeletal—enough, for the living.
Afterward, she bent down, tipped his limp, newly

printed form toward the metal, turned her face
away from his, stepping back. In his daze,
he thought he could hear her praying, murmuring,
no, Lord, you get nothing back, or was it
yes, Lord, here's the nothing that you get back. . . .

SPIDER OF DOUBT

*Lust in the long run spins a kingdom of lull
and dither,* I was saying, when down it slid:
the blond spider, arriving apropos of
all its eights, innocent as pinprick.
Notwithstanding you and I—weatherworn,
window-seated, couched in a kind of progress—
after qualms and wavering, who can blame
us for naming it our pet? We nurtured
it as our nature, loved its search, so be-
fuddledly running the span of sofa,
nightstand, bottom of bed . . . You came and went,
biting like a mate. I'm webbed to the edge.
Tell me again why we're never the we that's needed
to weave, never putting us, our trust, at stake.

SAM TRUITT (b. 1960)

FROM *Anamorphosis Eisenhower*

I. THE KERF

But her favorite poems take place underwater
This one is called *Holding Your Nose at Forty Fathoms*
It is Easter afternoon & we walked to McDonalds
Beneath a sky of graphite clouds
But her favorite poems take place underwater

Before blood had become the 7th element after money
An ancient poem when it was still bereaved
That everything that happens is matted with meaning &
where-would-my-life-be-if-I-turned-around
But her favorite poems take place underwater
This one was written while we were taking a shower
Slippery with soap washing   The Black Bird
Its throat its beak its heart slamming against
Four hours watching the set   drank 1 beer smoked 8 cigarettes &
where-would-my-life-be-if-I-turned-around
& against her thighs splashed

The mind.
                    And I found
My body again under your hand &
The circuits of my body entered   The Poem
Its throat its beak its heart slamming against
My body again under your hand &
The angry men in their goggles pursue
Their mad career around the raceway
Of life! of life! of breath divided in & out
The loops of distraction as
The scenery & the angry men in their goggles pursue
The spectators at the edge of their lungs
Whipped in & out of view of
The screaming cars & Handsome Hanson in his Marvelous 8
Car-grime streaking his lovely flushed face
The angry men in their goggles pursue
With a red scarf streaming behind him

The violent flowers in our mouths & in the sky &
What is fun but taboo speed & love we must
Beneath a black umbrella ghosting through the rain
In his Marvelous 8 car-grime streaking his lovely flushed face
Teeth clamped to a stogie smoking through the foam
& the blocks   of 20th Century houses
& Bob is in the basement filming a subway chase in Boston
We've run out of oil. Forsythia blooms on the fences
& that's not all. But I meet Mark in an hour
& Bob is in the basement tearing out the curtains
Picking up where we left   clothes strewn on the subway floor
Everything sad is "remembered" somehow
We must blaze a trail through the banks of marigolds
& sometimes we must crawl   on our bellies through the dirt
Picking up the polka left off on Central toward
What was left of the palace

The embattlements the ringed garden & the Black Bird perched
In a window-well at the Last Call Saloon
Winks to me like my old granddad in bathrobe & slippers
Picking up where we left off picking
Up where we left off o brother from
Somewhere near the solar plexus (straightening his shoulders)
For granted in the big baffled smile
Of an old man slipping down through the graces
Whipped in & out of view of
The plow an old man slipping down through the grease hole
Watch out son the tail-fuselage is on fire!
What is the Nature of Rime in the hive's gold cluster?
The moon that rose between each of our days
The night we held beyond each embrace
What is the Nature of Rime in the hive's gold cluster
Beneath graphite clouds, Madam?

VII. OLD WORLD MONKEYS

In Geneva I pawned my pocket watch & passport
& those dreams were going on. So we finished high school
A row of fence stood around the keg on a hilltop
The road below in the streetlight shining   "Black Macadam"
A row of fence stood around the keg on a hilltop
& where are we if we are not there chewing the fat
The mind shapely & 5-leafed. So we smoked some pot
A hand its palm turned up stroking the belly
Keto if you can hear this don't get married!
Shapely & 5-leafed   a carburetor the senses flood
What we think I tell you comes back tanned adorned dressed up in
    other clothes
Other times the road grows more strong slick &
We give mouth-to-mouth resuscitation for   the displacement of the
    figure is
The form. I have watched it through the keyhole grow
"What we do I tell you comes back skinned broiled
Behind the eyes from one pale tendril. There are

More & the demons roar "In Geneva I pawned my pocket watch &
    passport"
I have gone through the form   The displacement of the figure is
The Providence Bruins get beautifully battered
What we do I tell you comes back caressing the line
What we do I tell you"   thinking about that movie I saw last night

            we could go on like this forever
The dark nights loom like refrigerators   Are yours?
I snap on my facemask smoking Freud
We live lives of mild exaltation the 3rd
Door to the left of which drops in on men who've learned
To give to their suffering mild exhalations   read "aneurism"
Men stand up in their dreams to run down their houses
With red scarves caressing algorhythmic paper-clips
Are yours? Freedom is a word men have learned
To give to their wandering an esprit-de-coeur
With red scarves caressing algorithmic paperclips
History is the consternation of famous men

                  & a fold-out leaf of color illustrations!

When she offered you the apple you should have said no to her you dip
I look out at the world through a chink in the arbor
It is curious. It fits. It follows. The room floods with
History is the consternation of famous men Madam
When she offered you the apple you should have said
"Julia I love this camera!" She boarded the plane to L.A. wearing
            overalls
"In the apple is the worm & the worm is good" said the Rock
What is natural is   the dog up on its haunches
Dreams fade like islands nothing holds
When she offered you   the apple you   loved her more
Like a 3-day beard wandering along the River Were
& slept for 7 years among the dwarves of the wood
They were curious. They were lecherous. They fit
They were knocking the heads off parking meters
Dreams fade like islands nothing holds up against the sky a tree a cross
What we have here is a slice of the swoon

When the snake coiled himself inside Eve's womb
Waving a white flag of nothingness she could not see
I have gone through the door & it is good &
The beatitudes sleep in the blown grass like abandoned marine mammals
Waving through a last shred of mist a white flag of
Nothingness we could not see   :through
& the white picket-fence where marigolds once weighed sags
Flynn is a great name for a dog & snow flurries wave
At an open boxcar door the soundtrack to   "There was a Tree in Ohio"
Shining torches through the rain the search party wept
Picking our past to pieces that fit   the last 12 years we crashed
The mind a mosaic flashing between dimensions

When you are spun in a cornfield is the only direction you can count
    on up?
& those dreams were going on. So we finished high school
Shining through the rain the black slab against which
Nothing will fade   the sky   Apollinaire's plane

ALPAY ULKU (b. 1964)

SPRING FORWARD, FALL BACK

Be a facilitator, not a roadblock, says the lady who runs the news stand,
                            when the children
    reach for the comics,

BROTHER, CAN YOU SPARE A DIME playing as she dances sixty years ago,
                            her hair falling over
    her soldier's arm,

the scent of peaches. Are you my son? she whispers. The *Times*,
                            please, smiles the man.
    Are a changin', she always replies.

And after three days of unpaid "training," the new telemarketers are
                            replaced with more of where
    they came from.

Even his secretary, fresh from college, knows to clock herself out and
                            stay, though the light falls
    at 5 P.M., falls and falls.

Hard times are hand-me-downs tossed to the youngest and the poorest.
                            The 1960s were a crock
    of shit.

Tune in, turn on, drop out, smiles the son. Clean, don't lean, the lady
                            replies, hands him
    the *Times* and his change back,

the first snow wheeling over the city, how if you look just right, you
                            could believe we were moving.

HISTORY

Even this far from that burning place
the dogs would not stop howling.

When we gathered by the river
our captors told us our captors had been destroyed.

O City of Pure Light,
they razed what they had rebuilt in your name.

When the tinsmith's son stole from the grocer's cart,
we cut off his right hand, and fed it to the dogs.

I'm not saying it was wrong.
I knew the tinsmith's son, learned a song from the grocer.

But what we did to the woman who read the future in our coffee
    grounds
and spoke of what she saw.

I'm not saying what: I am no fool:
I did not want to die:

I took my harp down from the willow tree
and sang.

When they flung their copper coins at my feet,
I thanked them.

When they laughed to see me scramble in the mud,
I looked in their eyes and I laughed, too.

LULLABY

You are safe.
You are lying in a hammock
far from the cult of the black sun,
the folded wings of the sky over Portland.
Far from the mantra *information*.
You don't have to justify your life.
You could be a flower,
your own thoughts falling around you like rain.
You could be the timber wolf

who has lain in ambush a hundred thousand years
for the flying horse to land once more.
Sleep steps lightly over the wet grass, cocks its head.
The highway ribbons through the mountains
and vanishes into the afternoon.
The light is pale and clear.
It feels good to listen to the thunder.

R E E T I K A   V A Z I R A N I   (b. 1 9 6 2)

MRS. BISWAS OF MARYLAND ON THE PHONE

I.

That Sindhi boy is keen on you.
I saw his mother at Sari Town;
nowadays she is chubby as fruit,
worrying constantly for her son.
I discussed that you are up at school
just like your Nana was. Now he is lame,
and any second he could fall,
he rambles about lorries on our road,
hiccups for several days at a time,
only three Bengali words he says to me.
I am with your Nana this century
so I know what it is to be married.

II.

Are your foods good in Cambridge?
You are getting mustard seed and cabbage?
If not, I can send you mustard seed
by post, but for delays on this end;
I am thinking worldwide postal strike—
last month critical letter to X
of D.C. bank, regarding Nana's checks,
came back to me with Philippine postmark.
Mix-ups like India only but very
much worse: last week I sent my sari
to new dry cleaner, and I was in shock
to be billed for two tablecloths.

III.

I must buy eighteen nylon saris
and Walkmans for my India trip;
hope customs won't take my batteries.
For years I collected lipsticks to give—
Avon, Ultima, and Maybelline;
I ordered heart attack tablets
and Dramamine pills—handy for seven-day
weddings of Hindus; and I retain fluid;
lately my thumb expanded to such an extent,
I answer the phone with my oven mitt.
Labana, Cheekoo, paying respects: believe me,
they're hinting of fashions from Delhi.

IV.

You do one thing: come with me to Delhi
while Blue Cross is carrying my health;
I must procure your husband or else
you settle on that Sindhi boy, no doubt
his father is leading in pathology
(and their import business is nationwide).
At twenty-one I finished botany
and engaged. You are nearly twenty-eight,
reading, reading, how do you live,
you will get cataracts from scholarship;
no money, then you go blind. Your Nana was
a scholar, but that Sindhi, tsch, clever in accounts.

Mrs. Biswas Goes through a Photo Album

1. Holidays at Lake Nageen, 1925-1938

You see us in this picture,
four girls with matching frocks,
four cousin-brothers wearing cricket caps
all at Kashmir on holiday.
We hired a boat with thirteen
rooms and took our own cook, Tirupati.

2. Christian Life

It was fresh air days, and streets
were clear for evening walks,
not like the problems we are having now,

Hindus rioting with Musselman.
We were Baptists from the start
though we respected goddess Kali,
very prominent goddess in Calcutta
seen in every temple.
We snapped her photo at *Durga Puja*.
Whatever you may think of it,
we retained our Christianity.
And when we walked outdoors at eight
in the evening, Mashi wore her crucifix
outside her sari blouse, and we walked
with the Buntings who had lately
turned to be Jesuits.

3. Business Life

You ask about the childhood days—
you recall my father died.
His brother had a soda factory
so we lived with Uncle Jiten,
such a house he kept on Park Street.
(See nine cousins on the marble stairs.)
And he dispensed our pocket money
at the season's final cricket match;
we stood behind the soda sellers
and gathered the bottlecaps:
one anna per dozen, and the coins
among us lasted all year.

4. Marriage

My sister keeps the college photos
so this next one is my marriage day:
note the length of receiving line,
so large was our family
even I cannot recall the names.
Some say numerous impostors joined
to partake of our prestige.
The Governor himself arranged
the date; he even matched your Nana
to me—such marvelous governors
we had those times. My portrait
was shown at the Reception Hall.
Photos are one thing, but painted
canvas—only that one kept my beauty.

Mrs. Biswas Breaks Her Connection with Another Relative

Nobody can please her except God,
she is that type of girl.

This is what news I have heard:
she is expecting only seven months
after the wedding.
Did she come to my house
to tell me of the wedding?
No, she phoned me up.
She is a daring girl—
from the beginning when she came
to this country she was always
rebellious and disobedient.
Who can instruct her
who has her own ideas on life? For that,
I am breaking my connection.
Nobody can please her except God,
she is that type of girl.

Anthony R. Vigil (b. 1968)

El Hogarcito de La Madrugada

is the mother of earth, moon, and stars
disappearing a ball of quetzal feathers
under the waistband of skyscrapers,
flesh of serpent fire and macana buses,
rolling the moon and streetlamps to flight,
day of flower and tainted water.

I can hear the spirit of dead bones
beneath the holes of sewers,
the stones of flint knife planted
under an old tree. Beyond its roots,
shadows of prisoners and the souls
of jefitas walk the serpent fire
into the tomb of sky.
They are arrows of light opening

arteries of stars, the nectar of elote
seeping further into the mouth of earth.

Before the government building, there is
the lip-clawed spirit, the shield of serpent fire
and ocelotl skin of feathers, copper rims
and golden fenders on stellar ranflas, placas
of water and movement; I can hear their tongues
scraping against the boulevard of night, the first world
airbrushed with the sun of spotted skin.

I've seen the sun hewn down in the water,
watched it sprout teeth and skin
to devour giants between the fingers
holding a forty of booze as love.
The pata of darkness uproots
trees, cardboard chantes,
and the white stream of bones.

The wind, clay ground between teeth,
spreads the dust of cornseed, the whisper
of exhaust. The eagle ladders of breath,
taloned sunflowers in front of the projects,
are laurels of light, balls of copal
and liquidambar to the mother and father of gods.

And even through the smudged glare of oily light,
el hogarcito de la madrugada is the maguey
spines of blood and liquid coral before concrete;
it is the brazier of fire blossoms, quinto sol
stem of light, pure fire of the world:

ocelotl spots of ash
black-tipped feathers of eagle.

THAT'S THE WAY, UH HUH, UH HUH, I LIKED IT,

uh huh, uh huh, my jefitos
shakin' they booty above concrete

draggin' dust up to K.C. and the Sunshine
cold iron keg flowerin' joy
into legs, hips, and lips

spillin' the plastic cupped birongas
threads and hands pushin' up
bodies hustlin' back-n-forth

me shakin' my lil' grove thang
hittin' up my jefito for mo' sips
holdin' the silk hand of my jefita

leanin' our hearts into night
shufflin'-n-spinnin' above brick
bottles, and cracked walls

brown circle of light
boogie'n stars staggerin'
mano a mano halo drifting

still gettin' all the way down
on clogged walks of tar
lappin' up grooves con todo mi alma

me hopin' our halo never dries
like the sweat of skin on stars.

AT THE STOP LIGHT, THE BRAIDED BLOND MAN

driving an orange bug, passes
his smoke to the tusk smooth
woman in the passenger seat.
I can see rings of salt on his suede vest,
sweat inside the shovel of his upper lip,
and black dirt under his fingernails.

Smoothing back her bleached hair
with long and thin fingers,
the bracelets and rings of the woman
burnish the smoke into silver light.
She takes a long drag. Blows
it out the cracked window.

They laugh louder than their radio
cranking up songs on the street.
The woman points at our gold Ford,
at me, as the man turns his head
and glances with eyes of blue fire.
When they return to her,

they both smile, turn back
and wave hello.

I roll my window all the way down,
push out my head and chest
of raised arms and folded fingers:

¡*Viva la raza!*

The light flashes green,
as I watch both of their fists
rise from the windows,
until their reflection in the mirrors
of skyscrapers is an orange
butterfly, flapping towards
heaven.

AS THE BEER TRUCKS ECLIPSE THE
LIGHT OF MORNING,

una jovencita across the street sinks into the dark mouth of her bus.
She sleeps until gringolandía.
Yesterday is newspapers twisting along cracked streets,
black tumbleweeds bleeding the ink
of nuestro cuento into trapped gutters.
Y ahorita, the heat of day cruises in as pesadilla,
blurring everything into despair:

Young homies y veteranos hitting yesca & forties in the park.
Hermanas walking to a nowhere jale.
Chingao, esta sociedad no nos respeta.

Pero, sabes qué, todavía hay resistencia a la violencia,
the accumulative small deaths.
Because when the sun burns elote-white,
it traces el quinto sol, profecía de nuestra sangre.
Los chamacos run through the water of Lake Texcoco.
They are flower and song, blossoms of brown and proud legacy.
Their cool-breathed laughter sings el corazón del barrio,
gallitos awakening la raza al canto de la belleza,
el ritmo de la vida, a songvoice for nuestro barrio
to help us remember why we were born:

straight-up born for beauty, love, and each other, homie.

K A R E N V O L K M A N (b. 1 9 6 7)

SEASONAL

Much melting, and crows close to home.
Snow giving its fingerprints this March morning.
If I could, I would take your arm
in the manner of our European forebearers,
linked elbows, fist pressed close to the heart,
singing songs to the springtime, singing old songs.
It would be this much to give to the world,
to the dead in the ground who need consoling, need consoling.
It would be this much to give to the world
which is not like a boot in the face, but a blessing.
The wordless birches rise up, a pure promise, but it is
early, the day collects in puddles, you are far off.
And remembering noise in the wind, and remembering.
Your eyes which are paler than sleep
kissed from the forehead of one who is still dreaming.
If I could, I would take your arm.
Then the crow in the pine would know us, saying
These are the ones who knew so little, all the time.

THE PREGNANT LADY PLAYING TENNIS

The pregnant lady playing tennis
bobs on her toes at the court's left side,
raises the green ball high, and sets it

spinning. Then moving in circles
of deliberate size, she returns the lob
with the same giddy grace. In the quiet glide

of the lady playing tennis,
there's a knowledge of speeds and angles,
arcs and aims. From the other courts,

the players watch, dismayed, half-fearing
for the safety of the lady playing tennis,
half-wishing this odd distraction shut away.

Tennis, they notice, is a dangerous game.
But the ovals close
on the lady playing tennis, as if

the tight-knit mesh of her racket
were a magnet, with the ball
a perfect pole veering home. Watching

each hard-shot lob clear the net,
the pregnant lady playing tennis
braces in the pure sensation of her game,

in her body's stretch and haul, and plants
a crazy slam past the net: past the lines,
past the out zone, past the court's steel network wall.

THEFT

Two men filched pumpkins from the grocery display.
It was late night, harsh. The sprawled orange stack
preached of plenty while the moon
looked sarcastic. What loss! What lucid absence!
What roaming of suburban streets
with crazy globes. I thought of it next morning,
fixing oatmeal and coffee. Necessity. Surfeit.
I'd watched, one long year, my lover
feed his dying mother, the mashed food
laced with useless medications, the spoon
small in his hands. The old woman must have
barely known, stunned with age and her body's breaking.
The common slander of a failing heart,
her throat so choked with phlegm
even soft food could barely be taken.
But still her mouth sought each spoonful,
automatic and ready. What did she crave?
Peace or new life? Sometimes she called
for her father or long-dead friends. I remember
her faded eyes, the white hair oddly set.
Her mouth was thin and chipped with wrinkles,
it opened vaguely like a bird's or baby's
as my friend offered again and again the tiny bites.
There were stark hibiscus and a view of the inlet.
Early boaters and easy chatter and daily fear.
There was casual sunlight. We took meals
every morning. Nothing simple about it.
Something stolen. We must have known.

(Untitled)

I was watching for it, everytime watching, for the neck that was bent, for the nape that was bare. The hand holding a cup was holding a thin cup, then the cup was broken, and the fluid gone. So things were the same—eyes stayed blue, limbs retained their curves, slacks and sleeves. Someplace more thoughtless something would happen, less full of couches and women and legs. The windows were waiting, and the lamps, and the hat donned once, discarded, and the hesitant hips, and the whisper which forebore. For all was intent, potential, not fulfill.

I go out sometimes, like a shadowless ghost, less remnant than lip, in the incomparable midnight of intransigent mist, and the doomsayers and lockpickers, cloud-like in clairvoyance. Lad, you keep the latch hanging, keep the curtain drawn. Beyond blue night, when the puppets are sleeping, the stars all coiled in their tremulous wheel, the thin moon summers in my goldenest gaze, awakening dreaming oceans, to drown, to roam.

Sky-eyed scholar, pale Confucius: Put down your book.

DAVID SCOTT WARD (b. 1961)

HUNTING IN TWILIGHT

I walk among dark shapes
along this bank in the coolly fading
afternoon, the unbroken language
of water staying with me. I kneel
and see the gray light
of the evening, too heavy
to allow my dark reflection,
here where the current runs
against itself, turned
by some obstruction in the shallows, flowing
into a perfect moss-grown laver.

Among the rounded sand stones
a shape fastens itself
in my sight. In the strange refraction
in hand becomes another hand, reaching
into another stream, in a place grown
black and silent with the past.
My hand brings back the stone,

and I am kin to the Creek hunter who waded
the stream all day, searching
for a flint of good dimension,

my hands are one with those that chipped
and knapped the stone
into perfection, honed the point
and fastened the shaft with a length
of sinew or thew, I am he who moved
against the wind, stepping ahead
of my scent, drawing
the bowstring to my cheek, my eye
taking sight from the shaft.

The cold of the small stone
seeps into my palm. Some cord
in me snaps tight, unbends the curve
of my imagining. Though I know
I have not passed one night beneath
the stars or walked these hills
in darkness, though I feel no respect
for cold, I would know the burning
of those pure lights, feel my own warm shape
against the world and follow

the shaft's far shadow into forest.

My Brothers Make a Lantern

For Margaret Renkl

All light has left the yard.
Only the sky holds the blue
of light turning back into dark
and shaping in hard shadow every edge
of roof top, every leaf and tree limb,
shaping my two young brothers
as they sway in silhouette bodies
after fireflies.

A green light opens in air.
They dart with a tin lid
and a mason jar, quick as fish
to trap the insects. Above them
the light of the moon is broken

in tangles of pine, and they appear
and disappear among the trees
far away to the dark of the woods.

Their voices have tapered away
into distance; the forest takes in
the night air. Far off, a woman
is calling her children home,
and the sound of a train labors
into the dark. I want to call out
to my brothers, but I see,
very faintly, their light.

This darkness lies thick on my skin.
I move slow under its cover, an outline
in the cool air; I go where the green
spark has shifted beyond the last
boundary of dark, holding my eyes wide open
to take in the field of pure black.
When the green light crosses back to me,
I enclose it inside of my hand.

Slowly, by a living mantle of light,
my brothers return from the woods.
The circle their lamp is throwing
shows a different side of the night
where objects are one in the darkness
and change in the green of our sight.
I add my fly to the lantern and we walk
in the pulse of that glowing.
I move in the light with my brothers
and feel myself fill my whole shadow.

THOM WARD (b. 1963)

DARK UNDERFOOT

The impulse among us is to throw eyes
skyward. Shaggy heads of maples,
the summer's blue turban, we tug
the sleeve of another as kestrels
float over fields. Icarus and Earhart.
At night in our rooms cherubs assemble,

hover like little dirigibles,
our last thought the space
from Adam's finger to God's touch.
The infant looks up toward the breast,
and the man in the open casket
watches satellites drift

across the back of his lids. What
can we say about the ruts
in the old, dirt road? No one
paints the apostles on sidewalks.
Children freeze before cellar steps.
Maybe our blindness is astral, snow-capped,

and wandering we miss
the mushrooms' inveterate work.
More Light! More Light! Goethe cried.
And so do we. But who will trace
what is dark underfoot?
Who will wait for the nightcrawler to sing?

STRAY DOGS, FOAMING

The poor man has misplaced the silk
    fingers his father wove. Dry rot
splits the joist and shingles crack.
    The sick woman has drunk a river.
Still, fires in her body popple and jet.
    Not all are guilty, but all
are responsible, Dostoevski said.
    Our clocks keep their jobs, and we walk
with efficient prophets. Come autumn
    the hemlock will take the laurel.
What to do with old Styrofoam,
    the cowbird stealing the finch's nest.
When the battered kid blows his flute,
    only stray dogs hear the sound.
They rush through dark streets,
    mouths foaming. The air has always
been scratched, the water swollen.
    And as much as we'd like to believe
otherwise, we aren't the first to wake
    with wounds we thought sleep would salve.

In the Interest of Possibility

a young engineer receives a wooden crate marked: *unusual cargo handle with care.*

> At the eastern slope of a garden
> snow falls where a cherry tree has perished.

He asked for a slice of the West, and his mother-in-law delivered.

> Against the dead bark the old samurai
> sits and knows his life has filled enough days.

With this tumbleweed, he'll have something, come summer,
to roll across the yard.

> Running in the garden, children stop and snap
> their fingers, but the old man doesn't blink.

One more thing with shit stuck to it is his wife's reply.

> Quickly, the dagger sends the samurai's ghost
> into the tree.

Two hours after making love, they dig at the frozen ground,
drop manure in a cart.

> Each year people travel hundreds of miles
> to stand in thick sweeps of snow while
> the cherry blossoms open.

What could be better, he says, than a beer, a lawn chair,
and a good tumbleweed.

> Huddled, they watch and dream of crushed
> fruit, breast milk.

She reminds him that amaranths scratch, and this weed
in the hands of their kids will be trouble.

> It is the 16th of January.

It is the 19th of March.

> A pink star flares
> at the eastern slope of a garden.

The Rottweilers sniff, squat.

TACIT

The ice and the scotch, the fable
and the farce, three diamonds,
two no trump, Moe's fingers
and Curly's sockets,
what the judge expects, the plaintiff
seeks, remora and shark,
noose and neck, Rubens' brush
and the frost on the polders,
their tabby and the couch,
our poodle and his balls,
this knife, that piece
of muffin wedged
between the coils, a neighbor's
lamppost, a boy's slingshot,
how the tux stratifies, the bra
enhances, album, cassette, compact
disc, the mold and the grout,
the march and the Mace,
his bonds, her stocks,
my last legitimate
maneuver, my next
felonious thought.

JOE WENDEROTH (b. 1966)

AESTHETICS OF THE BASES LOADED WALK

Four times the pitch is outside the strike zone:
high, low, outside, low—four balls.
The man must be given a base, a base on balls.
But there is no base to be given,
no base unoccupied, the bases are full.
Some cannot understand this.
They believe it must be a shameful thing,
lowly forfeit,
the humiliation of man-made rules and chalk boundaries.
They imagine confrontation itself has failed.
Some, even most, don't understand the bases loaded walk,
and they proceed to hiss

or to mock their earlier earnest applause.
But I love it.
They've got no room to put him on.
They put him on. They put him on
and here comes the lowly run
home. Certain, uncontested,
and incomparably calm.
A home-run would have been unbelievable—
the grand slam, loveliest of moments
to glimpse—
but it leads quickly, inevitably, away from us.
Bases empty.
Rally as good as over.
But a walk! a walk! Bases still loaded!
Rally never at a more urgent or capable point!
This is the beauty of it.
The maintenance of a simple danger by way of a good eye.
The inning, the game itself,
hangs in the indelicate balance
of this subtlest method for staying alive,
in the casual implication of unending loss,
in the terrible patience of an anonymous victory.

DEATH

the indifference
of rain
for where

it falls
not going
unnoticed

DISFORTUNE

the year I was sick
and you took care of me
the most beautiful thing I saw
I saw   lying in the gutter
near a small public basketball court
I played on   alone on weekdays
in a neighborhood where working people lived
it was a blurry Polaroid
of two children at a birthday party

one looking at the other
the birthday boy
lustfully

it was over-exposed   scratched up and torn
and had some kind of oil on it
but I took it home
and pinned it up on a cork bulletin board
in the hall outside my rented bedroom
in east Baltimore

then I moved   and left it there
to the unoriginal
oblivion   that made it
and never really ever
let it alone

DETAILED HISTORY OF THE WESTERN WORLD

where the river gets swift
my grandfather stops rowing
turns round
and with one oar
sweeps a row-boat full of cats
into water so black
you could say
it was almost anything

RACHEL WETZSTEON (b. 1967)

URBAN GALLERY

When the wind invades the treetops
and the trees agree, shivering
take me, take me, when their
stealthy perfume drifts down to waft
among mortals, they come out in droves:
the boy whose bouncing keys speak a language
all their own, the novice who gets her tricks
from magazine molls (their haughtiness, swirl

of cleats), the gigolo with eyes lowered,
the better to judge his prey, the woman
whose hemlines rise as her age does,
the bad girl whose only remaining option
is to get worse: despite the string of cheats
and lukewarm reactions, she still has
the power to pound, the knack of
funneling her frustration into
the arrogant click of a heel. . .
at this armada of proud, unyielding soldiers
I have cast ferocious stones, holding forth
on barricaded gardens and souls' communion
until, heaving my bones from garret to gutter
I took to the street and saw it, too, was worthy.
Chasers out for a good time, flirters in
for a life's catch, strutters so skilled your
lurid designs burn holes, kill the cold
in the pavement, it does not matter
what fever you feed, so long as
you feed it freely; I hid my eyes
but sickness is catching; lovers, permit me entrance.

SURGICAL MOVES

Lights dimmed, the scraper scraped, and I could feel
the change begin; it was the kind of pain
you brace yourself and bear, imagining
all the unfolding options that the cuts
make possible. The red that rolled away
gave rise to thoughts of rolling hills, and so
I told myself, it is a pinch that pays.
Just in the nick of time, I'm hardly doomed
but free to choose my way and free to find
great pleasure in the choosing: jumping off
the table, throwing down the bloody smock
and bolting from the operating room,
I'm the poor fool who stumbles up the aisle
and I'm the sweet face at the other end
who blesses and forgives; I'm in a cloak
behind a pillar, spying on a thief
who answers to my name. Come find me on
the summer lawns, the moonlit winter rinks
and drag me back to where the spongy lumps
coagulate and darken; counsel me

to get down on my knees and look at what
I left behind; implore me to admit
that all the red is realer than the roads
I hastily, unthinkingly pursued;
however many stumps are floating in
the pulp like ghosts of shapes that might have been,
however many stares are telling me to
clean up the mess, it is no mess of mine.

COMING BACK TO THE CAVE

Coming back to the cave is when the hard part
begins. What can be said to your bosom companions
the howling mouth, the thumb-twiddler and the dim-witted rhapsode
that cannot be translated into one cruel sentence:
I have been there, envy me? In the thick of the
ignorant night, icicles clinging ever more
stubbornly to the walls, what can be done
to bring the sunlight in? It would be easy
to fashion earplugs out of worn-out clothing,
to striate the walls with a record of hated days,
to pare down one's speech to a one-note lament
of long ago and someday perhaps. But
punishing a cell and the prisoners in it
only gives old bars a new coating—shrunk
to a cynical husk, spitting out teeth and discourse,
you would throw back your head and think, thank God it's doomsday
and be stripped of sun forever. Come back,
then, tenderly, to your old home; looking around
at the hungry and the hobbling, always be ready to speak,
and when they make ribald comments about the curious gleam
in your eye, gather them up and begin:
partners in darkness, friends, I have seen such wonders.

DRINKS IN THE TOWN SQUARE

No sooner had they carried their martinis
over to the café's remotest table
and huddled close to praise the coming sunset,
red as a famous letter, than it happened:
empty when they had entered it, the square now
quivered with life. What she saw: burly spinsters,
big books in hand, refusing to be selfless,

women in white and, lurking in the shadows,
elegant lady spies. What he saw: strutting
Romeos, hearts for rent, devoted scholars
for whom high windows could outshine rich windows,
cynics for whom all cities were the same.
They had come all this way, by plane, by marriage,
hoping to pit their love—with all its thriving,
colorful avenues, unending crops—to
everything else, but now the square was teeming
with all the faces they had left behind!
Visitors from their own obstructed futures
dazzled their eyes and scarred their hearts much more than
glamourous strangers they could never have,
and when the square began to reassemble
they butted heads and called each other darling,
as if to cover private crimes with public
blandishments. But there was no denying
that each grinning face was a murderer.
When all the ghosts got up and walked out, they were
left with a vivid sense of screen doors closing,
and when they staggered homeward, there were trembling
fists in their pockets, daggers in their eyes.

WITNESS

I crawled out of the wreckage whistling
a bouncy tune, I shut the barbed wire gate
with plots of operas forming in my head.
It was the only way I could go on
without a helpless, horrified look back.
But soon a crowd of mourners blocked my path
and weakened my resolve with their lament:
no song can sound the depths of what you saw,
and even if it could, a song would be
a guilty pleasure after what occurred;
nothing but silence keeps a crime alive.
I walked away with cotton in my mouth
and whispered "No!" when inspiration came;
I told myself that singing would be like
collaborating in calamity.
Time passed. I spoke in grunts and I grew thin,
and then one day I passed a mirror and,
not thinking for a second, thought I saw
one of the walking dead approaching me.
In a great flash of shame I realized that

my thinness was like giving in, and that
my meekness would make men in tall boots smile.
No, it was right to go on singing, and
aggressive, soulful, proud, brash, adamant,
stern, melancholy, loud, not to be stopped,
I filled my lungs with healthy air and gave
my passionate detractors all I had:
they put my broken body in a cage,
but they could never cage my spirit's fugues;
they halted time and bent it out of shape,
but time (not without agony) bent back;
they hated us if we were loud, and so
to quiet down is to admit defeat;
of course it is no easy task to sing,
but singing well might soothe a scar or two;
they burned my family and baked my friends,
but I was lucky, I got out alive;
they thought that, though alive, I posed no threat;
I'll threaten them by proving them dead wrong;
they muffled all the sounds that they could hear,
but never heard the music in my head.

SUSAN M. WHITMORE (b. 1962)

THE BIRD

I dreamed there was a bird
caught in my throat, hysterical
because it couldn't get out.

Oddly, there was room for it
to fly about in there.
I felt it flutter and flutter,

again and again spreading
paper-thin wings out and in;
I saw it, too, in the strange,

bright-colored way of dreams.
It stopped flying by thrusting
its long beak into the dark muscle

that leads to my lungs,
and hung there, resting and mute.
I woke, sick on the beaten air

of my breath and nauseous
in the soft spot under my tongue,
wondering what it is I cannot say.

GAMELIA
The Marriage of Earth and Sky

Longing achieves nothing;
lovers must first give up
any idea of each other.

In deep winter the world
no longer believes in spring,
and each day of the cold

is forever. Once
one knows they can live,
regardless, alone

and even lonely, still
going on, companionship comes,
god's gift to the strong.

So the earth was surprised,
when, after months of
hardening herself against

the cold and exposing
her sturdy bones,
a warm rain fell from heaven,

loving and opening her;
so she was amazed to feel
the seed bursting inside her.

And as the ground began to move
about her, in her swelling,
she grew abundant and beautiful.

LENAIA
Pentheus Sings

Having built my city and named my god,
the panther walks into my limbs
on steady, padded paws

and runs a thin flame
along the length of my veins.
The heart inside starts, remembers,

grows wild. Soon it is raging.
I place my chest on the cool ground,
but the wind rushes around in the storm,

drives the reed
clean through the tree trunk,
and the city walls fall inward,

the faces of god are turned to stone.
Again I am drawn to the wine
and the wild way of the forest.

CRYSTAL WILLIAMS (b. 1970)

IN SEARCH OF AUNT JEMIMA

I have sailed the south rivers of China and prayed to hillside Buddhas.
I have lived in Salamanca, Cuernavaca, Misawa, and Madrid.
I have stood upon the anointed sands of Egypt and found my soul in
                                        their grains.
I am a global earth child who is still excluded from conversations on
                                vacation hot spots.

I have read more fiction, non-fiction, biographies, poetry, magazines,
                                essays, and bullshit than
imaginable, possible, or even practical. I am beyond well read and am
                                somewhat of a
bibliophile. Still, I'm gawked at by white girls on subways who want
                                to know why and how I'm
reading T. S. Eliot.

I have shopped Hong Kong and Bangkok out and sent them to
                                        replenish their stock
in heat so hot the trees were looking for shade—I was the hottest
                                        thing around.
Still I'm followed in corner stores, grocery stores, any store.

I can issue you insults in German, Spanish, and some Japanese.
Still, I'm greeted by wannabe-hip white boys in half-assed ghettoese.

I've been 250 pounds, 150 pounds and have lived and loved every
                                        pound in between. I am still
restricted by Nell Carter images of me.

I've eaten rabbit in Rome, paella in Barcelona, couscous in Morocco,
                                        and am seated at the worst
table by mentally challenged Maitre' dee's who think my big ass is
                                        there for coffee.

I am still passed up by cabs
passed over for jobs
ignored by politicians
guilty before innocent
Black before human.

I am still expected to know Snoop Dog's latest hit
Mike's latest scandal
to believe in O. J.'s innocence.
And I am still expected to walk white babies
up and down 92nd street as I nurse them, sing a hymn and dance a jig.

Sorry, not this sista, sista-girl, miss boo, miss it, miss thang, honey,
                                        honey-child, girl, girlfriend.

See, I am not your militant right-on sista wearing dysikis and 'fros
                                        with my fist in the air
spouting Black Power while smoking weed, burning incense and
                                        making love to Shaka—formally
known as Tyrone.

I am not your high-yellow saditty college girl flaunting Gucci bags
                                        and Armani suits
driving an alabaster colored Beemer with tinted windows and A.K.A.
                                        symbols rimming my
license plate.

I am not your three-babies-by-fifteen, green dragon lady press on nails

welfare fraud ghetto Ho
whose rambunctious ass is stuffed into too tight Lycra with a lollipop
hanging out the side of my
mouf and a piece of hair caught in a rubberband stuck to the top of
my head.

I am not your timberland, tommy hilfiger, 10K hollow-hoop wearin
gansta rappin
crack dealin
blunt smokin
bandanna wearin
Bitch named Poochie.

I am not your conscience clearer.
I am not your convenient Black friend.
Notyourprototypenotyourselloutcause
massa and the big house is too good.
I am not your Aunt Jemima.

In my (8957) days of Black Womanhood I have learned this:
Be careful of what you say
of what you think
of what you do
because you never know who you're talking to.

FOR THE WHITE LADY HOLDING ME

Momma is a big-boned, Nordic looking
woman, stands five-nine with a head
full of used-to-be auburn hair. Black Irish.
Years ago she wore a conservative bun.
When loose it shimmied like oil, was dense
as swamp marsh, was the extent of her
extravagance.

All her life Momma has been solid.
After her mother died she cared for
the seven brothers, worked herself
through school, married my father.
I loved him, she says. Race didn't enter
the equation, only age but she weighed
the 30-year-fault & concluded:
she loved him enough to lose him.

A photo of their wedding shows
her towering over daddy, both peering
tentatively through the lens as if searching
the world beyond their yard, smirking
like they know something good.

I have questioned her surreptitiously,
trying to ferret out some rabble-rousing.
She was too old to be a hippy. Still,
some act must account for us.
All I can conjure from her pressed lips
is she once had a black friend
who couldn't eat at the counter.
Their protest was never returning.
Political? No, I wasn't political.

At five I asked,
"When will the dirt wash off my skin?"
She searched out the best public school
in Detroit. Of Roper City & Country Day
I remember only how white
the children were, the bubbled domes
of classrooms, & saying goodbye to no one
in particular.

This photo was taken in Alabama
my father's folks surrounding us,
their black skins withered & soft.
They're long since gone; their music/stories
lost to me. I was too young. Just a bright black
baby under a southern sky,
extending my mother's hip.

When I ask why
the Afro wig & Curtis Mayfield sunglasses,
she sighs sweet breath on my face,
*That's just how it was, Crys. I didn't always
wear it. In the car . . . well . . .*

silence and memory snatch at her eyes

*. . . down there, Daddy drove up front
& I rode in back with you.*
This is all she'll say. I take it greedily.

When friends see the photo, colored folk

flanking a light-skinned Cleopatra Jones,
"Who's that pretty, light-skinned lady
holding you?" they ask.

My mother. She's my mother, I say
& she's white. Isn't she something
to behold. Isn't she fierce.

LISA WILLIAMS (b. 1966)

CRATER

Old moon, old moon,
what do I tell you?
You sit there, scribed with night.

Do you expect invention?
Beauty as its own reign
or arrangement? No praise

then, just this stutter
between stare and star, the imprint
of my heel on relative dark.

Fool moon, fool moon,
what do you know
of me or my crumbled ladders?

You're not a smile, or a grimace,
you're not even a leap,
just some bruiting glow

that hangs from its one
dichotomy. You can't figure
the tunes, the variant

weights on a tongue.
Poor moon, poor moon,
what does your one eye mean?

To have half a sense,
a cruel bright, your whole vision
wandering or, dispersed

into clueless trinkets
you can never collect.
Won't you always be

swivelling? Bold mood, your flood
is the flood of the mind
in its black habit:

lighting all, but uplifted by none.
Lantern of the odd soul,
miner of discontent,

don't come out, don't come out.
Stay hidden, in my cold coat
pocket.

INTERRUPTION OF FLIGHT

The woman with no feet sits on the porch.
Before her, on the new-mown lawn,
her son polishes his motorcycle
until its chrome facets gleam
under the sun, display a world
playing on surfaces, things shining along
and across, their parameters warped,
motions churning and strange. The tall trees
fringe space, fringe the blue
with its frills of white mist,
its patched lace. The old woman
watches over the humming engine
while her son revs it up,
dark roar in our ears full of wind.
The space around shapes
is of interest, the space between leaves
imprecise, planes of pale air notched
by the green, a geometry raised,
what might be an angle
interrupted by branches grown past
plain. The woman's legs jut out:
one longer, cut off below the knee,

the other lost mid-thigh. And above,
the air writhes with birds, the sky's alive
with flying into, flying through.
Robins, dark robins, and sparrows,
like strong priests, loop together
the light between edges,
gathering sense, making of the jaggedness
something defined only by feeling.
Or the crowd of the self's lifting off,
carrying an image it believes
is immense. Now the woman
with feet made of air, with no speech,
is being helped out of a car.
(When did she disappear?)
"Lean forward. *Lean forward*," the son orders.
(I was watching the birds.)
"*Push yourself out! Push yourself out!*"
And the world above the words, the real sky
trailed by robins, by two crows
and by fat pigeons scuttling
the attic, feathering the heart's box.
One particular tree across the street
from the woman with no feet
stands in front of me. In the tree's
knotted limb is a hole, and in that waits
an additional hunger
deepening. Sparrows dart
in and out of the hole in the limb
where the restless chicks wait
with black throats. The parents
are solicitous, swooping down
every few minutes. They will not stop
so much emptiness, or the young naked song,
song so sure of the spirit's
primacy, of the terrible wish.
"*Good job. That makes it easier on everyone.*"
Now the brusque son has placed his mother
in a wheelchair, pushed her back to the porch
where she'll sit and observe
the sun's anger increase,
the mechanical fruit. And her feet made of air
have flown off with my heart
like the birds who are priests.
May we scatter in peace.

GREG WILLIAMSON (b. 1964)

NEIGHBORING STORMS

Dark clouds are gathering. The trick knee aches.
The hackles itch. She's breezed in drunk again,
Precipitating fears of other men.
Doors slam. A thunderclap of dishes shakes

The wall. And when the storm outside surmounts
Their rain of insults and their muffled threats,
The downpour eavesdrops on their epithets,
The wind delivers blow by blow accounts—

Until it all blows over and sachets
Of honeysuckle scent the morning air.
They chirp like birds, and all is peaceful there.
But me? I'm rattled. I scan the sky for days.

UP IN THE AIR

Gin-weary, temple on the pane,
  I watch the props begin to shake
  The sunlight. As we climb, the plane
Trolls its crank bait shadow across a lake.

  It drags an airy grappling hook
  Over the churches of white towns
  Tucked away in the hills that look,
For all their pleated folds, like dressing gowns

  Where all the clouds are shaving cream
  And powder, periwigs and lace,
  The fragments of a lazy dream
That conjures up a ballroom in their place

  And finds, across the dreamt parquet,
  In a cirrus gown, a girl. Then all
  At once this cloying matinee
Dissolves, as if the episodes I call

  My life were just such master strokes
  Of whimsy, false and protean,

And all I think I love a hoax
Invented by the shadow of a man

Muttering in a windowseat,
Watching a toothless anchor comb
A lake, fooled by his own conceit.
At most, from all of this, someone at home

May shake his head in a reading chair
Or glance up from a gin and lime
At this annoyance in the air,
A minor thing which happens all the time.

DRAWING HANDS

Way on back in the reign of Mrs. Duke
All of the small subjects went in fear
Of her, her stormy eyes, her thunderhead
Of hair. Daily on the wall's clean slate,
She wrote the language he would learn to live
With: words and rules and examples of the rules
Whereby nouns adverbly verb their objects,
So that he might call things as he saw them.

There in the classroom, under a cloud of chalk,
How smoothly his attention used to glide
To the glass, to water braided on the glass,
Clearly clear, and standing still as it ran
Away, and deeper into the misted day
Where fields began dissolving into felt
And a stonefaced house reflected on the street.
Then the ruler would crack across his hand.

That boy lived my life ago, and whether
I leave him soloing at his desk today
Under the unbroken rules of Mrs. Duke
Or walking home through the mystifying day,
He finds his winding way back here somehow,
Where I sit high in the head of the house,
Writing and rewriting him, and watching the rain,
Which is what I came in out of for.

THE COUNTERFEITER

When he was starting out, still green,
He used to make a signature mistake
So that his hidden talent could be seen,
Reversing the flag above the White House roof.
It made him feel ingenious and aloof
To signify his forgeries as fake.

He always liked his jokes, but they are private.
Sometimes, when he is pressed about his trade,
He answers with a shrug, "I draw a profit"
Or "I trust in God." Nobody ever laughs.
In the den, above two ebony giraffes,
Hangs the first dollar that he ever made.

But making money is an enterprise
Of tedious, grave concerns. To reproduce
These symboled reproductions, his hands and eyes
Must settle on what others merely see,
The couples, columns and the Model T,
And all the framework, intricate, abstruse,

And difficult to copy by design,
With fine acanthuses and cycloid nets.
He must account for every tiny line
To duplicate the sad and distant stare
Beneath the breaking waves of Jackson's hair,
If he would tender these to pay his debts.

He has invested his adult career
In being perfect when he goes to press,
An artistry both humble and severe.
Down at the basement desk, long hours pass
With a burin and a magnifying glass.
No one suspects his notable success.

He profits by his anonymity,
But deep regret competes with honest pride:
To labor toward complete obscurity
And treasure a craft that will efface his will,
Render his name unknown and all his skill
Unrecognized, long after he has died.

BELVEDERE MARITTIMO

My dear, you would not believe the weather here.
The postcard doesn't do it justice, nor
Can I. But notice how the sun's great mint
Is stamping silver coins upon the sea,
Scooning away whole treasuries of change
On pelicans, bikinis, the lacy flounce
Of surf. And notice, too, in the flowerbed
How lady-slippers and narcissi blush
Beside the bedsheets luffing on a line,
And how the watercolor limes and pinks
Of the little summer cottages appear
To be the very picture of repose.

For seven days I've looked out of my room
On none of this. A bankrupt, dishrag sky
Wrings out a steady mizzle on the beach,
An indigent hachure which drains away
The washes of pastel to shades of grey
As bleary, wet and untranslatable
As every sodden page of *il giornale*.
Sinister, small black birds clothespin the line.
"The piers are pummelled by the waves." I write,
Perhaps, to weather this foul weather, dear.
The rain runs down the glass. Wish you were here.

STEVE WILSON (b. 1960)

THE PICTURE ON THE PURPLE WALL

A painting of an endless field where grass waits
Always for the touch of a wandering child.
And delighting like a motion might, down the trail
To the horizon, nothing but air is there.

In the glow of the sun how the sky carries
The white fire of her star off
Into the distance like a mother cradling
Her sleeping child through a storm. This storm

Hides in the bark of sycamores and the leaves
Of elms, but still the child sleeps, and dreams
The wall, a wine-dark ocean, drinks in
Daylight while this room holds everything

The world has ever been or seemed—
That chair, this porcelain angel, this space
That breathes cracked ice. There is
A house where his mother's kiss will drift him

Calmly out toward velvet light.
What will he meet on the waters of night?

EXPERIMENTS IN THE IMPERSONAL

until today. On the table
a piece of paper: a few lines
about the insistence of strangers, of women
on downtown streets—you've imagined them,

how they pause before the florist's,
the shoe store, pass the two children
in brown wool coats on their way home.
But we're here in the bedroom.

I can see the heels of her black slippers.
I can see her as she leans across the bed
to open the window. Will I tell her
someone has to make a move, make a run for it?

No. I'll sit in the low lights and remember,
remember in the low lights those ladies
in their dresses—wrapped in silk dresses—
who now have turned down an avenue.

A man walks by with his dog. He thinks about
the rain. That's all you need to know.

A CONTEMPORARY POET

No sharp edges to this poet, who strolls
into a restaurant and correctly orders
the coq au vin with tarragon asparagus.
Purged of germs, of the detritus of coffeehouses,

I've repented every sin, recounted each
miniscule transgression against friends,

colleagues, mailmen and Labradors. I renounce
drugs, alcohol, and more drugs. The sexual pirouettes
in Boulder. The lifting of rosary beads, a woman's
St. Christopher medal. Now I stand at bus stops

and wait my turn for a seat. I comfort the frightened
boys lost on the subway. I reach out my hand in welcome

to bankers and military men, see myself in those
well-polished shoes. Free to blend and disappear
into crowds, shoppers, browsers at a neighborhood swap,
I've nothing to do, everyone to do it with.

Observe the miraculous diminishing of expectations.
This modest verse squirms languidly before me.

RECREATIONAL MATHEMATICS

Start slowly and simply—warming up is crucial.

Count the squares on the kitchen floor.
Divide the contents of the refrigerator into spoiled and
        fresh, solid and liquid.
Calculate the weight of the clothes in your closet, or the
        length of time since you last made love.

Finally, find the value of x.
By now, the numbers should be coming quickly, easily.
You are ready to begin.

Quantify the intersections of light and dark on the
        stairway.
Chart the potential course of sun across the table.

Enlarge photographs of former lovers to enormous
        dimensions, horrifying expanses of eyes and ears
        growing exponentially, geometrically. Codify the
        distortions in the faces as each conforms to the
        rough skull of your wall.

Balanced unbelievably, compute the arc your hands will
        form as they wrap around the curve of your
        shoulders with a force as fragile as logic.

CHRISTIAN WIMAN (b. 1966)

HEARING LOSS

Only the most obvious questions
were asked her, how she felt
or if she'd slept, and even these words,
before they reached her, wavered free of meanings
as if a wind were in them. Friends and family
came close and called to her
as they would call down a well, peering
into some darkness their own altered voices
might rise out of. In time,
even the echoes faded, until
any moment's simple music—
a bird singing, her grandchildren laughing—
faltered before her, trembling
somewhere in the very air she breathed.
She felt sounds she was hardly conscious of
before: the deep-freezer's door hummed
when touched, and the dry heartbeat
of an old clock ticked lightly into her fingers.
Her son, old himself, would lean over her
trying to make her understand an hour
was all he could stay, it was Sunday
or Monday, or a particular silence
was the silence of rain,
and on the long drive out here
the wet road whispered him home.
                                        Waking alone,
dawns so quiet she hears
leaves breathing light, or drifting
alone through days unchanging as smooth water,
she can almost believe the life she remembers
is life. Lovers on the television screen
know only the words she gives them, birds
in the trees sing her memories
of their song. She answers the softest knocks
at her door, surprised each time
that no one is there, she listens intently
to mirrors, stands at a window
bringing the wind inside. Until,
in the muted light of late afternoon
she lies resting, resisting

sleep like a small child
who has stayed up too long, who half dreams
the arms that hold her, the room full of voices
and laughter, but cannot bring herself wholly
into the world where they are.

In Lakeview Cemetery

This is the time of year
the lengthening dark appears
as light in all the trees.

Enameled chestnuts ease
from their skins
and I am holding again

the deep-casked color and shape
a low note might take
before becoming its sound.

Today the rain came down
in clean, elliptical lines
through sunlight, a sign

of something, I remembered,
as the brief shower ended
and the sky cleared.

Now, as I walk here
in the rain-scented air
I hear the sound of water

in the windy trees.
How can I learn to grieve?
The damp shadows of leaves

are printed on stones,
on sidewalks where leaves have blown,
fallen and actual, gone.

SWEET DREAMS

Voices fade as he walks
into them. He hears his name
in the air above him, passed
from parents to guests
and back to him like a ball.
The plates have faces. In his
father's he sees his own.
The candle's shadow is talking
and laughing with the wall.
There are kind questions
for him, shared silences he hears
himself speak into: he blinks,
whispers to the floor,
a small fist blooms with years
he's stored in fingers. Somewhere
in their watches are the hours
he can't enter. In awkward
pauses some stare into his sleep.
A red-nailed finger slowly circles
the rim of a glass, but the red
bell of wine won't sing.
They look at him and smile.
His mother stands, her hand enclosing
his. His father's cheek cuts
into his kiss. The hardwood floor
shines eyes of light. The dark
doorway is the wall's yawn.
He walks into their wishes.

SUZANNE WISE (b. 1965)

I WAS VERY PROLIFIC

Legislators say they want women to have second thoughts.
—headline from *The New York Times*, January 28, 1998

I was very prolific in my generating qualities.
I was sprouting here and there.
They said I was developing.
They said my heterosexual adjustment

was quantitatively well above average.
Of course, they said, there is always the possibility
she won't cooperate. But I did my best
to acclimate. I said to them: *Just don't rip my nylons.*
I said to myself: *This is not my self.*

Afterwards, no matter how much I gargled
or apologized I couldn't get that force field
out of my head: it sucked and dragged.
It depleted most of the memory banks
and then installed my functions
in the outskirts of a category
called *unknown or other.*

Basically I was subletting
a very unlisted condition. I signed up
for Public Resistance, for Confessional
Help, for Social Insecurity.

At headquarters, the police said: *Welcome*
to our favorite prefab events.
The doctors said: *Let's make a deal.*
The technicians said: *The Traumatic Image*
Resource Room is now out of order.

After the treatments and a brief dreamy
episode involving armed forces,
a parasite shaped like a subway system
built its home in my lungs.

No matter how precisely I cross-referenced,
no matter how many official reports
I downloaded, I was still not clear.
I was vaporware, I was the pre-data
part of a package deal.

And so I have learned to distrust
the blinking signs, the free-floating quotations,

I have learned that my gender is still a risky situation
marred by sexuality, like those B movies,
dominated by chase scenes and ending in predictable
disasters. And, despite the best of intentions,

it is not true that groups of humans behave
in an aimless, non-goal directed manner.

Nor is it true that being stripped and strapped down,
flown like a flag and projected onto the big screen,
is without reward: just look

at the audience turning its one
gigantic head, from left to right, then back again.

50 Years in the Career of an Aspiring Thug

1. Burned Christ to a crisp. 2. On the Betty Crocker burner.
3. Tied a body to the railroad tracks. It wore the clothes of a girl.
4. Later found naked and weeping in the fields. 5. It was a body
of straw. 6. It wore a note that said: *I am God.* 7. Drove Father's
golf cart into the pond. *My final hole in one,* said the note stuffed in
the ninth hole. 8. Stole prize roses from Mother's garden. Wore
them on the head, as a wreath, in secret, admiring the Romanesque
profile in the bathroom mirror. 9. In the diary: *I will conquer.*
10. Dreamed of making the rank of Eagle Scout. 11. Stole brother's
b.b. gun. 12. Shot the lights out all over town. 13. Disappeared.
14. Didn't leave a note. 15. Got a job in the city working for the
glass company. 16. Checking panes for cracks. 17. Etched curses
into every self reflected. 18. Got a job working for the car company,
answering the phone. 19. *I'm Henry Ford, on this earth to eat your soul.*
20. Got a job working for the baby food company, counting cans of
mashed beets, broccoli, meats. 21. Kept that job. 22. Wrote neat
columns. 23. Of numbers. 24. Added with precision. 25. Punched.
26. The. 27. Clock. 28. The. 29. Clock. 30. The. 31. Clock.
32. *One more spot in the spotty night,* scribbled on the forehead in the
mirror. 33. Sad brow of the girl on the job in the boss's bed.
34. *I am beads on an abacus.* 35. *Clicked.* 36. *From left to right.*
37. Wore a crown. 38. Of sweat. 39. Bars of the headboard trapped
in small hands. 40. Woke as the only one inside the body of mulch,
the body of palm smears, the rewired body of blue veins and split
hairs, the body of loose and multiplying terms. 41. Breathed zeros in
the damp. 42. Monitored ceiling stain's spread. 43. Pondered the
unwritten book of the distant. 44. Time card. 45. *That little priest
hungry for sins.* 46. Wielded the stolen grease pencil. 47. Blackened
the stolen roll of fish-wrapping paper, a record of the end. 48. Of
hiding places. 49. *Because street lights got replaced.* 50. *Because fields
grew parking lots.*

Closure Opening Its Trap

The pigeons have survived.

Or something that is like pigeons, things
small and gray, things perforating the horizon

until the backdrop of creamy
stucco clouds unseams

and black-eyed buildings collapse
down into themselves, bottom levels bombed out
and vanishing into the upper parts,
like arms pulled back inside sleeves.
Then the bites or scratches

that might be pigeons turn suicidal, turning
downward, falling slowly like a description
of rain, followed by faded, illegible, off-
white names, followed by THE END,

block-faced, heavy-
handed then melting
in the sudden downpour,

then dispersed as wet, bready lumps
drifting out to sea, where the pigeons,
no, gulls now,
aim at what appears to be food.

But, the tiny birds, beaks packed
with debris, fan out into flocks of feathery
smears, wake of the erasure
paving over the flood, a highway

of nothing that bawls
and bawls and bawls,
then coughs, hiccups, chokes.

This is the theme song—
a dirge mixing itself up
with canned laughter—
beginning to skip,

to skip,
to skip

MARK WUNDERLICH (b. 1968)

THIRST

In the painting above your bed a woman pauses,
lifts her arms upward in a gesture of infinite reticence,
protesting winds that are stagnant and a ship that won't move.

Why do you study me like this? While snowy pullets in the yard
    flare up
into white fires, you roost there, a jewel at the throat, a sad thing.
I stare down at your body's wreckage,

a field gleaned for its small nourishment, while the sun through
    the window
recoils its tail of far heat. I am no clean numeral. No simple boy.
You ask for a glass of ice, for water turned cold hardened water.

ONE EXPLANATION OF BEAUTY

Everywhere the material world is speaking to me—
the cry of a door or the floorboard's groan
with the slightest pressure of a foot,

or the pear tree blooming on the Avenue,
its cells bursting and multiplying,
the kindest thing I know. Here in this world capital

a new version of beauty reveals itself—
one of action, and people
shedding their lives like skins—a fury

recalcitrant as an animal circling its bed,
too stubborn to go down. In my heart,
its dumb fist pounding in me now,

I know what you are saying—that calm and stasis
are beautiful, like horses
with their platters of muscle and wet eyes.

That inactivity offers a window to look through
without opening, and permission to touch no thing.
That an image of a city is better than the city

itself, with its crude happenings and pain.
My choice has been made, for this
immeasurable velocity—because images burn,

and lives like ours
shatter like houses in a desperate wind—
But here, I leave you with this

because I know you will love it—a horse,
her bowed neck white and rippled
picking through wet grass, toward a looming grove.

SUTURE

Someday I will leave this town and not look back
but for now I keep hurtling toward
the red center, the road unfolding,

the ice raining down in crystals
while the bridge heaves itself onto the bank;
river of mud, river of sad oily pleasures

where a kingfisher cuts through the water's brown skin
clean as math, and I want to say
this is like logic, but something fails me.

Listen to the unforgivable birds
piercing cold sky and singing like needle and thread
and feel for the scar splitting my eyebrow.

(You remember the doctor tying his knots, don't you?)
This is always mine—the shadow of an animal,
smell of newly shorn wool, the workhorse pawing air

and stomping in his stall. Somewhere in the marsh
cress sharpens green in this age of stunted miracles.
But how to get there from here?

M. WYREBEK (b. 1960)

AN EXAMPLE

The train sneaks through farm country
heading for Boston, snaking behind houses
early every weekday morning. I see
what the home owners pretend not to see:
lawns barren of flowers and shrubs, bald
tires leaning against tree trunks softened
by moss, rusted hubcaps and decaying chassis.
Steeped in murky water, the backyards merge
with marshes. I saw a heron once, its legs slender stalks
holding the lute of its body. In the still semi-darkness
it shone pale as driftwood, a splinter in the sky.
I was going into the light, riding the train east
toward the hospital overlooking the Charles
where I would splay my body on a gray table
for all assembled to look at me,
an example, waiting for the bliss
of anesthesia to whisk me to that place
where memory does not exist.
When I woke I had forgotten what I saw
on my way in: a man kissing a half-opened screen door
which hid a half-dressed woman who could have been me.
After I was discharged, on the train home,
I saw what was no longer
there on the marsh: a lone heron standing stick straight
as the wind's feathered tail trailed across the water.

TRENDELENBURG POSITION

There I was midsummer skating on a lake,
inscribing my joy across the surface, unaware
my shadow had gone—it was somewhere
out of sight, a black naked whisper of a girl
writing her story across the blank age of ice.
Then I heard cracking, as though the presence
of this mirage startled the ice,
but it was my skin, it was the sound of my flesh
recognizing my self, back after a long absence.
In this glass-domed world of infection the body
does anything to get attention, my fever rising

to 105, then dropping to 92. I see the girl
skating, white sparks shooting from her
ankles as she curves through air,
her shadow swaying, blades not recording
the cuneiform of swirls. I see them
meeting, each suddenly finding in the other
what it lacked, something gone unrealized
till that precise moment. That's when my mind
read the frantic writing of my nerves,
and woke in my hospital bed ringed by a cloud
of nurses and doctors, head low to the floor,
feet high in the air: Trendelenburg Position,
used to raise blood pressure and increase blood flow
to the heart—all my blood in a hurry
to get to the head and rouse me
so I can know where I am
and who I was.

A HEALING LOGIC

Today I stopped.
I call my niece to tell her I'm through
with treatments. She wants to know
why I got sick in the first place.
What can I say?
I know nothing new or unpossessed
by her logic, or I know the same
things more intimately.
All nine years of her ask
if I have lost any more hair.
At her house she keeps a calendar,
crossing out each day on the way
to one square emblazoned with a star,
yellow-orange, I imagine, the last day
of my chemo glowing like the methotrexate
that burned through my veins.

She told me once to tell her
if my doctors said I would die
                              her to believe them.
                              ched from its cradle
                           n my bed, my body filled
                              two tired kidneys.
                              nask over her face

and breathed in slowly, pressing
the little poker of her finger into my hand
then smiling, as if surprised
by the bone beneath my flesh.

RECOVERY

Tonight I walk home through the park
along a gravel path, stopping to sit under a lamp
that casts its net of light over a cement bench. Resting
in the glow, I lean back, spreading my limbs
across the bench. The cement releases its hoarded cool
and my pain uncoils. The ache swims free.
I absorb the night as if it were water,
as if I were lying on a wide stair
in the shallow end of an immense,
emptied pool. The world seems upside down—
the starless sky a deep blue ocean above me,
the black air like night submerged
below me. I think I know how oceans feel
when sky pours darkness into their vast basins.
I am buoyed by slow waves that lure away my hurt
easily as the moon coaxing water away from the shore.

No, I'm not thinking this at all.
I'm reveling in how quickly
I can make myself imagine I don't feel
what I'm feeling, amazed
by truth, how it floats to the surface
like air rising from the mouth
of a person drowning.

KEVIN YOUNG (b. 1970)

AN ALMANAC, 1939

The midwives all were scarecrows
or spinsters, as if years
of marriage to pain
had left them

without wanting. The other
women slowly turned to trees
thickening their hollows
with plum children

whose shade spilled across their feet.
Had the fathers read
the shifting winds
they too might have grown

to regret this sunless
reaping. But the birds
kept on bringing babies
with such bruiseless skin

that no one saw how far
the children had to fall.

DEGREES

The weather in my head
is always summer: tan,
electric, mosquitoes buzzing
steady as family. My heart
an ant-filled apricot. Outside,
west of here, killing stays
in season, birds plunging
like stones into the pools
of our upturned faces.

And to think I dreamt
the cold might just miss us
this time, that somehow I could
step outside the steady swirl
of leaves & into a season
that never ceases, hands fanning
faces, waving away each yellow–
jacket year. Instead ash
trees bend toward me almost
praying to be lit, craving to be set
free. *Please.* If you must know

I still plan to go out beyond
the pale, just jump the fence
& wade through fireant

fields, keeping on past
my mind's stuttering storm—
it slows, turns thunder then
effortless, suffocating snow.

from THE ESCAPE ARTIST

beyond the people
swallowing fire   past the other acts
we had seen before   we found the escape
artist   bound to a chair   hands tied
behind his back   we climbed onstage
to test the chains   around his ankles
and tongue   watched on
as they tucked him   in a burlap sack
and lowered it   into a tank of water
he could get out of   in his sleep

EDDIE PRIEST'S BARBERSHOP & NOTARY
Closed Mondays

is music   is men
off early from work   is waiting
for the chance at the chair
while the eagle claws holes
in your pockets   keeping
time   by the turning
of rusty fans   steel flowers with
cold breezes   is having nothing
better to do   than guess at the years
of hair   matted beneath the soiled caps
of drunks   the pain of running
a fisted comb through stubborn
knots   is the dark dirty low
down blues   the tender heads
of sons fresh from cornrows   all
wonder at losing   half their height
is a mother gathering hair   for good
luck   for a soft wig   is the round
difficulty of ears   the peach
faced boys asking Eddie
to cut in parts and arrows
wanting to have their names read
for just a few days   and among thin
jazz   is the quick brush of a done

head   the black flood around
your feet   grandfathers
stopping their games of ivory
dominoes   just before they reach the bone
yard   is winking widowers announcing
cut it clean off   I'm through courting
and hair only gets in the way   is the final
spin of the chair   a reflection of
a reflection   that sting of wintergreen
tonic   on the neck of a sleeping snow
haired man   when you realize it is
your turn   you are next

Central Standard Time

Down below, everywhere, all
the black skycaps have disappeared
since last time, last time being always,
or at least your childhood of air. Gone
like that. At the curb, a mother

overtips the new white luggage hands
as if to say We know who this is no longer
feeding, to say The face on this bill, turned
just so, figured he freed us too. Will you
always wander like an eye,

a rumor? You always seem to be
on the side without a view, only houses
with pools round & unstirred as the water eyes
of the blind, the pale tongues of abandoned
drive-in screens. Must gaining light mean

setting the clock back? The young, balding,
peroxide saint in 5F the window,
reads his Bible with easy-reference finger guides
to all the psalms, mouthing words
like some cross-country horror movie

minus airplane crash, that you don't
pay to hear. Only watch, guess what
those tongues must be saying,
what monsters they must be
warning us about.

KATAYOON ZANDVAKILI (b. 1967)

NO TRESPASSING (PRIVATE BEACH)

Today:
            the Valley
in front of the ocean—

            (your back)

A man/watching
his fields/water:
a yellow hat.

Finnish lips.
Eagle candy.

COUNTY

Finding the stars over and over again
Nothing succeeds

You throw stones into the bed

A year later, she got married—

I could talk to you, and you
wanted to leave

"Wildly in love," you say, you
always stay, and I look out
from the porch at the mountain rising

Brandy the hot water under
the stars your neck. That I am toothless
in this sentence

The coast raves,
is the coast, an old ocean gazing:
the young man next day a boxer

You were granted three wishes

and used only two.
I was wasted

A kiss in the middle
of the highway: the spine of a road.
Five lights in the ocean

LOVE LETTER

once haunted,
my face will take form

     ruins and a few fiend birds glued onto

     this fish's eye: iris

this girl's voice again

to stare at exotic cloth and when
we are horrible, to be very horrible together

intricate furniture of heart space

     (days forged from goodness)

CONTRIBUTORS NOTES

RICK AGRAN is the author of *Crow Milk* (Oyster River Press, 1997). He lives in an apple orchard in Lee, New Hampshire with a Jersey steer named Cocoa. He has a whole tricycle as a front door knocker, bakes a mean apple pie, and drinks plenty of cider.

ELIZABETH ALEXANDER is the author of *The Venus Hottentot* (University of Virginia Press) and *Body of Life* (Tia Chucha Press, 1996), as well as numerous essays on African-American literature and culture.

SHERMAN ALEXIE's poetry books include *First Indian on the Moon* and *The Summer of Black Widows* (Hanging Loose Press, 1993, 1996). He has also published a book of stories and a novel, and he wrote the screenplay for *Smoke Signals*.

RICK ALLEY was born in Kingsport, Tennessee. He is the author of *The Talking Book of July* (Eastern Washington University Press, 1997). Currently, he lives in Norfolk, Virginia, where he teaches literature and creative writing.

ALICE ANDERSON was born in Tulsa, Oklahoma. She is currently residing in Northern California. She is the author of *Human Nature* (New York University Press, 1994), winner of the Elmer Holmes Bobst Award for Emerging Writers.

DANIEL ANDERSON's first book, *January Rain*, won the Nicholas Roerich Poetry Prize and was published by Story Line Press in 1997. He is presently the Tennessee Williams Fellow and a visiting professor at the University of the South.

TALVIKKI ANSEL grew up in Mystic, Connecticut. She received an MFA from Indiana University and was a Wallace Stegner Fellow at Stanford University. *My Shining Archipelago*, her first book, won the Yale Series of Younger Poets competition in 1996.

AARON ANSTETT was born in Chicago. His collection of poems, *Sustenance*, was published by New Rivers Press in 1997. He lives in Colorado with his wife, Janet, and their daughter, Molly.

CRAIG ARNOLD's first book, *Shells*, won the 1998 Yale Series of Younger Poets Prize. He recently received a fellowship from the National Endowment for the Arts (NEA). He lives in Salt Lake City, where he sings and records with his band, Iris.

DAVID BARATIER is the founder and editor of Pavement Saw Press. His books include *A Run of Letters* (Poetry New York Press, 1998) and *The Fall of Because* (Pudding House Press, 1999). He is the editor of *Hands Collected: The Books of Simon Perchik*.

DAVID BARBER is the author of *The Spirit Level,* which won the Terrence Des Pres Prize from *Triquarterly* (Northwestern University Press, 1995). He is an adjunct lecturer at Emerson College and staff editor at *The Atlantic Monthly* in Boston.

PAUL BEATTY was born in Los Angeles and currently lives in New York. He is the author of *Joker, Joker, Deuce,* a book of poems (Penguin, 1994), and *The White Boy Shuffle,* a novel (Houghton Mifflin). He was the winner of the 1990 New York Poetry Slam.

JOSHUA BECKMAN is a poet and book artist living in Phoenix, Arizona. He is the author of *Things Are Happening,* published in 1998 by the *American Poetry Review.*

ERIN BELIEU was raised in Nebraska and studied writing at Boston University. She has published two poetry collections, *Infanta,* a National Poetry Series selection, and *One Above and Below* (Copper Canyon, 1995, 2000). She teaches at Kenyon College.

MOLLY BENDALL's two collections of poems are *After Estrangement* (Peregrine Smith, 1992) and *Dark Summer* (Miami University Press, 1999). She teaches at the University of Southern California.

DINA BEN-LEV is the author of three award-winning books, *Note for a Missing Friend* (1991), *Sober on a Small Plane* (1995), and *Broken Helix* (MidList Press, 1997). She has received the Elliston Poetry Prize and an NEA Fellowship.

JACQUELINE BERGER's first book, *The Mythologies of Danger,* won the Bluestem Award and was published in 1998. This collection also won the 1998 Bay Area Book Reviewers Association Award. She lives in Brisbane, California.

CAROLE BERNSTEIN is the author of *Familiar* (Hanging Loose Press, 1997) and a chapbook, *And Stepped Away from the Circle,* winner of the 1994 Sow's Ear Chapbook Competition.

MARK BIBBINS lives in New York City. His first collection, *Swerve,* appears in *Take Three: 3* (Graywolf/*Agni*). His work has been nominated for a Pushcart Prize and has appeared in *Poetry, The Paris Review,* and *The Yale Review.*

DAVID BIESPIEL was born in Tulsa, Oklahoma and grew up in Texas. He has published one book, *Shattering Air* (BOA Editions), and has received an NEA Fellowship and the Wallace Stegner Fellowship in Poetry.

RICHARD BLANCO was born in Madrid to exiled Cuban parents and raised and educated in Miami. His first book, *City of a Hundred Fires,* won the Agnes Lynch Starrett Poetry Prize from the University of Pittsburgh Press in 1997.

JOE BOLTON was born in Cadiz, Kentucky. The University of Arkansas Press published *The Last Nostalgia: Poems 1982-1990* in 1999. He took his own life in March 1990 at the age of twenty-eight.

GAYLORD BREWER is an associate professor at Middle Tennessee State University, where he founded and edits *Poems & Plays*. His poetry publications include *Presently a Beast* (Coreopsis, 1996) and *Devilfish* (Red Hen, 1999).

JOEL BROUWER was born in Grand Rapids, Michigan. He has received fellowships from the Wisconsin Institute for Creative Writing and the NEA. *Exactly What Happened*, his first book, was published in 1999 by Purdue University Press.

STEPHANIE BROWN was born in Pasadena, California and grew up in Newport Beach. She is the author of *Allegory of the Supermarket* (University of Georgia Press, 1998) and was co-winner of the Jessica Nobel-Maxwell Memorial Poetry Prize for 1994.

LISA BUSCANI is a national poetry slam champion and the author of *Jangle* (Tia Chucha Press), as well as two solo shows, "Carnivale Animale" and "At That Time." She has toured poetry venues throughout the United States and Europe. She lives in Brooklyn.

ANTHONY BUTTS, the seventh of nine children, grew up in southwest Detroit and was educated in classes for visually and mentally impaired students until entering Detroit Renaissance High School. His book, *Fifth Season*, was published by New Issues.

RAFAEL CAMPO teaches and practices medicine at Harvard Medical School and Beth Israel Medical Center in Boston. His poetry books include *The Other Man Was Me* (Arte Público Press, 1994) and *What the Body Told* (Duke University Press, 1996).

NICK CARBÓ was born and raised in the Philippines. He immigrated to the United States and married the poet Denise Duhamel. His books include *El Grupo McDonald's* and *Secret Asian Man* (Tia Chucha Press, 1995, 2000). He has received a fellowship from the NEA.

KENNETH CARROLL, a DC native, is director of the Urban Scholars Program for the Humanities Council of Washington, DC. His book, *So What: For the White Dude Who Said This Ain't Poetry*, was published in 1997 by The Bunny & the Crocodile Press.

KEITH CARTWRIGHT has served as a Peace Corps fisheries volunteer in Senegal. He currently teaches at Roanoke College in Salem, Virginia. He is the author of *Saint-Louis: A Wool Strip Cloth for Sekou Dabo* (Xavier University Press, 1997).

HAYAN CHARARA was born in Detroit, Michigan. His first book of poems, *The Alchemist's Diary*, was published in 2000 by Hanging Loose Press. He edits the annual literary anthology, *Graffiti Rag*.

LISA CHAVEZ is a Chicana Mestiza writer and teacher born in Los Angeles but raised in Fairbanks, Alaska. She is the author of *Destruction Bay* (West End Press, 1999) and currently teaches at Albion College in Michigan.

JUSTIN CHIN is a writer and performance artist. He is the author of *Mongrel: Essays, Diatribes, and Pranks* (St. Martin's Press) and *Bite Hard* (Manic D Press). Born in Malaysia and raised in Singapore, he now lives in San Francisco.

A. V. CHRISTIE's book, *Nine Skies*, was a National Poetry Series selection in 1996 (University of Illinois Press). She received an NEA Fellowship in 1997 and currently lives in Malvern, Pennsylvania.

JOSHUA CLOVER was born in Berkeley, California, where he currently lives. He teaches at Saint Mary's College of California, and he writes about music for *The Village Voice* and *Spin* magazine. His first book, *Madonna anno domini*, was published by LSU Press.

LISA COFFMAN grew up in East Tennessee, the setting for many poems in her first book, *Likely* (Kent State University Press). She has received fellowships from the NEA, the Pew Charitable Trust, and the Pennsylvania Council on the Arts.

NICOLE COOLEY grew up in New Orleans, Louisiana. Her book of poetry, *Resurrection*, won the 1995 Walt Whitman Award and was published by LSU Press in 1996. Her novel *Judy Garland, Ginger Love* was published by Harper Collins (Regan Books) in 1998.

LESLEY DAUER's poetry has appeared in a number of journals, including *New England Review, Poetry,* and *Seneca Review*. Her first book of poems, *The Fragile City*, won the Bluestem Award and was published in 1996. She teaches at Foothill College in California.

CHRISTOPHER DAVIS' first book, *The Tyrant of the Past and the Slave of the Future*, won the 1988 Associated Writing Programs Award, and his second collection, *The Patriot*, was published in 1998 by the University of Georgia Press.

OLENA KALYTIAK DAVIS, author of the Brittingham Prize-winning collection, *And Her Soul Out of Nothing*, is a first-generation Ukranian-American. She was educated at Wayne State University, The University of Michigan Law School, and Vermont College.

CONNIE DEANOVICH is the recipient of a Whiting Writer's Award and a GE Foundation Award for Younger Writers. She is the author of *Zombie Jet* (Zoland) and *Watusi Titanic* (Timken).

MARK DECARTERET works at a bookstore where he hosts and coordinates poetry readings. He also teaches at the Heartwood College of Art in Kennebunkport, Maine. His book, *Review: A Book of Poems*, was published by Kettle of Fish Press.

JUAN DELGADO was born in Guadalajara, Mexico. He came to the United States when he was five and currently lives in Southern California. His books include *Green Web* (Georgia, 1994) and *El Campo* (Capra Press, 1998).

TOM DEVANEY is from Philadelphia. He writes for the experimental puppet group, "The Lost Art of Puppet." He lives and teaches in Brooklyn. His first book of poetry, *The American Pragmatist Fell in Love*, was published by Banshee Press in 1999.

ELIZABETH DODD was born in Boulder, Colorado and grew up in southeast Ohio. She lives in the Flint Hills region of eastern Kansas with her husband, Christopher Cokinos. Her first book, *Like Memory, Caverns*, was published by NYU Press.

SEAN THOMAS DOUGHERTY grew up in an inter-ethnic politically radical family, with a mother of Moldavian-Jewish/Okie descent and an African-American stepfather. His books include *The Body's Precarious Balance* and *Love Song of the Young Couple, The Dumb Job*.

DENISE DUHAMEL is the author of ten books and chapbooks, including *The Star-Spangled Banner* (Southern Illinois University Press, 1999), *Exquisite Politics* (with Maureen Seaton) (Tia Chucha, 1997), *Kinky* (Orchises, 1997) and many others.

THOMAS SAYERS ELLIS was born and raised in Washington, DC. He is a cofounding member of The Dark Room Collective. His collection of poems, *The Good Junk*, was included in *Take Three: Agni New Poets '91*.

HEID ERDRICH grew up in Wahpeton, North Dakota, where her parents taught at the Bureau of Indian Affairs boarding school. She is Metis/Ojibway from Turtle Mountain and German-American. Her book, *Fighting for Myth*, was published by New Rivers Press.

SASCHA FEINSTEIN's poetry collection, *Misterioso* (Copper Canyon, 2000), won the Hayden Carruth Award. He is the author of two critical books, including *Jazz Poetry: From the 1920s to the Present*. He edits *Brilliant Corners: A Journal of Jazz and Literature*.

LISA FISHMAN's book of poems, *The Deep Heart's Core is a Suitcase*, was published by New Issues Press. She teaches at Beloit College and lives with her husband on a small farm in Orfordville, Wisconsin.

NICK FLYNN's first book of poems, *Some Ether*, was published by Graywolf Press in 2000. He has received the PEN/Joyce Osterweil Award from the PEN American Center as well as a "Discovery"/*The Nation* Prize. He lives in Brooklyn.

RUTH FORMAN was the winner of the 1992 Barnard New Women Poets Prize. Her books include *We Are the Young Magicians* (Beacon, 1992) and *Renaissance* (Beacon, 1997). She is also a filmmaker.

KENNY FRIES is the author of *Anesthesia: Poems* (Advocado Press, 1996), which includes "The Healing Notebooks," for which he received the Gregory Kolovakos Award for AIDS Writing. He also wrote *Body, Remember: A Memoir* (Dutton, 1997, Plume paperback).

JOANNA FUHRMAN grew up in New York. Her first book, *Freud in Brooklyn*, was published by Hanging Loose Press. She is a graduate of the University of Texas at Austin and the University of Washington in Seattle.

SUZANNE GARDINIER was born in New Bedford and grew up in Scituate on the coast south of Boston. She is the author of *The New World* (University of Pittsburgh Press, 1993) and *A World That Will Hold All People*, essays on poetry and politics (University of Michigan Press, 1996).

STEPHEN GEHRKE was born in Mankato, Minnesota. His first collection, *The Resurrection Machine* (BkMk, 2000), won the John Ciardi Prize for Poetry. He is also the recipient of a kidney from his older sister, Gwen.

TIMOTHY GEIGER is the author of the poetry collection *Blue Light Factory* (Spoon River Poetry Press, 1999). His work has received a Pushcart Prize and a Holt, Rinehart and Winston Award. He is the proprietor of the literary fine-press, Aureole Press.

LISA GLATT, a poet and fiction writer from California, has held residencies at Yaddo, MacDowell, and Fundacion Valparaiso in Spain. She is the author of *Monsters and Other Lovers* and *Shelter* (both from Pearl Editions).

DOUGLAS GOETSCH grew up in Northport, Long Island and resides in Manhattan, where he teaches English and writing at Stuyvesant High School. He is the author of *Nobody's Hell* (Hanging Loose, 1999) and *Wherever You Want* (Pavement Saw, 1997).

RIGOBERTO GONZÁLEZ was born in Bakersfield, California and raised in Michoacán, Mexico, the son and grandson of migrant farm workers. His first book of poetry, *So Often the Pitcher Goes to Water Until It Breaks* was a 1998 National Poetry Series selection.

DEBRA GREGERMAN holds a BFA in painting from the Rhode Island School of Design and an MFA in creative writing from the University of Arizona. Her first book, *Jealousy and the Things You Are Not*, was published by Owl Creek Press in 1999.

MAURICE KILWEIN GUEVARA was born in Belencito, Colombia and raised in Pittsburgh, Pennsylvania. His books include *Postmortem* (University of Georgia Press) and *Poems of the River Spirit* (University of Pittsburgh Press). He is also a playwright and fiction writer.

BETH GYLYS' book of poems, *Bodies That Hum*, won the Gerald Cable Poetry Award and was published by Silverfish Review Press in 1999. Wind Press published her chapbook, *Balloon Heart*, in 1998. She teaches at Mercyhurst College in Erie, Pennsylvania.

JIM HARMS was born in Pasadena, California. He is the author of three books of poetry, *Modern Ocean* (1992), *The Joy Addict* (1998), and *Soon* (forthcoming, 2001), all published by Carnegie Mellon University Press.

TERRANCE HAYES is a native of South Carolina. His first book of poetry, *Muscular Music*, was published by Tia Chucha in 1999. After earning his MFA from the University of Pittsburgh, he lived for a year in Japan with his wife, poet Yona Harvey.

BRIAN HENRY has edited *Verse* since 1995. He was a Fulbright Scholar in Australia in 1997-98, and is the editor of *The Polygon Book of Younger American Poets*. In 1999, his first book, *Astronaut*, appeared in the United Kingdom from Arc Publications' International Poets Series.

BOB HICOK's books are *Plus Shipping* (BOA Editions, 1998) and *The Legend of Light* (Wisconsin, 1995), which won the Felix Pollak Prize and was an ALA Notable Book of the Year. He was an NEA Fellow in 1999. He owns an automotive design business.

M. C. HILL's first book of poems, *If You Return Home with Food*, won the 1998 Bluestem Award. She lives with her husband in Shawsville along the old Great Road in Virginia. She teaches writing at Roanoke College.

ELLEN HINSEY's volume, *Cities of Memory*, won the Yale Series Award in 1995. She was awarded a Rona Jaffe Foundation Writer's Award in 1998. She teaches literature and writing in Paris.

CHRISTINE HUME's first book of poems, *Musca Domestica*, was published by Beacon Press. She lives in Denver, Colorado.

AUSTIN HUMMELL was born in Florida. His first book, *The Fugitive Kind*, was published by the University of Georgia Press in 1995. He teaches at the University of North Texas.

BRUCE JACKSON grew up in Chicago, spent many years in Los Angeles, and currently lives in San Francisco. His book, *Growing Up Free*, was published by Manic D Press, which also featured his prose poem about living in his car in *The Sofa Surfing Handbook*.

J. L. JACOBS was born in the Ouachita Hills of Oklahoma. She holds an MFA from Brown University. Her first book of poems, *The Leaves in Her Shoes*, was published by Lost Roads in 1999.

JONATHAN JOHNSON lives in a remote log cabin in northern Idaho. His first book, *Mastodon, 80% Complete*, was published by Carnegie Mellon University Press in 2000. He teaches at Eastern Washington University.

JUDY JORDAN was born on a small farm near the border between the Carolinas. In 1996 she received a Virginia Commission for the Arts Fellowship in Poetry. Her book *Carolina Ghost Woods* won the 1999 Walt Whitman Award from the Academy of American Poets.

ALLISON JOSEPH was born in London, England to parents of Caribbean heritage. She grew up in Toronto, Canada and the Bronx, New York. Her books include *What Keeps Us Here* (Ampersand, 1992), *Soul Train* (Carnegie Mellon, 1997), and *In Every Seam* (Pitt, 1997).

JULIA KASDORF was born in Lewistown, Pennsylvania. Her first book, *Sleeping Preacher*, won the 1991 Agnes Lynch Starrett Prize and the Great Lakes Association Award for new writing. Her second book, *Eve's Striptease*, was published by Pittsburgh in 1998.

LAURA KASISCHKE is the author of two novels and four books of poems, including *Housekeeping in a Dream* and the forthcoming *What It Wasn't*, both from Carnegie Mellon University Press. She lives in Chelsea, Michigan.

DAVID KEPLINGER's first book, *The Rose Inside*, won the 1999 T. S. Eliot Prize and was published by Thomas Jefferson University Press. From 1995 to 1997, he was a Soros Fellow in Frydek-Mistek, the Czech Republic. He lives in Philadelphia.

GER KILLEEN was born in Limerick, Ireland and is now a United States citizen living in rural Oregon. He is the editor of *Continental Drift*, an on-line literary magazine, and is a journeyman herbalist. His first book, *A Wren*, was published by Bluestem Press.

JAMES KIMBRELL's first book, *The Gatehouse Heaven*, was published by Sarabande Books in 1998. He has won a Whiting Writer's Award, and his book was runner-up for the Norma Faber first book award.

GERRY LAFEMINA, author of three chapbooks and two full-length collections, received a 1997 ArtServe Michigan Creative Artist Grant. He lives in Northern Michigan with his wife, Mary Ann Samyn, and edits the national literary journal, *Controlled Burn*.

LANCE LARSEN is the author of *Erasable Walls*, published in 1998 by New Issues Press. He has received fellowships from the Utah Arts Council and the Cultural Arts Council of Houston. He serves as poetry editor of *Literature and Belief*.

DANA LEVIN grew up in the Mojave Desert in Southern California. Her first book, *In the Surgical Theatre*, won the 1999 *American Poetry Review/ Honickman First Book Prize*. She lives in Santa Fe, New Mexico.

MARK LEVINE was born in New York and was raised in Canada. He's received a Whiting Writers' Award, the Hodder Fellowship from Princeton, and an NEA Fellowship. He's an active magazine journalist for *The New Yorker* and *Outside* magazine.

KATE LIGHT is a violinist in the New York City Opera and is involved in modern dance and theater. Her book, *The Laws of Falling Bodies*, was co-winner of the 1997 Nicholas Roerich Poetry Prize and was published by Story Line Press.

FATIMA LIM-WILSON's first collection, *Wandering Roots/From the Hothouse*, won the 1992 Philippine National Book Award for poetry. Her second book, *Crossing the Snow Bridge*, won the 1995 Ohio State University Press/*The Journal* Award in Poetry.

BETH LISICK is a writer and performer. She is the author of *Monkey Girl* (Manic D Press) and fronts a band, The Beth Lisick Ordeal. She resides in Berkeley, California and is working on her first theater piece, a show about a washed-up lady rock star.

TIMOTHY LIU's books of poems are *Vox Angelica* (Alice James, 1992), *Burnt Offerings* (Copper Canyon, 1995), and *Say Goodnight* (Copper Canyon, 1998). He is the editor of *Word of Mouth: An Anthology of Gay American Poetry* (Talisman House, 2000).

M. LONCAR's first book, *66 galaxie*, was the winner of the Katharine Bakeless Nason Poetry Prize and was published by Middlebury College Press. He lectures in English literature and composition and film studies at the University of Michigan.

JOEL LONG's book, *Winged Insects*, won the 1998 White Pine Press Poetry Prize and was published in 1999. He teaches creative writing and art history in West Jordan, Utah, where he founded the Lake Effect Writers Conference.

PETER MARKUS' book, *Still Lives with Whiskey Bottle*, was published by March Street Press in 1996. He's received a Michigan Creative Artist Grant from ArtServe and teaches as writer-in-residence at three Detroit high schools.

DAVID MARLATT lives on the farm near Richland, Michigan, where he was born and raised. As well as being a writer, he is a musician who plays bass sackbut, trombone, and fiddle. His first book, *A Hog Slaughtering Woman*, was published by New Issues Press.

VALERIE MARTÍNEZ's book, *Absence, Luminescent,* won the Levis Prize from Four Way Books (1999). She has translated the work of Delmira Agustini and was assistant editor of *Reinventing the Enemy's Language*, an anthology of native women's writing.

KHALED MATTAWA's first book of poems, *Ismailia Eclipse*, was published by Sheep Meadow Press. He emigrated to the United States in 1979 at age fifteen and after spending his childhood in Libya. He was awarded the Alfred Hodder Fellowship at Princeton for 1995-96.

ELLYN MAYBE is the author of *Cowardice of Amnesia* (2.13.61 Publications), the *Ellyn Maybe Coloring Book* (Sacred Beverage Press), and *Putting My 2¢ In.* She works at Beyond Baroque Literary Arts Center in Venice, California.

SHARA MCCALLUM was born in Kingston, Jamaica and emigrated to the United States at the age of nine. Her first book of poems, *The Water Between Us*, won the 1998 Agnes Lynch Starrett Prize and was published by the University of Pittsburgh Press.

JEFFREY MCDANIEL is the author of *Alibi School* and *The Forgiveness Parade* (both published by Manic D Press). Active in the poetry slam scene, he has performed his work in over forty-five American cities and ten cities abroad. He lives in Los Angeles.

CAMPBELL MCGRATH is the author of four full-length collections, most recently *Road Atlas* (Ecco Press, 1999). His awards include the Kinsley Tufts Prize, the Cohen Prize, and fellowships from the Guggenheim Foundation and the Library of Congress.

LESLIE ANNE MCILROY's first book of poems, *Gravel*, was published by Slipstream Press. She won the 1997 Chicago Literary Awards Competition, and she is co-founder of HEART, an organization devoted to encouraging artists to address issues of discrimination.

PAULA MCLAIN has been a resident at The MacDowell Colony and the Vermont Studio Center. Her first book of poems, *Less of Her*, was published by New Issues Press in 1999.

MARK MCMORRIS' books include *Figures for a Hypothesis* (Leave, 1995), *Moth-Wings* (Burning Deck, 1996), and *The Black Reeds* (Georgia, 1997). He received the Gertrude Stein Award for Innovative American Poetry from Sun and Moon Press.

CONSTANCE MERRITT was born in Pine Bluff, Arkansas and educated at the Arkansas School for the Blind in Little Rock. *A Protocol for Touch*, winner of the 1999 Vassar Miller Prize in Poetry, is her first collection of poems.

MALENA MÖRLING was born in Stockholm and grew up in southern Sweden. Her first book of poems, *Ocean Avenue*, was published by New Issues Press. Her translations of Tomas Tranströmer appeared in his book, *For the Living and the Dead* (Ecco Press).

JULIE MOULDS, author of *The Woman with a Cubed Head* (New Issues Press), taught children's literature many years. She served as librettist of the operetta, *Baba Yar*, and has been beating cancer for seven years.

RICK MULKEY was born in Bluefield, Virginia. He has lived and taught at colleges and universities in Poland, Kansas, Ohio, and South Carolina. His first book, *Before the Age of Reason*, appeared in 1998 from Pecan Grove Press.

MAGGIE NELSON was born in San Francisco, California. Her poems have appeared in a collection with the poet Cynthia Nelson entitled, *Not Sisters* (Soft Skull Press, 1996), and most recently in *Agni*/Graywolf Press's *Take Three: New Poets Series*. She lives in Brooklyn.

RICK NOGUCHI was born in Los Angeles, California. His first collection of poems, *The Ocean Inside Kenji Takezo*, won the 1995 Associated Writing Programs (AWP) Series and was published by the University of Pittsburgh Press.

JENNIFER O'GRADY's collection of poems, *White*, won the 1998 First Series Award and was published by Mid-List Press in 1999. Her poems have appeared in *Poetry, Harper's, The Yale Review, The Kenyon Review*, and other publications. She lives in New York City.

JOE OSTERHAUS has worked in scholarly publishing and taught at Boston University and Washington University. Graywolf Press published his first collection, *The Domed Road*, in *Take Three: Agni New Poets Series: 1*. He lives in Washington, DC.

FRANKIE PAINO was born in Cleveland, Ohio. She has published two books of poems, *The Rapture of Matter* (Cleveland State University, 1991) and *Out of Eden* (Cleveland State, 1997).

ALAN MICHAEL PARKER is the author of two books of poems, *Days Like Prose* and *The Vandals*. He co-edited *The Routledge Anthology of Cross-Gendered Verse* and is editor for North America of *Who's Who in 20th Century World Poetry*.

G. E. PATTERSON's awards include fellowships from the MacDowell Colony and the Minnesota State Arts Board. *Tug*, his first book of poems, was published by Graywolf Press.

V. PENELOPE PELIZZON's book, *Nostos*, won the 1999 Hollis Summers' Prize and was published by Ohio University Press. She received a 1997 "Discovery"/*The Nation* Award. In addition, she has published critical essays on literature, photography, and film noir.

TRACY PHILPOT works at South Peninsula's Women's Services as a rural outreach counselor for victims of domestic violence, sexual abuse/assault. She lives with her husband and two-year-old son in a cabin with no running water in Seldovia, Alaska.

D. A. POWELL's first full-length collection of poems, *Tea*, was a finalist for the AWP Award in Poetry and was published by Wesleyan University Press. He is the author of two chapbooks from Norton Coker Press.

KEVIN POWELL is a poet, journalist, and essayist. He edited, with Ras Baraka, *In the Tradition: An Anthology of Young Black Writers*, published a volume of poetry, *recognize*, and is the author of *Keepin' It Real: Post-MTV Reflections on Race, Sex, and Politics*.

ROHAN B. PRESTON, Jamaican-born, New York-reared and Yale-educated, makes his living as a stringer for *The New York Times* and literary, arts and music writer for *The Chicago Tribune*. *Dreams in Soy Sauce* (Tia Chucha Press, 1992) is his first book of poetry.

467

KEVIN PRUFER grew up in Cleveland, Ohio. His first book, *Strange Wood*, won the 1997 Winthrop Poetry Series Award. He is also editor of *The New Young American Poets* (Southern Illinois University Press, 2000) and *Pleiades: A Journal of New Writing*.

CHARLES RAFFERTY's *The Man on the Tower* won the 1994 Arkansas Poetry Award. He has also published two chapbooks, *The Wave That Will Beach Us Both* (Still Waters Press) and *The Bog Shack* (Picadilly Press). He works as an editor at a computer consulting firm.

HEATHER RAMSDELL's first book of poems, *Lost Wax*, was a National Poetry Series winner in 1998 and was published by the University of Illinois Press. A native of northeastern Massachusetts, she now lives and writes in Brooklyn.

CLAUDIA RANKINE, born in Jamaica, West Indies, is the author of *The End of the Alphabet* (Grove Press) and *Nothing in Nature is Private* (Cleveland State Poetry Center). She teaches in the English department at Barnard College.

JOANNA RAWSON was born in Kansas and raised in Iowa. She currently lives in Minneapolis and works as a journalist and editor. Her first book, *Quarry*, won the AWP Award Series in Poetry in 1997 and was published by the University of Pittsburgh Press.

WILLIAM REICHARD's first collection, *An Alchemy in the Bones*, won a Minnesota Voices Project Prize and was published by New Rivers Press. His novella, *Harmony*, won the Evergreen Chronicles Novella Prize and was published in 1995. He lives in Minneapolis.

REBECCA REYNOLDS was raised in Washington, DC. Her book, *Daughter of a Hangnail* (New Issues Press, 1997), won the Norma Faber First Book Award from the Poetry Society of America.

KIM ROBERTS runs literary programs for the Cultural Affairs Division of Arlington County, Virginia, including Say the Word, a series of readings, performances, and workshops; an annual national poetry competition; and Moving Words, a poetry on the buses project.

ELIZABETH ROBINSON is the author of *Bed of Lists* (Kelsey St. Press, 1990) and *In the Sequence of Falling Things* (paradigm press, 1991). She lives in Berkeley, California with her husband and two sons.

MATTHEW ROHRER grew up in Oklahoma. His book, *A Hummock in the Malookas*, was a National Poetry Series winner in 1994 and was published by W. W. Norton. He lives in Brooklyn, where he is poetry editor of *FENCE* magazine.

LEE ANN RORIPAUGH's first volume of poetry, *Beyond Heart Mountain* (Penguin, 1999), was a 1998 National Poetry Series selection. Other honors include the 1995 Randall Jarrell International Poetry Prize and an AWP Intro Award.

CATIE ROSEMURGY grew up in Escanaba, Michigan. She currently lives in Maryville, Missouri, where she co-edits *The Laurel Review*. *My Favorite Apocalypse*, her first collection of poems, was published by Graywolf Press.

SARAH ROSENBLATT's first book of poems, *On the Waterbed They Sank to Their Own Levels*, was published by Carnegie Mellon University Press. Her videos have been shown at the Anthology Film Series and the Andrea Rosen Gallery in New York City.

SARAH RUDEN's book, *Other Places*, won the 1995 Central News Agency Award in South Africa, where she teaches at the University of Capetown. Her writing honors include the Voss Memorial Writing Award (1984) and the Roberts Memorial Poetry Prize (1989).

JOHN RYBICKI's first book of poems, *Traveling at High Speeds*, was published by New Issues Poetry Press. He works as a teacher and a carpenter and has been pulled over by the police twice for writing while he's driving.

MARY ANN SAMYN is the author of *Captivity Narrative* (1999 Ohio State/ *The Journal* Award) and *Rooms by the Sea* (1994 Wick Prize, Kent State). She lives in Northern Michigan with her husband, Gerry LaFemina.

MARGOT SCHILPP lives in Salt Lake City where she edits *Quarterly West* and teaches at the University of Utah. Her first collection of poems, *The World's Last Night*, was published by Carnegie Mellon University Press.

RUTH L. SCHWARTZ won the AWP Poetry Competition for *Accordion Breathing and Dancing* (Pittsburgh, 1996). She has received a writing fellowship from the NEA. After working for many years as an AIDS educator, she now teaches at Cleveland State.

LISA SEWELL was born in California. Her first book, *The Way Out*, was published by Alice James in 1998. She has received fellowships from the NEA, the Massachusetts Cultural Council, and the Fine Arts Work Center in Provincetown. She lives in Philadelphia.

PATTY SEYBURN's first book of poetry, *Diasporadic*, won the 1997 Marianne Moore Prize given by Helicon Editions. A native of Detroit, she currently lives in Costa Mesa, California with her husband, Eric Little, and teaches at California Institute of the Arts.

BRENDA SHAUGHNESSY's first book of poems, *Interior with Sudden Joy,* was published in 1999 by Farrar Straus Giroux. She was raised in California and currently lives in New York City.

REGINALD SHEPHERD was born in New York City. His first book, *Some Are Drowning*, was published by the University of Pittsburgh Press in 1994 as the winner of the AWP Prize. His other books, *Angel Interrupted*, and *Wrong*, were also published by Pittsburgh.

MARTHA SILANO's first book, *What the Truth Tastes Like* (Nightshade Press), won the 1998 William and Kingman Page Poetry Book Award. She has worked as a proofreader, legal secretary, CPS caseworker, and word processor, and now teaches English in Washington.

ROSE SOLARI is a poet, fiction writer, playwright, and journalist. She has won many awards for her writing, including the 1995 Columbia Book Award for Poetry for *Difficult Weather* (Gut Punch Press) and the 1998 Randall Jarrell Poetry Prize. She lives in Bethesda.

ANGELA SORBY's first book, *Distance Learning*, was published by New Issues Press in 1998. She has received a "Discovery"/*The Nation* prize, and her work was included in *Best American Poetry 1995*. She lives in Milwaukee.

PHILIP STEPHENS was raised in Missouri. His first book of poems, *The Determined Days* (Overlook Press, 2000), was chosen for the Sewanee Writers' Series. He currently works as a free-lance writer in Kansas City, Missouri.

ADRIENNE SU is the author of *Middle Kingdom* (Alice James, 1997). Her poetry awards include a Pushcart Prize and fellowships from Dartmouth College and the Fine Arts Work Center in Provincetown. She lives in Iowa City, Iowa.

VIRGIL SUÁREZ's books include *Garabato Poems* (Wings Press, 1999), *You Come Singing* (Tia Chucha Press, 1998), and *Spared Angola: Memories from a Cuban-American Childhood* (Arte Público, 1999). He has also published five books of fiction.

LARISSA SZPORLUK's book, *Dark Sky Question*, won the 1997 Barnard New Women Poet's Prize. She is the recipient of a Rona Jaffe Award and her work appears in *Best American Poetry 1999*. She lives with her husband and two children in Bowling Green, Ohio.

RICHARD TAYSON's first book of poetry, *The Apprentice of Fever*, won the Wick Poetry Prize and was published by Kent State University Press (1998). His nonfiction book, *Look Up for Yes*, appeared in paperback from Viking Penguin (1998).

J. TARIN TOWERS was born and raised in rural Maryland. She is the author of *Sorry, We're Close* (Manic D Press, 1999) and received a Pushcart Prize for her piece, "Mission Poem." She is also the author of *The Dreamweaver Visual Quick Start Guide* (Peachpit Press).

ANN TOWNSEND was born in Pittsburgh. Her book of poems, *Dime Store Erotics*, won the 1997 Gerald Cable Poetry Prize and was published by *Silverfish Review*. She has won a "Discovery"/*The Nation* award, and her poems, stories, and essays are widely published.

PIMONE TRIPLETT's book, *Ruining the Temple*, was published by Northwestern University Press. She teaches in the Program in Creative Writing at the University of Oregon.

SAM TRUITT is the author of two chapbooks, *The Song of Rasputin* and *Blazon*. His full-length collection, *Anamorphosis Eisenhower*, was published by Lost Roads Publishers in 1998. He lives and works in New York City.

ALPAY ULKU's first book, *Meteorology*, was published by BOA Editions in 1999. He was born in Turkey, grew up in Canada, and now lives in Chicago, where he works as a real estate appraiser. He was a fellow at the Fine Arts Work Center in Provincetown.

REETIKA VAZIRANI, author of *White Elephants* (Beacon 1996), received a Barnard New Women Poet's Prize. Her many awards include a "Discovery"/ *The Nation* Award, a Pushcart Prize, and fellowships from the Sewanee and Breadloaf Writers' Conferences.

ANTHONY R. VIGIL was brought up in Denver. While completing his MFA at Colorado State University, he won the Dr. Martin Luther King, Jr. Award for academic excellence and humanitarian activism. His book, *The Obsidian Ranfla*, was published by Cleveland State.

KAREN VOLKMAN was born in Miami. Her first book of poems, *Crash's Law*, was a National Poetry Series winner and was published by W. W. Norton in 1996. She received a 1993 NEA Fellowship and was included in *The Best American Poetry* in 1996 and 1997.

DAVID SCOTT WARD's first book of poems, *Crucial Beauty*, was published by SCOP Publications in 1991. He is managing editor of the *Eckerd College Review* and Assistant Editor of *Shenandoah*.

THOM WARD's poetry collection, *Small Boat With Oars of Different Size*, was published by Carnegie Mellon University Press. He is editor/development director for BOA Editions, Ltd. He lives with his wife and three children in Palmyra, New York.

JOE WENDEROTH's books include *Disfortune* and *It Is If I Speak* (Wesleyan, 1995, 2000), and a chapbook, *The Endearment* (Shortline Editions, 1999). He lives in Mt. Horeb, Wisconsin and Marshall, Minnesota, where he teaches at Southwest State University.

RACHEL WETZSTEON was born in New York City. Her first book, *The Other Stars*, was a National Poetry Series selection in 1993 and her second book, *Home and Away*, was published in 1998, both by Penguin. She has received an Ingram Merrill grant.

SUSAN WHITMORE is executive director of The Writers Place, a non-profit literary arts organization in Kansas City. Her publications include two books of poems, *The Invisible Woman* (Singular Speech Press) and *The Sacrifices* (Mellen Poetry Press).

CRYSTAL WILLIAMS is the author of *Kin* (Michigan State University Press, 2000). She is a Nuyorican Poet and regularly gives readings. Her work appears in the anthologies, *Beyond the Frontier: African-American Poets into the Millennium* and *Poetry Nation*.

LISA WILLIAMS grew up in Tennessee and California. She has received an Elliston Fellowship, a Henry Hoyns Fellowship, and the May Swenson Poetry Award. Her book, *The Hammered Dulcimer*, was published by Utah State University Press.

GREG WILLIAMSON grew up in Nashville, Tennessee. His first book, *The Silent Partner*, won the Nicholas Roerich Poetry Prize and was published by Story Line Press in 1995. He teaches in The Writing Seminars at Johns Hopkins University.

STEVE WILSON is the author of *The Singapore Express* and *Allegory Dance*, both published by The Black Tie Press. He teaches in the writing program at Southwest Texas State University.

CHRISTIAN WIMAN was born and raised in West Texas. He has held a Wallace Stegner Fellowship, a Dobie-Paisano Fellowship, and a Ruth Lilly Fellowship. His book, *The Long Home* (Story Line Press), won the 1998 Nicholas Roerich Poetry Prize.

SUZANNE WISE's first poetry collection, *The Kingdom of the Subjunctive*, was published by Alice James Books in 2000. She was a fellow at the Fine Arts Work Center in Provincetown from 1997-1999.

MARK WUNDERLICH is the author of *Anchorage* (University of Massachusetts Press, 1999). Born in Fountain City, Wisconsin, he has been a fellow at the Fine Arts Work Center and a Wallace Stegner Fellow at Stanford University. He lives in San Francisco.

M. WYREBEK's first book of poetry, *Be Properly Scared*, won the 1995 Intro Competition from Four Way Books. Her work has appeared in both literary and medical journals. She received a fellowship to the Breadloaf Writers Conference. She lives near Boston.

KEVIN YOUNG's first book, *Most Way Home*, won the National Poetry Series and the Zacharis First Book Prize from *Ploughshares*. His second book, *To Repel Ghosts*, based on the work and brief life of Jean-Michel Basquiat, will be published by Zoland Books.

KATAYOON ZANDVAKILI's collection of poems, *Deer Table Legs*, won the University of Georgia Press' Contemporary Poetry Series Competition (1998). The book's title poem was included in the 2000 Pushcart Prize anthology. She lives in Piedmont, California.

PERMISSIONS

The selections by ★RICK AGRAN are copyright © 1997 by Rick Agran and are reprinted from *Crow Milk* by permission of Oyster River Press and the author. The selections by ★ELIZABETH ALEXANDER are copyright © 1996 by Elizabeth Alexander and are reprinted from *Body of Life* by permission of Tia Chucha Press. The selections by ★SHERMAN ALEXIE are copyright © 1996 by Sherman Alexie and are reprinted from *The Summer of Black Widows* by permission of Hanging Loose Press and the author. The selections by ★RICK ALLEY are copyright © 1997 by Rick Alley and are reprinted from *The Talking Book of July* by permission of Eastern Washington University Press and the author. The selections by ★ALICE ANDERSON are copyright © 1994 by Alice Anderson and are reprinted from *Human Nature* by permission of New York University Press and the author. The selections by ★DANIEL ANDERSON are copyright © 1997 by Daniel Anderson and are reprinted from *January Rain* by permission of Story Line Press and the author. The selections by ★TALVIKKI ANSEL are copyright © 1997 by Talvikki Ansel and are reprinted from *My Shining Archipelago* by permission of Yale University Press and the author. The selections by ★AARON ANSTETT are copyright © 1997 by Aaron Anstett and are reprinted from *Sustenance* by permission of New Rivers Press and the author. The selections by ★CRAIG ARNOLD are copyright © 1999 by Craig Arnold and are reprinted from *Shells* by permission of Yale University Press and the author. The selections by ★DAVID BARATIER are copyright © 1999 by David Baratier and are reprinted from *The Fall of Because* by permission of Pudding House and the author. The selections by ★DAVID BARBER are copyright © 1995 by David Barber and are reprinted from *The Spirit Level* by permission of TriQuarterly Books/Northwestern University Press and the author. "Independent Study," "Why That Abbott and Costello Vaudeville Mess Never Worked with Black People," and "Stall Me Out" are from *Joker, Joker, Deuce* by ★PAUL BEATTY. Copyright © 1994 by Paul Beatty. Used by permission of Penguin, a division of Penguin Putnam Inc. The selection by ★JOSHUA BECKMAN is copyright © 1998 by Joshua Beckman and is reprinted from *Things Are Happening* by permission of *The American Poetry Review*/Honickman First Book Prize and the author. The selections by ★ERIN BELIEU are copyright © 1995 by Erin Belieu and are reprinted from *Infanta* by permission of Copper Canyon Press and the author. "After Estrangement," and "Conversation with Isadora" appeared in *After Estrangement,* Gibbs-Smith Publisher, copyright © 1992 by ★MOLLY BENDALL. "Matinee Idylls" is reprinted from *Dark Summer*, published by Miami University Press, copyright © 1999 by Molly Bendall. The selections by ★DINA BEN-LEV are copyright © 1997 by Dina Ben-Lev and are reprinted from *Broken Helix* by permission of Mid-List Press and the author. The selections by ★JACQUELINE BERGER are copyright © 1997 by Jacqueline Berger and are reprinted from *The Mythologies of Danger* by permission of Bluestem Press and the author. The selections by ★CAROLE BERNSTEIN are copyright © 1997 by Carole Bernstein and are reprinted from *Familiar* by permission of Hanging Loose Press and the author. "The Pathology of Proximity" and "Geometry Class" by ★MARK BIBBINS appeared in *Take Three: Agni New Poets Series, 3* published by Graywolf Press, 1998. Reprinted by permission. The selections by ★DAVID BIESPIEL are copyright © 1996 by David Biespiel and are reprinted from *Shattering Air* by permission of BOA Editions, Ltd. and the author. The selections from *City of a Hundred Fires*, by ★RICHARD BLANCO, copyright © 1998 by Richard Blanco, are reprinted by permission of the University of Pittsburgh Press and the